P9-DDD-995

Acclaim for Linda Colley's

CAPTIVES

"Engaging, gracefully written. . . . Sharp-eyed. . . . There is marvelous detail on every page."
—*The New York Times Book Review*

"*Captives* is another important and beautifully written book by this first-rank British historian." —*The Irish Times*

"A sort of *White Teeth* version of imperial history. . . . A completely original intelligence." —*Financial Times*

"A brilliantly illuminating study by one of Britain's most distinguished historians." —*New Statesman*

"Consistently enlightening. . . . An insightful and stimulating book that presents history with a fresh perspective."
—*BookPage*

"Innovative. . . . Colley brings a contemporary edge to her writing. . . . [She is] one of the most interesting historians at work today." —*The Wilson Quarterly*

"Colley's fascinating book links captivity with imperial expansion and underscores the Britons' ultimate dependence on loyal 'natives.'" —*The New York Review of Books*

"*Captives* is an invitation to think again about an old story too often told in the same old way. . . . It is a book which should alter the way in which the history not only of the British, but of all the European empires is written."
—*London Review of Books*

"Superb . . . coruscating." —*The Independent on Sunday* (London)

"Abounds in fascinating human stories and constantly requires the reader to reconsider accepted dogma."
—*The Daily Telegraph* (London)

"Sublimely well written: cunningly paced, beguilingly fluent, deftly allusive, vividly evocative. It is a major contribution to understanding the paradox of the British: the weak who wangled the earth." —*Literary Review*

"Linda Colley is a great storyteller and she breathes life into the manuscripts she has discovered by captives in the early days of the Empire." —*The Observer* (London)

"Dexterous, wonderfully subtle." —*The Sunday Times* (London)

"This fine, thought-provoking book—at once readable and educative—is crammed full of telling insights."
—*The Sunday Telegraph* (London)

"Stunningly revisionist. . . . Almost every page of *Captives* challenges a settled orthodoxy or opens up a fertile new field for research." —*History Today*

Linda Colley

CAPTIVES

Born in Britain, Linda Colley has taught and written on history and current events on both sides of the Atlantic. Previously at Cambridge, Yale, and the London School of Economics, she is now Shelby M. C. Davis 1958 Professor of History at Princeton University. Her previous books include *In Defiance of Oligarchy: The Tory Party, 1714–1760*, *Namier*, and *Britons: Forging the Nation, 1707–1837*, for which she won the Wolfson Prize.

ALSO BY LINDA COLLEY

In Defiance of Oligarchy: The Tory Party, 1714–1760
Namier
Britons: Forging the Nation, 1707–1837

CAPTIVES

CAPTIVES

Britain, Empire, and the World, 1600–1850

LINDA COLLEY

Anchor Books

A DIVISION OF RANDOM HOUSE, INC.

NEW YORK

FIRST ANCHOR BOOKS EDITION, JANUARY 2004

Copyright © 2002 by Linda Colley

All rights reserved under International and Pan-American Copyright Conventions. Published in the United States by Anchor Books, a division of Random House, Inc., New York, and simultaneously in Canada by Random House of Canada Limited, Toronto. Originally published in Great Britain by Jonathan Cape, an imprint of Random House U.K., London, in 2002, and subsequently in the United States by Pantheon Books, a division of Random House, Inc., New York, in 2003.

Anchor Books and colophon are registered trademarks of Random House, Inc.

The Library of Congress has cataloged the Pantheon edition as follows:
Colley, Linda.
Captives / Linda Colley.
p. cm.
ISBN 0-375-42152-1
1. Great Britain—Colonies—History.   2. Captivity narratives—Great Britain—History
3. British—Foreign countries—History.   4. Imperialism—History.   I. Title.
DA16.C65 2003
941—dc21
2002075960

Anchor ISBN: 0-385-72146-3

Author photograph © Niall McDiarmid

www.anchorbooks.com

Printed in the United States of America
10   9   8   7   6   5

In memory of my mother
Marjorie Colley, née Hughes
1920–1998

Contents

List of Illustrations   xi

Acknowledgements   xv

Introduction   1
Small is vulnerable, small is aggressive   4
People and stories matter   12
Re-appraising empire   17

Part One

MEDITERRANEAN
Captives and Constraints

1   **Tangier**
    Breakers   23
    Another sea, another view   33
    Pressure points   37

2   **The Crescent and the Sea**
    Barbary   43
    Counting   48
    Britons can be slaves   56
    Sea raiders and a sea empire   65

3   **Telling the Tale**
    Going public   73
    Church and state   75
    The captive's voice   82
    Readings   88

4   **Confronting Islam**
    Dis-orientations   99
    Mixed messages   104
    Testimonies   113
    Transitions?   125

Part Two

AMERICA
Captives and Embarrassments

5   **Different Americans, Different Britons**
Looking beyond the Atlantic   137
Taking captive   141
Divisions   152

6   **War and a New World**
Confrontations   168
Into the wilderness   172
The captive and the captivated   186
The spoils of victory, the toils of insular constraints   198

7   **Revolutions**
Mistaken identities   203
Who is to count?   208
Catching the lion in the net   216
Blackening the empire, building empires anew   227

Part Three

INDIA
Captives and Conquest

8   **Another Passage to India**
Sarah's story   241
Limits   245
Riding the tiger   257

9   **The Tiger and the Sword**
Mysore and its meanings   269
Fighters as writers   277
Adjusting to defeat   287
Re-writing to win   296

10 **Captives in Uniform**
  Winning the numbers game   308
  The ones that got away   317
  Whipping the legions into line   328
  Re-envisioning the imperial soldiery   341

  Epilogue: To Afghanistan and Beyond
  More captives, more stories   347
  What remained the same, what was different   354
  Nineteenth-century conclusions   367
  Twenty-first century issues   374

  Appendix: The Captivity Archive   380

  Notes   386

  Index   425

List of Illustrations

The illustrations in this book form an integral part of the text and have been captioned accordingly. Their full titles and provenance are as follows.

I am most grateful to the libraries, art galleries and private owners listed below for allowing me to reproduce images in their possession. Images with no provenance cited are from my own collection of prints, books and photographs.

1.   Britain as global empire: a detail from an 1893 map (British Library, Maps, 17.c.13).

2.   The Peters World Map, © Akademische Verlagsanstalt, supplied by Oxford Cartographers.

3.   The title page of *Madagascar: or Robert Drury's Journal*, London, 1729 (Cambridge University Library).

4.   Title page of Wenceslaus Hollar, *Divers Prospects in and about Tangier*, London, 1673 (National Maritime Museum, Greenwich).

5.   *The South-east Corner of Tangier*, etching by Wenceslaus Hollar (National Maritime Museum, Greenwich).

6.   *Prospect of ye Inner Part of Tangier*, etching by Wenceslaus Hollar (National Maritime Museum, Greenwich).

7.   *Prospect of ye Bowling Green at Whitehall, by Tangier*, etching by Wencelaus Hollar (National Maritime Museum, Greenwich).

8.   Plan of the mole at Tangier (Public Record Office).

9.   Dirck Stoop, *Demolishing Tangier's mole in 1684* (National Maritime Museum, Greenwich).

10. The frontispiece of John Ogilby, *Africa*, London, 1670 (British Library).

11. C. Runker, *View of the City of Algiers*, 1816 (British Library, Maps. K. Top. 117.73.e).

12. *The Going into Slavery at Algiers*, an engraving of *c.* 1700 (National Maritime Museum, Greenwich).

13.   A battle between Barbary corsairs and Royal Navy warships, *c.* 1670s (National Maritime Museum, Greenwich).

14.   A bird's eye view of Tripoli, *c.* 1660 (British Library, Maps. K. Top. 117.62).

15.   Lorenzo A Castro, *Seapiece: A Fight with Barbary Corsairs* (by permission of the Trustees of Dulwich Picture Gallery).

16.   Illustration from Thomas Troughton, *Barbarian Cruelty: or an Accurate . . . Narrative of the Sufferings*, London, 1751 (Beinecke Library, Yale University).

17.   Title page of *The History of the Long Captivity and Adventures of Thomas Pellow*, London, *c.* 1740.

18.   Frontispiece of William Okeley, *Eben-ezer: or a Small Monument of Great Mercy*, London, 1675 (British Library).

19.   Title page of Joseph Pitts, *A True and Faithful Account of the Religion and Manners of the Mohammetans*, Exeter, 1704.

20.   A section of the Mechouar at Meknès.

21.   The massive walls of one of Moulay Ismaïl's storehouses.

22.   Illustration from Joseph Pitts, *A True and Faithful Account of the Religion and Manners of the Mohammetans*, London, 1731 (British Library).

23.   R. Ball, *A Plan of Algiers*, 1776 (British Library, Maps. K. Top. 177.72).

24.   Francis Bird's Indian (Conway Library, Courtauld Institute of Art)

25.   The severed head of a captive: detail from Francis Bird's Indian (Conway Library, Courtauld Institute of Art).

26.   Illustration from Mary Rowlandson, *The Sovereignty and Goodness of God* (courtesy of the American Antiquarian Society, Worcester, Massachusetts).

27.   John Verelst, *Tee Yee Neen Ho Ga Row, Emperor of the Six Nations* (courtesy of the John Carter Brown Library at Brown University).

28.   John Verelst, *Sa Ga Yeath Qua Pieth Ton, King of the Maquas* (courtesy of the John Carter Brown Library at Brown University).

29.   *A Presentation of Several Humorous Heads*, 1765 (courtesy of the Print Collection, Lewis Walpole Library, Yale University).

30.   George Townshend, *Unknown Native American* (courtesy of the National Portrait Gallery, London).

31.   Benjamin West, *General Johnson Saving a Wounded French Officer from the Tomahawk of a North American Indian* (Derby Museum and Art Gallery).

32.–33. Two British portrait prints of an Iroquois ally, Hendrick, during the Seven Years War.

34.   Frontispiece of *French and Indian Cruelty Exemplified in the Life . . . of Peter Williamson*, Edinburgh, 1762.

35. Benjamin West, *The Indians Delivering up the English Captives to Colonel Bouquet* (Yale Center for British Art, Paul Mellon Collection).

36. Major John André, self-portrait (Yale University Art Gallery; gift of Ebenezer Baldwin, B.A. 1808).

37. The execution of John André (courtesy of the Print Collection, Lewis Walpole Library, Yale University).

38. Lieutenant Moodie rescuing a British prisoner: a 1785 print (courtesy of the Director, National Army Museum, London).

39. *The Commissioners Interview with Congress*, 1778 (British Museum).

40. James Gillray, *The American Rattle Snake*, 1782 (British Museum).

41. John Vanderlyn, *The Murder of Jane McCrea*, 1803–4 (Wadsworth Atheneum Museum of Art, Hartford, Connecticut; The Ella Gallup Sumner and Mary Catlin Sumner Collection Fund).

42. *A View in America in 1778* (courtesy of the Print Collection, Lewis Walpole Library, Yale University).

43. Frontispiece of *The Female Soldier*, London, 1750 (British Library).

44. Paul Monamy, *English East Indiaman, c.* 1720 (National Maritime Museum, Greenwich).

45. George Lambert and Samuel Scott, *Bombay, c.* 1731, oil on canvas (reproduced by permission of the India Office Library and Records, British Library, F48).

46. J.M.W. Turner, *The Loss of an East Indiaman* (by permission of the Trustees of the Cecil Higgins Art Gallery, Bedford).

47. *Sepoys of the 3rd Battalion at Bombay* (courtesy of the Print Collection, Lewis Walpole Libray, Yale University).

48. George Stubbs, *Tigress* (© Christie's Images Ltd, 2002).

49. James Ward, *Fight between a Lion and a Tiger* (by permission of the Syndics of the Fitzwilliam Museum, Cambridge).

50. Wood and clockwork effigy made for Tipu Sultan (© The Board of Trustees of the Victoria & Albert Museum).

51. A tiger-headed Mysore cannon at Madras.

52. *The Battle of Pollilur*: detail of an 1820 copy by an unknown Indian artist (Collection Otto Money; photograph: A.I.C. Photographic Services).

53. Victorian photograph of the Darya Daulat Bagh, Seringapatam (by permission of the India Office Library and Records, British Library, Photo 96/1 [94]).

54. Detail from *The Battle of Pollilur* (Collection Otto Money).

55. British School, *Mrs. Louisa Brown Holding the Journal of her Son* (by permission of the India Office Library and Records, British Library, F825).

56.–57. Exterior and interior of the officers' dungeon at Seringapatam.

58.   Pages from Cromwell Massey's prison journal (by permission of the India Office Library and Records, British Library, MSS. Eur. B392).

59.   Unknown Indian artist, *Richard Chase, Prisoner of Tipu*, late eighteenth century (private collection).

60.   Thomas Rowlandson, *The Death of Tippoo or Besieging a Haram!!!*, 1799 (Library of Congress, Washington).

61.   Robert Home, *Drawing of North-east Angle of Seringapatam*, 1792 (by permission of the India Office Library and Records, British Library, WD3775).

62.   Edward Penny, *Clive Receiving a Legacy from the Nawab of Murshidabad*, 1772, oil on canvas (by permission of the India Office Library and Records, British Library, F91).

63.   Frontispiece of William Francklin, *Military Memoirs of George Thomas*, London, 1803 (British Library).

64.   *Governor Wall*, 1810 (courtesy of the Print Collection, Lewis Walpole Library, Yale University).

65.   *Governor Wall Contemplating on his Unhappy Fate* (courtesy of the Print Collection, Lewis Walpole Library, Yale University).

66.   Painting of a Company sepoy and his wife by an unknown Indian artist, 1780s (by permission of the India Office Library and Records, British Library, Add. Or. 3923).

67.   British officers captured in Afghanistan: a romanticised 1844 print based on an earlier Afghan sketch (courtesy of the Director, National Army Museum, London).

68.   Florentia Sale by Vincent Eyre (courtesy of the Director, National Army Museum, London).

69.   A sketch of his cell in William Anderson's captivity narrative (by permission of the India Office Library and Records, British Library).

70.   Emily Eden, *Dost Muhammad Khan together with Members of his Family*, 1841 (by permission of the India Office Library and Records, British Library, WD1291).

71.   Captain Bygrave by Vincent Eyre (courtesy of the Director, National Army Museum, London).

72.   Lieutenant Vincent Eyre: self-portrait (courtesy of the Director, National Army Museum, London).

73.   Lieutenant Muir by Vincent Eyre (courtesy of the Director, National Army Museum, London).

74.   Diagram from J.M.D. Meiklejohn, *A Short Geography*, London, 1913.

Acknowledgements

As befits its subject, this book has been pondered over and written in many different countries and continents, and I have accumulated many debts.

I had long wanted to explore the global context of British history, to move beyond these small islands to a broader vision but, in 1997, two gracious and unlooked for invitations gave me the vital incentive to do so. I was asked to deliver the Trevelyan Lectures at Cambridge University, and the Wiles Lectures at Queen's University, Belfast. Historians traditionally use these occasions to decant the accumulated wisdom of a lifetime. I, however, seized upon them to try out some raw ideas, positions and arguments that none the less proved crucial to the making of this book. I am therefore all the more grateful for the attention, helpful criticisms – and patience – bestowed on me by my Cambridge and Belfast audiences. I am particularly indebted to David Armitage, Chris Bayly, Stephen Conway, Marianne Elliott, Roy Foster, Ian Kershaw, Dominic Lieven, Peter Marshall, Peter Jupp, Terence Ranger and John Walsh, who commented on each Belfast lecture as it was delivered, and in some cases were rewarded only by being sent drafts of this book to read. I hope that the electors to the Trevelyan and Wiles Lectureships will accept my belated thanks for all that their invitations and generosity provoked and made possible.

My second major debt is to friends, former colleagues and students at Yale University. In the sixteen years I had the honour to work there, I was never allowed to forget that Britain and its one-time empire were only episodes in a wider global and temporal drama. Time and time again, I was asked questions, forced to engage in arguments, supplied with booklists, and offered valuable ideas and insights. I am especially grateful to Abbas Amanat, David Bell (now of Johns Hopkins University), John Blum, Jon Butler, David Brion Davis, John Mack Faragher, Maija Jansson, Paul Kennedy, Howard Lamar, John Merriman, Edmund Morgan, Stuart Schwartz, Jonathan Spence, David Underdown, and Robin Winks. I must also thank Alison Richard, Provost of Yale, who granted me leave at a crucial stage in this project, and whose scholarly concern and resilience under fire were a constant inspiration. John Demos however deserves special thanks. It was he, over a New Haven lunch table a long time ago, who first introduced me to captivity narratives. That was the beginning.

The end has been primarily the gift of the Leverhulme Trust of Great Britain which in 1998 awarded me a Senior Research Professorship. This allowed me a span of concentrated time in which to mull over and write up an ambitious topic, and also made it possible for me to visit the various sites discussed in this volume. It was R.H. Tawney who said that historians require a stout pair of boots, and I now understand why. Unless one makes oneself familiar with Britain's own dimensions, and then walks, trains, sails, and explores across those huge regions into which its peoples once intruded, a proper appreciation of the workings, dynamics, and meanings of its one-time empire is not possible. I am therefore most grateful to Barry Supple, former Director of the Leverhulme Trust, and to its other members for their tremendous kindness and generosity. I am also immensely grateful to Tony Giddens and the London School of Economics for giving me such stimulating shelter during the course of my award, and for the opportunity to spend time at London University which brings together so many distinguished scholars. Particular thanks go to Mia Rodriguez-Salgado, Joan-Pau Rubiés, and Patrick O'Brien of the LSE; to David Bindman, Michael Brett, David Feldman, Catherine Hall, Shula Marks, Peter Robb and Miles Taylor; and to the members of the seminar on 'Reconfiguring the British', which has supplied me with so many ideas. I must also thank the British Library and the Paul Mellon Centre of British Art, which – together with the Lewis Walpole Library at Farmington, Connecticut, and the Yale Center for British Art – have supplied wonderful places in which to work, as well as visual images crucial to this book.

As with all big books that take a long time to write, specifying particular individuals and debts in this fashion is in some ways invidious. So many people have contributed to my work over the years. I have indicated particular debts in the end-notes whenever possible, but some who helped me must remain nameless. There was the bus driver in Tangier who lectured me in French on how the English were driven out of his city, as if that event had happened yesterday, rather than in 1684. There was the immaculately polite guide who escorted me around Bangalore, and with whom I argued – ridiculously – over how many sons of Tipu Sultan of Mysore were killed by the British in the 1790s (none in my history books; all of them in hers). And there were year upon year of wonderfully engaged Yale students with whom I discussed sharply varying interpretations of the American Revolution. This book draws upon stories that individual Britons told in the past in order to relieve their anxieties and apprehensions about engaging in global enterprise, and in due course to make it possible. I have been constantly reminded while writing *Captives* – and have sought throughout to make clear – that other, very different stories exist about the empire that the British once made.

Without the encouragement, wise advice and entrepreneurship of my literary agents, Mike Shaw in London, and Emma Parry and Michael Carlisle in New York, and the enthusiasm, skill and professionalism of my editors, Will Sulkin and Jörg Hensgen at Jonathan Cape and Dan Frank and Andrew Miller at Random House, this book would not have proved possible. Without David Cannadine, I would never have been able to travel so far or complete this journey.

L. J. C.
2002

'When the prison-doors are opened, the real dragon will fly out.'
Ho Chi Minh, *Prison Diary* (Hanoi, 1962)

CAPTIVES

INTRODUCTION

Two parables exist about the making and meanings of the British empire. In one, a man sets out on an eventful trading voyage, and is ultimately shipwrecked. He finds himself the lone survivor on a desert island, but despair soon gives way to resolution, Protestant faith, and busy ingenuity. By becoming 'an architect, a carpenter, a knife grinder, an astronomer, a baker, a shipwright, a potter, a saddler, a farmer, a tailor', and even 'an umbrella-maker, and a clergyman', he subdues his unpromising environment and renders it fruitful. He encounters a black, and promptly names him and makes him a servant. He uses force and guile to defeat incomers who are hostile, while firmly organising those who defer to his authority: 'How like a king I look'd . . . the whole country was my own mere property . . . [and] my people were perfectly subjected.' This is Daniel Defoe's *Robinson Crusoe* (1719). This is also how the British empire is commonly envisioned.

Empire-making in this parable – as in much of history in fact – involves being a warrior and taking charge. It means seizing land, planting it, and changing it. It means employing guns, technology, trade and the Bible to devastating effect, imposing rule, and subordinating those of a different skin pigmentation or religion. 'The true symbol of the British conquest', declared James Joyce famously, 'is Robinson Crusoe.' Yet if Crusoe seems at one level the archetypal conqueror and coloniser, he is also representative of British imperial experience in a very different sense. Before his shipwreck, Crusoe is captured at sea by Barbary corsairs and becomes 'a miserable slave' in Morocco. He escapes his Muslim owners only to become 'a prisoner locked up with the eternal bars and bolts of the Ocean, in an uninhabited wilderness'. And even as he transforms his desert island into a colony, Crusoe remains uncertain whether to regard his life there as 'my reign, or my captivity, which you please'.[1]

The hero of the second parable about British Empire is left with no doubts on this score. This man sets sail from Bristol, centre of transatlantic commerce and slaving, bound for successive zones of European imperialism: Spanish America, the West Indies, coastal India. He never reaches them. Instead, his voyages are aborted, time and time again, by events and beings beyond his control. First, an apparently puny tribe, the Lilliputians,

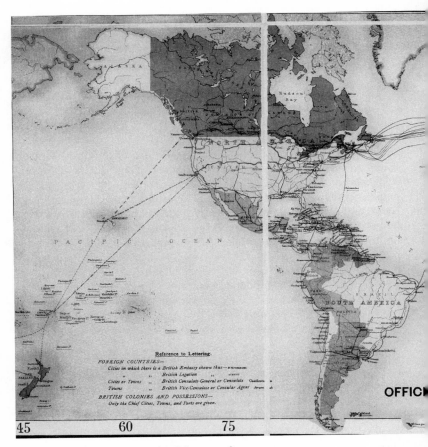

OFFIC

1. Britain as global empire: a detail from an 1893 map.

capture him, tie him down and reduce him to their will. Then a people much larger in stature than himself, the Brobdingnags, overwhelm him, sell him like a commodity, turn him into a spectacle, and sexually abuse him. But it is his last captivity that is most devastating. Confined on the island of the Houyhnhnms, creatures utterly unlike himself and far superior, he becomes so caught up in their society that he succumbs to its values. Forced at length to return to Britain, he can barely tolerate the stench of his one-time countrymen or the ugliness, as it now appears to him, of his own family. For this man, overseas venturing brings no conquests, or riches, or easy complacencies: only terror, vulnerability, and repeated captivities, and in the process an alteration of self and a telling of stories. This second

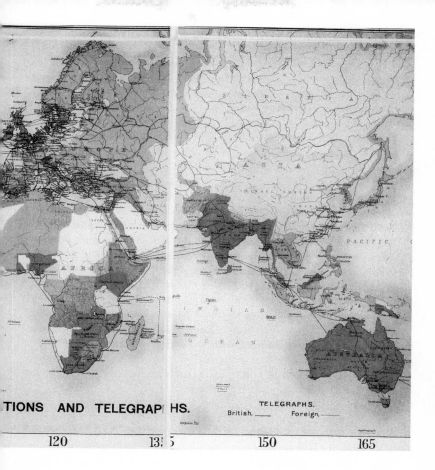

TIONS AND TELEGRAPHS.

TELEGRAPHS.
British. _____ Foreign. _____

| 120 | 135 | 150 | 165 |

parable about Britain's empire is of course Jonathan Swift's *Gulliver's Travels* (1726), and its subject and themes are also mine.[2]

The primary actors in the pages that follow are those hundreds of thousands of English, Welsh, Scottish and Irish men, women and children who were taken captive in different regions of the extra-European world during the first quarter millennium of British imperial enterprise. The sources I am mining are pre-eminently – though never exclusively – these captives' own extraordinarily rich and virtually unexplored writings and drawings. And my intention throughout is to supply a work both of individual recovery and of imperial revision. As Defoe and Swift recognised, captivity was an integral part of Britain's overseas experience which cannot be

3

properly understood or assessed without it. Nor is it possible to understand this empire's impact on the various non-European peoples it collided and colluded with, unless the full meanings of captivity are uncovered and explored. Captives and captivities were the underbelly of British empire, and they set us free to explore another vision.

Small is vulnerable, small is aggressive

The fundamental reason why their pursuit of empire involved Britons in so many different confinements is contained – but also concealed – in one of the most famous maps ever produced. It shows Britain and Ireland situated close to the centre of the displayed world and coloured red or pink. Around the outer circle of the map are a succession of land masses – Australia, New Zealand, Canada, the Indian subcontinent, large swathes of Africa, assorted Caribbean islands and more – all coloured an identical red or pink to Britain itself. Some late nineteenth- and twentieth-century versions of this map also include the shipping routes and telegraph lines operating between Britain and these various overseas territories, marked out in black or again in red. The visual effect is rather like spokes jutting erratically from the hub of a wheel, or a scarlet spider at the centre of a massive, global web. Britain is made to appear physically connected to the distant lands it claims as its own and that literally take their colour from it.

This map has long since disappeared from the atlases, along with the empire it depicted, but it remains a standard feature of history books and school texts. It is part of our mental furniture even now. And superficially the story behind it is straightforward and unilinear. Before the late sixteenth century, few of the English, and even fewer Scots, Irish and Welsh displayed much interest in the world beyond their own continent. Even in 1630, there were probably little more than 12,000 settlers and traders from these islands clinging to outposts in North America, Guiana, the Caribbean and coastal India: 'a few dispersed men . . . altogether without Government', as one contemporary described some of their number.[3] By the early 1700s, however, the British state and the major trading companies associated with it, claimed authority over more than half a million white settlers, as well as hundreds of thousands of free and enslaved non-whites scattered over four of the five continents of the world. By the 1820s, British dominion had dramatically expanded to encompass a fifth of the population of the globe. A hundred years later, when close to its widest extent in terms of patches of red or pink on the map, the British empire covered in total over fourteen million square miles of the face of the earth.

Summarised thus, Britain's expansionist trajectory appears inexorable, and its ultimate if very temporary global hegemony overwhelming. There seems negligible space in this version of events and power relations for white captives: only for the colonial captivity of millions of men and women who in the main were not white. But look again at the famous map of Britain's empire. Like most cartographic exercises, it is not a simple depiction of the lie of the land, but in some respects a lie, or at least a calculated deceit.

The map deceives because it gives the impression that Britain's empire was the only substantial one existing, which was never the case. It deceives, too, because its Mercator projection together with its use of the Greenwich meridian put Britain arbitrarily but not accidentally near the centre of the displayed world. It further deceives by using an identical colour for all of the territories claimed by Britain, thereby making them appear a single, homogeneous unit, which this empire never was in fact. But there is still another sleight of hand involved here that is critical. Because Canada, New Zealand, Australia, the Indian subcontinent, large sectors of Africa, and parts of the Caribbean are coloured the same red or pink in this map as Britain itself, the spectator's eye is adroitly distracted from the smallness of the latter, to the size and global spread of the former. It is the world-wide expanse of this imperial system we are encouraged to focus on and admire, not the relatively tiny islands at its core. Yet in order to under-stand this empire – and its captivities – the proper place to begin is with the smallness of Britain itself. Britons were captured overseas in very large numbers during this period because they were at once uniquely ubiqui-tous intruders, and inherently and sometimes desperately vulnerable.

In terms of geography, Britain's smallness becomes easily manifest if it is compared with today's great powers. The United States is over 3000 miles from sea to shining sea, and – like China – covers more than 3.5 million square miles. The borders of the Russian Federation are still in flux, but it remains close to six million square miles in extent; while India, which Britain sought to govern before 1947, contains some 1.2 million square miles. By contrast, Great Britain and the island of Ireland together make up less than 125,000 square miles. Great Britain itself, which contains England, Wales and Scotland, is smaller than Madagascar. It would fit into the state of Texas twice over with ample room to spare.[4] Of course geo-political size has never been the only or even the prime determinant of global power, and by the standards of present-day giants, *all* of the European states that once presided over maritime empires would appear small. But the scale of the disparity between Britain's massive imperial pretensions on the one hand and its modest domestic size and resources

5

2. Cut down to size: Britain and Ireland as shown in the Peters projection of the world.

on the other was remarkable. By the early twentieth century, the Dutch empire was perhaps fifty times bigger than the Netherlands, while the French colonies were some eighteen times the size of France itself. Britain's authority, however, was stretched over a global empire 125 times larger than its own islands.[5]

This imperial overstretch was sharpened by another aspect of Britain's smallness: demography. By European standards, much of early modern Britain and Ireland experienced a rapid rate of population growth. Whereas France's population is estimated to have expanded by 79 per cent between 1550 and 1820, and Spain's may have risen by just 56 per cent,

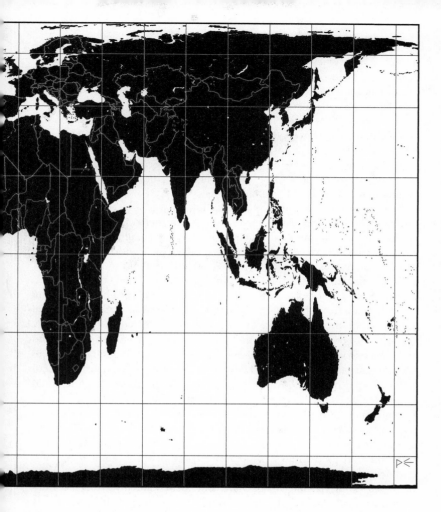

the population of *England* almost trebled over this same period. But it needs remarking that this impressive English population take-off occurred from a very small base, barely three million souls. By 1820, when the British empire contained one in every five beings on the face of the globe, there were still fewer than twelve million men and women living in England itself. This was in marked contrast with Spain, or France, or the various German kingdoms, or the Italian states, which by that stage each averaged some twenty million inhabitants apiece.[6] Political union in 1707 between England and Wales on the one hand, and Scotland on the other, and a further Act of Union with Ireland in 1800, guaranteed London

7

access to additional and indispensable domestic supplies of manpower. None the less, throughout the seventeenth and eighteenth centuries – and occasionally after – Britain's rulers remained uncertain whether their home population was sufficient to generate the armies, navies, settlers, and taxes demanded by large-scale imperial enterprise. Many politicians and commentators convinced themselves indeed that the drain in men and money was too great, and that Britain's population was actually in decline. There was no census here until 1801, in part because of the fear that counting heads might expose an embarrassing demographic deficit to Britain's rivals – and to its colonial subjects.[7]

Britain's limited population and its inhabitants' objections to maintaining large standing armies, provided for a further respect in which this was always an empire challenged at its core by smallness. The size of Britain's own armed forces never remotely kept pace with its global interventions. This was true even at sea. As Daniel Baugh remarks, the very scale of Britain's expanding maritime presence after the seventeenth century itself caused problems. These islands were never able to generate enough seamen by themselves 'to supply the wartime needs of both the navy and the merchant service'. And although by 1700 the Royal Navy was the most powerful in the world, it never possessed sufficient ships both to protect Britain itself from European enemies, and simultaneously to preside in strength over the world's oceans. For most of the quarter millennium covered by this book, the bulk of Britain's fleet was not, and could not be engaged in conquering and coercing the non-European world. Instead, most Royal Navy warships remained in home and European waters monitoring the movements of Dutch, Spanish, and French rivals.[8]

But the pressures on Britain's navy were as nothing to those on its army. Over time, as John Brewer has described, the British became supremely and necessarily adept at recruiting domestic manpower and hiring foreign mercenaries for specific, major wars. But these suddenly swollen legions (which were anyway usually bigger on paper than in the field) were strictly special occasion fare.[9] They could not be afforded, and were never routinely forthcoming for everyday, imperial needs. In 1715, when Britain already claimed authority over some half a million men and women in North America, plus large parts of the West Indies, coastal settlements in India, and vital outposts in the Mediterranean, its army is estimated to have been no bigger than the king of Sardinia's. In 1850, when this book ends, Britain's home-produced army was still conspicuously modest in point of numbers by comparison with that of Russia, or France, or even Prussia. 'At no time', as one military historian writes, '. . . were the land forces available for the peacetime policing and defence of the [British] empire . . .

sufficiently strong for the task'.[10] Even at the height of its imperial power, Britain's military and naval resources would have appeared negligible if set against the bristling overseas garrisons and staggering oceanic naval presence currently possessed by the United States.

These limits in military manpower might not have mattered had Britain commanded throughout the sort of easy and invariable technological supremacy still sometimes attributed to early modern Western empires, but it did not. At sea, to be sure, the major European powers had established a marked lead over other regions of the world by 1600 (though for a long time their wooden ships remained vulnerable on long voyages, and instruments of navigation were crude and sometimes fallible). On land, however, it was a different matter. Part of the excitement and sentimentality with which Britons and other Europeans reacted to Captain James Cook's encounters with Pacific islanders in the 1770s and '80s may well have been due to a gratified recognition that here were societies whose weaponry was indeed indisputably primitive in quality. By contrast, in parts of Africa, in North America, and above all in Asia, British intruders in this period had regularly to confront peoples whose weapons were similar to their own, and occasionally better.[11] The familiar image of ill-provided non-European peoples being casually and terribly mowed down by white imperialists equipped with gatling guns and similar quick-firing weapons belongs in the main to the later nineteenth century and after. For most of the quarter millennium covered by this book, land warfare remained conspicuously low-tech, and there was no necessary gulf between Western and non-Western armaments. As late as 1799, guns, cannon and ammunition together accounted for less than 5 per cent of Britain's land warfare budget. The rest went on horses, carts, uniforms, swords, knives, pikes and soldiers' pay: virtually the same staples of land warfare as in the Ancient World – and in much of the non-European world.[12]

Some might argue that these material factors – Britain's marked limits in terms of geographical size, population, armed forces, and, for a long time, military technology – were of only secondary importance. That manifestly a vast British empire came into being, and therefore that these constraints must have been of less significance than the 'will, self-confidence, even arrogance' that allowed growing numbers of Britons to view the overseas world as a site for action, conquest and exploitation. Yet those living in the seventeenth and eighteenth centuries, and even in the early 1800s, were rarely able to see things this way. There is certainly abundant evidence throughout this period of individual Britons asserting their unbounded superiority to all foreigners, both European and non-European. But as more thoughtful or battle-hardened spirits amongst them acknowledged, where global power relations were concerned, arrogance and jingoism were never enough. Language, culture and complacency had no automatic witchcraft capacity by themselves to magic away more rudimentary deficiencies in terms of numbers and available force. 'The maxim believed by the common people of this country, "That one Englishman is equal to two foreigners" . . . may . . . be useful in some cases,' wrote an experienced imperial soldier and diplomat wearily in 1810, 'but it is . . . devoid of truth.'[13]

As this suggests, alongside routine declarations of Britain's political, religious, economic, and ultimately racial superiority, there were always other voices, sometimes very powerful ones, pointing out that its varieties of domestic smallness were bound to make sustaining a large overseas territorial empire a challenging and chancy business. 'We are a very little spot in the map of the world,' writes the marquis of Halifax in the 1660s, and therefore could make 'a great figure only by trade'. 'We want not the dominion of more countries than we have,' cautions Daniel Defoe in 1707. 'We want nothing but numbers,' laments a British army officer about his country's forces abroad in 1744.[14] Britain's normal 'military establishment', remarks Adam Smith during the war with Revolutionary America that would demonstrate the imperial costs of this, was: '. . . more moderate than that of any European state which can pretend to rival her either in wealth or in power'. 'The extension of our territory and influence has been greater than our means,' observes the future duke of Wellington grimly in 1800.[15] But it was a less senior analyst of military power and empire who summed up the dilemma best. In regard to the size and resources of Britain itself, he wrote in an influential survey published in 1810, its global pretensions resembled 'an oak planted in a flower-pot'.[16] A swollen empire was nonetheless constrained by the smallness in which it was rooted.

There were, to be sure, some respects in which being small – being a flowerpot – actually worked to foster Britain's imperial involvement and success. If emigrants, entrepreneurs and adventurers of all kinds left it in large numbers for other lands (as they still do), if its slavers haggled for chained manpower on the western coasts of Africa, and if its traders ruthlessly invaded other seas and other shores in search of raw materials and new markets, this was in part because the home islands could seem too modest to afford the land, opportunities, manpower, raw materials, and markets that were wanted. Domestic smallness and a lack of self-sufficiency made for continuous British extroversion, not to say global house-breaking, violence and theft. And Britain's compact, physical insularity did more than fuel restlessness and greed, it also provided the means of escape, and the means as well to global commerce and conquest. Nowhere in Britain is more than seventy miles from the sea: and this was a vital advantage in a period when – for a long time – travel by sea was infinitely faster than journeying by land. The sea, the one commodity apart from coal and sheep they had around them in abundance, allowed the British to compensate for sparsity of numbers by sheer mobility and ubiquity.

Britain's compactness facilitated its imperial enterprise in other ways too. The physical smallness of these islands encouraged the rich, powerful and ambitious of England, Wales, Scotland and Ireland to filter into just one extraordinarily large metropolis, London. Magnetised to a conurbation that was at once the site of government and the court, and Britain's biggest port, ship-building centre, money market, and source of print, the different elites of these islands developed, from very early on, a shared avidity for imperial investments, ideas and adventures. This was just one respect in which physical smallness advanced the evolution in Britain of a markedly centralised state, and ultimately a precocious national ideology, with all the cohesion and belligerence that naturally went with these things.[17] The same compactness, together with state-driven political union, also ensured that the island of Great Britain became one of the world's most efficient free-trade areas from very early on, a hive of internal as well as external commercial energy. Even Britain's military vulnerability may have aided in some respects its imperial drive. Self-consciously small, increasingly rich, and confronted with European enemies that were often bigger and militarily more formidable than themselves, the British were frequently on edge, constantly fearful themselves of being invaded, necessarily alert and ready for a fight. A sense of inferiority, suggested Alfred Adler in regard to troubled individuals, breeds aggression and above all an urge to compensate. So arguably it proved with the British as a people.[18]

It is these mixed consequences of Britain's smallness – its cohesiveness, restless extroversion, busy commerce, and aggression on the one hand, and its demographic, military and resource inadequacies on the other – that account in part for the very large numbers of real-life Crusoes and Gullivers seized in regions outside Europe after 1600. Too many small, unarmed merchantmen venturing gamely into hostile or unknown waters, with not enough Royal Navy convoys to protect them, led – as Part One of this book describes – to substantial numbers of Britons being captured at sea. Civilian settlers and traders intruding determinedly but often in very small numbers into lands that other people regarded as their own, or endeavouring to establish themselves there without sufficient or sometimes any British army cover, resulted over the centuries – as Part Two details – in large numbers of captivities and casualties on land. While, throughout this period, under-strength British regiments, dispatched to different regions of the world equipped with weapons of no great sophistication, together with insufficiently manned and poorly supplied colonial cantonments and forts, regularly resulted in sharp imperial reverses, heavy casualties, and high captivity rates, not just among men in uniform, but also among various womenfolk and children.

'The body is a model which can stand for any bounded system,' writes the anthropologist Mary Douglas, and in times of stress the body's 'boundaries can represent any boundaries which are threatened or precarious.'[19] In just such a way, the bodies of English, Welsh, Scottish and Irish men and women, seized in successive captivity crises overseas, mark out the changing boundaries over time of Britain's imperial aggression, and the frontiers of its inhabitants' fears, insecurities, and deficiencies. But these encounters are revealing about far more than just the British themselves. What subsequently happened to these same captive bodies also illumines how those non-European peoples whom the British sought to invade or exploit, sometimes proved able to resist and punish them, and even find their own uses for them.

To this extent, this book uses captive individuals and their tales to investigate and reassess far wider national, imperial and global histories.

People and stories matter

Yet the captives in this book were more than symptomatic and emblematic bodies. All of them participants in first English and subsequently British maritime and imperial enterprise, these were also men, women and children from widely varying social and ethnic backgrounds, of different ages, religious denominations, politics, occupations, education, outlook and even language. How these myriad and miscellaneous individuals reacted to their respective captors was in practice as diverse as how the captor societies involved responded to them. So how can we recover the quality and content of these manifold contacts and confrontations over time?

Like captives from other cultures – like those whom they themselves colonised indeed – Britons seized in the course of overseas enterprise recorded what happened to them in many different ways, not all of them verbal. Some told their tale – or had it told for them – in drawings, or in graveyard inscriptions, in songs, or in sermons. Some scratched evocative and anguished lines and images on coins, or on the walls of places where they were confined. Some even tattooed their reactions on their own entrapped bodies. Captives who were rescued or eventually returned to

Britain might speak rather than write their stories: in order to appease an army court martial, or on the instructions of suspicious magistrates, or to entertain impatient passers-by on busy streets as a means of attracting charity; and these spoken testimonies were occasionally set down on paper by others. But the most complex and comprehensive testimonies of overseas capture, and thus the most valuable as far as this book is concerned, were captivity narratives.

These are substantial accounts usually written in the first person and completely or in part by a one-time captive, but sometimes dictated to others. A mode of writing rather than a genre, captivity narratives commonly describe how a single individual or a group was seized, how the victim/s coped (or not) with the challenges and sufferings that ensued, and how they contrived in the end to escape or were ransomed or released. Such narratives vary widely in length and quality but, at their best, they form the closest approximation we have for the past to the kind of analyses supplied by anthropologists and ethnographers immersed in alien societies today. In Mary Louise Pratt's words:

> The authority of the ethnographer over the 'mere traveller' rests chiefly on the idea that the traveller just passes through, whereas the ethnographer lives with the group under study. But of course this is what captives . . . often do too, living in another culture in every capacity . . . learning indigenous languages and lifeways with a proficiency any ethnographer would envy, and often producing accounts that are indeed full, rich, and accurate by ethnography's own standards. At the same time, the experience of captivity resonates a lot with aspects of the experience of fieldwork – the sense of dependency, lack of control, the vulnerability to being isolated completely or never left alone.[20]

Along with many other sorts of testimonies and evidence, both Western and non-Western, I have drawn extensively in this book on over a hundred printed and manuscript narratives written or dictated by Britons between 1600 and the mid-nineteenth century in response to captivity experiences in the Mediterranean and North African region, in North America, and in South and Central Asia.

By definition, these are subjective, sometimes highly charged writings, and I discuss their authenticity (and what that means) in Chapter Three. But it needs stressing from the start that, while these texts sometimes contain fictional interludes, together of course with a tithe of lies and errors, their overall factual anchorage can usually be tested, and has been tested in these pages throughout.

MADAGASCAR:

O R,

Robert Drury's

JOURNAL

DURING

Fifteen Years Captivity on that ISLAND.

Y Defign, in the enfuing Hiftory, is to give a plain and honeft Narrative of Matters of Fact; I fhall not, therefore, make ufe of any artful Inventions or borrow'd Phrafes to lengthen or embellifh it; nor fhall I offer any other Reflections than what naturally occurr'd from my many uncommon and furprifing Adventures. And,

B

3. Robert Drury's narrative.

Consider as an example the captivity narrative of Robert Drury, an English midshipman who was shipwrecked on the southern coast of Madagascar when he was just sixteen, and held for fifteen years there as a slave by the local Antandroy people. When this work, which is over 460 pages long, was published in London in 1729, Drury expressed his anxiety in the preface that, even though it was nothing else but 'a plain and honest narrative of matters of fact', it might be received as just 'such another romance as Robinson Crusoe'. His misgivings proved justified. Even some contemporary readers declined to believe Drury's story; and in 1943 a scholarly monograph 'proved' it to be a literary pastiche written by Daniel

Defoe himself. Libraries worldwide promptly changed their catalogue entries of Drury's work, and the *Encyclopaedia Britannica* downgraded it from respectable anthropological notice to a romantic fiction. Then, in 1991, a marine archaeologist called Mike Parker Pearson went back to Robert Drury's narrative and took it seriously.[21]

His team of archaeologists and ethnographers has now validated the wreck of Drury's ship, a 520-ton East Indiaman called the *Degrave*, lost in 1703 on the return voyage from Bengal to London. They have checked Drury's accounts of early eighteenth-century southern Madagascar's fauna, flora, climate, clothing and cuisine, the details he supplies of river names and mountains, and his descriptions of Antandroy rituals of warfare, circumcision, and death, and of their suspicion of Europeans: 'Every white man is looked on as not less than we think a cannibal.' In addition, Pearson has examined Drury's eight-page lexicon of Malagasy language, its spellings inflected by the seaman's own native Cockney. And the result of all this scholarly detective work? It is clear that Drury or his editor borrowed material from other published works, which was standard practice in the eighteenth century, omitted details, and exaggerated 'quantifications of distance, size and weight'. None the less, Pearson concludes, *Madagascar: or Robert Drury's Journal* is 'not a work of fictional realism nor is it a fancifully embroidered account based on a few authentic pegs'. It is 'a largely accurate historical document', by which is meant not an impeccable source, but a usable and important one.[22] The same is true of most substantial captivity narratives. These are imperfect, idiosyncratic, and sometimes violently slanted texts. They are also astonishingly rich and revealing, both about the British themselves, and about the mixed fortunes and complexities of their dealings with other peoples.

For it is emphatically not the case, as has sometimes been suggested, that captivity narratives were comprehensively 'safe' texts that only corroborated pre-existing and dismissive European viewpoints about other societies. Read scrupulously, indeed, they usefully disrupt the notion that there was ever a single, identifiable British, still less 'European' perspective on the non-European world, any more, of course, than there was on anything else.

In part, this is because their authors were so various. British attitudes to empire have often been reconstructed – and over-homogenised – on the slender basis of testimonies by a few conspicuous actors in positions of power or notoriety: politicians, pro-consuls, generals, colonial governors, monarchs, celebrated authors and intellectuals, merchant princes, industrial magnates, intrepid explorers and the like. Such dominant, confident and predominantly masculine creatures regularly, and necessarily, strut through these pages also. But one of the advantages of investigating captives, and the texts associated with them, is that doing so brings us into contact with the rather different people who always made up the majority of British imperial personnel in fact. Not all captives were obscure individuals, but many of them were. They were minor settlers and farmers, common seamen and private soldiers, junior officers and small traders, itinerants and exiles, convicts and assorted womenfolk. As a result, many of these individuals experienced what one twentieth-century Irish captive called being 'a tiny, insignificant pawn in a global game over which I had no control' in a double sense.[23] At one level, they found themselves at the mercy of non-European captors; but, at another, some of these British captives also felt constrained and subordinated by their own society of origin, and wrote accordingly.

And, irrespective of the social status and sentiments of their authors, captivity narratives were *always* disturbing texts at some level simply by virtue of what they described. For those Britons directly involved, overseas captivity meant not just sudden exposure to danger and extreme vulnerability, but also being dragged across a line of sorts. This might be the line between Christian Europe and bastions of Islam in North Africa and the Ottoman world; or the line between regions of British settlement in North America and more mobile Native American societies. After 1775, the line in question might be that between American territory as British imperialists envisaged it, and as those rebelling against their rule wished to reconfigure it; or it might be the line between regions of encroaching British influence in South or Central Asia, and areas of indigenous power and resistance there. Many of the individuals who feature in this book remained bitterly resentful throughout at being forced to cross into trauma and difference. Some captives, however, chose or were compelled to adjust to their new settings, while others learnt from their experiences to question the very validity of divides between peoples, and the meaning of what they had once regarded as home. Virtually all British captives though were compelled by the nature of their predicament to re-examine – and often question for the first time – conventional wisdoms about nationality, race, religion, allegiance, appropriate modes of behaviour, and the location of power.

These were individuals caught up bodily in zones of imperial contest, forced into protracted encounters where they were at the bottom, and other people who were generally not European, and usually not Christian, or white, had power of life or death over them. What those who survived such encounters wrote, or otherwise recorded about their experiences, proved persistently absorbing and often disquieting to their compatriots back home. 'Autobiographical forms,' remarks James Amelang, 'played a crucial role in circulating information in early modern Europe about the world beyond': and, as far as captives' autobiographies were concerned, this remained true for the British well beyond the early modern period.[24] Until they succeeded in convincing themselves (though never totally and not for long), that global empire was a feasible option for a small people like themselves, all kinds of Britons were drawn to scrutinise, and anguish over the captive's story. We should pay attention to it too.

Re-appraising empire

This book, then, combines the large-scale, panoramic and global, with the small-scale, the individual, and the particular. At one level, it is a macro-narrative of some of the constraints and crises that Britain confronted during the quarter millennium that made it the world's foremost power, and what followed from these both as regards its own peoples, and for other peoples. At another level, this book is an exploration of micro-narratives produced by just some of the very many English, Welsh, Scottish and Irish men and women who got caught and caught out because of this power's amalgam of incessant extroversion and aggression, and frequent and intrinsic vulnerability.

Men and women from these islands were held captive over the centuries in every continent of the world, but I have concentrated on the three vast geographical areas in which London and its rulers took successively the most interest, and sunk the most imperial effort, imagination and expense. Accordingly, Part One of this book focuses on North Africa and the Mediterranean. This region is often left out of the history of English and British commercial and imperial endeavour, yet it witnessed both the most costly (and catastrophically unsuccessful) colonial settlement attempted by the English state in the seventeenth century, and the biggest concentration of British troops overseas before 1750. Part Two is devoted to mainland North America, focusing on those Thirteen Colonies which decolonised so violently after 1775. Part Three belongs to South and Central Asia, and sweeps from British captivities in southern India in the four decades after 1760, to British failures in Afghanistan in the 1840s.

In order to convey changes in power-levels and imperial attitudes over time, I have looked at each of these three regions according to when captivity crises there proved the most dangerous for the British, and provoked the most attention and alarm. Thus Part One stretches from 1600 to the early eighteenth century, a period when English commercial and imperial ambitions in the Mediterranean and North Africa became threatened by, but also dependent upon, local Islamic powers. Part Two examines English and British captivities in North America from the later seventeenth century to the end of the American Revolutionary War in 1783. Throughout these years, captivity crises here – as in the other regions in this book – were linked to much wider issues and anxieties. Captive bodies in America were caught up with clashes between advancing, land-hungry British settlers and angry and retreating indigenous peoples, but also with the tensions and differences emerging between these same assertive white settlers and their fellow Britons on the other side of the Atlantic. Part Three of this book, on South and Central Asia, moves from the mid-eighteenth century into the early Victorian era, a period in which the quality of imperial captivities and domestic reactions to them changed markedly, along with the direction and intensity of Britain's aggression, and the level of its global power.

Since this is a big book that requires readers to travel across several continents as well as through a quarter millennium of time, I have supplied guide-posts. Each of the three sections begins with an orientation chapter, a scene-setting for the captives, captors, countries and cultures involved. Throughout, I have sought to convey both the growing scale of Britain's global reach and its persistent limitations; I have also stressed connectedness, weaving together histories that are often reconstructed only separately. I have ranged impertinently but with purpose over America, Asia, and the Mediterranean world, because patterns of British overseas enterprise in these regions – and patterns of resistance to it – were interconnected. I have sought to consider and complicate the line between aggressors and the invaded, the powerful and the powerless, because it was sometimes crossed and compromised in fact. And I have stressed the linkages between the actions, confinements and writings of English, Welsh, Irish, and Scottish individuals in different parts of the world on the one hand, and events and reactions back in the home islands on the other. This book is written in agreement with those who argue that the segregation of British domestic history from the histories of varieties of Britons overseas cannot stand.

There is another set of connections that I have wanted to stress. I take for granted that the British need to know far more about their impact in the past on different regions of the world, and about how peoples and developments in these same regions have in turn impacted over the centuries on them. But, by the same token, those wanting to understand the histories – and the present – of large parts of Africa, or Asia, or America, or indeed the Caribbean and the Pacific regions, need to reassess the complex roles once played in them by the British, and see the latter clearly for what they actually were, in their real diversity and limited dimensions, as distinct from how they wished to appear then, and from what they are still stereotypically viewed as being now. This book offers a different perspective on Britain's imperial impact and experience, without in any way suggesting that this is the only one that can be adopted. But *Captives* is also concerned to rewrite the British themselves, so that they may be put more accurately in their place in global history.

There is a final point. The people who feature in this book were radically different from men and women today in all kinds of respects, and not least in that – whether European or non-European – many of them tended to take the existence of empire for granted. This was hardly surprising. Britain's maritime empire existed in tandem with, and competed against, the maritime empires of France, Spain, Portugal, Denmark and the Dutch. These Western European seaborne empires coexisted in turn with the great land-based empires of the East. There were the Chinese, Russian and Ottoman empires; and there was the Safavid empire in Persia, and the Mughal empire in India: all of which in 1600 were infinitely more formidable powers than England and its adjacent countries, and all of which continued to expand thereafter for different lengths of time, and with different rates of success. And there were land-based empires within Europe itself: the empire of the Hapsburgs that encompassed Austria and parts of Eastern Europe and Italy, and the empire built up so violently by Napoleon Bonaparte after 1796, that subdued 40 per cent of all Europeans, and threatened for a time to overrun Britain itself.

As this last example suggests, imperialism in this period – and after – was espoused by revolutionary and republican regimes as well as by monarchical, ancien regimes. America's revolution against George III and British rule after 1776 did not lead it to reject empire as such. Its white inhabitants simply continued to invade ever westwards under their own flag, displacing Native Americans and other peoples as they went, intent on constructing what Alexander Hamilton (who had fought against the British) described unabashedly as 'an empire in many respects the most interesting in the world'. The sheer ubiquity of empire in this quarter millennium needs bearing in mind when assessing how the British themselves thought and acted. But the degree to which empire 'has been a way of life for most of the peoples of the world' throughout recorded history also needs bearing in mind and pondering now, in the early twenty-first century.[25]

We are perhaps too ready to believe that, because colonisation by force is no longer a real danger, the substance and tendencies of empire have therefore ceased entirely to exist. This book deals with the relationship between size and power, and with the penalties and paradoxes of the pursuit of global dominance, not just for those encroached upon and invaded, but also for the invaders themselves, the warriors who so easily became captives in one fashion or another. It would be nice to believe that such issues could be safely consigned to the realm of history. It would also be unwise.

Part One

MEDITERRANEAN
Captives and Constraints

ONE

Tangier

Breakers

The strip of sea that brought them to the shores of their new prize and the entrance to the Mediterranean is famously volatile. Even today, crossing or passing through the straits of Gibraltar, the narrowest stretch of water between Europe and Africa, is a slow and turbulent business. However bright the sunshine at embarkation, strong winds and rain can move in swiftly, blotting out coastlines and turning the oil-flecked, ultramarine sea into a choppy slate grey. In bad weather, the trip churns the stomach and can be dangerous. Migrant workers from Morocco and Algeria, their belongings tied up in immaculate brown paper parcels, together with some hardier backpackers will still entrust themselves to the larger, older ferry boats, huddling below deck amidst the cigarette smoke and old coffee stains. But comfortable tourists looking forward to a sea excursion from Gibraltar to Tangier ('Your Day Out In Africa') cancel their bookings in droves, while the smaller, faster hydrofoils linking Tangier with Tarifa and Algeciras in Spain sometimes cease operating. As for amateur craft, they can vanish altogether. Hundreds of men and women still die on this eight-mile stretch of water every year.

It was the unpredictability of its offshore waters, the sudden, violent rainstorms, and the quirks of the landscape that most impressed the English occupation force when it first arrived in Tangier in 1662, yet these things did not make the soldiers, officials and families feel any more at home. The fact that, at a distance and shrouded in mist, the low mountains behind Tangier might almost have passed for those of North Wales, only accentuated the strangeness of the rest: the clarity of the Mediterranean sunlight, the expansive sands, the luminosity of the settlement's white and ochre-coloured buildings, fruits and vegetables most of them had never tasted before, roses that bloomed even in winter. Sir Hugh Cholmley, though, remained undistracted and was immediately busy, for his mission was to regulate the sea itself.

Cholmley was a Yorkshire landowner from a moderately royalist background, a highly intelligent and driven man whose idea of relaxation was

Divers Prospects in and about
TANGIER
Exactly delineated by W: Hollar his May:
designer   and by him afterwards
to satisfie the curious etsbd in Copper.
And are to be Sold by John Overton at the
White Horse without Newgate London.

Prospect of y.ᵉ North side of Tangier regarding the mayne Sea.   from the hill as you come from Whitby or the West, toward the Towne.

4. Prospect of Tangier by Wenceslaus Hollar.

pegging away at mathematical puzzles. He was also a gentlemanly capi-
talist of a kind, as concerned to invest in England's intermittently
expanding empire overseas, as he was to diversify his income at home. He
developed the alum mines on his family estates at Whitby, married off his
daughter to a speculator in Indian diamonds, and, most of all, applied
himself mind and muscle to Tangier.[1] Charles II, King of England,
Scotland and Ireland, had acquired the settlement along with other colonial booty in 1661, as part of the dowry of his sad, barren Portuguese
bride, Catherine of Braganza. One year later, Cholmley signed a contract
with the government to build a mole at Tangier at the rate of thirteen
shillings for every cubic yard completed. As Cholmley noted down with
typical thoroughness, the word 'mole' comes from the French and Latin
for a great mass. The idea was to construct a substantial artificial outcrop
or breakwater from Tangier's natural shoreline, lined with cannon and
other defences, and thereby make the harbour deep enough for the Royal
Navy's largest warships, and a safer, more congenial haven for what was
expected to become an ever-growing share of the world's trade.[2]

For Tangier was and is a special place. Its now dated reputation for
transgressive sexualities and international intrigue masks its extraordinary
strategic and geographical significance, but does at least acknowledge the
city's role as a meeting-place for different cultures. Adjacent to the point

where the continent of Africa comes nearest to Europe, it is bounded on the one side by the Atlantic, while commanding on the other the western entrance to the Mediterranean. So its attractions for its English occupiers were profound and plural. At one level, Tangier offered a base from which they could look to make further commercial and colonial advances into the North African interior. At another, it supplied them with a naval stronghold from which to monitor the fleets of richer and more powerful European rivals, Spain, and above all France. At yet another level, Tangier guarded the entrance of what one contemporary called 'the greatest thoroughfare of commerce in the world', by which he meant not the Atlantic Ocean, but the Mediterranean, at this stage still the most profitable arena by far for English imports and exports.[3] Trade with southern Europe and the eastern Mediterranean seaboard, Turkey and the Levant, had been expanding since before 1600. England shipped its cloth here of course, as well as fresh and salted fish for the Catholic ports, and by the second half of the seventeenth century an ever-growing supply of colonial re-exports, pepper, tobacco, sugar, East Indian silks and calicos. In return, the English looked to the Mediterranean for imports of Levantine silks and dyestuff, for Turkish cotton and Spanish short wool, for Italian wine and Portuguese Madeira, for leather and fine horses from Morocco, and raisins, figs, oranges and olives to diversify the diet of the well-off. Tangier appeared an ideal base and mart for this rich and varied commerce, and one of the first things that London did after 1662 was proclaim it a free port.

On expansionist, strategic, and commercial grounds, then, Tangier seemed to the English an impeccably prudent acquisition that would in due course pay for itself many times over, 'a jewel', as Cholmley put it. Samuel Pepys, writing as a naval administrator and member of the council responsible for the new colony, rather than in his more familiar guise as a man-about-town, confided in his diary that Tangier was 'likely to be the most considerable place the King of England hath in the world'. Catherine of Braganza's other bonus, Bombay, struck him by contrast as no more than 'a poor little island', too distant ever likely to be made properly useful.[4] In seventeenth-century sailing-ship time, Bombay was at least half a year from London; and even England's North American colonies were three months away. Tangier, though, offered proximity as well as seemingly limitless potential. A fast merchantman setting out from London could reach it in well under two weeks. Not surprisingly, then, in the early years of its occupation, the new colony was talked of in official circles 'at a mighty rate as the foundation of a new empire'. It would be easy, urged one supporter in the 1670s, for Charles II so to exploit Tangier as 'to command our northern world, and to give laws to Europe and Africa'.[5]

1. Catharine Port,
2. The Irish Battery.

Prospect of yᵉ lower part of Tangie

5. Tangier fortified.

Money was lavished on the colony on a scale appropriate to these ambitions. The Portuguese had allowed the place to decay, and major rebuilding began almost as soon as the 4000-strong occupation force arrived, many of the troops veterans of Oliver Cromwell's New Model Army. Long, fortified walls began to coil around the settlement 'one without another, as there are [skins] to an onion'. The Bohemian engraver turned English court

the hill west of White-hall ⊕ — 5 The head Court of Guard,
W: Hollar delin: 4 The Bay.

artist, Wenceslaus Hollar, sketched some of them on an official visit in 1669,
together with the newly named towers and fortresses they interlinked,
Peterborough Tower, York Castle, Henrietta Fort, Charles Fort, James Fort.
Intricate and precise, the last substantial works Hollar ever completed, these
drawings suggest something of the scale of the English investment in
Tangier, and their confidence at this stage in its permanence.[6] The draw-

ings convey something else as well. Hollar's panoramic views of the new fortifications are clearly designed to impress, yet at the same time he makes Tangier appear familiar and even domestic. A workman and his wife dressed in sombre English fashions trudge homewards arm in arm, their only protection an ambling dog. Carts trundle usefully along well-built roads. And the neatly tiled roofs of the houses inside the city's fortified walls cluster together as reassuringly as if they were located in Hollar's adopted London or his native Prague. Looking at these scenes, there is precious little to indicate that they are set on the northernmost shores of Africa.

Nor did Hollar's employer, Charles II, intend that there should be. Tangier's royal charter, issued in 1668, confined office-holding and voting in the colony to Christians and of course to men. The region's Muslim inhabitants, it insisted, were 'so barbarous and so poor and so continuously embroiled in civil wars, that no near prospect can be imagined to make them apprehended'. In the official mind, Tangier was projected as a substantial colony of settlement with an agenda from the start of expansion, commerce and anglicisation; and initially some roots were put down. By the 1670s, there were almost as many civilian settlers in Tangier as there were soldiers, including over 500 women and children.[7] They lived in a city marked out now with English street names and with its own corporation. Every Sunday, Tangier's mayor, aldermen and common councilmen would put on specially designed scarlet and purple robes and process stickily to its Anglican church, where a pew lined with green velvet cushions awaited the colony's governor and his lady, and a carved and painted image of Charles II's coat of arms was prominently displayed. Through the leaded windows, the more inattentive worshippers could catch a glimpse of an ancient monument inscribed in Arabic still standing firmly in the new Anglican churchyard. But, if their eyes strayed in that direction, it was probably only for an instant, for after the service there were other pursuits to look forward to, especially if you were male. There was Tangier's new bowling-green, where the resident army officers played against the more affluent inhabitants, or the city's growing range of brothels or, for the chaste and studious, a visit to its library from which some unknown settler stole away with the single copy of John Milton's *Paradise Lost*.[8] These colonisers, it seemed, were making themselves at home.

Never before in its history had the English state, as distinct from private investors and trading companies within it, devoted so much effort and thought, and above all so much money to a colonial enterprise outside Europe. The surviving accounts, which are incomplete, suggest that in the 1660s Tangier cost on average over £75,000 every year. Cutting down on its military garrison and establishing a civilian administration failed to

6. Inside colonial Tangier.

7. The bowling green.

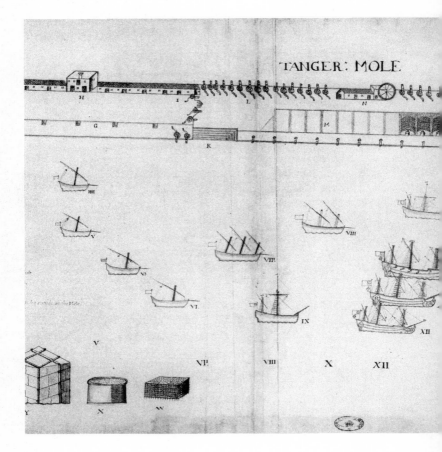

reduce the drain on the Crown. Average annual expenditure on the colony between 1671 and 1681 rose to almost £87,500. Altogether, this North African episode appears to have sucked in close to two million pounds, a substantially greater sum, as Tangier's last governor, Lord Dartmouth, remarked, than Charles II spent on his other overseas outposts, or on all of his garrisons on home territory put together. Over a third of this money went on funding Sir Hugh Cholmley's stupendous mole.[9]

Outwardly at least, the man behaved as though unrelenting energy and technical ingenuity were enough to transform and possess an alien landscape. He removed so many rocks from Tangier's beaches that its city walls began to subside. Undeterred, he blasted out a new quarry to the west of the settlement, and built a road to transport stone from there to

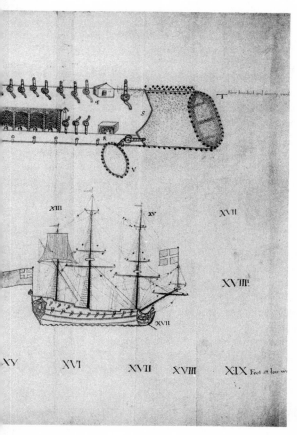

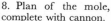

8. Plan of the mole, complete with cannon.

the mole. When the garrison troops, who laboured on the project in their hundreds, still proved insufficient for the task, Cholmley imported skilled workmen from Yorkshire, building them a dormitory town that he named after his native Whitby. Nothing, it seemed, was to get in his way. An uncle summoned to Tangier to assist him sickened and died. His own wife had the temerity to fall pregnant. The family's maids were captured at sea by Barbary corsairs. Yet still Cholmley pressed on. By 1668, in defiance of atrocious weather and at a huge cost in money and lives, Cholmley's mole already extended some 380 yards from the North African shore. By the mid-1670s, it stretched 457 yards out to sea, was 110 feet in width, and rose eighteen foot out of the water. Twenty-six cannon guarded one side, while two batteries of 'great gunnes' protruded from the other.[10]

This was by far the most ambitious engineering work ever carried out up to this point by Englishmen working outside Europe: and in this, as in other respects, Tangier's significance in imperial terms was much greater than itself. Its astonishing mole was the first of those ambitious constructions in stone, brick and iron – bridges, dockyards, railways, roads, dams and canals – which the British subsequently scattered over every part of their overseas empire, means to facilitate trade, transport and control, but also attempts to compensate for their own intrinsic smallness and sparsity of numbers by imposing on the landscape large, enduring monuments in their own technological image. In one draft of his memoirs, Cholmley even compared himself to Nebuchadnezzar, the Babylonian ruler of the Old Testament, who built a mole to subdue the inhabitants of Tyre. A more appropriate analogy, as it turned out, would have been King Canute, except that what was advancing against the English at Tangier was more than just the power of the sea.

Winter gales and fierce coastal currents breached the mole some thirty times during its construction, reducing Cholmley to bouts of despair that he was wasting his youth and energy on an 'endless feeding of the sea with stones'. Not until 1677 was his surveyor, Henry Sheeres, able to inform London that the project had finally been completed. Tangier's mole, all three million cubic foot and 170,000 tons of it, now stood firm in the water, crowed Sheeres unoriginally, 'like a rock'.[11] Just seven years later, the rock shattered into rubble. Forced to evacuate Tangier in 1684, the English exercised the only power left to them and destroyed what they had previously built up at such cost. The intricate houses, the splendid forts, the ringed, defensive walls that Wenceslaus Hollar had found so sketchworthy, and finally Cholmley's engineering triumph, the great mole itself, were all detonated and demolished so as to avoid yielding them up to those Moroccan armies that had always been in wait and watching as the English focused on the dangerous, commerce-laden sea. On Charles II's orders, new-minted coins bearing his engraved image were buried deep in what was left of Tangier: 'which haply, many centuries hence when other memory of it shall be lost, may declare to succeeding ages that [this] place was once a member of the British empire'.

Now, alas, Tangier!
That cost so dear,
In money, lives, and fortunes . . .[12]

It is a strange picture. Men in salt-stained, dust-encrusted uniforms scrambling over smoking ruins, feverishly digging small graves for samples of the king's coinage, as colonial ambition dwindles into the stuff of archaeology. But then the entire Tangier episode appears strange in the light of conventional and current narratives of empire, so much so, that it is usually left out of them altogether. Despite its drama and importance at the time, the unprecedented amounts of state money poured into it, and Cholmley's extraordinary, vanished marine masterwork, only one major book has ever been written about Tangier's rise and fall as seventeenth-century England's most elaborate and expensive extra-European colony. Even this was published before the First World War, and it is suggestive that the E.M.G. Routh whose carefully neutral initials grace the title page of *Tangier: England's Lost Atlantic Outpost* (1912) was a woman, someone who worked outside the then almost entirely male establishment of imperial historians. Routh's solitary and scrupulous investigations have had little impact. The most recent and authoritative survey of England's fledgling empire in the seventeenth century, compiled by a team of American and Irish as well as British scholars, glances at Tangier barely half a dozen times in well over 500 pages.[13] As for Sir Hugh Cholmley, that strange, maniacal imperial projector and builder, his name has long since disappeared from the history books and is absent, too, from *The Dictionary of National Biography*. It is a powerful demonstration of just how effectively Britain's sporadic imperial disasters and retreats were expunged from the historical record and from national and even international memory.

Yet this lost Tangier episode is vital to a proper understanding of Britain's empire in its early modern phase, and a natural starting-point as well from which to explore its varied imperial captivities. Tangier was not a one-off, any more than it was just a cul-de-sac along Britain's uncertain route to temporary global dominion. A post-mortem of this failed colony reveals directions and characteristics that prevailed more widely, and stresses and vulnerabilities that proved persistent.

To begin with, Charles II's monetary and imaginative investment in Tangier is a reminder of the importance of the Mediterranean as a cockpit for contending states and religions, as a place of commerce, and as a site of empire. This point has been largely obscured because the master-narrative of British imperial expansion in the seventeenth and eighteenth centuries has always been the rise of the American colonies and their ultimate revolution, an approach that has been further reinforced by the current primacy of the United States. The fact that Fernand Braudel

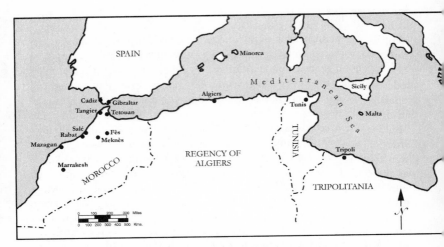

The Mediterranean and North Africa in the early eighteenth century.

ended his superb geo-historical saga of the Mediterranean world in 1598, and suggested – at least initially – that the sea declined abruptly in importance after 1650, has also encouraged historians to concentrate attention thereafter on the Atlantic and on the rise of extra-European commerce and colonies.[14] Yet the Mediterranean remained a major zone of activity for the British and other maritime powers long after the mid-seventeenth century. We have already seen one reason why this was so: the profitability of this zone in commercial terms. In 1700, Southern Europe and the Mediterranean accounted for as much of Britain's trade in terms of value as India and North America did put together; and, even at the end of the eighteenth century, there were probably as many British ships and crews active in the Mediterranean as there were in the Atlantic.[15]

Like other zones of British imperial enterprise, however, the Mediterranean was never just about trade. Here, as elsewhere, empire was also driven by the rivalries and insecurities of the major European powers. An essential part of Tangier's appeal had been that it offered a base from which the Royal Navy could monitor the Spanish fleet at Cadiz and Cartagena, and the French fleet at Toulon. Established at Tangier, with proper resources for ships to re-fit, re-provision and winter over, England hoped to be able to intervene rapidly in the event of either or both of these states massing their fleets for an assault on its colonies or against its own coastlines. Just how well Tangier functioned as a naval base in fact has been a matter of debate, but there can be no doubt that it was the prototype for a succession of similar and more enduring Mediterranean strongholds – Gibraltar, Minorca, Malta, Cyprus, and the Ionian Islands. These bases would constitute Britain's empire *inside* Europe, a territorially modest, often forgotten, but strategically indispensable element of its global enterprise, which would become even more important once India and the Suez canal had been seized.

But, in the seventeenth century and after, there were other empires bordering on, and involved in this sea. As Braudel chronicled with such magnificent sweep and arresting detail, the early modern Mediterranean was above all a region where the different states of Western Christendom confronted and sometimes co-operated with the Ottoman empire and with Islam. And it was this complex and protracted engagement, between the Mediterranean ambitions of the Western powers and the forces of the Crescent, that lay at the heart both of the failure of colonial Tangier, and of seventeenth- and early eighteenth-century Britain's most significant captivity fears.

At the time that Sir Hugh Cholmley was constructing his doomed masterwork at Tangier, the total population of the Ottoman empire may have been approaching some 30 million souls, as against the 5.5 million men and women who lived in England and Wales at that point. On paper, at least, the Ottoman armed forces – the janissaries, provincial militias and timariots – were well over 150,000 strong, many times as large again as the armies at the disposal of early modern England's monarchs.[16] Because of its size, wealth and populousness, the Ottoman empire was a rich market for overseas traders, but it controlled most of its own inland trade, just as it generated its own advanced manufactures, paper, glass, gunpowder, sugar and the like. It also possessed a sophisticated administrative structure that for a long time coped expertly with the demands of imperial conquest. Within a few years of seizing western Crete from Venice in the mid-seventeenth century, for instance, the Ottomans had implemented a tax census of the island itemising its property down to the last beehive. Not until the eighteenth century would the British come close to matching this degree of fiscal zeal and efficiency even in their own islands, never mind in their overseas territories.[17] The Ottomans regarded the Mediterranean as peculiarly their own. They controlled its north-eastern coastline through Serbia, Albania, Morea and Turkey. They secured access to its easternmost part through their conquest of Egypt and Syria, and to the western Mediterranean through their North African provinces, Tripoli, Tunisia, and Algiers. It was in part from these last three outposts of Ottoman power and influence that fleets of Muslim corsairs issued into the Mediterranean and the Atlantic, and preyed for centuries on European shipping and exposed shorelines.

The other major North African corsairing power was Morocco. This was not a part of the Ottoman empire, but was culturally influenced by it, and attentive – as all Muslim states were – to the religious significance of its sultan. During the first two-thirds of the seventeenth century, Morocco had been disjointed by civil wars: but then came the Alaouites, the dynasty that rules the country to this day. The second Alaouite sultan, Moulay Ismaïl, was a correspondent of Louis XIV of France, as great, if not an even greater builder, and a mature ruler for almost as long, from 1672 to 1727. Moulay Ismaïl was also a brutally effective centraliser, coming down hard on challenges to his authority from his own population, stamping out Ottoman attempts at interference, and launching successful assaults against many of the small European fortified settlements that had been clinging to the Moroccan coast since the fifteenth century. The Spanish were driven out of Larache, Mamora and Asila. As for English Tangier, it was 'besieged so closely', exulted one Muslim chronicler, 'that the Christians had to flee on their vessels and escape by sea, leaving the place ruined from bottom to top'.[18] This put it too simply, but it was certainly the case that pressure from powerful Moroccan armies, equipped with weapons fully comparable to those of Tangier's English garrison, deterred many families from settling here, undermined the commercial and expansionist dreams of those in residence, and forced on the colony human and defence costs which in the end its masters in London were no longer willing to afford.

The English had always recognised of course that occupying Tangier would bring them into direct contact with Islamic societies, but they had been divided as to the likely consequences of this. Some felt confident that – as with the English East India Company's coastal settlements in Mughal India – proximity to rich, powerful Muslim empires was bound to foster commerce. Moreover, it was thought that if the Royal Navy could only succeed in establishing itself at Tangier, then the danger that North African corsairs presented to English ships and sea-goers would be much reduced. Others however – including Hugh Cholmley – appear to have been nervous from the outset about the threat to the English from Moroccan military power and resistance. When an experienced Scottish soldier, Andrew Rutherford, Lord Teviot, took up the post of governor of Tangier in 1663, he found the garrison's morale already shaken: 'such was the fear they harboured for the Moor'. Teviot's response was energetic and ultimately unwise. He built up the colony's defences, tried to win over and divide local Muslim war leaders, and in May 1664 led a force of 500 elite troops outside Tangier's city walls to prove that Charles II's imperial power in North Africa could stretch beyond them. Teviot and all but nine of his men were promptly wiped out by Moroccan armies.

Subsequent governors of Tangier reacted by constructing still stronger defences, but also by reining in ambition. Initial English projects of using the colony as a point of departure into the North African interior were now tacitly abandoned in favour of simply hanging on. 'We have never sent any to understand their country,' one writer admitted glumly, 'to search into their strength and dependencies, to examine their interest.'[19] Even hanging on came over the years to seem ever more unlikely. By 1680, Moroccan forces were strong enough to seize three of Tangier's forts. Its then governor, Sir Palmes Fairbourne, had offered to surrender one of these – Henrietta Fort – if the men defending it were allowed to go free. The Moroccan commander brushed the offer aside: 'He wanted not stone-walls, but slaves for his master's service, that he could destroy them when he pleased.' Three days later, he did just that. Although eventually driven back, Moroccan armies went on to kill Fairbourne, as well as hundreds of English troops, and seize a further fifty-three men as slaves.[20] Such episodes of bitter defeat, violent deaths, and multiple captivities would be repeated many times in Britain's imperial history.

But this was not the only way in which this brief colonial adventure in Tangier proved both a failure and a portent. For as Moroccan force was exerted, the morale and cohesion of the English frayed and sometimes snapped entirely.

Pressure points

Britons and other Europeans engaged in imperial enterprises outside their own continent are sometimes imagined as monolithic contingents, their solidarity only enhanced by contact and conflict with non-Europeans. This was rarely ever simply and straightforwardly the case; and in Tangier the fracture lines among the colonisers themselves were at once particularly acute, and in some respects extreme versions of tensions that would recur in other imperial locations at other times.[21] The fundamental problem here – as so often – was an insufficiency of manpower. Initially, Tangier's garrison was some 4000 men strong; and there was broad agreement in London that this number should ideally be maintained. In practice, however, there were rarely more than 1500 soldiers in the settlement after 1670, because there was insufficient money available for more, or even to pay the existing ones on time. During the seventeenth century, the English state had become more actively concerned with overseas ventures, and less willing to concede the initiative in such matters to private enterprise. But its ability – as distinct from its desire – to exert and expand control outside its own domestic boundaries, whether in the Mediterranean, or North America and the Caribbean, or Asia, remained a constricted one. In 1670, Charles II would commission a magnificent silver medal from John Roettiers making clear the scale of his imperial aspirations. *Diffusus in Orbe Britannus*, proclaimed its motto: Britons spread throughout the world. Just two years earlier, however, the king had been obliged to give up attempts at direct rule over Bombay. The royal budget could not stretch to Indian adventures at this stage, and neither could the Crown's armed forces. A land attack on Bengal in 1686 in which royal troops participated proved a disaster; and so did a naval campaign against Western India two years later.[22] Set against this context, the fate of Tangier was just another, if more spectacular demonstration of the limits at this stage of the overseas power and personnel of the English state.

Starved of manpower, its garrison's pay always in arrears, hemmed in on the one side by the angry sea, and on the other by superior Moroccan military numbers, Tangier became a prey to festering internal divisions. Many of the garrison troops had fought in the civil wars of the 1640s and '50s for the sake of Parliament and a godly English republic. Sweating now under an alien sun, some of them wondered aloud why they should venture their lives for the sake of a king. 'When I served Oliver Cromwell', one Tangier corporal was heard to complain in 1663, 'I was paid like a man, but now I serve I do not know whom, I am paid like a turd.' Charles II was 'no Englishman' grumbled another Tangier soldier, accurately enough, 'but a Scotchman or a Frenchman'. Both of these men were executed.[23] Some of the settlement's womenfolk also rebelled, mainly it seems out of poverty, boredom and quarrels with neighbours or lovers, but sometimes again for the sake of politics. In June 1664, one Margaret Summerton was found guilty of sedition and of trying to raise a mutiny. She was flogged in front of Tangier's assembled garrison, before disappearing into its prisons and from the archives.[24]

But it was national differences and religious differences that caused the most persistent trouble. On paper, Tangier was an English colony, but like all English, and ultimately British colonies at all times, it contained a medley of nationalities, religions and cultures. There were Dutch, French, Italian, Portuguese and Jewish settlers, as well as fluctuating numbers of Muslim slaves and traders; and there were Welsh and Scottish settlers and soldiers. The main groupings though were the English and Irish, with

9. Demolishing Tangier's mole in 1684, by Dirck Stoop.

Protestants and Catholics well represented in both camps. These religious and national factions constantly jostled against each other, not always in predictable ways. During the siege of 1680, Irish Catholic soldiers and officers defending one of Tangier's forts on behalf of the King of England were obliged to call out instructions to each other in the Gaelic language, so as to avoid being understood by some English Protestant renegades who were serving with the Moroccan forces outside the gates.[25]

As this incident suggests, desertion was a major problem at Tangier. To begin with, a few dozen of the garrison's troops slipped away every year; but much higher numbers defected as the years went on, as pay fell into arrears, and excitement and professionalism faded into boredom and loss of hope. At all times, as the English high command admitted, far more of their men deserted to the Moroccan forces and to Islam, than there were Moroccan defectors willing to try their luck in Tangier as Christian converts.[26] English deserters unlucky enough to be caught by their own side and found guilty were executed, their bodies left hanging from scaffolds until consumed by the sun and carrion birds. Those who managed to convince the courts that their passage beyond Tangier's walls had somehow been innocent, or that they now bitterly repented of their actions, might have their penalty commuted to slavery – and this was the term actually employed in sentencing. They would be put to work without pay on the ceaseless task of repairing fortifications, iron shackles fixed to their wrists and ankles. Thus were English (and Irish, Scottish and Welsh) actors in empire reduced to slavery by their own kind.

It is striking indeed just how much of the language applied to Tangier by its occupiers resonates with images of confinement. For Lord Dartmouth, in his final speech to the colonists before dismissing them in early 1684, the very walls around Tangier which the English had built at such cost, together with the hills behind the settlement, evoked claustrophobic narrowness and irksome restraint. This was in reply to an address from Tangier's settlers thanking Charles II for recalling them 'from danger to security, from imprisonment to liberty, and from banishment to our own native country'.[27] Such complaints may have been partly sour grapes, but other, earlier comments made about the colony by those with direct experience of it strike a very similar note. Tangier was a 'perfect prison' declared some of its early occupiers. And a one-time settler in the colony claimed that the garrison troops viewed it as 'an ill prison, from which they could only hope to be freed by a grave'.[28] For the British, such prison analogies proved to be the colony's most durable cultural legacy. Until the end of the eighteenth century, one of the worst sections of Newgate prison in London was colloquially referred to as Tangier. Airbrushed out of polite histories of the British empire with a thoroughness that misleads to this day, Tangier continued for a while to be remembered at demotic level as a place of confinement and duress, as a site for captivities.

In this respect too, this initially cherished and celebrated colony that came to grief, possesses a much wider imperial relevance. Tangier demonstrates, as would so many later emergencies and disasters, the risks and dangers that England and later Britain could incur in combining overseas territorial ambitions with inadequate military manpower and parsimonious funding. It illustrates how the business of empire sometimes laid real as well as metaphorical chains on the activists directly involved, especially but not uniquely on poor whites. It shows how, when men and women were stranded hundreds of miles from home, and under pressure, discipline and loyalty could fray and fail, and ethnic, religious and political divisions come to the surface. And it demonstrates how, in these circumstances, Welsh, Scottish, English and Irish men and women could become vulnerable to capture, or change sides of their own volition. Tangier was the spectre at the imperial feast, a grim and embarrassing reminder of how difficult, in practical terms, sustaining empire at this early stage could be for Britons, and conversely of just how much effort, adjustment and expense would be required if a greater measure of success was to be achieved in the future. Little wonder, then, that when the rise of British imperial power came finally to be re-imagined as inexorable and inevitable, the story of this particular colony was quietly covered over and left undisturbed.

Which is why disinterring this episode is important. Investigating Tangier, and recognising the degree to which many of its problems were portents of things to come, obliges us to begin approaching the British empire in a more varied, more open-minded, and less over-determined way, and to seek out new things. It reminds us that – for the British – there were paths not taken, interludes of retreat, sporadic failures and significant limits, as well as formidable and indisputable exertions of power, and that those who made this empire were always diverse and sometimes at odds with each other. Investigating Tangier also brings us into contact with the Mediterranean, with its commercial, naval and strategic importance, and with the power and aggression displayed here by the forces of the Crescent, as well as by the states associated with the Cross. All of these elements – trade, naval and strategic imperatives, and the complex relationship between the Western powers and Islam had been closely involved in the rise and fall of colonial Tangier. They also provide the essential context for the British experience of the Mediterranean as a zone of captivity. The sea that enticed them could also entrap.

10. The frontispiece of John Ogilby's *Africa*.

TWO

The Crescent and the Sea

Barbary

In 1670, John Ogilby published a sumptuous volume entitled simply *Africa*. A Scot, turned London printer and entrepreneur, Ogilby pirated sections of this compendium of real and bogus information from earlier works, while adding material and illustrations of his own. He could easily have chosen to preface it with a view of Tangier, at this stage still an English colony and widely expected to lead to further imperial and commercial gains in North Africa. Instead, he selected a very different and much less complacent frontispiece.

A resplendent black ruler, in leopard-skin cloak and with sceptre in hand, sits enthroned amidst a vision of Africa's people, animals and landscape. There are large-eyed ostriches, supercilious camels, oddly attenuated pyramids, coiling snakes and strange birds; and there is a 'Hottentot' or Khoikhoi woman, whose breasts are so pendulous and elastic that one is stretched back across her own shoulder by a fiercely suckling infant.[1] In this imagined Africa, all is magic, menace and monstrous deviations from European norms. Yet more is on show here than simply the white man's prejudices. In the lower right-hand corner of the engraving, an individual stands gazing up intently at his regal black master. High cheek-boned, mustachioed, broad-shouldered and therefore strong, he wears a turban, the accepted emblem of Islam. Casually, he holds the chains of some fettered, naked slaves. Only these slaves are white; and they are also male. For Ogilby's English readers at the time, the act of opening his book on Africa would have meant being confronted at once with a representation of their own kind in captivity and slavery.

They would have understood the allusion instantly, though by now we have largely forgotten. Throughout the seventeenth century and in the early 1700s, England's (and subsequently Britain's) most widely known and controversial contacts with Islamic cultures were with the so-called Barbary powers, Morocco, Algiers, Tripoli, and Tunisia, the last three all regencies or military provinces of the Ottoman empire. Between 1600 and the early 1640s, corsairs operating from these North African territories seized more than 800 English, Scottish, Welsh and Irish trading vessels in the Mediterranean and Atlantic, confiscating their cargoes, and taking their crews and passengers into captivity. Some 12,000 English subjects may have been captured over these decades, and in most cases subsequently enslaved for life in North Africa and elsewhere in the Ottoman empire. Between 1660 and the 1730s, at least another 6000 Britons fell foul of Barbary corsairs. In all, over the course of the seventeenth and eighteenth centuries, there were probably 20,000 or more British captives of Barbary. These represented only a fraction of the total number of European men and women confined in North Africa over this period. There were also French, Neapolitan, Dutch, German, Scandinavian, Portuguese, American and above all Spanish captives and slaves. As late as the 1760s, 1400 Spaniards had to be redeemed from Algiers alone.[2]

Europeans who commented on this trade in humanity at the time – like many who have written on it since – rarely took the trouble to locate it in its full Mediterranean context. They simply branded the men responsible, whether they were Moroccan, Algerian, Tunisian or Tripolitan, as Barbary or Turkish pirates, terrorising the seas, preying on legitimate, peaceful trade, and selling innocent Christians into Muslim slavery. The term 'Barbary' referred originally to the Berbers, North Africa's indigenous people.[3] As the British commonly used it, however, 'Barbary' served as a blanket term for the entire North African region (excluding Egypt), and for all of its diverse peoples, Arabs, Berbers, Moriscos, Ottoman soldiers and officials and more. And the assonance between Barbary as a geographical signifier and the insult 'barbarian' was a gift of which generations of polemicists made abundant and predictable use. 'The sink of trade and stink of slavery,' wrote the clergyman and voyage-writer, Samuel Purchas, of Algiers in the early 1600s:

> the cage of unclean birds of prey, the habitation of sea-devils . . . the whip of the Christian world, the wall of the Barbarian; terror of Europe . . . scourge of the islands, den of pirates.[4]

'Pirates', like Barbary, was a convenient and common epithet, but not an accurate one. It put the men who set sail out of Algiers, Morocco, Tunisia or Tripoli to hunt down European shipping on a par with England's own sea-robbers, who were still common enough around its own coastlines in 1600, and active in the Caribbean and other waters for much longer. Greed, need and aggression linked all of these sea-goers, but most North African 'pirates' were not independent agents operating outside of their home communities' laws, so much as a vital and officially recognised part of their revenue-raising machinery. In the regency of Algiers, the biggest threat to English shipping before the 1680s, the governor received a share of the profits on all cargo and captives seized by crews based in his territory. Morocco's rulers also levied taxes on men and merchandise taken by their subjects at sea. Barbary 'pirates' are therefore more properly styled corsairs or privateers; and North African corsair attacks, unlike pirate attacks, were rarely indiscriminate. It was Christian shipping that these corsair fleets targeted, especially ships from countries with which they and their sponsors regarded themselves as being at war.

Not for the last time, Western powers were more ready to condemn aggression on the part of Muslim forces, than acknowledge the parallels existing between it and their own actions. For Europeans practised Mediterranean corsairing too, though not all of them to the same degree. As Peter Earle has described, Malta's sea-going Knights of St John routinely preyed on Muslim vessels, seizing their crews and passengers and selling them in the open market. There were an estimated 10,000 Muslim slaves in Malta in 1720. Those European powers which possessed substantial Mediterranean galley fleets – France, Genoa, Venice, and the Papal States – also drew heavily on slave manpower seized at sea from Ottoman and Moroccan vessels.[5] But it was Spain, so long a meeting-point between the Crescent and the Cross, that was most intricately involved in this Mediterranean slave trade. Most of the Muslims expelled from its shores in successive waves after 1490 had settled along the North African coast. Some of these men and their descendants (the Moriscos) turned to corsairing in order to make a living in what was always a poor area agriculturally, and to act out a holy war of revenge. At least 15,000 Spanish men and women had to be redeemed from North African captivity in the seventeenth century alone; thousands more, snatched in corsairing raids on coastal villages in Andalusia, or from small craft operating off its shores, died before they got the chance to go home. The other side of all this however was Spain's own population of captive Muslims seized in turn from North African vessels. Searching in 1714 for Moroccan slaves to exchange for some of his own enslaved countrymen, a British naval captain remarked unemotionally that 'amongst the several towns situated on the coast of Spain, there may be Moors purchased at very reasonable rates, such as are aged, blind or lame. It's no matter, all will pass so they have life'.[6]

And what of Britain itself? Unlike Spain, France, or some of the Italian states, it possessed no galley fleet for which a pool of captive Muslim labour might have seemed attractive. Moreover, as we shall see, imperial and strategic considerations increasingly made the British more likely to liberate any North Africans they encountered in captivity than enslave them. But this had nothing to do with scruples about Muslim slavery as such. Moroccan slaves were employed in Tangier throughout its time as an English colony; and in periods of open war with one or more of the Barbary powers, the Royal Navy often sold any of their seamen and traders it captured to European states that did employ Muslim slave labour.[7] There are even stray examples of men and women from North Africa falling into the hands of British transatlantic slavers, and ending up labouring on plantations in the American South.

In Abdallah Laroui's words, then, captive-taking and slave-making were emphatically 'a Mediterranean . . . phenomenon' in the early modern era, and never exclusively a Muslim one.[8] Frenchmen, Spaniards, Portuguese, Italians, Dutchmen, Britons, and even Americans were all involved in the business, as well as crews operating out of the North African powers. But men and women experiencing captivity and enslavement in this region, or living and sailing in fear of it, rarely adopted a considered, comparative perspective on their plight. Most thought only of their own terrors and, if they moved on from this at all, of fellow sufferers of their own country of origin and religion. This was especially true of the British. By contrast with France, Spain or the Italian states, it was rare for Britain to retain North African or any other Muslim slaves and captives on its own soil, so men and women from these islands were unlikely to view North African corsairing as a natural response to their own state's violence and cruelties. And only a minority of Britons seem to have acknowledged any parallel between their own risk of being captured at sea by North African corsairs, and the much greater threat that British slaving ventures increasingly posed to men and women in West Africa. To most Britons, it is clear, Barbary corsairing and captive-taking were simply monstrous acts, a sort of terrorism. Moreover, Barbary corsairs provoked an altogether different level and quality of anxiety than did the privateers employed by Britain's European enemies. It is unlikely that all of the Barbary powers put together captured more English, Welsh, Scottish and Irish vessels over the centuries than did French privateers operating out of the single port of St Malo, who seized 2000 British ships between 1688 and 1713 alone.[9] But such losses to European privateers were confined to periods of open war and viewed in Britain overwhelmingly in commercial terms. Cargoes and vessels might be lost forever; but people rarely were. By contrast, the Barbary threat was more persistent, much less predictable, and always perceived as involving more than just economic risk and damage.

Barbary corsairing alarmed and angered out of all proportion to its actual extent because it seemed the negation of what England and ultimately Britain and its empire were traditionally about. 'Britons never will be slaves', proclaimed James Thomson's 'Rule Britannia' (1740), but North Africa's corsairs could reduce individual Britons to exactly that servile condition. Barbary corsairing also affronted British Christianity and Protestantism, since slaves and captives in North Africa were believed to be at risk of forcible conversion to Islam or, still worse, of opting voluntarily for that faith if exposed to its influence long enough. Most of all, this mode of captive-taking provoked anxiety because it happened at sea. As David Armitage shows, from the sixteenth century onwards, maritime references were regularly employed by writers and theorists on British national and imperial destiny. Those who wanted the island made up of England, Wales and Scotland to be a single, united state – something not achieved until 1707 – invoked the encircling waves as irresistible proof that God and Nature were in favour of this political arrangement. Quite literally, it was the sea that gave Britain its shape. The sea was also the vehicle of Britain's cherished and totemic commerce, and it was vital as well to British mythologies of empire. This was not simply because this empire rested on the power of the Royal Navy. For generations of publicists and politicians, sea-power was what made British empire distinctive and benevolent. The empires of Ancient Rome and Catholic Spain, they argued, had nourished atrocity, corrupted their makers, and ultimately declined, because of their reliance on military conquest. Britain's empire, by contrast – because it was predominantly maritime – would confer freedom and prosperity, and consequently endure. 'Such as desire Empire & Liberty', wrote Sir William Petty in the 1680s: 'let them encourage the art of ship building'.[10]

At one level, then, Barbary appalled because its corsairs converted the sea from an emblem of commerce, freedom, power and proud British identity, into a source of menace and potential slavery. The corsairs also provoked fear because – like Tangier – they brought Britain into sharp and initially disadvantageous contact with the power and politics of Islam. In contrast with central and eastern Europe and the Iberian peninsula, England, Wales, Scotland and Ireland had never before the seventeenth century been exposed to serious manifestations of Ottoman and Muslim physical force. The onset of major losses to North African sea predators after 1600 was thus experienced with peculiar acuteness. At exactly the same time as the English began encroaching as traders and marginal settlers into one great Muslim empire, Mughal India, they also had to deal with Muslim predators in the Mediterranean and Atlantic, and with the warlike, frontier provinces of the most formidable of all Islamic empires, the Ottomans.

Yet to understand the full imperial significance of this particular captivity panic we have to probe rather more deeply. Instead of approaching the Mediterranean in the past primarily as a site for contest and conflict between the Crescent and the Cross, Fernand Braudel insisted, we should regard this remarkable, inland sea as a stage for more complicated encounters:

> The actors on this stage speak many tongues and do not always understand each other; nor do we, the audience, always realise what is really going on, for the plots and story-lines are complex and not always what they seem.[11]

The Barbary powers threatened commerce and the lives and liberties of unlucky individuals, English, Welsh, Scottish, Irish, and many more: yes, indeed. More profoundly, they were feared and hated over a very long period because their chosen medium of manoeuvre and attack was the sea, and because they were Muslims. Yet, as far as Britain and its empire were concerned, Barbary gradually became something more and something different than just a threat and a focus of hate. So we have to do more than count its victims and explore the kinds of captivity and slaveries it inflicted, important though these were. We also need to explore Barbary's changing relationship with the British state, a small European power that was ever more intent on overseas empire, but always dependent on non-European auxiliaries of different kinds in order to attain it.

Counting

All Barbary captives remain imprisoned in substantial historical ignorance. There is much about them that we cannot know and will never know.[12] When British and other European slave-traders purchased men and women from West Africa and shipped them into bondage across the seas, they usually listed their victims and filled out ledgers of the monetary costs involved. This taste for documentation, for writing up the unspeakable, has allowed historians of the transatlantic slave trade to reach a broad if not a complete consensus about its dimensions over time. No such lists or ledgers exist for the very different, but sometimes no less lethal trade in human beings carried out by North African corsairs, though when the Ottoman archives in Istanbul become better known, a surer statistical base

11. The corsair city of Algiers.

for at least some of these captivities may eventually emerge. But while anything approaching a comprehensive head-count of Barbary captive-taking will always be beyond us, the broad outline of its impact on Britain is clear enough.

Stray English ships and seamen had been captured by Ottoman and Barbary vessels in the sixteenth century, a natural consequence of this country's growing involvement in Mediterranean trade.[13] It was dynastic and diplomatic changes at the start of the following century, however, together with a temporary decline in English naval effectiveness, that raised the risk of capture to an entirely different level. When James VI of Scotland also became James I of England, Wales and Ireland in 1603, he made peace with Spain, and thereby aligned his kingdoms with the prime Christian empire of the period and the state most at odds with the Ottoman empire. Retaliation was swift. By 1616, Algiers alone was estimated to have seized over 450 English vessels, and this was just the beginning.[14] Between the 1610s and '30s, Cornwall and Devon, both sea-going counties heavily involved in trade with southern Europe, lost a fifth of their shipping to North African corsairs. In just one year, 1625, nearly a thousand sailors and fishermen from the major West Country port of Plymouth were seized, most within thirty miles of its shore. Overall, David Hebb calculates, in the two decades before the outbreak of the Civil War in 1642, Barbary corsairs inflicted well over one million pounds of damage on English shipping, a sum that needs to be multiplied more than a hundredfold to gain any sense of its meaning in today's values.[15]

Not all of the 8000 or so English, Welsh, Scottish and Irish captives taken to North Africa during these early decades were seized at sea. At this stage, the Algiers fleet was strong enough to stage occasional raids on England's West Country, on the Channel Islands, and the coast of Ireland. Among nineteen women redeemed from Algiers in 1646 were two, Ellen Hawkins and Joan Brabrook, who had been seized fifteen years before from Baltimore, County Cork; six more of the women brought back that year hailed from Youghall further along the southern Irish coast.[16] It was partly these Barbary depredations – on ships, cargoes, lives, and domestic coastlines – that prompted James I's successor, Charles I, to levy ship money so controversially on his subjects in order to raise additional revenue for his failing navy. By the same token, the massive damage that Barbary corsairs inflicted on lives and commerce after 1603 helps to account for growing popular alienation from and disillusionment with these early Stuart kings. To this extent, the power of the Crescent – so often left out of British history entirely – helped to provoke the civil wars that tore England and its adjacent countries apart after 1642.

In the aftermath of these convulsions, English responses to North African corsairing became more systematic. Parliament levied a duty on imports and exports to raise ransoms for the captives, and the Royal Navy became increasingly formidable, equipped with warships which soon outclassed any available to the North African powers. It is easy to assume, and it sometimes has been assumed, that this burgeoning naval power translated swiftly into suppression of Barbary corsairing. 'And who dares choose, through the broad earth to roam', boasted Daniel Defoe in 1707:

> Shall sail safe under British ships of war;
> Then no damn'd Algerines or corsaire dare
> Attempt our persons, or assault our goods . . .[17]

But this was propaganda designed to persuade Scotland's sea-traders, who were vulnerable to Barbary corsairing, to accede to union with England. In reality, rising British sea-power did not and could not immediately wipe out the threat posed by the corsairs.

I have already drawn an analogy between early modern perceptions of the Barbary corsairs, and Western perceptions of terrorism today. There are other analogies. Barbary corsairing resembled modern terrorism in that it was at once so diffuse and so rooted a phenomenon that even substantial naval and military force for a time won only temporary advantages against it. Indeed, and again like terrorism today, the corsairs were able to turn some of the very sources of Western power to their own advantage. After 1650, the English built up an increasingly powerful navy: but this navy had much more to defend. There were 115,000 tons of English merchant shipping in the 1620s; sixty years later, there were 340,000 tons. These statistics are usually cited as straightforward proof of England's expanding wealth and global reach at this time, yet as Gerald Aylmer pointed out: 'the larger a country's merchant marine and the more far-flung its overseas trading interests, the more potentially vulnerable it is to commerce raiding.'[18] Every additional English ship in the Mediterranean and even the Atlantic increased the corsairs' potential harvest.

This was especially the case since most of these ships were small, with limited crews, and few or no cannon to defend themselves. And it was small ships on which North African corsairs increasingly preyed. A list of twenty-seven vessels from Britain and New England captured by Moroccan corsairs between 1714 and 1719 shows that on average each was crewed by fewer than ten men. A similar pattern emerges in later decades. A British envoy sent to ransom some 150 captives from Morocco in 1734 reported that they came from twelve different ships. Easily the biggest of these had a crew of twenty-five. Far more typical, though, was the *Ann* with its crew of six, or the *John*, captured off Malaga with just eight Scottish seamen aboard.[19] For ships of this type, the only real defence against the corsairs was a naval convoy system, and this was not always available or even practicable. Vessels carrying highly perishable cargoes could not afford to wait for a convoy to assemble. Nor were traders always eager to arrive at a foreign port at the same time as a convoy of their competitors, since this naturally lowered the price their cargo could command. None the less, whenever Britain was at odds with a North African power, there were always shrill appeals to the Admiralty from ports involved in Mediterranean trade. 'Such ships are entirely unprovided for making any defence', wrote Bristol's Merchant Venturers in 1754, when another war with Morocco seemed imminent: 'and must unavoidably fall a prey to our merciless enemies (to the great loss not only of the property but lives of many of His Majesty's subjects) unless your lordships will be pleased to send a sufficient number of ships of war.'[20]

The date of this plea – 1754 – suggests just how long fears of North African corsairs persisted, but calculating the actual number of British and Irish captives of Barbary over time is extremely difficult. The last all-out North African assault on shipping from these islands occurred between

1677 and 1682, when England was at war with the regency of Algiers. This conflict cost the English over £800,000, at least 160 merchant ships (some estimates go as high as 500), and some 3000 captives.[21] It ended with a treaty between England and Algiers in 1682. From now on – as well as paying certain subsidies – the English state bound itself to provide its subjects' vessels with formal passes which Algiers agreed to, and usually did, respect. But this was not the end of British and Irish captivity in North Africa. Instead, the main scene of conflict shifted to Morocco. After 1680, its formidable sultan, Moulay Ismaïl, systematised corsairing as a weapon of state finance. All captives seized by Moroccan corsairs now became the sultan's property, and European states were no longer allowed to redeem nationals on an individual or group basis. Instead, they had to pay for all of their captives detained in Morocco at any given time.

The consequences for British shipping were never as lethal as earlier attacks by Algerian corsairs, but they remained serious for much longer. In 1711, corsairs operating out of Morocco cost Britain £100,000 in lost ships and cargos, and this was a year of formal peace between the two countries. During periods of open war – between 1715 and 1719 for instance – British trading losses were much higher.[22] Since Morocco's rulers were always eager to exchange captives for ransoms, the number of Britons within its borders at any given time was usually limited but regularly replenished. In 1690, Morocco held at least 500 British captives. In 1720, some 300 men and one woman from these islands are known to have been confined there; and in 1759 – after a marked lull in captive-taking – there were over 340 British detainees. Yet, as is true of all such estimates, these figures are mere snapshots of captivity, conveying little of its quality or its real dimensions.

Christian prejudice, fear and ignorance inflated many early assessments of the number of captives in Barbary, but later, more conservative estimates could also err and this time on the downside. As far as England was concerned, many of these apparently more judicious totals were supplied by envoys in North Africa who spoke no Arabic, or derived from petitions by the captives themselves. Thus in 1662, 300 men held in the city of Algiers dispatched a petition to London begging to be redeemed. But these men will have represented only a portion of the total number of English captives held throughout the regency of Algiers at this time, some 1200 according to one estimate.[23] Establishing the number of men and women redeemed from captivity over time is rather easier. Before the outbreak of the Civil War in 1642, barely a quarter of all Britons seized by North African corsairs seem to have got the chance to return home, but after 1650 the English state applied itself more systematically to the business of redemption. Between 1670 and 1734, government records suggest that *at least* 2200 captives were shipped back to Britain.[24] These are individuals whose names and places of origin we can establish with a fair degree of certainty. Yet to say that 2200 men and women returned from North Africa over this sixty-year period is far from saying that this was anywhere near the total of English, Welsh, Scottish and Irish captives seized during this time.

To begin with, this figure of 2200 redeemed captives excludes an incalculable number of Britons and Irishmen who made their own escape from North Africa during this period, as well as those who turned renegade and chose to stay on there. It also excludes an unknown number of Scots, since – before and even after the Treaty of Union in 1707 – the Presbyterian Kirk and prominent individuals north of the border often made their own arrangements to bring local seamen back home. Manifestly, this total of 2200 redeemed captives also leaves out individuals killed in the course of capture. Corsair targets only occasionally made a fight of it, but some encounters were bloody and mortal. James Amos, an Englishman taken captive in Morocco in 1718, was the only survivor from a crew of twenty-seven. The rest of his comrades were blown up along with their ship when they tried to resist the corsairing vessel attacking them.[25] More crucially still, not everyone captured was subsequently redeemed. The treaty with Algiers in 1682 stipulated that its inhabitants were not liable 'against their wills, to set any [slaves] at liberty', and that the English state was under no obligation to ransom its subjects, a let-out clause repeated in later treaties. Such provisions help to explain why England had a reputation in Barbary for being more miserly than other states in its response to its captives. In 1674, the governor of Algiers complained to Charles II that an earlier agreement to redeem his city's English captives had still not been honoured: 'In this condition, your men . . . are neither clearly slaves, nor clearly free . . . in this matter you have taken no care, but have gone on in neglect.'[26]

The English state's meanness on this issue was partly a function of its limited resources at this stage, but it was also simply that: meanness. Before 1700, and especially before 1650, ransoming captives held hundreds of miles away sometimes received low governmental priority. Sporadic official inertia in this connection was in some respects made worse by this culture's Protestantism. Catholic European states vulnerable to Muslim privateering had long ago either organised civic societies to look after the business of ransoming, as Genoa did, or relied like France and Spain on two religious orders which had devoted themselves to Christian captives of Islam since the thirteenth century, the Mercedarians and the Trinitarians.[27] After the

Protestant Reformation, these redemptionist orders were no longer available to assist English subjects held in Ottoman and Barbary captivity. The Church of England, the Presbyterian Kirk in Scotland, and various dissenting churches all played major roles in raising ransoms and publicising the plight of Barbary captives, but they lacked the contacts and linguistic skills of the Catholic redemptionist orders in Continental Europe. Without full-time religious activists working on their behalf, captives from Britain and Ireland sometimes felt bereft. 'All nations is provided for', scrawled a desperate and semi-literate captive to his wife from Morocco in 1716, 'but the poor English has no assistance from their nation.'[28] This man never got home.

This was one example (we will encounter many more) of how the politics of English and British captivity overseas overlapped with the politics of social class back home. As was true of all peoples caught up in it, most British and Irish victims of this Mediterranean trade in captive bodies were poor, labouring men. There were some conspicuous exceptions. The earl of Inchiquin was seized by Algiers corsairs *en route* to Lisbon in 1659, together with his son and heir who lost an eye in the attack. But the majority of captives were, predictably, petty traders, fishermen, soldiers in transit to overseas postings, and above all seamen. 'These are the men who make you rich,' William Sherlock told a congregation assembled in St Paul's cathedral in 1702 to celebrate the return of hundreds of North African captives:

> who bring the Indies home to you, and clothe you with all the bravery of the east. These are the men that defend your country in their wooden walls, the great strength and glory of this island.[29]

It was an eloquent summing-up of why Barbary corsairing appeared a particular affront to Britain's essence. Seamen were instruments of Britain's overseas commerce and manned its navy, and these in turn made possible its empire. Yet seamen were the corsairs' pre-eminent victims. They were also overwhelmingly poor men and consequently vulnerable.[30] If seized at sea and held in North Africa, it was extremely unlikely that a common seaman would be able to assemble his own ransom. Unlike prisoners taken in a conventional European war, he could rarely hope to be exchanged for men from the other side. And even if they got to learn of his predicament, his family back in Britain would find it hard to raise money on his behalf. So when the authorities in London were slow to intervene, Barbary captives could be stranded and enslaved in North Africa for many years, and sometimes for ever.

Here is an example. In 1701, five men who had been captured while serving as soldiers in English-occupied Tangier finally returned to their native country from Morocco. The official reporting this noted without comment that they had been 'in slavery for these twenty-four years'.[31] This was an extreme case, but captives from Britain and Ireland often found themselves held in North Africa for five years or more; and, before 1700, ten years was not exceptional. More than anything else, it is the duration of these Barbary captivities that makes the number of men and women eventually redeemed a poor guide to the total captured in the first place. The longer captivity lasted, the more likely it was that those enduring it would cross over and turn renegade or, far more commonly, simply not survive to be freed. In the mid-seventeenth century, one in every five European captives held in Tripoli is known to have died every year. By the eighteenth century, the death-rate among Barbary captives was lower, except in plague years, but it remained substantial. A list of 263 British and colonial American captives in Morocco between 1714 and 1719 shows that fifty-three of these men died over this five-year period: just over 20 per cent of the total number detained. This same list also illustrates how the risk of dying in captivity increased relentlessly along with its duration. Forty-eight of these fifty-three casualties were men and boys whose captivity ordeal had begun in 1716 or earlier.[32]

In many years, plague was the biggest killer of captives and captors alike. Recurrent epidemics reduced the city of Algiers' population from perhaps 100,000 in the early 1600s – about half the size of London's at that time – to some 40,000 by 1800. But, as far as the captives were concerned, major killers also included food poisoning, sudden exposure to a hot climate, shame, despair, and mistreatment. When John Whitehead's boat smashed on Morocco's western coast in February 1691, he and his nine shipmates were seized and marched for weeks on end through Marrakesh to Meknès, a journey of over 200 miles along the foothills of the Middle Atlas mountains. Exhaustion, shock and contaminated water meant that only two of the ten men made it.[33] The trauma involved in being taken by force and reduced to varieties of enslavement in a foreign country, away from friends and family, could also prove lethal. One example of this emerges from the same sample of 263 Anglo-American captives in Morocco just cited. For while, on average, one in five of these men died, among those who had previously been shipmasters, the mortality rate was almost double that: 38 per cent. Shipmasters were generally older than the average crewman, but their previous experience of command may also have made these men particularly sensitive to the terrible loss of status and autonomy involved in captivity. As the Africans whom their countrymen were shipping ever more busily across the Atlantic could have told these British victims, capture and slavery killed through their impact on the mind, not just on the body.

If we factor in those Britons who died during captivity or who were killed while being captured; if we remember that our base figure of 2200 British and Irish redeemed captives between 1670 and 1730 excludes escapees, renegades, many Scots, and those whom the London authorities never knew about, ignored, or were unable to recover; if we remember, too, that this total leaves out English, Welsh, Scottish and Irish seamen who were captured while working or travelling on vessels belonging to foreign states – Spain, Venice, Holland or wherever – and consequently dealt with (or not) by their representatives rather than by Britain: then it seems likely that during this particular sixty-year period well over 5000 Britons and Irishmen spent some of their lives confined in North Africa as captives and slaves. Given that some 12,000 men, women and children from these islands appear to have suffered a similar fate between 1620 and the 1640s, and that another 1200 men were reported captive in Algiers in the early 1660s, it seems almost certain that we should be thinking of a total of at least 20,000 British and Irish captives held in North Africa between the beginning of the seventeenth century and the mid-eighteenth century. How many Britons were held as captives and slaves in addition to this total in other parts of the Ottoman empire after 1600 still remains to be explored.[34]

Britons can be slaves

What did it mean for Britons to be captured and put at risk of enslavement in this fashion, and how were these experiences understood and imagined by their countrymen back home? These questions have never been seriously posed, in part because Britain's notorious role as a dealer in black slaves before 1807 has understandably diverted attention from its own inhabitants' earlier and very different exposure to the threat of slavery. In this, as in other respects, we are not accustomed to scrutinising sources of weakness, fear and failure in rising and ruthless empires, even though they were certainly present, and men and women at the time took their existence for granted.

Moreover, although the Ottoman and North African trade in both white and black slaves existed over a longer period than the transatlantic slave-trade – and was at times comparable in scale – far less is currently known about it, and about the kinds of slavery and forcible confinement operating in these zones over the centuries. Some sites remain of course. If you visit Rabat in Northern Morocco, once a major corsairing centre, you can still enter the medina or old city through the Bab Mellah, and stroll along the narrow and tumultuous Rue des Consuls to one of the places where white captives are known to have been sold, the Souk el Ghezel. But even if you can resist being distracted along the way by the smells of fresh mint, ground spices and new-baked bread, or by displays of goods ranging from tacky, imported toys to jewel-coloured, geometrically patterned carpets, you will still find precious little to see when you finally arrive. The place where unknown numbers of British and other European captives were once stripped, fingered, and haggled over, is now a tree-shaded car park and home to some of Rabat's best wood-carvers, quite lacking in any indicators of its former use.

In contrast to the meagreness of indigenous written and physical evidence, British and other Western sources on Barbary captivities and slaveries are abundant, but shaded with varying degrees of bias. Fear, anger, ignorance and prejudice all worked to distort, and so too did desperation. In the 1670s, the parents and wives of almost a thousand English captives in the regency of Algiers, most of them poor people, dispatched an emotional appeal to the House of Commons:

> The said patrons [Algerian slave-owners] do frequently bugger the said captives, or most of them . . . run iron into their fundaments, rip open their bellies with knives, cut their britches across, and washing them with vinegar and salt, and hot oil, draw them in carts like horses.

Those who drew up this petition can have had little or no direct experience of North Africa or of how the captives were actually faring there. They were merely rehearsing anti-Barbary and anti-Islamic atrocity stories in the frail hope that Parliament might be jolted into ransoming their menfolk. Captives, too, embroidered their sufferings. 'Your petitioners are there to the number of about three thousand in miserable captivity,' wrote some English seamen trapped in Algiers to the House of Commons in 1641:

> Undergoing diverse and most insufferable oppressions as rowing in galleys, drawing in carts, grinding in mills, with diverse such unChristian-like labours . . . suffering much hunger, with many blows on our bare bodies.[35]

There will have been an element of truth to these complaints, but again these men will have wanted to give an unalloyedly negative picture of

12. White slaves being unloaded at Algiers: an English drawing of 1700.

what they were enduring in the hope of persuading Parliament to act. Not until the early eighteenth century, when the threat from Barbary was recognised as receding, did British and other European writings on white captivity and slavery in North Africa become conspicuously more nuanced. In *Robinson Crusoe* (1719), Defoe was careful to distinguish between Barbary captivity in practice and the sensationalist versions on offer in folklore and traditional polemics. His hero falls victim to Moroccan corsairs, and undergoes two years enslavement in Salé in advance of his more lengthy island captivity, but remains throughout phlegmatic: 'the usage I had was not so dreadful as at first I apprehended.'[36]

As this suggests, it is the variety of Barbary captivity experiences, more even than contemporary bias or the paucity of indigenous information, that makes reconstructing them so challenging. At no time – and especially after the early 1720s – were all British captives in North Africa sold into slavery or forced into hard labour. Even those who were experienced markedly diverse fates of widely differing duration. Under Islamic law, to be sure, infidels taken in war, whether on land or sea, and whether white or black, could be enslaved. Certain things followed on from this. All slaves, in whatever system or region of the world, become commodities. Uprooted from where they belong, they are stripped of control over some or all of the most important aspects of their lives. The *Qur'an* recommended that kindness be shown to slaves, but these were still people of inferior status who could be sold, inherited, lent to another owner, or gifted away. Any property they owned was at the disposal of their master or mistress. Both in law and practice, female slaves were at the sexual mercy of their masters, though they were not supposed to be put out to prostitution. British and Irish female victims of Barbary corsairs were always a tiny minority, but – like other European women in this position – many of them before 1720 seem never to have got home. And whether male or female, young or old, black or white, slaves and captives in Islamic regimes, like slaves and captives everywhere, ran the risk of falling into the power of bad owners, guards and supervisors and of suffering sexual and other kinds of abuse.[37]

All this said, both white and black slaves in North Africa lived more diverse lives, and sometimes much freer lives, than the majority of plantation slaves in the Caribbean or American South. Slaves under Islamic law could marry with their owner's permission and own property. There was even a special Arabic term (*ma'dhūn*) for slaves who set up a business, a shop say, or a tavern catering to other Christian captives as well as errant Muslims, and who then handed a percentage of the profits over to their owners. This was the fate of two late seventeenth-century Anglo-Jamaican merchants, a Messrs Nash and Parker. Sailing back from the West Indies to England, their fortunes swollen by exploiting one kind of slave economy, they were captured by Moroccan corsairs and became slaves in their turn in Tetouan. Only in their case, this brought the chance to learn Arabic and local business practices. Once their freedom had been purchased, the two men chose not to return home, but instead set up a trading house in Tetouan which endured into the eighteenth century.[38]

But the most crucial difference between the experiences of white slaves and captives in North Africa, and black plantation slaves across the Atlantic, was that – for the former – deracination and loss of freedom often, though not always, had a temporal limit. After 1650, English, Welsh, Scottish and Irish male captives of Barbary, together with more affluent and protected women detained there, could usually look forward to being ransomed at some point. It bears repeating that such ransoms sometimes took a decade or more to arrive, and consequently arrived too late for those who were unlucky or weak. Nevertheless, the hope of securing them at some point did give owners and employers in North Africa an incentive to keep their British and other European captives alive and moderately healthy. The ransoming system held out the prospect of freedom for captives, and a bounty for their employers. It gave both of them a vested interest in servile survival.

Britons captured by North African powers experienced, then, a wide variety of fates. How they were treated might be influenced by their perceived social class and level of wealth, by their age and gender, and by such skills as they possessed. Those viewed as useful by their captors – such as medical men, boat-builders, fluent linguists and armourers – could be offered all kinds of advancement. In the 1720s, an Anglo-Irishman named Carr, whose brother served in the Royal Navy, was working as Moulay Ismaïls's chief gun-founder in Meknès. 'A very handsome man, very ingenious, and much of a gentleman in his behaviour', this individual had long since buried his captive status, along with his original nationality and religion, in lucrative collaboration, casting 'mortars, shells, cannon etc. as well as can be done in Europe'. Carr's appears to have been a reasonably contented, self-chosen existence, but highly qualified captives of this sort were sometimes excluded from ransoming agreements against their will, precisely because they were too useful to be given up. 'I do keep his accounts and merchandise', complained an unusually well-educated English slave of his Algerian owner in 1646, 'and that keeps me here in misery, when others that are illiterate go off upon easy terms . . . so that my breeding is my undoing.'[39]

The experience of Barbary captivity was also shaped by factors other than the captives' own characteristics and qualifications: by *when* in time they were captured, by *where* exactly they were captured, and by *who* took control of them.

Any moderately healthy European male seized by Barbary corsairs in the first two-thirds of the seventeenth century was at acute risk of becoming a galley slave. Before 1650, Algiers' corsair fleet, for instance, was some seventy vessels strong. Like the galley fleets of France, Spain and the Italian states, it relied on forced labour, with up to twenty-five banks of oars per ship, and three to five men shackled to each oar who might row for more than twenty hours a day. 'Not having so much room as to stretch his legs', remembered the Englishman Francis Knight of his time as a galley slave in the 1630s:

> The stroke regular and punctual, their heads shaved unto the skull, their faces disfigured with disbarbing, their bodies all naked, only a short linen pair of breeches to cover their privities . . . all their bodies pearled with a bloody sweat.[40]

The only blessing of life as a galley slave was that it was often short. Heart-attacks, ruptures, broken limbs, malnutrition and insufficient rations of water to replace what the rowers sweated out were standard occupational hazards. Given levels of intra-state and corsairing violence in the

13. A battle between Barbary corsairs and Royal Navy warships, c. 1670s.

Mediterranean, galley slaves also risked being injured or killed by their own kind. When the English naval commander Sir Thomas Allin attacked the Algiers fleet in 1671, his squadron is estimated to have killed, along with large numbers of Muslim seamen, some 400 of their European rowers, chained helplessly to their benches and unable to escape the cannon-fire and the sea.[41]

By 1700, the risk of British and other white slaves being doomed to the oar was shrinking fast, along with the North African galley fleets themselves. But most male Barbary captives, whether sold formally in a slave market or no, could still expect to be exposed to a period of hard, physical labour, particularly if they were of low status or fell under the control of the state. Moulay Ismaïl employed substantial numbers of European captives on his lavish building projects in Meknès and elsewhere. They were used to make and carry bricks, dig foundations and cut marble, build walls, courtyards and arched gateways, and spade those irrigated Andalusian gardens, that remain beautiful to look at now, but would have been back-breaking to establish. The horror stories emerging from all this that were perpetuated in British and Continental European accounts must be exaggerated, but not always or absolutely.[42] A powerful ruler with thousands of slaves at his disposal was likely to be less attentive to their individual welfare than a small private householder with perhaps just one slave in his employ and an eager expectation of securing a ransom at some point. (In the same way Louis XIV, Most Christian King of France, devoted scant attention to the Muslim captives manning his galleys, or indeed to the Huguenot heretics rowing alongside them.) And for Northern European captives in Barbary, hard labour on public works under an overseer's whip could be lethal in a climate for which most of them were utterly unprepared. When the 350-ton London privateering ship *Inspector* was driven aground in Tangier Bay by a storm in January 1746, almost half of its 183-man crew were killed instantly. Of the ninety-six men left alive and sent as captives to the sultan of Morocco, twenty-one had turned Muslim by 1751. In most cases, religious conversion will not have been the prime motive. These men were put to work for long, hot day after long, hot day, repairing fortifications outside the great medieval city of Fès.[43] Changing faiths in the hope this would lead to better treatment must have struck some of them as their only means of self-preservation.

Captivity in Barbary, then, was not a single fate, and neither was enslavement. All men and women seized by North African corsairs, or wrecked on their shores, underwent a measure of terror; and some went on to experience physical and mental suffering, forced labour under the whip, permanent loss of contact with their country of origin, and premature death. But Barbary captivity might be a very different experience from this. It might involve only a brief stay, being reasonably well cared for, followed by a speedy return once a ransom was paid. And even captives confined to North Africa for several years might learn new languages and attitudes, or adjust to Muslim households where they were treated less as slaves than as family members, or convert to Islam out of conviction or in order to marry a cherished Muslim woman, or enter well-paid employment as mercenaries, medical experts, architectural advisers, or armourers.

The diversity of captive experiences is a warning against any simple, monochrome judgement on the quality and significance of this Barbary threat. Suggestions made at the time, and occasionally since, that Barbary corsair assaults and the enslavement of whites that sometimes ensued were comparable to the transatlantic trade in black slaves are, for instance, unsustainable. By 1670 – though probably not before – the number of blacks being shipped out to slavery annually from West Africa by British and other white traders was indisputably in excess of the total number of Europeans seized every year by Barbary and Ottoman corsairs. Moreover, white corsair victims were increasingly allowed a hope of redemption and return, as black slaves shipped across the Atlantic in this period never were. But while it is wrong to draw comparisons between the North African system of seizing and exploiting human beings and the triangular trade in black slaves, it is no less inappropriate to marginalise Barbary depradations and the slave-systems they serviced, or to suggest – as some have done – that Barbary captivities were simply invented or exaggerated by Europeans as a means of vilifying Islam.[44] Barbary corsairs were highly effective predators who succeeded over the centuries in extorting very large amounts of ransom and protection money from virtually all Western European governments. Even a relatively distant and secure state like Denmark devoted about 15 per cent of its profits from Mediterranean trade to paying them off.[45] Such sums would simply not have been forthcoming had the Barbary threat not been judged to be substantial, or had fears of Barbary slavery simply been manufactured.

For early modern Britons, the fear of Barbary was very real. So visceral were these terrors, indeed, that they long outlasted the corsairs' capacity to do serious harm. This inflected the British vision of slavery in ways that have scarcely been acknowledged. It is often suggested that, after 1600, slavery became 'geographically and racially marginalised', a fate that whites in Europe were able to inflict on people of a different skin colour in regions of the world safely distant from their own. A concept 'of us – white, English, free', writes Orlando Patterson, grew up alongside a conception of 'them – black, heathen, slave'.[46] Yet this neat, binary formulation of white, Western slave-traders on the one hand, and black slave victims on the other, gives insufficient attention to Ottoman and North African slave and forced labour systems. For seventeenth- and early eighteenth-century Britons, slavery was never something securely and invariably external to themselves. They knew, all too well, that this fate sometimes befell people like them. Britons could be slaves – and were. Moreover, before 1730, men and women in Britain and Ireland were exposed to far more information about white Barbary slavery than about any other variety of slavery. This was partly because so many Barbary captives hailed from London, the centre of Britain's print culture, as well as of its shipping and its trade. So what happened to these people received – as we shall see – extensive newspaper, pamphlet, and ballad coverage, as well as prompting church sermons and appeals for ransom money on a nationwide basis. In the seventeenth and early eighteenth centuries, far more Britons must have met, seen and heard about fellow white countrymen who had undergone, or were still experiencing Barbary slavery, than were in a position to encounter personally the relatively few black slaves resident in their islands at that time.[47] Barbary slavery was able to become a nationwide concern at this point to an extent that was not true of black slavery until much later in the eighteenth century.

Let me be clear what I am arguing here. I am not suggesting that Barbary captivity and slaveries were comparable to black slavery in the

Caribbean and North America. Clearly, they were not. The point is rather that slavery at this early stage was not viewed in Britain as racially restricted. Before 1730, at least, the face of slavery – as far as Britons and other Europeans were concerned – was sometimes white. Public and private language bear this out. References to English, Scottish, Welsh and Irish men and women being enslaved in North Africa were common propaganda currency. 'A great number of our good subjects peaceably following their employment at sea', stated a royal proclamation in the 1690s, were now '. . . slaves in cruel and inhumane bondage . . . driven about by black-a-moors, who are set over them as task-masters' – a reference to Morocco's black slave soldiers who sometimes served as overseers to white captives. Similar vocabulary crops up in official documents not intended to serve a polemical purpose. In 1729, an envoy dispatched to Morocco to ransom British subjects there described his mission in a private memorandum as 'to demand His Majesty's subjects unjustly taken and detained in slavery'.[48] The existence of white slavery involving Britons was taken for granted.

For some, this must only have made acquiescence in black slave-trading easier. The business of slavery – like the business of making empires – was undoubtedly facilitated in the early modern era by widespread recognition that such practices were ubiquitous and had always existed in some form. But awareness that slavery could be racially promiscuous sometimes had very different consequences. It encouraged some writers to question the very connection between slavery and presumed inferiority. If 'some one of this island [Britain] . . . should chance to be snapt by an Algerine, or corsair of Barbary, and there to be set on shore and sold, doth he thereupon become a brute?' enquired an Oxford academic in 1680: 'If not, why should an African?' Like many other anti-slavery arguments, this one faded out for much of the eighteenth century, but resurfaced at its end. 'A negro, although in a state of bondage in his own country, is as feelingly affected at being sold into European slavery', argued a writer in 1806, 'as an Englishman would be at becoming a slave to the Moors or Algerines.'[49]

In the intervening era, it became less common, and less acceptable for British writers to refer in print to the possibility of their own kind being rendered subject in anything approaching the fashion of black slaves. And after the 1730s, slavery became rhetorically established as a polar opposite to Britishness to such a degree that men and women still falling victim to Barbary captivity found it very hard to make sense of their predicament. 'A poor slave, as I am at present in the hands of barbarians', wrote a semi-literate English sailor in servitude in Algiers in 1789, '. . . which is contrary to the laws of Great Briton to have a true Briton a Barberish slave.'[50] 'Contrary to the laws of Great Britain': the certainty is striking. It was also a comparatively recent growth. Back in the seventeenth century, and earlier in the eighteenth century, things had been very different. At that stage, the scale of Barbary captive-taking, together with the rumours, writings and campaigns surrounding it, had meant that neither British nationality nor white skin colour could be viewed as reliable guarantees against the experience of slavery. Britons at that stage had not securely ruled the waves, still less the world. They could be slaves, and some of them were.

Sea raiders and a sea empire

Individual Britons might be forced to stand, then, half-naked in a public space while strangers methodically assessed their flesh and musculature, waiting under a harsh North African sun until an auctioneer sold them; or forced to labour in fear of a whip wielded perhaps by someone who was not white. For their countrymen at the time, these were the most dramatic and obvious respects in which Barbary had the power to turn their world upside down. And, as we have seen, individual liberty was not the only fetish the corsairs outraged. They preyed on commerce, the god of British idolatry; and they attacked at sea, which the British aspired to dominate. In retrospect, however, there is a more significant respect in which Barbary can be viewed as having turned things upside down. After 1600, the islands of Britain and Ireland changed progressively from being marginal European lands into a highly aggressive and supposedly united state avidly pursuing and for a while possessing prime global power. How, then, was Barbary able to attack British trade and seamen so successfully and so profitably for so long? What did it mean that they could get away with what they did?

One reason for the corsairs' continuing menace, and for Britain's failure (along with other European states) to extirpate them once and for all, was the resilience and reputation of the Ottoman empire. As current Ottomanists are now making clear, this empire was emphatically not in serious decline in the seventeenth century, or even, in some respects, for much of the eighteenth century.[51] To be sure, Ottoman armies were turned back from the gates of Vienna in 1683, their terrible advance into Continental Europe halted forever. But the decisiveness of this defeat was much less apparent to men and women at the time, than it has sometimes been to historians since. The Ottomans remained strong enough to seize all of Morea from Venice in 1715, to make good their annexation of

Western Iran in 1727, and to recover Belgrade from Austria in 1739. Not until the disastrous wars with Russia in the 1760s and '70s did they begin to lose substantial portions of their territory.

The British, like other western Europeans, were certainly more attentive by 1700 to signs of incipient Ottoman decay, and they were also aware that Ottoman control over the three North African regencies, Algiers, Tunisia and Tripoli, was slackening. But although the Ottoman empire was now increasingly condescended to in prose, western European governments remained diffident about challenging it in any more substantial fashion, and early modern Britain never seriously contemplated doing so. Unlike the maritime empires of Spain, France, Portugal, the Dutch, and Britain itself, the Ottoman empire was not dispersed over the globe, and thus dependent on sea-power. It was one vast, alarming bloc, a 'jigsaw of interlocking land masses', as Braudel puts it.[52] Its sheer territorial dimensions, like its huge, ill-disciplined armies, and the size of its population, continued to provoke awe, especially in a small, under-populated country like early modern Britain.

This helps to explain why English (and later British) retaliation against the Barbary powers was often sporadic and consciously limited. Behind the corsairs, and their busy, infuriating, expensive sea-raids, Britain continued to discern the enduring shadow of Ottoman grandeur, and held back much of its fire accordingly. Even in 1816, when the Battle of Waterloo had been won and European and global primacy seemed assured, the British government still resisted hawkish suggestions that it should convert a naval assault on Algiers and its corsairs into a full-blown colonising expedition. 'Are the Christian nations to plant colonies along the [North African] coast', enquired a London journalist sarcastically, fully endorsing this official policy of restraint: 'or is it meant to replace the Turk in full and quiet possession of them?' Evidently he, like the men in Whitehall, regarded such a prospect as wholly unrealistic. Even at this stage, the Ottoman sphere of influence still appeared something to be approached with caution, and left in general judiciously alone.[53]

Moreover, and as the fall of Tangier had demonstrated, the North African powers could be formidable in their own right, and not just because of the Ottoman connection. By the late seventeenth century, their corsairing vessels were no match for British and other Western European warships, but this was less decisive than might be expected. As the Pentagon has been repeatedly reminded in the past and may discover again in the future, even the most high-tech weaponry sometimes fails to achieve success in determinedly low-tech conflicts. Late twentieth-century America possessed sufficient nuclear capability to obliterate Vietnam many times

14. The corsair base of Tripoli.

over, but it could not defeat the Vietcong by conventional warfare, any more than it could invade Baghdad during the first Gulf War at an acceptably low cost to itself. By the same token, after 1650 the Royal Navy was increasingly in a position to destroy whole fleets of Barbary corsair ships, had they been foolish enough to meet it in set-piece sea-battles. But this signified little, as the corsairs rarely operated in this fashion. Like stinging insects, their light, rapid vessels were designed to strike at unarmed or lightly armed merchantmen, while being able to flee very speedily at the mere approach of a warship. Barbary corsairs simply refused to play the Western naval game. They had their own.

As a result, there was not much the Royal Navy could do except sporadically bombard the coastal cities from which the corsairs came. Thus in 1655, Admiral Blake attacked Porto Farina, near Tunis, and destroyed several corsair galleys at anchor there. The effects of such bombardments tended however – as in this case – to be localised and temporary, and the risks involved were high. Before the discovery of longitude in the 1760s, which enabled vessels to establish more precisely where they were in relation to the shore, any ship of the line sailing close to the dangerous North African coastline, especially in poor weather, was at risk of smashing there. Immediately before the British warship HMS *Litchfield* hit the Moroccan shore in 1758, *en route* to Gorée in West Africa, its trained navigators reported confidently that the vessel was still 'thirty-five leagues distant from the land'. This dire miscalculation, a comment on the limits of Western technology at this time, cost the lives of 120 men, as well as supplying the sultan of Morocco with 220 lucrative British captives.[54] Nor was Barbary an easy region for Britain to contemplate attacking on land. Algiers always maintained a sizeable army and this, together with its substantial coastal defences, proved strong enough even in 1775 to repel a Spanish invasion force of 300 ships and 22,000 men.[55] Morocco, too, possessed at intervals a much bigger army than Britain disposed of in time of peace. As a Moroccan official remarked evenly to a British envoy in 1718: 'he knew very well by sea the English would be too hard for them, but by land they did not at all fear 'em.' Why should they, when – at this point in time – Britain's standing army was well under 30,000, while Moulay Ismaïl's forces were estimated by some diplomats to exceed 150,000 men?[56]

This military capacity not only worked to keep the British and other Europeans for a long time at bay, but was also directly and indirectly sustained by them. Morocco and Algiers especially made a point of demanding ransoms for their captives in the form of armaments as well as cash, and for a long time they got what they wanted. In 1700, Britain was obliged to provide 100 gun-locks 'each according to the pattern given by the Emperor [of Morocco]', in return for every single captive it wanted back; while in 1721, a British mission to Morocco to recover over 300 captives handed over 1200 barrels of gunpowder and 13,500 gun-locks.[57] If you visit the Bordj Nord, Morocco's military museum in Fès – and it is a fascinating place, ordered with impressive scholarship – you can still see some of these 'donated' Western weapons today. There are rows of early Georgian muskets on show, each bearing the mark of the Tower of London, as well as displays of French, Spanish, Dutch, Portuguese and Italian guns, mortars, and cannon. Some of these were purchased or captured in battle, but many of the armaments on show were supplied to Moroccan sultans at different times by British and other European governments as payment for captured and enslaved nationals.

Here, then, was a trade in arms between Europe and North Africa that was parasitic on, and positively fostered a trade in people. Barbary corsairs seized British and other European ships' crews and passengers. These captives were then exchanged for money and armaments, which in turn helped the North African powers to equip themselves so as to repel military and naval assaults on their shores, and also to maintain their own corsair fleets. It seems an extraordinary system, yet – like so much else that occurred in this vital Mediterranean zone – this trade in arms possesses a wider significance. It demonstrates a point that we will encounter many times in these pages: namely, that until the end of this period, and so far as land warfare was concerned, there was no invariable gulf between the armaments of Western and non-Western powers. Morocco and Algiers were able to secure (and at times manufacture) sufficiently advanced military equipment to keep British and other European forces at bay until the early nineteenth century, just as they were able to counter superior European naval technology by avoiding fighting in the fashion for which that technology was designed. There is another, equally important point. Looked at closely, this trade in men and arms illustrates how Barbary corsairing facilitated communication and barter between different cultures, while seeming only to precipitate conflict between them.

Because so much imperial history is conceptualised in a manichean fashion so as to emphasise opposition and antagonism – whether it be the rise of racial conflict, or the growing divergence between the West and the rest – it is easy to overlook the parallel stories of deals and compromises constantly going on between European and non-European cultures. Yet, as Braudel always insisted, below the surface of its sharp political and religious divisions, the Mediterranean region was characterised by crossings and collaborations between governments as well as individuals.[58] Muslim corsairs preyed on Christian shipping and treated their captives like commodities: yes. Western European powers dealt in Muslim slaves and sporadically bombarded North African cities: yes, again. But, at another level, at least some of the Christian and Islamic societies involved in this Mediterranean cockpit were interdependent. As we shall see later, in 1756 the Moroccan ruler, Sidi Muhammad, would embark on a furious campaign of captive-taking against the British, not in order to sever relations and provoke war, but so as to pressure them into appointing a consul in his country with whom he could do business.[59] By the same token, fierce British propaganda assaults on the Barbary powers, and sporadic naval violence against them, went hand in hand with a persistent logistical and commercial dependence on them. For without the aid of Barbary, Britain could never have maintained its Mediterranean empire.

Just as Tangier, England's earliest, expensive and abortive Mediterranean colony, has been neglected by historians of empire, so there has been a tendency to gloss over Tangier's more durable successors, Gibraltar and Minorca.[60] These were seized from Spain during the War of Spanish Succession, and confirmed in British possession by the Treaty of Utrecht in 1713. They were deemed vital for the same reasons that Tangier had been. They protected and fostered Britain's commercial interests in the Mediterranean, and they provided bases from which this small, expanding but always nervous power could monitor the fleets of its bigger rivals,

France and Spain. Minorca's Port Mahon, which remains a stunning site to visit, is the second largest natural harbour in the world, and France, Spain and Britain fought each other for it repeatedly until the early nineteenth century.

Yet the importance of these places is often passed over now because they fit uneasily into conventional notions of what British empire was about. Far from being commercially profitable, Gibraltar and Minorca – as Adam Smith complained in *The Wealth of Nations* – soaked up British taxpayers' money at a relentless rate. These minute territories offered no raw materials of value, and no land for hungry settlers. They were also white, European colonies, snatched from a Roman Catholic power. For ordinary Britons, this indeed was why they mattered so much. 'Long live the King and let Gibraltar and Minorca stay English for ever,' roared out the crowd as George II processed through London to open Parliament in 1729.[61] Not a word appears to have been said on this occasion about the importance of the American colonies.

Gibraltar and Minorca were also treated with deep seriousness by those in charge of the British state. It was the short-lived French conquest of Minorca in 1756 – in which two hundred ships as well as the future marquis de Sade were involved – which marked for the British the real commencement of the Seven Years War. Admiral Byng, who was made a scapegoat for the island's loss, would be tried and shot to encourage other British naval commanders never to forget the Mediterranean's absolute centrality to British imperial pretensions, sea-power and trade.[62] Gibraltar and Minorca were viewed as equally vital in Britain's subsequent global contest, its lost war with America; and the former even more so when Minorca was lost to Spain. In 1781, the British effectively gave up Yorktown to its besiegers by dispatching a crucial segment of their fleet from its American station to Gibraltar which was also grievously besieged at this time by the French and the Spanish.[63] This decision makes no sense if we adopt present-day perspectives on the absolute centrality of America. It makes perfect sense if we remember how vital the British viewed the Mediterranean in strategic, imperial and commercial terms.

These same imperatives made it indispensable for the British to maintain some kind of constructive engagement with Barbary. Before 1750, more British troops were stationed in Gibraltar and Minorca than in the whole of North America; while British naval vessels regularly docked and reprovisioned here both before and after that date.[64] Without regular supplies from the North African powers – grain, cattle, fish, fresh fruit, and mules for transport – it would have been impossible to feed these British garrisons in Gibraltar and Minorca, or to run these places as provisioning and repair centres for the Royal Navy. As a British official conceded wearily in 1758, as he contemplated paying out yet more substantial ransoms to redeem captives from Morocco:

> It has been found convenient, for the protection and advancement of our navigation and commerce in general, as well as for supplying His Majesty's garrison of Gibraltar, and his fleets when in the Mediterranean, with fresh provisions, to be at peace with these people.[65]

Here, then, was a Protestant empire, Britain, needing to rely on supplies from Islamic societies – in this case the Barbary powers – in order to control territories seized from and inhabited by Catholic Europeans. It is a powerful reminder that, at this time – as since – the polarity between Western states and Islam was often more pronounced on paper and in polemic than it was in terms of substantial politics. It is also a reminder that, for the British, the business of making and maintaining empire always involved dependence on non-whites and non-Christians, and not merely the experience of ruling them.

Thus Barbary which – like the Mediterranean itself – is often left out of the story of early modern British empire, urgently needs incorporating within it, not least because it alerts us to so many paradoxes and limitations to do with power. The protracted assaults of Barbary corsairs, always expensive and sometimes deadly, illustrate how the downside of fast-growing British maritime trade was sometimes increased vulnerability to attack. The difficulties that the Royal Navy experienced in eradicating the corsairs and in bombarding their North African bases indicate some of the restrictions on Western naval power and technology at this time. Then, as now, the possession of advanced firepower did not automatically confer success against opponents who played and fought by different rules, and who were in this case ingenious and resolute as well in maintaining their own military hardware. Barbary captivities, so often treated as the stuff of picturesque, marginal detail, seemed profoundly menacing to seventeenth- and early eighteenth-century Britons, in part because they suggested that whites as well as blacks might be enslaved. The British state often tolerated these attacks on its trade and its personnel, preferring in the main to pay substantial ransoms rather than declare all-out war, because it continued to be wary of the Ottomans, but also because it had little choice.

For even as they contended with the Barbary powers, the British came increasingly to need them. Britain's relations with these North African societies illustrate some of the contrivances to which a small country was compelled in order to construct a large empire. Charles II's England had not been strong enough to establish a Mediterranean colony at the expense of Muslim North Africa. Tangier had failed, despite all the money, blood and engineering efforts poured into it; and the British would have to wait almost 200 years before establishing another settlement in North Africa itself. None the less, building up a Mediterranean empire did become possible for the British after 1700, but only at the expense of Roman Catholic Europeans, and with North African and Muslim aid. Emphatically not for the last time, its own limited resources required Britain to be dependent on non-European assistance in order to play the imperial game. Like other zones of captivity, then, Barbary challenges, modifies and problematises the story of Britain's empire.

But what of the captives themselves and the tales they told?

THREE

Telling the Tale

Going public

The sea was so vast. The vessels they sailed in were small. Yet still the corsairs tracked them down, by magic and conjuring some sailors believed. It would begin with one or two ships, rarely more, appearing on the horizon. If they flaunted the sign of the Crescent, men straining to identify them knew these were Ottoman vessels, and so possibly from Algiers or Tunisia or Tripoli. Once in range and their identity was clear, the sight of their cannon and heavily armed crews was enough to make most unescorted, civilian ships surrender immediately. But sometimes there was gunfire, splintering timber and killing; and there might also be trickery. In the aftermath of England's treaty with Algiers in 1682, some Moroccan corsairs made a practice of sailing under Algerian colours. They would wait for the approach of a trusting victim, dispatch a boarding party ostensibly to check its sea pass (as the treaty allowed Algiers captains to do), and then suddenly roll out their cannon, overpower the English crew, and fling their futile pass overboard.[1]

This was when terror might be least controllable, the transitional moment when an individual's mundane freedoms and pursuits were overtaken by something utterly different but still largely unknown. Forced below deck on the *John of London* with dozens of other captives in June 1670, his voyage from Lisbon aborted by Moroccan corsairs, a future Anglican clergyman called Adam Elliot found it at first impossible to comprehend what was happening to him. Only when the corsairs adopted a lengthy and circuitous route back to Salé so as to avoid European warships and take more prizes, was Elliot able at last to impose some order on his thoughts: 'There it was that I began to reflect upon my condition, for before the change was so sudden, and the strange uncouth accidents so surprising I had scarce leisure to consider.'[2] Whether seized at sea, as this man was, or on land in other zones of commercial and imperial enterprise, this was usually how individuals began the process of converting their ordeal into a story, desperately trying to make sense of the act of capture itself. If

15. *Seapiece: a fight with Barbary corsairs*, by Lorenzo A Castro.

they survived, this initial, unspoken narrative would be supplemented and reshaped many times over. Reshaped, in order to take account of whatever confinement, mistreatment, new employments and encounters followed, as well as all the other shocks and adjustments involved in being forced into a subordinate and vulnerable position in another country and continent.

Captives who managed to return to Britain might communicate these interior narratives of trauma, endurance, and discovery privately to family, lovers, friends or neighbours, almost always censoring in some respects as they went along. Or they might be ordered to tell something of their story more widely by authority figures of some kind: employers, law officers, courts martial, churchmen or politicians. Sometimes, however, they themselves chose to go public about what had happened to them by means of pen and print. Or others did this for them, using their experiences as the stuff of sermons, political speeches, novels, ballads, drawings, travel accounts and other books.

The matter of Barbary, in other words, was never something just external to Britain, or the business only of politicians, diplomats, the Royal Navy, and those traders, seamen and passengers directly involved. Like other captivities in other parts of the world, like empire itself, Barbary corsairing and its victims impacted richly and diversely on British culture at home, in this case influencing images and fears of Islam, and supplying men and women with information on North Africa and the Mediterranean region more broadly. Before examining the imperial impact of all this, it is important to look in more detail at the modes of communication in Britain itself. The captive's tale took many forms and was the work of many voices. Let us begin with the most powerful.

Church and state

One very basic way in which ordinary Britons learnt about Barbary and its captives was through their pockets. In the 1670s, the political economist, Sir William Petty, calculated that it cost at least £60 to redeem each and every detained prisoner in North Africa, and while this was probably an exaggeration, captives were certainly too numerous at the time Petty was writing for the state to be willing or able to ransom them all out of ordinary revenue. Consequently, and until the 1720s, it was the churches that assumed prime responsibility for raising the necessary ransom money. Every Protestant denomination was involved – Quakers, Presbyterians, Huguenots, non-conformists of all kinds – but it was the

Church of England that did most to mobilise and synchronise fund-raising.[3] Anglicans throughout England and Wales had organised collections for mariners captured by 'the Turks' as early as 1579; and there were other major collections in 1624 and 1647. But Church involvement became more important after 1660, when political and public pressure to redeem captives increased. During the next half-century, a committee appointed by the Privy Council, on which a member of the royal family and the current Archbishop of Canterbury and the Bishop of London always served, presided over five nationwide campaigns to raise ransoms to bring home English, Welsh, Scottish and Irish captives of Barbary.

These campaigns were influential in shaping attitudes and enormously successful in raising money. The collection initiated in 1670 'towards the relief of captives taken by the Turks and Moors of Barbary' secured over £21,500 – several million pounds in present-day values – some of this coming as big donations from wealthy individuals, but most from public collections organised at parish and diocesan level. Predictably, it was the regions most heavily involved in Mediterranean trade and consequently vulnerable to corsairing that gave most: the diocese of Exeter, home to the great West Country ports; the diocese of Norfolk, because of the big merchant communities at Norwich, Yarmouth and King's Lynn; and above all London, hub of trade, hub of government. But every region participated in this emergency effort to some degree, even tiny, impoverished St Asaph in Wales, which managed to contribute £113. The collection begun in 1692 achieved less impressive results, perhaps because heavy wartime taxation at this time eroded the capacity and will to give. Just over £8000 trickled in for the captives over a space of five years. Another nationwide collection, initiated in 1700, did capture the public's imagination, despite the coming of the War of Spanish Succession. By 1705, £16,500 had been donated, some of which went the following year on ransoming 190 men from Morocco.[4]

For the captives and those who loved them, this was what mattered most. Public generosity, mobilised by the churches, set individuals free and brought them home – if they managed to survive long enough. But these campaigns were never just about money. Because of how they were organised, virtually every man, woman and child in Britain and Ireland, within reach of some kind of church, was exposed to arguments, assertions and rudimentary information about Muslim North Africa, the Ottoman empire more generally, and commercial and naval activity in the Mediterranean. Not since the crusades, had the power and content of Islam been ventilated in these islands at such a broad and popular level.

The device used for these early disaster appeals was the Charity Brief, a royal warrant authorising collections for a specified charitable object in every place of worship, and frequently by way of house to house visits as well. It was signalled by the King's Printer issuing a special form, about 12,000 copies for each appeal. This set out in highly coloured language why North African captives were such particular objects of Christian and national concern. Bishops, parsons and ministers would then appeal for donations at successive church services, often preceding this with a special sermon. Church wardens and curates would then visit every household within reach, as the 1692 Brief put it: 'to ask and receive from all the parishioners, as well masters and mistresses . . . lodgers, sojourners, or others in their families, their Christian and charitable contributions, and to take the names of all those which shall contribute thereunto'. As the last requirement makes clear, this was closer to being an additional tax than a strictly voluntary donation. Those individuals who remained unnamed were expected and encouraged to feel shamed. Even live-in servants, who generally paid no taxes, were urged on this occasion to give alongside their employers.[5]

Nor was this all. Charity Briefs were authorised not just for collections on behalf of large numbers of people, but also for private initiatives. The five big campaigns to help Barbary captives between 1660 and the early 1700s were thus only the most dramatic demands for mass action on this issue. In addition, there were hundreds of individual appeals, many of them instigated by captives' womenfolk. In 1676, a Brief was issued to help one Joan Bampfield raise a ransom for her son Edward, a captive in Morocco. Four years later, men and women throughout the land were urged in church to help Mary Butland get her husband Ambrose back from Algiers. Every year then, and often several times a year, church-goers would be reminded of how their countrymen were suffering under the yoke of Islam, and exposed to captivity and slavery. In Tavistock, Devon, congregations dipped into their pockets for North African captives on over thirty different occasions between 1660 and 1680.[6] The breadth of the response was sometimes staggering. In 1680, 730 of Tavistock's citizens – a substantial part of the town's adult population – clubbed together to raise over £16 for the captives. As this suggests, most could not give very much, but almost everybody gave something, from Lady Mary Howard who topped the list of donors with ten shillings, down to poor Elizabeth Harris who could only afford a single penny.[7]

Charity Briefs were used to raise funds for all kinds of emergency: flood victims, for instance, or survivors of an outbreak of plague, or a town devastated by fire. But collections on behalf of North African captives seem to have elicited higher levels of generosity and more varied donors than others, and not just because of the element of persuasion and emotional blackmail involved. The enslavement of their own kind – and most of these campaigns made no bones about the fact that Britons were being enslaved – struck men and women right across the social spectrum as peculiarly terrible; just as, when the trade in black slaves came finally and far too belatedly to be perceived as a rectifiable evil, the response in Britain also conspicuously spanned both sexes and all social classes.[8] Fire, plague and flood were acts of God: but captivity and slavery were the acts of men. And since victims of Barbary were held in bondage under the Crescent, their hopes of salvation were seen as being at risk as well as their mortal bodies. 'Above all', thundered the Charity Brief of 1680, the faithful should call to mind 'that accursed tyranny used towards the souls of these miserable wretches . . . who are daily assaulted by these professed enemies of Christ.'[9] Again, there are similarities here with the British abolitionist movement at the end of the eighteenth century. For the latter, too, one of the strongest weapons in its propaganda armoury would be the argument that black slaves were perishing without any opportunity of being introduced to Christianity. As with white Barbary slaves, immortal souls, and not just chained and suffering bodies, were at stake.

Yet some of the multitudes who gave money to free Barbary captives (like many later abolitionists) were moved, more than anything else, by the helplessness and ordinariness of most of the victims involved. Labouring men standing awkwardly at the back of an English, or Welsh, or Irish, or Scottish church, at the easy mercy of landowners or magistrates, could identify all too well with individuals, poor like themselves, who had been suddenly snatched from their work at sea and enslaved. Women, under pressure, coping alone, or grieving for dead children, had little difficulty imagining what it must be like to lose a husband or a son to Barbary, to hope that he was still alive somewhere, but never to be able to communicate with him, or know for certain if he would return. There was a sense in which Barbary captives embodied in a particularly dramatic form the vulnerability of the labouring poor in general. In this respect, as in so many others, the culture of captivity served to interweave the foreign and the domestic, the general and the deeply personal.

More than any other cause at this time, then, Barbary captives were a people's charity. The captives' plight was publicised and addressed by the institution that still possessed, at this stage, unquestionably the strongest pull on mass loyalties and attention, and an unrivalled nationwide organisation, namely the Church. But the issue of how these captivities were to be presented to the public and interpreted was also the business of the secular authorities. Returning captives were greeted with elaborate, public rituals that involved the monarch, politicians, and local dynasts as well as churchmen, and were designed to transform these forlorn representatives of national humiliation into emblems of triumph, self-congratulation and patriotic self-assertion. The men would journey under escort from their port of arrival to the city of London and then, on an appointed day, process through crowded streets to a special service of thanksgiving held at St Paul's cathedral. These ceremonies were carefully choreographed. In the redemption processions held in December 1721 and again in November 1734, the former captives were instructed to wear their 'Moorish' or 'slavish habits', the clothes they still had left from their time in North Africa.[10] This made them more intriguing and pitiable objects to the 'vast multitudes of people that crowded to see them', and so helped attract generous donations on their behalf. But the strangeness of the captives' costume on these occasions also served as a visual reminder of their previous subjection to an alien power and religion, just as its ragged condition could be read as a denunciation of both these things. Now, though, the captives were redeemed. A Christian service, in a Christian church, in the Christian capital of a godly nation would reclaim them as Protestant Britons, and the vestiges of Islamic influence would, surely, be cast off like the ugly rags clinging to their backs.

If these points were not already clear, the sermon at St Paul's cathedral (which was always printed) was explicitly designed to make them so. 'The happy occasion of our present meeting', thundered William Berrington before hundreds of redeemed captives and the rest of his congregation in 1721, was 'to congratulate you . . . upon your return from slavery under the yoke of infidels, to enjoy the liberty of your native country'. 'You are restored to the enjoyment of English air, and English liberty,' he told them, 'free from the despotick rule of your imperious lords.'[11] But not free of obligations. For the aim was at once to reincorporate the captives into the polity and remind them of their duty to it. William Sherlock spelt out the contract succinctly in a Thanksgiving Service in 1702:

'Tis not only the charity of private Christians, but the care the government hath taken of you, to which you owe your liberty. And therefore pray consider what it is you owe your country . . . to be loyal to your prince, obedient to government, ready to defend it against all enemies . . . They redeemed you, that you might serve them, not as slaves, but as free-born subjects.

Here, indisputably, was Islam conjured up as usefully defining Other. North African and Ottoman slavery, aggression, and tyranny were invoked so as to throw into even clearer contrast the liberty, benevolence and true religion characterising Britain itself (though not yet, as we shall see, to advocate its global expansion). Free again, yet also subjects again, the captives would rise to their feet in the chill, cavernous cathedral and, clutching their rags to their sunburnt bodies, make ready for the final stage of the ceremony, yet another procession, this time to salute the king of England for his efforts on their behalf. 'His Majesty viewed them from the palace windows', reported a London newspaper on a procession of ransomed captives in 1734, 'and was graciously pleased to order 100 guineas to be distributed amongst them.'[12]

Officially, then, the embarrassment of having large numbers of civilian subjects repeatedly seized by corsairs and held captive in North Africa, and of having to pay substantial ransoms to secure their release, was contained, reinterpreted and put to political use by way of the religious and secular wings of the British state. Yet although these church-run campaigns and public redemption ceremonies were important and carefully orchestrated, they were less spectacular and protracted than comparable events in Continental Europe. This was partly a function of numbers. At no time, except perhaps in the early decades of the seventeenth century, did Britain lose as many captives to North Africa as France, the Italian states, or above all Spain. A more significant difference, however, was the absence in Britain of the Mercedarian and Trinitarian Fathers who played a vital ceremonial and literary role in every Catholic state affected by Muslim privateering.

Their rituals would begin in North Africa itself. Groups of Catholic Fathers from France, or Spain, or Portugal, or Naples, would journey to Tunis, or Meknès, or Algiers, to hand over ransom money collected from the faithful back home. They would arrive in Barbary carrying royal and papal banners, and with the colours of the Trinity much in evidence: white for the Father, blue for the Son, red for the Holy Ghost. They would then assemble their respective countries' captives, dress them in the fresh white robes they had brought with them in order to proclaim their innocence and Christianity, and finally escort them back across the sea to their place of origin. The Fathers would also cut a deal with the captives themselves. Roman Catholics ransomed from Barbary in this fashion were contractually bound to participate in special rituals once they returned home. These might last for a year or longer. In France, for instance, there was not just one elaborate procession and one major church service celebrating the captives' return, as in Britain, but a succession of them. The first took place in the port of re-entry, usually Marseilles. The procession of redeemed captives then followed a traditional route that had evolved over the centuries: Toulon, Avignon, Lyons, and so on to the sacred heart of France, Paris itself. At each and every stopping-off place, there were ceremonies in which local elites participated and ordinary folk watched. Bells rang. Soldiers assembled. Strewn flowers were crushed into scent under milling crowds. Small children struggled protestingly into fancy dress as cherubs and saints. And at the heart of it all were the white-robed captives and their Father-minders, the latter itching to write up and publish accounts of their real and reputed sufferings.[13]

In Britain, it was very different. In this strictly Protestant culture there was simply no provision for year-long spectacles of this kind, occurring both in the capital and the provinces. 'We have no Trinitarian Fathers of Redemption', declared a pamphleteer in 1736, 'to roam up and down, and beg money for the relief of our captive brethren . . . nor any who make it their business to parade with them, when redeemed and brought home, in pompous, solemn, and expensive processions.'[14] As this somewhat perverse piece of Protestant boasting implied, returning British captives of Islam were left far more to their own devices, and not just because of the lack of Redemptionist orders. Relations between the British state and the Barbary powers were, it bears repeating, ambivalent. On the one hand, the former naturally resented Barbary corsair assaults on its reputation, trade and personnel, just as its churches were always anxious in case enforced exposure to Islam polluted Protestant, British subjects. On the other, North Africa and the Ottoman world in general were valued outlets for trade, and the former was an ever more indispensable auxiliary in Britain's Mediterranean empire. Partly for these reasons, governmental orchestration of anti-Barbary sentiment and attentiveness to the captives were on a moderate scale, particularly after the acquisition of Minorca and Gibraltar. The captivity issue could never be allowed to embarrass the entente between Britain, Barbary, and the Ottoman empire.

Official restraint, combined with the lack of busy Redemptionist Fathers, influenced indirectly how the captive's tale was told in Britain. In Catholic cultures, state and the church were more proactive in compiling and disseminating accounts of Barbary captives. In Britain, intervention from above – though present – was less pronounced, while commercial press networks were precociously advanced. In this culture, it was easier to tell the tale through a rich variety of unofficial media. Here, captives were more likely to find, however imperfectly, a voice of their own.

Vincent Jukes was the eldest son of an innkeeper and in the view of most of his neighbours in Myddle, Shropshire, no good. A restless, nimble spirit, he first tested the bounds of rural society by trying his hand at petty burglary, and soon found it expedient to go to sea. This turned out to be a passage to another kind of confinement. In 1636 he and thirty-three other crew members were captured off the coast of Tangier, yet more victims of Algerian corsairs. Except that Jukes was nobody's victim. Sold as a slave in Algiers, he converted to Islam, submitted to circumcision, and adopted local dress, actions that did not automatically make him free, but did confer greater mobility and choice of occupation. He resumed his life as a sailor, working on a corsair ship along with three other renegade Christians and ten Algerians. On one trip, for whatever reason, the four renegades changed sides yet again. According to their own account, they killed some of their Muslim fellow crewmen and managed to lock the rest below deck. One-time captives turned captors, Jukes and his partners sailed to Spain where they sold their stolen vessel – and the surviving Algerians. Richer by £150, Jukes returned to England in 1638, purchased new clothes and a good horse and set off back to Myddle, aching to see its burghers' customary disapproval give way to sour envy at his good fortune. But as he rode through one small market town after another, Jukes experienced himself a kind of theft. He discovered that his Barbary exploits, which he had gossiped about so freely in London's taverns, had already been converted into a ballad which was being sung and distributed in print even as he passed. What Jukes had projected as *his* story was being shaped and disseminated by others over whom he had no control.[15]

The tale of Vincent Jukes went on to inspire a sermon by a London divine and several pirated versions, and was finally written down towards the end of the seventeenth century by Richard Gough, the chronicler of Myddle, whose family had known the man and plainly disliked him. Perhaps because of this, Gough's version is full of holes. He never enquires how Jukes reacted to his brief stay in an Islamic society, or whether motives other than self-interest prompted him to convert, or why exactly such an essentially rootless man should have wanted to return to England. No sooner had Jukes settled back in Myddle, sniffs Gough, than he 'went . . . to sea again, and was heard of no more'. But Gough's account does convey how easily official interpretations of North African (and other) captivities were supplemented and even subverted in Britain by very different versions spread verbally or by print. Those listening to the ballads and sermons spawned by Jukes' adventures, or watching him return, well-mounted and in spanking new clothes, may have felt thrilled to the core by an Englishman's success against superior Barbary numbers and by his bloody-minded determination to return. They may equally well have been struck by the fact that Jukes' stay in an Islamic society and swift abandonment of Christianity when it suited him had apparently done him no harm, and ultimately made him rich.

The ballad of Vincent Jukes is now lost, but scores of other English, Welsh, Scottish and Irish ballads survive celebrating the experiences of Barbary captives. The most famous, the so-called 'Lord Bateman' ballad, appeared in at least 112 different versions between the seventeenth and nineteenth centuries. Here, again, capture by North African corsairs is described not as a source of unalloyed suffering, but as an unlikely and unexpected means of self-betterment, in this case sexual as well as pecuniary. A young man from the North Country goes to sea, is captured by 'Turkish pirates' and flung into prison. There he is visited by the governor's beautiful daughter:

> When she came to the prison strong,
> She boldly ventur'd in,
> How do you like, oh! then she said,
> How do you like to be confin'd . . .

She helps him to escape and, in certain versions of the story, follows him to England, where he abandons his local, Christian fiancée for this 'Turkish' bride, who brings with her a jewelled belt worth more than all the wealth of Northumberland.[16]

At one level these persistently popular verses give a North African twist to the Western world's recurrent Pocahontas fantasy: a European male in peril is rescued by an influential non-European female who promptly falls in love with him and comes over to his society. Yet to read the 'Lord Bateman' ballad only in this fashion is to miss important complexities. In these verses, it is the white man who is initially vulnerable, and the 'Turkish' female who possesses superior power, initiative and wealth. She employs these for the Englishman's benefit, to be sure, but she does not die or get cast aside in the process. Instead, the white man crosses boundaries too, ultimately abandoning a woman of his own kind for her sake. As with the story of that seventeenth-century Shropshire lad, Vincent Jukes, we are a considerable distance in these verses from the public statements on North African corsairing so carefully formulated and advanced by Britain's secular and religious authorities. As evoked in the multiple variations of 'Lord Bateman', captivity in an Islamic power is not a fate worse than death, nor a confrontation with an uncompromising and monolithic Other.

Instead, individual Christians and Muslims break ranks, compromise allegiances, and collaborate for mutual benefit.

Yet while ballads like 'Lord Bateman' obviously differed sharply in tone and emphasis from Church of England sermons, or royal proclamations on Barbary, these media were alike in distorting what being a captive there entailed. Balladeers transmuted the bitterness and hardship of captivity into romance and adventure, while government and clerical propagandists glossed over the complex diplomatic, imperial and commercial ties actually existing between Britain and the North African powers, taking refuge instead in stock and traditional contrasts between the Crescent and the Cross. Rarely did those advancing these equally selective interpretations of Barbary captivity have any personal experience of what it meant, or any first-hand knowledge of North Africa itself. So how could someone like Vincent Jukes retrieve his experiences from the various official and commercial agencies wanting to appropriate and exploit them? How could captives seize control of, and tell their own tales?

Doing so might seem essential. Translating any experience of trauma into one's own words is cathartic. It gives victims back a measure of control. They can tell their side of the story, put themselves at the centre of the plot, and make clear that they still matter.[17] Individuals seized by Barbary, like captives in other regions, seem often to have felt this way, and been eager to tell their version of events, even if only in a brief, unconventional fashion. Forced to build houses in Mustafa Superieur, a suburb of the city of Algiers, an English slave called John Robson wrote his story in the only way available to him. He pressed into the still damp plaster his own name, together with the date: 3 January 1692.[18] This was an act signifying something very different from a builder's usual proud marking of his handiwork. As a slave, Robson would have been renamed by his Muslim owner, stripped of the most obvious emblem of his identity. So impressing on the very stone of Algiers his surname and his *Christian* name, together with the Christian rather than the Islamic date, was an act of defiance and a declaration that what had happened to him had not obliterated what he still considered himself to be.

Captives who returned to Britain might also write their story or cause it to be written in stone. Until destroyed by World War II bombing, a monument in Greenwich, London, read as follows:

> Here lyeth interred ye body of Edward Harris . . . mariner.
> . . . Was 18 years a slave in Barbary,
> And steadfastly kept to ye Church of England,
> . . . died in ye faith of ye said Church, 1797.[19]

One detects in these lines a note of anxiety as well as a testament. Individuals held in an alien society as long as Edward Harris was, might feel on their return home under pressure to tell their version of events. Not just as a form of therapy, but as a means of reassuring friends, relations and neighbours that they were still the same people as before, with the same loyalties, even though this was rarely true in fact. Some one-time Barbary captives were even compelled to tell their story. Since many were labouring men, and returned from North Africa to no money or job, and in some cases to find their families dead or dispersed, descending into vagrancy was a common enough fate. In which case, they might end up telling their tale to a clergyman to obtain charity, or explaining their Barbary past to a bench of sceptical magistrates. Poor John Kay, for instance, experienced virtually his entire adult life as a succession of captivities. He was first bound as an apprentice to a Northumbrian industrialist and landowner, then was swept into the British army. Briefly freed by an outbreak of peace, he went to sea working for a Venetian trader and was promptly captured by Algerian corsairs. This led to three and a half years of slavery in North Africa. In 1724, Kay finally returned to the north of England, only to be snatched up and charged with begging. Justices of the Peace extracted his story from him, putting it into writing as he could not, and making him add his mark at the bottom of the page.[20]

For the illiterate, telling their captivity story through a third party, whether under coercion like John Kay or voluntarily, was the only way to get it recorded. Anyone who takes the trouble to explore seventeenth- and early eighteenth-century local records, especially from maritime counties such as Devon or Cornwall in England, or Fife in Scotland, will find dozens of small narratives like Kay's, tales recounted by one-time Barbary captives but not written down by them.[21] Some of these spoken narratives were probably fakes. It must have been tempting for beggars who were mutilated in some way, and who had perhaps heard ballads or sermons about North African captives, to tell an impressionable church minister or a sympathetic householder that they had lost a leg, or an eye, or teeth, through the cruelties of 'Turkish' pirates. But magistrates were generally cannier. Confronted with impoverished individuals claiming time in Barbary, they wanted names, dates, details of ships and their owners, information about where in North Africa they had been held, even some kind of supporting documentation.

Such assiduity on the part of long-dead officialdom can bequeath extraordinarily valuable insights into the experiences of those normally too poor and unlettered to enter the light of history. This point is neatly made by a captivity tale from the other side. In September 1753, a

Moroccan sailor called Hamet recounted to the Governor of Tetouan his captivity experiences in British America. Sailing southwards from Salé in 1736 with a boatload of corn for what is now Essaouira, he and six comrades were seized by a Portuguese cruiser and taken to Mazagan, one of Portugal's few remaining bases in North Africa. There, he and a friend escaped to a British ship whose captain, a man called Daves, promised to help them. At least this was what the two Moroccans thought he promised, for naturally they neither spoke nor understood English. Daves took them on a sea voyage that lasted months, seemingly always gesturing that they would soon see the shores of England, and return from there to Morocco. But Daves was a part-time slave-trader, and the sea they were crossing was the Atlantic. After landfall in America, Daves sold the two men to an isolated plantation some 150 miles outside Charleston, South Carolina. They worked there fifteen years, grinding corn to feed the plantation's black labour force. Only the accident of their owner's bankruptcy finally freed them. The plantation's seclusion was broken through by the arrival of irate creditors, and by now Hamet and his friend knew enough English to explain who and what they were.[22]

At one level, this is an exceptional story. Muslims as well as Christians living or working in the Mediterranean zone were vulnerable to capture in the early modern era, and to being dragged over the line into varieties of slavery and another society, but the evidence for this is often desperately one-sided. High levels of illiteracy and the lack of a print culture deprived most men and women from North Africa who were captured by western Europeans of any chance of leaving behind durable tales, even if they managed to return home. Yet the picture may turn out to be less bleak than this implies. As North African and Ottoman sources become better known, and as European archives are sieved more imaginatively for non-European material, more stories like Hamet's may emerge, more accounts by illiterate Muslim men and women who lacked print outlets, certainly, but who were sometimes able – like European illiterates – to tell their tales to officials of some kind who did write them down.

And *as a tale*, Hamet's story is more representative than it appears. It demonstrates something that we will see evidence of again and again: the centrality of linguistic capacity to captives' chances of survival. How easily they could be disoriented and entrapped by not understanding the language of their captors (as Hamet and his friend were entrapped by Daves), and conversely how captivity might itself lead to new language skills, and consequently to an enhanced capacity to survive and even prosper. Because they picked up some English during their fifteen years' hard labour on a South Carolina plantation, Hamet and his companion were ultimately able to explain who they were. They could present their case to the colony's governor, James Glen, and convince him to ship them home. Back in Tetouan, the two men could tell their story again, to the local Moroccan governor and to the British envoy, William Petticrew. The latter gave them over £30 in compensation, an enormous sum for two destitute seamen. He did this in part, he wrote, because they 'pretty well understand the English language which corroborates their declaration'.[23]

Petticrew also recompensed the two men in this fashion because of Britain's vital connections with Barbary. Successive treaties between Britain and Morocco after 1721 stipulated that the latter would refrain from capturing and enslaving Britons (an undertaking that occasionally lapsed). In return, Britain undertook not to seize individual Moroccans, and to aid any who were enslaved in Continental Europe and elsewhere and who appealed to its officers for help. Their awareness of these treaty provisions explains why poor Hamet and his friend immediately (and in this case mistakenly) ran to a British vessel for help after evading their Portuguese captors. Normally, though, and for their own reasons, the British did abide by these treaties. Indeed, it is a measure of just how much they wanted to maintain a working relationship with Morocco that first Governor Glen in South Carolina, and then William Petticrew, the British envoy in Tetouan, felt obliged to behave so scrupulously towards two desperately poor seamen, arranging for their passage back from South Carolina to Morocco, and compensating them for their sufferings. Britain at this time was becoming ever more mired in transatlantic slave trading, while Glen presided over, and would have taken for granted, a colonial economy rooted in black slavery. Quite clearly, however, these two particular Africans were recognised at British official level as being strictly off-limits as far as slavery was concerned, and were accordingly helped towards home and freedom.

Another, more broadly applicable point emerges from this selfsame narrative. Telling your own captivity story almost always paid in some way. At the very least, it made you feel better, and it might win you advancement, or help re-establish your credentials as a loyal, put-upon Christian (or Muslim). In addition, those who recounted their captivity experiences often did so with an expectation of receiving money. By telling their story to the right people, Hamet and his friend secured a passage home to Morocco and a substantial cash donation. British captives who succeeded in returning home also frequently obtained charitable hand-outs in return for recounting their hardships. But for the latter, another option was available. They could try to sell their stories in the open market. They could put them into print.

In 1640, an English merchant called Francis Knight wrote that 'none, to my knowledge, hath ever divulged in print, the estate and condition of captives in that place of Algier'. He proceeded to do just this, drawing on the details of his own seven years slavery there, and lending his text cachet by dedicating it to Sir Paul Pindar, a former ambassador to the Ottoman court.[24] Knight was not remotely as pioneering as he thought. Accounts of captivity in Algiers and elsewhere in North Africa, together with narratives of white captivities in the New World, had been circulating in Continental Europe since the sixteenth century. Even in England, the earliest known printed Barbary captivity narrative dates from the 1580s.[25] Yet Knight was correct in sensing that he was offering something distinctive as far as the English print market was concerned. His was a lengthy autobiographical account, which chewed over the multi-facetedness of Barbary captivity, rather than treating it in formulaic terms; and he or his publisher demonstrated a sensitivity to readership, inserting specially drawn illustrations and a preface headed 'To the Reader'.

This kind of complex narrative of captivity, usually printed or at least prepared for publication though not invariably so, flourished in England and later Britain from the 1600s through to the nineteenth century, and continued to appear occasionally after that. As far as Barbary captivity narratives were concerned, it is impossible now to establish exactly how many were produced. Some, particularly very early texts and those that remained unpublished, will not have survived. Others, still in manuscript, almost certainly await discovery; while some printed narratives are anonymous, so it is hard to establish their authenticity. And what, anyway, did authenticity mean in this context?

Readings

Whether in regard to the Mediterranean world, or North America, or India or elsewhere, narratives of the sort written by Francis Knight were at the apex of the culture of captivity in terms of sophistication and auto-biographical appeal, but always modest in point of numbers. Other kinds of printed accounts of captivity – be it newspaper and magazine reports, verses, books and pamphlets by third parties – were far more numerous; while it was still more common for these matters to be described, discussed and analysed orally, in sermons, in testimonies to civil and military courts, in parliamentary speeches, spoken proclamations, sung ballads, and ordinary neighbourhood gossip and private conversation. As far as Barbary is concerned, only fifteen substantial narratives by Britons who were unquestionably captives there, appear to have survived from the seventeenth and eighteenth centuries. These texts reflect quite well, however, some of the broad characteristics of this particular captivity experience.

Two-thirds of them were written by individuals seized before 1720, which is an apt indicator of when the corsairs were at their most dangerous as far as Britain was concerned. Like most Barbary victims, the writers were all under thirty when seized, and they were overwhelmingly male. Only one of these narratives is by a woman, Elizabeth Marsh, the daughter of a ships-carpenter from Portsmouth turned naval dockyard administrator in the Mediterranean, who went on to become a Mrs Crisp.

These accounts also confirm the diversity of Barbary captivities in point of duration, and consequently in quality. A third of the writers were held in North Africa less than a year; another third spent between one and five years there. The rest stayed much longer: one of them, Joseph Pitts, a West Country fisherman, for fifteen years; another, Thomas Pellow, for twenty-three years. Since producing a lengthy narrative usually (though not invariably) demanded a measure of literacy, the proportion of seamen among these authors was lower than among the total number of Britons held in this Mediterranean zone. None the less, six of them, Edward Coxere, Thomas Lurting, Thomas Troughton, James Irving, Thomas Pellow and Joseph Pitts, are known to have worked in the mercantile marine, all but one of them as common seamen. Two others, Adam Elliot and Devereux Spratt were clergymen. Five more, Francis Knight, William Okeley, John Whitehead, Francis Brooks, and Thomas Phelps appear to have been traders and men of business. Only one of the narrators, Lieutenant James Sutherland, was serving with the armed forces when taken. This was emphatically not – as we shall see – because British fighters were averse to becoming writers, even when this involved describing defeat and capture. The scarcity of military and naval testimonies of captivity in North Africa, reflects rather the distinctive imperial politics of the Mediterranean. Britain would find itself with military and naval captives galore as far as North America and India were concerned, because these were zones of conquest, war and occupation. But, between 1600 and 1800 – with the conspicuous exception of the Tangier episode – British soldiers and naval men rarely invaded and operated within North Africa itself. As a result, the overwhelming majority of British captives here were always civilians, more victims than aggressors.

To this extent, then, these fifteen accounts are broadly representative of North African captivity patterns. Their adequacy as descriptions of events and encounters in the non-European world is plainly another matter. 'The teasing gap separating a lived event and its subsequent narration',

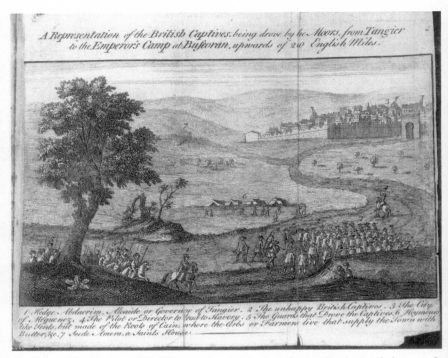

1 Hedge Abdacrim, Alcaide or Governor of Tangier. 2 The unhappy British Captives. 3 The City of Mequenez. 4 The Pilot or Director to lead to Slavery. 5 The Guards that Drove the Captives, 6 Heymours like Tents, but made of the Roots of Cain, where the Arbs or Farmers live that supply the Town with Butter, &c. 7 Seede Amera, a Saints House.

16. Thomas Troughton and his fellow captives in Morocco, from a drawing made by one of them.

in Simon Schama's felicitous phrase, was something of which these writers, like other captivity narrators, were painfully aware, and some tried desperately hard to contrive strategies of authentication.[26] As a middle-class woman, terrified that her brief Moroccan captivity had besmirched her reputation, Elizabeth Marsh declined even to raise the possibility of her account being in any way mendacious. She was (or wished to be) a lady: and consequently her veracity was not a matter for dispute even by herself. Instead, she adopted the delicate tactic of subtitling her captivity story 'a narrative of *facts*', which it only partly was. Some male narrators however were willing to tackle the issue head-on. 'Courteous reader,' declared William Okeley in the second edition of his account: 'I do readily agree with thee, that there is no sort of writing more liable to abuse than this of the narrative.' He offered, man of business as he was, to 'pawn his credit, not to wrong the narrative,' but in the end, could only refer those readers who were still sceptical to members of his own family, and ultimately to God: 'This book is Protestant, and hates a lie.'[27]

Some humbler narrators looked to social superiors to bestow legitimacy on their texts. Take Thomas Troughton, a sad, if clearly resilient man who laboured in turn as an apprentice tailor, a plasterer, a common seaman, and then – after five years' captivity in Morocco wore him out – as a failed painter, and died in due course in a Middlesex workhouse. In 1751, he swore to the authenticity of his captivity narrative in front of its printer, and before the Lord Mayor of London himself, Sir Francis Cockayne. He even took twenty-one of his fellow sailors and former comrades in captivity along with him to the Mansion House to 'attest to the accuracy of this account'. Their combined testimonies, which bore the names of the seamen able to write and the marks of those who could not, were inserted as a preface to Troughton's published text (which was still being reprinted in the nineteenth century), in a transparent attempt to reassure and convince readers before they embarked on it.[28]

Yet no matter how they strived, it was impossible for these or any other captivity narrators to prove the truth of all the experiences they laid claim to. The events in question had taken place too far away, amongst people who were unlikely ever to be available as witnesses, and whose perspectives on what had happened would anyway have been very different. Moreover, these accounts were bound to be distorted to some degree, and not just because their writers possessed – as all human beings do – their own preconceptions and prejudices. It was very rare, for instance, for early modern captives of Barbary to have access to pens, paper, or even the time and freedom to write. 'We must needs be very ill qualified to make a history,' remembered one Englishman of his time in Algiers in the 1640s: 'Such a design required leisure, liberty, privacy, retiredness . . . to all which we were perfect strangers.' All this man – William Okeley – could do, was consciously commit to memory a pattern of observations while he was undergoing slavery, which he finally put into print some thirty years later. A few individuals in Okeley's position were able to jot down notes in the margins of a prayer book or a Bible that their captors had allowed them to hold on to, but most narratives from this zone – more so even than from others – were composed from memory, often many years after the event.[29]

Narratives might be further compromised if they were the work of more than just the captives themselves. Since most of those seized by the corsairs were poor and of limited or no education, they often depended on others – friends, patrons, London publishers or whatever – to get into print, and sometimes to aid them with the business of writing itself. 'Till I could prevail with a friend to teach it to speak a little better English, I could not be persuaded to let it walk abroad,' admitted William Okeley of his story: 'the stuff and matter is my own, the trimmings and form is another's.'[30]

In Okeley's case, we can be reasonably sure who these auxiliaries were. A deeply religious man, he was urged to publish his experiences by some Anglican clergymen, and it was probably they who also helped him shape and style his narrative.

As this suggests, it is important to get away from the notion that these and other captivity narratives can usefully be characterised as either truthful or crudely mendacious. We all of us convert life's crowded, untidy experiences into stories in our own minds, re-arranging awkward facts into coherent patterns as we go along, and omitting episodes that seem in retrospect peripheral, discordant, or too embarrassing or painful to bear. Okeley was an intelligent, sensitive man who probably did try conscientiously to relate what he and his advisers saw as the quintessential truth of his six years' captivity. For him and them, however, this involved stressing above all the role of a Protestant God and his Providence. 'When I am tempted to distrust,' wrote Okeley (or his collaborators), 'I may encourage my faith from my own narrative, saying, Remember that God who delivered thee at the sea.' Zeal to testify to God's mercy must have prompted Okeley to cut and paste his memories of North African captivity. As an honest man, he admits indeed that this was what happened:

> I could relate a passage during our captivity in Algiers, that had more of bitterness in it than in all our slavery; and yet they were Christians, not Algerines, Protestants, not Papists, Englishmen, not strangers, that were the cause of it: but I have put a force upon myself, and am resolved not to publish it.[31]

In writing, or letting others write in accordance with this 'force', the desire to bear witness to the omnipotence of a Protestant deity and his merciful interventions in his own Islamic captivity, Okeley pruned and refashioned his experiences, but only so as to bring out what he regarded as their deeper, moral truth.

There is a further respect in which it is inappropriate to look for absolute, unadulterated verisimilitude in these narratives, or read too much into their authors' failure to provide it. As Lennard Davis observes, early modern readers did not expect a published text to be either comprehensively factual or unmitigated fiction to the extent that even in these postmodern times we still tend to do.[32] Authors of travel accounts in particular were well known for muddying the waters. Thus Jonathan Swift's novel *Gulliver's Travels* incorporated maps that were similar in design – right down to their professional-looking scale measurements and ornamental spouting whales – to authentic early eighteenth-century cartography, so his more credulous readers at the time may well have been convinced that Lilliput really was situated just south-west of Sumatra. Conversely, Daniel Defoe's *Tour of the Whole Island of Great Britain* (1724–6) is recognised now as an invaluable source on the social, economic and urban fabric of early Georgian Britain. But the detailed, empirical information it supplies on building practices, market-day customs, the growth of rural industry, and the condition of provincial roads was organised within the framework of a tour on Defoe's part which was a literary invention.[33]

In much the same way, highly factual and invaluable material in Barbary and other captivity narratives is sometimes intercut with fictional or pirated passages. Political, religious, cultural and racial bias is combined with reportage that can be substantially verified; and terrible ignorance is exhibited side by side with rare perceptiveness and serious insights. Like virtually every other source material historians ransack, these are not writings that can be swallowed whole, but they can – and should – be sampled and sieved. For I do not accept the argument that sifting for accuracy in such texts is a fruitless enterprise, or that these and other European writings on encounters with non-Europeans are revealing only about the observers and writers, and never of the observed.[34] No historical source should be automatically discounted on the basis of where its writers come from, or on the grounds of what their presumed ethnic group happens to be. Captivity narratives are fractured, composite sources, but it is inappropriate – indeed it is something of a cop-out – to analyse them textually but not contextually. Too much gets lost along the way.

Consider one of the most remarkable of Barbary narratives, Thomas Pellow's account of his detention in Morocco from 1715 to 1738, first as a captive, then as a renegade and mercenary soldier. Published in London in the early 1740s, its preface describes it as 'truly genuine . . . the real journal of the unhappy sufferer, written by his own hand'. Disproving this bold assertion is a simple enough exercise. Like many publications of the period, *The History of the Long Captivity . . . of Thomas Pellow* contains material pirated from other authors (and it would be pirated in its turn by Thomas Troughton when he came to write his own Barbary story). Pellow's narrative also contains its fair share of embellishments and inventions, particularly with regard to the formidable Moulay Ismaïl, the first sultan he served. Moreover the published text – which is the only version we have – suffered from the attentions of its London editor, whose insertions are pardonable only because they are so jarringly obvious. 'It is much to be regretted', this busy ignoramus interrupts at one point, 'that [Morocco] should go under any other denomination than that of a part of Christendom . . . [but] these digressions are quite out of my way, as well

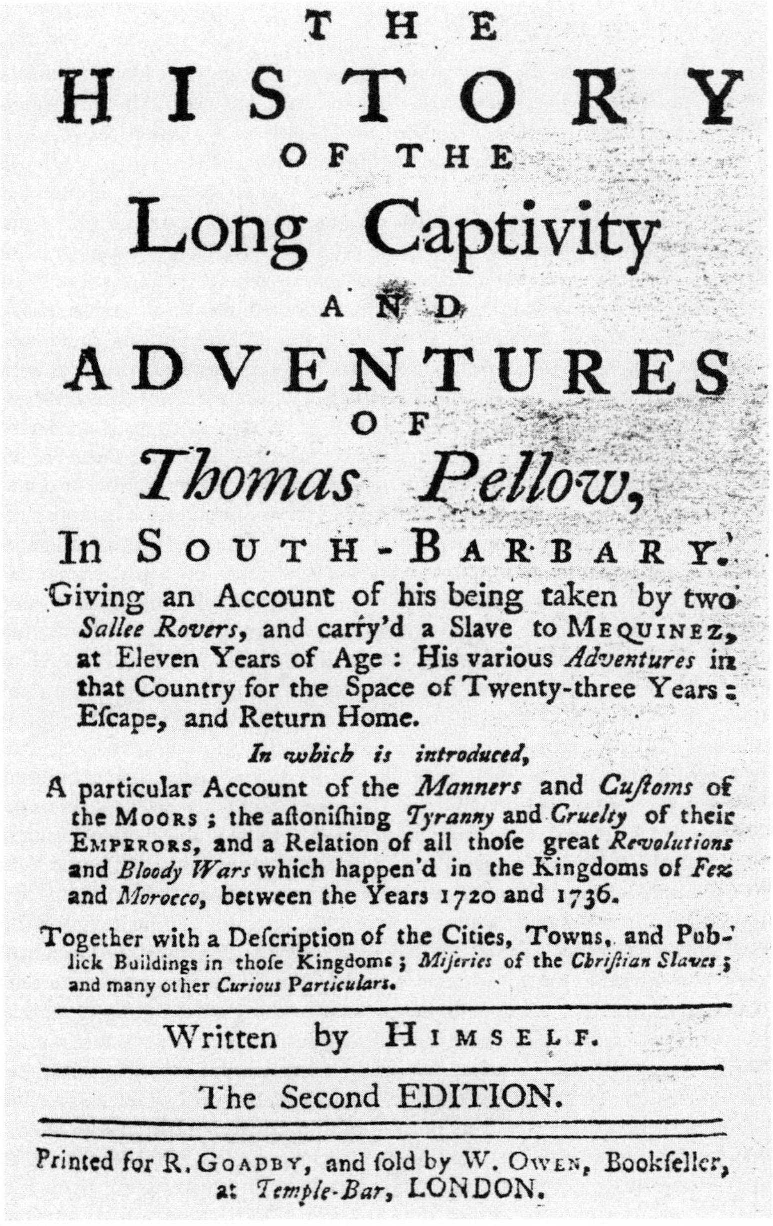

THE
HISTORY
OF THE
Long Captivity
AND
ADVENTURES
OF
Thomas Pellow,
In SOUTH-BARBARY.

Giving an Account of his being taken by two
Sallee Rovers, and carry'd a Slave to MEQUINEZ,
at Eleven Years of Age : His various *Adventures* in
that Country for the Space of Twenty-three Years :
Escape, and Return Home.

In which is introduced,

A particular Account of the *Manners* and *Customs* of
the MOORS ; the astonishing *Tyranny* and *Cruelty* of their
EMPERORS, and a Relation of all those great *Revolutions*
and *Bloody Wars* which happen'd in the Kingdoms of *Fez*
and *Morocco,* between the Years 1720 and 1736.

Together with a Description of the Cities, Towns, and Pub-
lick Buildings in those Kingdoms ; *Miseries* of the *Christian Slaves* ;
and many other *Curious Particulars.*

Written by HIMSELF.

The Second EDITION.

Printed for R. GOADBY, and sold by W. OWEN, Bookseller,
at *Temple-Bar,* LONDON.

17. Thomas Pellow's narrative.

as a subject far beyond my abilities.'[35] Quite so: because when Pellow's own voice re-emerges, it tells a very different story, and one that would not have been possible without deep and prolonged exposure to Moroccan society.

Magali Morsy's impressive, modern edition of Pellow's tale effectively separates its authorial wheat from its editorial chaff.[36] When Pellow was seized by Moroccan corsairs in 1715, he was just eleven years old, a Cornish schoolboy playing truant and accompanying his uncle on a trading voyage to Genoa. He carefully supplies the dates of his embarkation, capture and arrival in Morocco, and of his belated return to England as an embittered, hardened soldier in his thirties. His account of his time as a renegade, however, employs dates only rarely, and this has sometimes been viewed as proof that Pellow's narrative is little more than a picaresque fiction. Yet to argue thus is to apply Western criteria to the narrative of a man who lived a precarious existence for many years in a non-Western environment. Once Pellow converted to Islam, and joined the ranks of Morocco's 1500-strong army of European renegades, he moved outside the conventions of the Christian calendar, and into indigenous methods of marking the passage of time. His text conveys the changing of the seasons in Morocco by reference to when he was free to hunt game, or when he was allowed to live with the slave woman allocated to him as a wife. Above all, he charts his Moroccan life by reference to the seventeen military campaigns he fought in between 1720 and 1737, and the towns and villages he saw, lived in and sacked as he and his comrades traversed the country again and again harrying the sultan's enemies. For Pellow at this time, the business of tracking time became a spatial and a geographical one, rather than a matter for a watch and a calendar. There are 230 place-names in his narrative, including some unavailable in any other Western source on Morocco at this time.[37]

Thus a characteristic of this narrative that appears at first glance to mark it out as vague and largely fictional – its paucity of Western dating – suggests in fact the degree to which Pellow was caught up in and altered by his other, Moroccan existence. Close analysis of the text reveals indeed the tensions that resulted from his position as a human palimpsest, the original script of his English existence written over by twenty-three years of Moroccan state service, and this version of his life being in turn partially and unconvincingly expunged by re-entry into Britain in 1738. The end of his account relates how, as Morocco became convulsed in civil strife, he finally made the decision to escape, went on the run, and masqueraded for a time as a travelling healer. Pellow describes how he treated some Moroccan peasants who came to him with eye infections by pouring ground red pepper into their open eyes, and comments that their resulting agony moved him not at all: 'Just so (were it in my power) I would use most of the Moors in Barbary.'

Before we shudder at what appears to be a piece of racially motivated nastiness, we should understand what Pellow – or his editor – was trying to do here. Pellow had disowned Christianity and his country, and fought for more than two decades under different, alien banners. Attempting after 1738 to re-enter British society, he naturally sought to use his narrative to prove that in his heart he had never really turned renegade at all. He makes a point, for instance, of including an unlikely episode in which he tells Moulay Ismaïl to his face that he will never marry a black or mulatto slave woman, pleading with him instead 'to give me one of my own colour'. Yet this strenuous and naïve attempt to prove that his prolonged stay in Morocco had never modified his birth identity is compromised by Pellow's account of his red pepper cure. The use of a minute dose of red pepper for eye infections, especially of the inner eyelid, was not an innovative piece of racist cruelty on his part. It was a standard, Moroccan folk remedy for such ailments. An episode which British readers were encouraged to read as anti-Muslim, anti-Moroccan behaviour on Pellow's part, demonstrates in reality the extent to which this one-time Cornishman had assimilated Moroccan folkways.[38] Thomas Pellow had not just been captured by Barbary: he had in the process been changed. Irreversibly so, as it turned out, for he was never able to make a satisfactory life for himself on his return to Britain.

In part, this was because he had been captured so young, when he was only eleven years old, and held in North Africa for so long, well over two decades. As a result, Pellow found himself on his return to 'home' and 'freedom' in eighteenth-century Britain in much the same state of frightened and angry bewilderment that Joan Brady's grandfather seems to have experienced in late nineteenth-century America. The latter, she tells us in her astonishing book *The Theory of War* (1993), was sold as an infant to a mid-western tobacco farmer, and spent virtually all of his childhood and adolescence in what was effectively white slavery. After he escaped from his owner, this man – like Pellow – felt an initial surge of euphoria at the 'sudden freedom, the multiplicity of it, the dazzling, dizzying disorder of it'. But then came panic and fury, as he was forced to realise that freedom by itself could not give him back his past, nor provide for him a present in which he could feel comfortable:

> What once fit – what once was life itself – no longer fits, could never be made to fit again. Normality becomes another kind of bondage . . . Like God himself he had to build his world from scratch.[39]

Pellow seems to have undergone a similar shift from wild optimism immediately after his return to England, to feeling desperately and angrily unearthed. His parents failed to recognise him, and for a while his only solace was paying visits to Morocco's ambassador in London who was kind to him. Neither the place nor the date of his death is known.

Pellow's inability to settle back in and make good, may have been due to more, however, than his own alienation. In his absence, not only he, but also his country had been transformed. By the time his captivity narrative appeared, around 1740, Britain had become a first-ranking and increasingly aggressive state inside Europe, and more consciously intent as well on expanding its power outside Europe. This was scarcely a context in which the tale of a Briton who had turned Muslim, foreign mercenary, and defector, was likely to win easy acceptance, still less wide acclaim. As Pellow complained at the end of his narrative, when he finally returned to London in 1738, and with terrible naïvety presented himself at the Navy Office to ask for an interview with the king: 'all I could get from them at the last was the very extraordinary favour of a hammock on board of a man of war.'[40] As far as the British authorities were concerned, Pellow was an embarrassment who might at least have the decency now to get himself killed fighting for the country he had so impertinently (if involuntarily) abandoned.

As this episode suggests, captive-taking by foreign powers was always much more than a matter of individual sufferings and adventures. Then, as now, the capture of one country's nationals by the agents of another was a political issue, a matter for states, governments, diplomats and rulers. As far as Britain was concerned, captivity was also increasingly a matter of empire. Exactly the same points apply to the culture of captivity. As we have seen, this was partly an oral culture, a set of ideas, impressions and images that spread widely across the different social classes by way of sermons, speeches, sung ballads, the spoken accounts of returning captives, and the gossip and stories of those who knew them. Barbary captivity – like other captivity crises – also gave rise to abundant writings, sometimes in manuscript, but often in print. As I have sought to show, some of these texts were highly influential at the time and repay close reading and analysis now. Full-length captivity narratives especially are often moving and gripping sources, because of the intimate details they offer on cross-cultural collisions and collusions in North Africa and other parts of the world. Here are the halting, revealing testimonies of small but not unimportant people caught, sometimes literally, in the cross-fire. But these remarkable micro-narratives – like the rest of the culture of captivity – need to be located as well in a macro-narrative of contending states and empires.

From the very start, individual Barbary captives were caught up in much bigger stories than they themselves can often have been aware. On the one hand, English, Welsh, Scottish and Irish men and women were seized in increasing numbers in the Mediterranean after 1600 because the small, greedy islands from which they came nurtured first commercial and then imperial ambitions in this vital sea among the lands. On the other hand, these captivities also occurred because of the needs and imperatives of the Ottoman empire and its border provinces of Algiers, Tunisia and Tripoli, together with the formidable kingdom of Morocco. There was also a further twist. As Britain's power in the Mediterranean expanded, albeit unevenly and with major reversals on the way, a close relationship evolved between it and some of this region's Muslim powers. As first Gibraltar and then Minorca were seized, Britain became dependent on North African aid to provision and supply these white colonies, and so maintain them against its European enemies. If this tidy arrangement sometimes required that London look the other way when corsairs made sporadic hits against British ships, or strike curious deals to get its people back, or sometimes allow them to die unrevenged, then so be it. Whoever imagined that empire was to be achieved without cost?

In the Mediterranean world, then, as in other zones of British imperial enterprise, the captive's tale needs to be read and interpreted in a wider British and global context. These were never simply stories about individuals under stress, but commentaries on, and by-products of changing power relations over time. There was a particular respect in which this was so in this sector of the world. As we have seen, one result of the large numbers of English, Welsh, Scottish and Irish men and women being captured by Barbary corsairs after 1600 was that Islam came to be invoked and debated in Britain very broadly. The majority of seventeenth- and early eighteenth-century Britons did not approach the Islamic world initially with a view to possible conquests. They began devoting increasing attention to it in large part because the North African powers and the Ottomans, and the captivities they inflicted, allowed them no choice in the matter. Yet, over time, this would change. The great Muslim empires would come to seem less sources of danger to the British than vulnerable. It is this momentous shift over time, and the ways in which captivities can illumine it, that we now need to investigate.

FOUR

Confronting Islam

Dis-orientations

April 1751: it is cold in London this season, especially for the shabby, emaciated men waiting in the wings of Covent Garden Theatre, who hug themselves and stamp their feet as much as their fetters allow. The audience, though, is warm as well as restive. Not every box is occupied, but over a thousand people are packed into the pit and galleries, young men about town, dignified citizens and their wives, merchants and respectable shopkeepers, admiring rustics on their first visit to the capital, the odd army officer lounging in a blaze of scarlet, and – in the cheapest seats – the prostitutes, the servants, and the merely cash-inhibited. The matter of Barbary, as always, is set to play across the social spectrum. Briefly, the sound of the impresario's staff and some discordant and utterly inauthentic music cut through the chatter, then Thomas Troughton and his comrades are prodded on to the stage, caught fast and blinking in the bright candlelight. They know what to do, but find it hard not to be distracted by the particular smell of massed, barely washed Western bodies, and by the powdered faces of the women, eyeing them openly and without a veil. The audience, too, is transfixed. The men standing before them are bone-thin and burnt brown, dressed in rags that seem almost welded to their skins. Suddenly, each of them grasps the iron chains attached to their legs and arms, and rattles the links violently, smashing them down hard against the wood of the stage. Like Marley's ghost, these are spirits back from the dead, with a message of horror and of warning.

The man responsible for this theatrical coup was John Rich, Covent Garden's actor manager. He had sought out Troughton and his former shipmates as soon as they returned to London from almost five years' captivity and hard labour in Morocco, knowing their publicity value and audience appeal were bound for a while to be high. His interest in them may have been prompted by another consideration too. Rich had made his name and fortune staging the most famous musical satire of the century, John Gay's *The Beggar's Opera* (1728), where again the pains of capture and

Turks taking the English.

Selling slaves in Algers

Execution with A batoone.

Turks burning of A Frier er:

Divers Cruelties

Mayork

Making the boat & their Escape to May

18. 'Turkish' power and cruelty: the frontispiece to William Okeley's captivity narrative.

imprisonment are much in evidence. Its hero of a kind, Captain Macheath, spends a great deal of this musical drama in shackles and in fear of his life in Newgate prison.[1] It may be that Rich saw in Troughton and his worn-out companions an opportunity to revisit imprisonment and its metaphors. For just as the criminal underworld as evoked in *The Beggar's Opera* was also an attack on corruption in high places, so the spectacle of redeemed but suffering Barbary captives was more than ephemeral sensationalism. Behind the clanking chains, and the men's own eagerness to please and make a little money, was a political statement of sorts. In words, song, and mime, the enthralled habitués of Covent Garden were informed that these were the same loathsome irons and gaping rags in which the men had laboured for so long in Muslim North Africa, enslaved victims – to quote the title of Troughton's captivity narrative – of 'barbarian cruelty'.[2]

Here it was then. As represented in this pantomime version, North African Islamic society stood for tyranny, brutality, poverty and loss of freedom, the reverse and minatory image of Britain's own balanced constitution, commercial prosperity, and individual liberty. The fact that these claims could be rehearsed by a group of confused and hungry amateurs on a chilly London stage only demonstrated how well-primed their audience already was. For what Troughton and his comrades inexpertly acted out had been the stuff of cliché too long for any lack of understanding to be possible. Countless church sermons and royal proclamations whenever money was needed to ransom captives, and the plethora of commercial texts to which this issue gave rise, had all encouraged Britons to view Barbary as a source of aggression and menace, and as their own antithesis and nemesis. An unremarkable middle-class matron called Mary Barber summed it up nicely when dashing off one of her dreadful poems: 'On seeing the Captives, lately redeem'd from Barbary' in 1734:

> See the freed captives hail their native shore,
> And tread the land of LIBERTY once more
> . . . So, Albion, be it ever giv'n to thee,
> To break the bonds, and set the Pris'ners free.[3]

Barbary, in this stock and repeatedly recited view, was explicitly the 'Other', a place of 'inhuman, barbarous Moors'. It was the Other – or so it could seem – because it was not European. 'Wigs, cravats, or neck-cloths, gloves, breeches, nor stockings, they wear none,' one English captive observed conclusively in the 1690s. It was the Other, too, because the majority of its inhabitants were Muslims: 'our greatest enemies, I mean, those barbarous infidels, the Moors'. And it was made Other by its own unfreedom, for which the only compensation available was that it threw into still happier relief Britons' own unique privileges. Native liberty, mused a one-time captive in Morocco, Thomas Phelps, was a 'happiness only valuable by a reflection on captivity and slavery'.[4]

Such perceptions and language have struck some scholars in retrospect as both formative and portentous. For Edward Said famously, in his classic *Orientalism* (1978), these kinds of formulaic denunciations have to be taken seriously and recognised for what they were: 'a set of constraints upon and limitations of [Western] thought'. By consistently resorting to derogatory language of this type – he and others argue – Britons became able to view Islamic cultures over the centuries overwhelmingly in terms of strangeness, backwardness, and political and moral excess. By so projecting a 'settled, clear, unassailably self-evident' divide between 'us' (the West) and 'them' (the non-West), European and above all British imperialism became in due course possible. Because the Islamic world, and other parts of Asia and Africa, had been so thoroughly and persistently debased in cultural terms by the West, it became imaginable, as it would otherwise not have been, to invade and dominate them. Familiar hatreds and contempt bred and permitted expansionism once the other technical, economic and military preconditions were in place. By 1850, the United Kingdom, no more than a puny set of islands in terms of geography, would claim authority over more Muslims than any other state in the world.[5]

This is a powerful and seductive theory which has the great virtue of drawing attention to the minds and myths of those most obviously responsible for making maritime empire, rather than just their material power or short-term actions. For a small people like the British, learning how to think big and act big on the global stage was indeed vital, and required imaginative and intellectual effort, as well as military and economic force. Yet, by definition, concentrating on a persistent and traditional clutch of denunciations and misperceptions is not and cannot be an adequate way of exploring and accounting for change over time. The language and assumptions that the English, Scots, Irish and Welsh had recourse to in regard to North Africa and other Islamic cultures in the nineteenth century were similar in many respects to those their ancestors had deployed in 1600, and can be traced back in part even to classical times. But the power that governments in London exercised in the world was utterly different, and it is this British transition from marginality to global power that has to be investigated and explained. Moreover, as far as Islam and Islamic societies were concerned, language and attitudes were never homogenous or monolithic. The gut reactions to Barbary and Islam that John Rich appealed to so cannily at Covent Garden coexisted in practice with quite different and more varied responses. How, indeed, could it have been otherwise, given the nature of Britain's exposure to Islamic power in the Mediterranean world?

Before the 1750s, as we have seen, this was the sector of the globe where Britain's contacts with Islam were the most extensive, the most intense, and the most well reported among its home population. Up to this point in time, it was the Ottoman empire and North Africa that constituted, for the generality of Britons, the familiar and formidable face of Islam, not Mughal India, which was so much more distant geographically, and where the East India Company's power was still overwhelmingly commercial, rather than military or territorial. Accordingly, before 1750, Islam was more likely to be linked in British minds with aggression against themselves than with their own overseas ambitions. For it bears repeating that, in this Mediterranean zone, it was Britons who were for a long time at risk of being captured and even enslaved by Muslim powers, and not the other way around. Even when British power expanded in this zone in the eighteenth century, it was not at the expense of Islam. It was fellow Europeans and Christians whom the British succeeded in colonising here, not Muslims. Indeed, British empire in the Mediterranean – Gibraltar and Minorca – relied, as we have seen, on the Islamic regimes of North Africa for their basic sustenance. In this contested sea region, Islamic powers were never straightforwardly the 'Other', but rather vital auxiliaries in the business of British empire.

Understood in this way, encounters in the Mediterranean zone make both necessary and possible a more nuanced and more variegated view of relations between the British empire and Islam. They call into question the extent to which Islam was regarded and treated as a uniquely different and degraded 'them', and also the degree to which Britons saw themselves as a unified, superior 'us', possessed of a single, driving aim and interest. The sheer volume and variety of material existing about British–Islamic relations in the Mediterranean also provides for, and positively demands, a no less nuanced treatment of change over time. In the seventeenth century the English state had been bitterly humiliated at Tangier, and forced to pay exorbitant and regular ransoms to Muslim corsairs who preyed on its trade and traded in its people. It was still paying ransoms in the early eighteenth century, and still residually in awe of the Ottomans, a Muslim empire whose rulers regarded all Western Europeans with much the same disdain as did the Ch'ing emperors of China. But by 1750, attitudes and circumstances were alike changing, and we need to examine how and why.

Mixed messages

Cosmopolitanism, in the sense of an informed appreciation of rival religious and political systems, and a belief in their equal worth, was not a characteristic of any society anywhere in the early modern world. Popular and polite responses to Islam in Britain were often visceral and derogatory, but this sort of deep-rooted, almost instinctive prejudice was not a monopoly of Europeans, nor did the British themselves deploy it only against non-Europeans. The Muslim peoples of the Mediterranean exhibited a very similar verbal, written and symbolic disdain and contempt for Western Christians. When the new English ambassador to the Ottoman empire, Sir Daniel Harvey, arrived in Istanbul in 1668, he was made to wait a full year for an audience with the sultan, as a stern reminder of the latter's supreme religious and secular importance, and the disparity in grandeur and extent between Harvey's puny kingdom and this huge overland Islamic empire. It is far from clear that the subsequent rise in Western power modulated, at least initially, this traditional sense of Islamic superiority. 'They consider themselves the first people in the world', wrote an astounded British envoy to Morocco as late as 1814, the year before Waterloo, '. . . and contemptuously term all others barbarians.'[6]

Western European Christians and their Muslim neighbours in the Mediterranean were not just alike in often being ignorant, suspicious and contemptuous of each other: they were also equally chauvinist towards their own rival co-religionists. Just as Turks, for instance, looked down on the Egyptian population of the Ottoman empire (often accusing them of a similar indolence and sensuality as Western Europeans regularly attributed to Muslims as a whole), so polite and plebeian Britons frequently derided and despised those of their fellow Europeans who were Roman Catholic:

> What does one find, but want and pride?
> Farces of superstitious folly,
> Decay, distress and melancholy:
> The havoc of despotic power,
> A country rich, its owners poor;
> Unpeopled towns, and lands untilled,
> Bodies unclothed, and mouths unfilled.[7]

Despotism, superstition, backwardness, a timeless poverty: here, it would seem, is unabashed Orientalism, precisely the kind of stereotypical slurs that Britons so often applied to the Islamic world. Except that this particular verse was an English milord's verdict on Italy in the 1730s, and the target could equally well have been Catholic France, or Spain, or Orthodox Russia (or even, in our own day, reputedly bureaucratic Brussels). Then, as now, the British possessed a limited and very durable portmanteau of xenophobic language and assumptions that they drew on and deployed undiscriminatingly, and by no means – as in Lord Hervey's poetic put-down of Italians – invariably with imperial intent.[8] What lay behind these stylised and recycled insults was rather Britain's intense Protestantism, that fostered a sense of special election and grace, together with its conscious-ness of its own smallness and potential vulnerability. Characterising other peoples, whether European or non-European, as morally and politically defective and/or oppressive, while simultaneously vaunting their own achievements and virtues, was – for early modern (and perhaps some modern) Britons – as much a defence mechanism as an expression of serene superiority or considered aggression.

If, then, we are to trace shifting attitudes in Britain towards Islam in the Mediterranean (and anywhere else), we need to look beyond the stan-dard and formulaic language of denunciation, suggestive though it can sometimes be. Contemporary reactions must be explored more broadly and also in some depth, for after 1600 they multiplied rapidly.

One of the paradoxes of Barbary captive-taking was that it not only exacerbated pre-existing hostility to Islam, but also increased the volume and variety of information available about it in Britain, and transformed both the extent and the complexity of Muslim–British contacts. Thus, in the 1630s, Algiers corsairs attacked coastal villages in Western England and Ireland, and Morocco dispatched its first large-scale embassy to London to negotiate ransoms for its English slaves. But this same decade, the 1630s, also saw the establishment of the first ever chairs in Arabic at Oxford and Cambridge Universities, in part so that officials and interpreters could be trained up to deal with Barbary and the Ottoman empire in the future.[9] The 1640s saw both a parliamentary levy on trade to finance Barbary captives' ransoms, and also the first publication of the *Qur'an* in English, a poor translation from a French version, probably by an Alexander Ross. This went through several editions before being entirely superseded in 1734, when the London-based orientalist George Sale (himself 'half a Mussulman' in Edward Gibbon's later opinion) produced a new and remarkable version of the *Qur'an*. And this later publication coincided with a procession through the streets of London of 150 redeemed captives from Morocco, exhibiting their rags and shackles before massive crowds.[10]

This is not to say that Barbary corsairing was the sole cause of this brisk rise in interest in and information about Islam. Growing trade with the Islamic world in the Mediterranean and elsewhere (on which the corsairs sometimes preyed) was an important contributory factor, and so was the scholarly belief that learning more about Islam would enhance understanding about the Bible and Christianity. My point is that – at this stage – it was captivity, commerce and Christian scholarship together, far more than any urge to conquest, that informed British curiosity about and reactions to the matter of Islam.

There was also an element of awe involved, which never entirely went away. By the seventeenth century, the great Islamic empires together probably contained between one third and one quarter of the world's population, and sprawled across the globe on a geographical scale that dwarfed western Europe as a whole, never mind England and its adjacent countries. Here, in the Muslim empires, was a display of daunting territorial reach and military power, in the service of a religion that rivalled Christianity, and resembled it in being monotheistic and international. This explains why, *pace* Nabil Matar, it was rarely the case that 'the Muslim "savage" and the Indian [Native American] "savage" became completely superimposable in English thought and ideology'. To be sure, individuals did occasionally attempt such analogies. When Devereux Spratt (1620–88), an Oxford-educated Anglican minister based in Ireland, compiled a manuscript memoir of his captivity in Algiers, he debated with himself why God permitted his Protestants to suffer so much at the hands of North African Muslims, New England Indians and Irish Catholics. To Spratt, evidently, all of these groupings were alike heathen and malevolent.[11]

But such lack of discrimination was distinctly unusual. Native Americans were seen at this time and for long after as nomadic peoples, with no urge to build in stone or cultivate land over the seasons, and no written records as Europeans understood them. Muslims, by contrast, whether encountered in the Mediterranean, or India, or Persia, were markedly urban (a vital characteristic of civilisation in Western European eyes), highly commercial (ditto), and possessed of an influential written culture. 'That little smattering of knowledge we have', insisted Simon Ockley, Cambridge's Professor of Arabic, in 1717, 'is entirely derived from the East.'[12] Native American religions, insofar as they were recognised at all, appeared polytheistic and parochial. Islam, by contrast, was perceived by most Britons and other Europeans in the early modern era – and after – as inferior to Christianity, but wedded to one God, international, and formidable. As Samuel Johnson put it with characteristic trenchancy: 'There are two objects of curiosity – the Christian world, and the Mahometan world. All the rest may be considered as barbarous.'[13]

It followed that to have some acquaintance with Islam was a constituent part of polite British culture. Even when Arabic and Oriental studies, like so many other subjects, went into decline in the ancient English universities after 1700, this was compensated for to some degree by the greater availability of works on Islam issued by the commercial presses. There was Joseph Pitts' *A True and Faithful Account of the Religion and Manners of the Mohammetans* (1704), a wonderful and lengthy captivity narrative still worth reading, which provided the first authentic English-language account of the *hajj*, the pilgrimage to Mecca. There was a successful English translation of Boulainvilliers' *Life of Mahomet* in 1731, in which the Prophet featured as 'a great man, a great genius, and a great prince'. And there was Sale's seminal translation of the *Qur'an*, three years later, which informed its readers briskly that:

To be acquainted with the various laws and constitutions of civilized nations, especially of those who flourish in our own time, is, perhaps, the most useful part of knowledge.[14]

The assumptions here are worth underlining. For Sale, writing in the 1730s, Islamic societies were not equal to his own Protestant Christian culture in terms of spiritual revelation, but they were emphatically civilised, and they were no less emphatically flourishing. This was also the view of the foremost Grub Street commentator on Islam in Britain at this time, Joseph Morgan. Morgan – who deserves to be better known – had been a soldier in the British army during the War of Spanish Succession, and was taken prisoner by the Spanish in 1706. His subsequent experience as a prisoner-of-war among fellow Europeans brought him, as captivity so often did, both personal trauma and also an opportunity for reassessing his life and opinions. By Morgan's own account, he was used 'with such hardships and cruelties', that he emerged with a profound sympathy for Spain's traditional enemy, Muslim North Africa. He travelled there for many years, learned Arabic, and used the Spanish he had acquired as a prisoner-of-war to investigate the Moriscos. Once back in London, he wrote and translated a series of books on Islam and the North African powers, all of them informed by the wistful conviction that, if only his countrymen knew more about Islam, their prejudices would be much reduced: 'I am persuaded that were . . . persons to converse unknowingly with Mahometans in a Christian dress, they would look upon them to be just such creatures as themselves.'[15]

Coexisting with the derogatory stereotypes, then, and the fear and hatred provoked by Ottoman power and Barbary corsairing, was a more measured and multi-faceted British discourse on Islam, in which its believers were *not* viewed unambivalently as the 'Other' or wholly different. In part

A True and Faithful
ACCOUNT
OF THE
Religion and Manners
OF THE
𝕸𝖔𝖍𝖆𝖒𝖒𝖊𝖙𝖆𝖓𝖘.
In which is a particular Relation of their
Pilgrimage to Mecca,
The Place of *Mohammet's* Birth;
And a Defcription of *Medina,* and of his
Tomb there. As likewife of *Algier,* and
the Country adjacent: And of *Alexan-
dria, Grand-Cairo,* &c. With an Account
of the Author's being taken Captive, the
Turks Cruelty to him, and of his Efcape.
In which are many things never Publifh'd
by any Hiftorian before.

By *JOSEPH PITTS* of *Exon.*

EXON: Printed by S. *Farley,* for *Philip Bifhop,*
and *Edward Score,* in the *High-Street.* 1704.

19. Islam experienced: Joseph Pitts'
narrative.

– and as suggested by Morgan's remark that Muslims in Western dress
would be indistinguishable – this was because adherents of Islam were
not seen as invariably and visibly racially distinct. This was especially true
of those Muslims with whom Britons had most contact at this stage:
Ottomans and other North Africans.[16] 'They are not a people black like
those of Guinea,' Sir Hugh Cholmley reported from Tangier in the 1670s,
'but in features and manners more resembling some of their neighbours,
inhabitants of Europe.' A seaman and former captive, John Whitehead,
struggled some decades later to supply a more accurately nuanced description, in a way that demonstrates how fluid racial designations still were at
this time, and how bound up with analysis in terms of religious allegiance:

As the French, Spaniards and other papists call themselves Roman
Catholics, so the subjects of the Emperor of Morocco do all call themselves Moors: though they be of diverse nations, and colours, viz. Moors

or Arabians, and Barbarians. These are white, another sort of Arabians that are tawny.[17]

North Africa, as some Britons at least were made aware, was far from being the uniform region suggested by the loaded collective term 'Barbary'. This was particularly true of its coastal cities, where most European captives, envoys and traders were concentrated. Places like Tangier, Salé, Tunis and Algiers were markedly cosmopolitan, arrestingly so by British domestic standards at this time. Their populations included Ottoman janissaries, powerful Jewish communities, sub-Saharan black slaves, sometimes in positions of high authority, and Protestant and Catholic European merchants, bankers, smugglers, drop-outs and renegades aplenty, sometimes prosperous and usually tolerated. One of the aspects of her brief captivity in Morocco in 1756 that Elizabeth Marsh found most disorienting, was that of encountering so many European traders cheerfully cutting deals with her Muslim captors. Badly traumatised by her adventure, she wanted – as the early version of her captivity narrative shows – to make sense of it in retrospect in terms of villainous Muslims on the one hand, and put-upon virtuous Christians on the other. But what she herself had witnessed at first hand kept getting in the way. She describes in one draft how, while being detained in Marrakesh, she encountered a Dutch merchant who was negotiating with the sultan to establish a trading house there. 'The difficulties a Christian is exposed to in that country', she complains almost tearfully, 'were overlooked by him, as matters of no importance or consideration.'[18] Even when the Royal Navy arrived to rescue her, it was only to take her on to British Gibraltar, where again Muslim and Jewish traders normally operated freely. Marsh yearned for strict cultural and religious divisions. She discovered instead, as so many had before her, that this Mediterranean world was often a shared and interdependent one.[19]

This cultural and ethnic diversity, combined with its geographical location and historic connections with the Iberian peninsula, made it difficult for early modern Europeans to situate North Africa securely on their mental maps, and on real ones. Was Barbary African, for instance? And, if so, what did this say about conventional European imaginings of that continent? 'I saw here nothing of that rudeness', wrote one captive revealingly, 'which our people imagine to be in all the parts of Africa.' Or was Barbary – and perhaps the Ottoman empire in general – a kind of rebel sub-section of Europe itself, as some British maps of the continent certainly suggested?[20] In the nineteenth century, it became easier, for those wishing to do so, to advance firm divides between the West and the rest, not just because of the elaboration of racial ideologies, but also because of the pace of technological, scientific and industrial change. The coming of steam power, trains, mass-production, telegraphs, gas-light, efficient plumbing, medical innovation – and of course rapid-firing guns – proved vital, as Michael Adas shows, both to British and Western dominance in the Victorian era in practical terms, and to the ideas sustaining that dominance.[21] Earlier though, and especially before 1750, the characteristics in British and European eyes of efficient and powerful societies were more diffuse and less decisive. Trade and towns were viewed as vital: and these existed in abundance in all Islamic societies. Islamic powers also built and created on a scale that impressed Europeans, far more so and for longer than is sometimes recognised.

It can be hard, for instance, wandering around the imperial city of Meknès in Morocco today, to imagine the grandeur that astounded Western visitors here in the late seventeenth and early eighteenth centuries. Some of the city was destroyed by the Lisbon earthquake of 1755 (a Eurocentric label that ignores the devastation this and connected quakes wreaked in the northerly parts of North Africa). Meknès was also pillaged in the course of successive bouts of civil strife; and much of it is now overgrown and in need of further archaeological recovery. But if you walk through the kilometre-long passage that is the Bab ar-Rouah, the Gate of Winds, or stand in the vast colonnaded space of the Mechouar, you can still obtain a sense of the extraordinary scale of this city-palace complex built by Moulay Ismaïl. This was a project roughly contemporaneous with the building of Versailles by Louis XIV of France, and it was inspired by a comparable regal hubris and territorial ambition. The sultan's palace at Meknès was simply the 'largest he had ever seen', reported an envoy dispatched to redeem Britain's Moroccan captives in the 1720s. Even the stables, which he calculated were three-quarters of a mile long, seemed 'the noblest of the kind perhaps in the world'.[22] Set against this structure in its heyday, Versailles was unduly compact; while William III's extensions to Hampton Court near London would have seemed almost toy-like in comparison.

This, indeed, was a crucial point. To the extent that Islamic societies *did* appear different to Britons at this early stage, it could still be because they seemed bigger, stronger, or richer.

Early modern Britons, like the rest of mankind, had no way of foreseeing the future. Indeed, they were far more likely than we are today to assume that things would continue much as they had done in the past. Self-evidently, they had no way of knowing in 1600, or in 1700, or in 1750, that by 1850 they would rule on paper so many millions of Muslim men and

A section of the Mechouar at Meknès.

The massive walls of one of Moulay Ismaïl's storehouses.

women. Even at the beginning of the nineteenth century, many Britons felt unable to predict this with any confidence. So when previous generations of English, Welsh, Scottish and Irish men and women contemplated Islamic powers in the Mediterranean and elsewhere, it was rarely with any sense of manifest destiny or expectation of imperial dominance. They could not know that – in due course but briefly – theirs would be an empire on which the sun never set. Instead, they regarded the Islamic presence in the light of what they *did* know: the sheer scale and continuing grandeur of the Ottoman empire, the well-publicised depredations of Barbary corsairs, and the resilience and toughness of the regimes that backed them.

Their vision was also informed by a consciousness of the limitations of their own state. After 1750, the British became increasingly complacent about the calibre of their ostensibly balanced constitution and their political stability. Excesses such as over-mighty monarchs, civil wars, rebellions, mass killings, out-of-control nobilities, and frequent, violent switches of dynasties came – at this later stage – to seem comfortably alien, things that simply did not and could not occur in Britain. Consequently, the political violence, administrative malaise, and dynastic extravagance associated, rightly or wrongly, with many Islamic polities, whether in the Mediterranean or elsewhere, were easily interpreted as evidence of an intrinsic failure in development, and even as a rationalisation of imperial takeover. Since Britain was manifestly so accomplished at governing itself, it increasingly seemed – to its political class at least – that the more places it governed throughout the world, the better it would be for everyone.

But, before 1750, confidence in the stability and supreme desirability of Britain's own political arrangements was less widespread and pronounced: and for good reason. During the 1640s and '50s, Britain and Ireland witnessed lethal civil wars in which hundreds of thousands of people died and a monarch lost his head. In 1688, a change of dynasty was effected by force of arms; and yet another dynastic changeover in 1714 went on to provoke bloody rebellions in protest in 1715 and 1745. Moreover, successive regimes failed to win nationwide acceptance in England, still less in the three countries connected to it, Scotland, Wales and Ireland. As a result of all this, throughout the seventeenth century, and right up to the Jacobite Rising of 1745 and even beyond, despotism, assassination, decadence, court intrigue, corruption and bloody rebellion were unlikely to be viewed as peculiarly characteristic of Islamic regimes, demonstrating their otherness and essential inferiority. To Britons, at this point, such political upheavals and abuses seemed all too familiar, a case of analogy and not difference. 'Are the Algerians the only regicides?' mocked Joseph Morgan gently in 1750, defending their political system:

a king [Charles I] after a solemn trial, has lost his head upon a scaffold
... Remove the ceremony, pomp, and formality, with which these
proceedings were disguised among the Christians, and the act itself will
appear the same with that practised in Barbary.[23]

We come back, in other words, to the fact that the attitudes of Britons to
the outside world – and their capacity for, and interest in empire – can
only be properly assessed when due consideration is also given to the
internal conditions of their own state and their own self-image. British
responses to Islam, and to Islamic powers in the Mediterranean and elsewhere, were never static or uniform. They changed in tandem with shifts
in the intellectual scene, and in the power and reputation of the great
Islamic empires. But they also changed in accordance with the estimates
made by Britons of their own state and of its potential. In this, as in so
many other respects, messages about Islam were mixed and mutating rather
than monolithic. The voices of British men and women who were caught,
and caught up in, this Mediterranean zone are both vocal and varied. It
is time we listened to them – and listened carefully.

Testimonies

Capture, whether in the Mediterranean zone or elsewhere, initially and
unsurprisingly forced victims back on themselves and deepened any pre-
existing prejudices they held. In shock, wounded perhaps, dizzy with the
unaccustomed heat of North Africa, unable in the vast majority of cases
to speak Arabic or Spanish, few men and women seized by Barbary corsairs
can have registered much at first except terror, resentment and bewilderment at the strangeness of it all. When an English seaman briefly held
captive in Tunis in the 1650s, Edward Coxere, tried after his return home
to compose a simple narrative of his experiences, words failed him when
he came to describe his early days as a slave. All he could manage was a
primitive drawing of a large man flourishing a whip and wearing a turban
(the standard European emblem for a Muslim), and a group of small
Englishmen, still in the clothes they were captured in, weighed down with
chains.[24] Here, indeed, was Islam depicted as 'Other' – but also as superior power. Over time, however, Coxere's perceptions became more
nuanced than this cartoon representation suggests, not least because of
the greater religious toleration he, as a Quaker, received from his Muslim
captors, than from the authorities in England. But a crude divide between
Muslim oppressors on the one hand, and forlorn Christians in bondage

on the other, must have been all that most captives of Barbary were at first able to assimilate.

Some chose never to look any deeper. Individuals held only briefly or exposed to unusual harshness might never have the chance to do so; while some clung fast to their preconceptions irrespective of how they were treated or for how long. Devereux Spratt, the Anglican minister, was captured with 120 others in the 1640s by Algiers corsairs off the coast of Youghall, southern Ireland. 'I began to question Providence,' he wrote later, but not for long. An heroic, narrow man, once in the city of Algiers, he began ministering to its other English captives, refusing an early chance to be ransomed because he would not leave their souls untended. His captors allowed Spratt and his white slave congregation freedom of worship. He himself had, as he admits, a 'civil' owner who gave him 'more liberty than ordinary'. This remained the case even after Spratt connived in the daring escape of five other Englishmen. 'I was much suspected', he writes, '. . . but Providence so ordered that I was never questioned.' Yet none of this prompted in him any curiosity about his Muslim captors. He attributed every kindness shown him solely to the omnipotence of his Protestant God: 'God was pleased to guide for me.'[25]

By interpreting any good deed issuing from Algerian Muslims in this fashion, Spratt left himself free to despise them. Early accounts by English colonists seized by Native Americans frequently employ this same tactic of crediting Providence alone with any act of charity extended to them by their captors. In regard to Barbary, however, a 'closed' narrative like Spratt's – closed in the sense of being determinedly incurious about the captors' common humanity – was rare. This was largely because Barbary captivity represented a very different kind of peril. Colonists seized by Native Americans, and subsequently escaping, had an obvious interest even apart from revenge and anger in seeking to dehumanise them. Native Americans were near-neighbours and rivals for the same land, a perpetual, intimate danger. Barbary corsairs, by contrast, were external enemies who threatened British shipping, liberties and lives, but only occasionally and fleetingly British territory. Moreover, Muslims – unlike Native Americans – were rarely regarded as godless or outside of civilisation. British captives of Barbary might, and often did, still hate their captors: but they were also more likely at some point to relax into a measure of detached observation. Once the immediate shock receded, they might begin to look around them and pose questions.

This, however, was when real disorientation often began, as captives were made forcibly aware that they now had to live and labour exposed to another culture's othering that both mirrored and inverted their own.

'Prejudice against unbelievers', as John Hunwick writes, was the 'single great prejudice of Muslim peoples', and since by Islamic law only unbelievers could be enslaved in the first place, anyone held captive or put to hard labour in North Africa was *ipso facto* a creature to be suspected, the infidel, the unclean.[26] James Irving, detained in Morocco for a year along with his crew, was shocked to notice how the local inhabitants 'would never use any vessel that had touched our lips: so great was their detestation & contempt for us'. British and other European captives were also made to recognise that, in the eyes of many of those around them, their physical appearance singled them out and demeaned them. Especially in the less cosmopolitan, inland regions of North Africa, European styles of dress – close to the crotch and legs for men, and to the waist for women – were likely to be viewed as at best strange and ugly, and at worst immoral and obscene. 'She . . . was extremely inquisitive', snaps Elizabeth Marsh of one coolly appraising Moroccan woman, 'curious in examining my dress and person, and . . . highly entertained at the appearance I made.'[27]

There was a more inescapable sense in which British captives found themselves caught fast in a disapproving or ironical Muslim gaze: there was the matter of their skin. Ibn Khaldûn, the great Tunisian scholar of the fourteenth century, wrote in his masterpiece, *Muqaddimah*, of his distaste for the two extremes of skin colour as he saw them, those with black skin, and those whom a cold climate had bleached to whiteness, with their 'blue eyes, freckled skin, and blond hair'. Only people of an intermediate skin-shade, he argued, could claim 'an abundant share of temperance, which is the golden mean'. This kind of prejudice against very dark and very pale skin seems to have persisted in North African societies into at least the nineteenth century, and to have existed at different social levels. Joseph Pitts, the young Exeter seaman who was enslaved in Algiers between 1678 and 1693, was told by one of his captors that pink people of his sort resembled pigs, quintessentially unclean animals.[28]

Captivity in Barbary, then, brought with it a sudden turning of the world upside down and an abrupt education in another society's prejudices, with little or no chance of being able to retaliate. Even British envoys of the Crown visiting North African cities in the seventeenth and eighteenth centuries to negotiate treaties, or redeem captives, had frequently to run the gauntlet of crowds of young local males hurling insults at them as unbelievers, mocking their physical appearance, and firing guns over their heads to make them jump.[29] Individual captives, with no diplomatic status or guards to protect them, were inevitably far more exposed. How they coped depended on those with power over them, but also – often –

on themselves. When William Okeley forgot for a moment the defence-lessness of his new slave status, and insulted his Algerian owner's Muslim faith to his face, he was able both literally and metaphorically to roll with the punches that subsequently rained down on him. 'Well, I learnt from hence two lessons,' he recalled of his beating: 'one, that when the body is a slave, the reason must not expect to be free . . . Second, that it's fair for slaves to enjoy the freedom of their own consciences, without reviling another's religion.'[30]

James Irving, by contrast, never adapted to the strain of submitting to his Moroccan captors. It killed him. His captivity occurred some 150 years after Okeley's, in the early 1790s, by which time Britons of Irving's class possessed a far more inflated sense of national and often racial conceit. The acute shame he experienced derived however as much from what he did as from what he was. An uncompromisingly Protestant Scot, Irving was the captain of a Liverpool-based transatlantic slave-ship and, as his narrative makes clear, possessed a fundamental distaste for those he termed 'black cattle'. To have individuals whom he, at least, viewed as also black-skinned as well as pagan now threaten him with slavery in Morocco was an inversion quite beyond his bearing. The local British consul, who corresponded with him throughout, tried patiently to spell out the facts of his new captive status in words that can only have embittered him further. 'I must beg leave to caution you not to make use of the term infidels, either in your letters or discourse when speaking of the Moors,' Irving was told firmly. 'They look upon the term as the most opprobrious in their language, and *as they have the power in their hands*, it may operate to your prejudice.'[31]

There are two important points to notice about these individual agonies and adjustments. First, they illustrate yet again how the instinct to 'other' seemingly alien individuals and societies in debased terms, which is usually examined only as a Western trait, was not so at all. Britons seized by corsairs from the region they presumed to call 'Barbary' discovered to their dismay that one of the insults most commonly flung at them by their captors was in turn 'barbarian'. Second, while prejudice against those perceived as alien was – and is – ubiquitous, the degree to which different individuals believed in and acted in conformity with such prejudices varied enormously, as of course it still does. Britons taken captive in North Africa did not, in practice, always come 'up against the Orient as a European . . . first, as an individual second'.[32] Just like other human beings, different Britons combined and juggled different identities. For some, like Irving, being dragged across the frontier of an Islamic power did indeed sharpen their sense of themselves as Christian, British, European and white. Others – after they had recovered from the immediate shock – cared about these particular loyalties only some of the time. Still others gave priority to different considerations entirely; while a minority reacted to Barbary captivity by abandoning Christianity, Britishness, and notions of Europeanness altogether, or by adjusting their sense of what these allegiances involved. Here, as in other parts of the world, captivity, and the narratives emerging from it, never invariably aided the construction or reinforcement of 'a binary division between captive and captor . . . based on cultural, national, or racial difference'.[33] Captivity and its texts were just as likely to expose and bring to the surface divisions within the victims' own home society, differences of class, education and wealth, differences of precise national origin, and differences of religious outlook.

Devereux Spratt's utter passive resistance to his Algerian context, for instance, stemmed in the main from his intense, professional Protestantism, but also from his sense of himself as a University-educated clergyman and one-time tutor to the English gentry. Most Barbary captives were less programmed and less privileged than this. For them, limited expectations at home might inflect how they reacted to issues of difference in captivity abroad, not least because white captives in North Africa, like black slaves in North America, were sometimes confronted with the phenomenon of the good master. William Okeley wrote of the third Algerian who owned him, a small farmer, that 'I found not only pity and compassion, but love and friendship from my new patron. Had I been his son, I could not have met with more respect, nor been treated with more tenderness.' In his English life, Okeley's trade was deference. He was captured in the 1640s while carrying out a transatlantic mission for Viscount Saye and Sele and Lord Brooke, and would be employed after his escape from Algiers as a steward on a landed estate in Bedfordshire. His published narrative makes clear his sense that serving an aloof patrician who was a fellow Englishman was not necessarily an advance on cheerful household slavery with a good man who just happened to be a North African Muslim:

> There arose a scruple, nay, it amounted to a question, whether to attempt an escape from my [Algerian] patron, one that so dearly loved me . . . For, where could I hope to mend my self? Or better my condition? I might possibly find worse quarter in England . . . Liberty is a good word, but a man cannot buy a meal's meat with a word: And slavery is a hard word, but it breaks no man's back.

In the end, Okeley's decision to run appears to have been based less on revulsion against a new life that was fast becoming comfortably familiar, than on prudential motives that would always weigh with a subordinate man like himself: 'My patron's favour was no freehold . . . He might die, and leave me to another'.[34]

Among Britons who were seized very young, or who remained in North Africa for many years, the pull of the captor society might be stronger still. Joseph Pitts was captured and taken to Algiers in 1678 when he was just fifteen. He remained there until 1693, and converted – he claimed in print only nominally and under pressure – to Islam. Although he finally escaped, after a letter smuggled to him from his father tugged at strings he had thought broken forever, he, too, was open in his published narrative about the kindness of his last Algerian owner who promised to leave him money on his death, and the affection he felt for him. Pitts also confessed to a strong temptation to 'continue a Mussulman'. 'I was', he wrote, 'in a much fairer way for honour and preferment in Algiers, than I could expect ever to have been in England.' How accurate this claim was will never be known, though it seems likely that Pitts himself believed it. On his return to England in the 1690s, in the midst of a major war with France, he was immediately imprisoned and threatened with impressment in the Royal Navy. For a labouring man like this (as we have already seen in Thomas Pellow's case) release from captivity abroad did not necessarily result in a warm sense of liberty recovered and resumed at home. It is suggestive that Pitts' captivity narrative – which was highly successful when it was published in 1704, and reprinted in 1717, 1731 and 1778 – openly and explicitly represented Islamic society as sometimes offering superior opportunities to individual Christians. Pitts writes of at least three fellow English captives known to him who chose to stay in Algiers. One of these was actually ransomed and returned home, but 'came again to Algiers and voluntarily, without the least force used towards him, became a Mohammetan'.[35]

It is in the context of such behaviour that we can understand the many references in Barbary captivity literature to Joseph, the Old Testament figure taken captive into Egypt and enslaved. In 1627, for instance, an English envoy negotiating the redemption of captives from Morocco referred to its ruler as 'a second Pharoah which knew not Joseph', while Devereux Spratt in Algiers 'laboured . . . to remember ye afflictions of Joseph'.[36] These were hostile deployments of the scriptural reference, but men and women familiar with the Bible knew that the lessons of Joseph's tale were mixed. He is enslaved by an alien power, yes. But it is this self-same misfortune that leads to his owner Potiphar, a chief officer of the Pharoah, promoting him to be overseer. Joseph prospers in Egypt and grows powerful, and even has to repel the lustrous advances of his owner's wife: 'God', he boasts, 'hath caused me to be fruitful in the land of my affliction.'[37] As we have seen, ballads like 'Lord Bateman' popularised the notion that British captives of Barbary too might find the site of their affliction productive of worldly opportunity. Some poor whites might flourish under the Crescent, or at least do no worse than at home. The same could even be true of poor blacks.

What may be the only black British Barbary captivity narrative ever written has recently been lost.[38] But, thanks to the work of Marcus Rediker and Peter Linebaugh, we know that blacks formed a persistent minority in both the Royal Navy and in Britain's merchant fleet, and some of these men were certainly captured over the years. Thomas Saphra, a black servant, was seized on the London ship *Philadelphia* in 1716.[39] Three of the eleven crewmen taken captive alongside James Irving in Morocco in 1789 were black, and among the eighty-seven survivors from the *Inspector* shipwrecked there in 1746, were two black sailors, Thomas Jones and John Armatage. The latter 'turned Moor', and it seems likely that he was absorbed into the *'Abid al-Bukhari*, the black slave army of the Moroccan sultans. This was recruited in the main from the local black slave population, the *haratin*, but also seems to have drawn on blacks seized from captured European vessels.[40]

Joining the ranks of the *'Abid al-Bukhari* meant exposure to physical danger and brutality, but also the prospect of plunder and promotion. It might even bring the chance to oversee white slaves, a conspicuous demonstration that Islamic societies could offer opportunities that Western Europe did not. One has only to remember Olaudah Equiano's stunned excitement when he visited the Ottoman city of Smyrna in 1768, and observed how white slaves there were 'kept under by the Turks, as the negroes are in the West Indies by the white people'. Equiano seems to have been born to a black slave mother in South Carolina and was subsequently owned by a Royal Naval officer. Free now, but still a servant, he gained from his Ottoman journey not just insight into a very different slave system, but also a sense from witnessing it that power relations between the races might be mutable. Whites, he realised, could be made as vulnerable as he himself had once been. Not all slaves were black; and not all whites were free. For long after this – as he tells us in his own captivity narrative – Equiano cherished the idea of emigrating to the Ottoman empire.[41] In just such a way, some black seamen seized by the North African powers might feel drawn to Muslim society. It sometimes offered individuals like them more options, another world.[42] Here was an extreme version of a much broader and recurrent phenomenon: overseas captivity as a potential gateway to opportunity and a fresh start for those who were disadvantaged in some way in their home society.

The existence of British-based black captives of Barbary is a reminder that, then as now, the terms 'Briton', 'British', and especially 'English subject' or 'British subject' encompassed a patchwork of people. The quarter millennium covered by this book witnessed a dramatic rise in British national sentiment, but it also saw the British state becoming more composite, and composite in different ways at different stages. One of the more intellectual challenges confronting London in regard to Barbary captive-taking was indeed establishing exactly who it was responsible for redeeming at different times. The flux of Britain's ruling dynasties, state formation, international alliances and imperial acquisitions in the Mediterranean and elsewhere meant that the rules were constantly changing. After the Dutch stadtholder, William of Orange, ousted James II as king of England in 1688, for instance, the Moroccan sultan Moulay Ismaïl agreed that, when it came to ransoming, he would 'look upon the English and Dutch to be united, and in effect to be as one nation'.[43] This arrangement lapsed after William's death; but thereafter French Huguenots, Hanoverians, colonial Americans, and the multi-ethnic inhabitants of Minorca and Gibraltar were all claimed at different times by London as people it had a right and duty to ransom back as 'British subjects' if they were captured by Barbary.[44]

As demonstrated by the troubled internal politics of Tangier's garrison back in the 1660s and 1670s, the view from above of who qualified as an English or British subject could be at odds with the more visceral allegiances of those below. In 1747, British ministers approached the Ironmongers' Company of London, which presided over a lavish charitable fund specifically set up to redeem Barbary captives, for aid in a current ransoming campaign. The Ironmongers' grudging response is a wonderful example of how deep-rooted assumptions about national identity sometimes collided with more flexible and legalistic government notions of what 'Britishness' had practically to involve:

> They further object that in the number of the four score prisoners now detained [in Morocco] there may possibly be some Irishmen . . . and that there must therefore be proof made that they were all Britons before they apply the money.[45]

Quite clearly, as far as these Company members were concerned, the Irish – and no religion is specified in this passage – were not comprehended within the term 'Britons', and many others on the island of Great Britain, at this stage and later, would have concurred in this view.

As this suggests, approaching cross-cultural relationships and conflicts in the past in simple, bloc terms such as West and East, or Europe and non-European, or Britain and Islam glosses over important complexities and vital sub-divisions on all sides, and tends to hobble analysis. As politicians frequently have cause to remark even today, Europe, even western Europe alone, is not a unit and never has been. 'Europeans' did not think alike about Islam or anything else. As far as Britain itself was concerned, we have already seen how its marked territorial smallness helped to foster within it, as a countervailing advantage, a strong, centralised state, and a precocious, though never all-encompassing national unity and ideology. Even so, British unity was a partial and fractured thing, especially before 1750. Most particularly, it was persistently challenged by the divide between Catholic and Protestant, and like its other internal divisions, this complicated its responses to Islam and Islamic powers.

This tension can be seen, working itself out, at an individual level. Shared and fought over by rival states and faiths, the Mediterranean had traditionally always functioned as a frontier region where 'men [and women] passed to and fro, indifferent to . . . states and creeds', pursuing instead their own private, unofficial and sometimes rebellious vision of what they wanted from life.[46] After 1600, and still more after 1700, the volume of such individual crossings declined as states became more efficient at controlling and regulating their subjects, but at no time did they ever entirely cease. Those most likely to cross boundaries and turn renegade here, as far as the British state was concerned, were unsurprisingly the Catholic Irish. For just as some inhabitants of early modern England, Wales and Scotland had little desire to regard Ireland (especially its Catholics) as British: so the Irish (especially, but not exclusively the Catholics) sometimes returned the compliment. Take the case of the Butlers, a dynasty of Irish Catholic merchants who, by the mid-eighteenth century, were well established in Morocco, fluent in Arabic, and 'well acquainted' with the sultan's ministers. They delighted in helping visiting Continental European traders outwit British Protestant ones, and in assisting Spanish intrigues to recover Gibraltar.[47]

Some Catholic Irishmen who crossed over in this Mediterranean zone however did so more than once. From the 1730s, through to the 1750s, successive British envoys in Algiers struggled to determine what to do about a group of twenty-nine Irish Catholic mercenaries who had landed up there. These men had previously served Spain, doubtless at times against Britain. But once sent to the Spanish North African base of Oran – which was as bleak and brutal as garrison life in Tangier had been – these wild geese suddenly discovered the compelling attractions of Britishness. They deserted *en masse*, fled to Algiers where they were promptly enslaved, and appealed for help to the British consul there. Correspondence between him and his London masters about whether these individuals were indeed 'British subjects', and whether or not they – and other Irish mercenaries on the run in North Africa from French or Spanish service – should be ransomed, went on for decades.[48]

But the capacity of religious attachments to blur, rather than simply reinforce the divide between Britain and Islam, was exemplified in more than just the behaviour of disaffected individuals. This was a matter of state and even of theology.

Traditionally, the most persistent enemies of the Ottoman empire and Barbary were the Catholic powers, Spain, Austria, the Italian states, and on occasions France. For the rulers and the inhabitants of a Protestant polity like Britain, this Catholic hostility to the Islamic powers of the Mediterranean could seem a positive argument in the latter's favour. On the well-known principle of the enemy of my enemy is my friend, Elizabeth I sold weapons to the Moroccans in the late sixteenth century to use against the Catholic Portuguese; Charles I sought Moroccan aid against Spain in the 1620s; and, as we have seen, from 1704 onwards Britain relied on Algiers and Morocco to provision Gibraltar and Minorca, and so retain them against His Catholic Majesty of Spain. But there was more behind this Protestant–Islamic entente than just reasons of state or sectarian spite. There were aspects of Islam as a working faith that could seem to Protestants familiar and even congenial. Here, after all, was a religion that banned images from places of worship, that did not treat marriage as a sacrament, and had absolutely no time for monastic orders ('We shall have no Monk-ery,' the Prophet Muhammad is supposed to have declared). More radical Protestants might even relish Islam's contempt for the doctrine of the Trinity.[49]

This helps to explain why Protestant dissenters especially who got caught up in this Mediterranean world of crossings and captivities often adopted a markedly sympathetic perspective on their Muslim captors. Joseph Pitts, whom we have already encountered, used some of his captivity narrative to compare Islam with Roman Catholicism – very much to the former's advantage. He commended Muslims for excluding religious images from their mosques. He remarked on the practical toleration North African regimes extended to other faiths, which seemed to a Presbyterian like himself so much more impressive than the treatment meted out by the Anglican establishment at home. Autodidact as he was, Pitts also noted the zeal with which even some of the poorer Muslims he had known in Algiers studied the *Qur'an*, the primacy they gave to the word. It was a mode of faith and life, he thought, utterly unlike and far superior to 'the poor Romanists . . . [who] live and die in an implicit faith of what they are taught by their priests'.[50] The degree to which Pitts allowed himself to observe and empathise with his Muslim captors rather than judging them emerges most, however, in the tone and the detail of his narrative.

He published it in 1704 to justify the Algerian segment of his life to his Exeter non-conformist neighbours and make 'reparation for my past defection'. Yet, although this was his avowed aim in writing, the memory of how he had once been caught up in and stirred by Muslim North Africa kept impacting on and colouring his prose:

> A few days after this [that is, after a twenty days journey on the Red Sea] we came to a place called Rabbock [Rabigh], about four days' sail this side of Mecca; where all the hagges [pilgrims] excepting those of the female sex . . . take off all their clothes, covering themselves with two hirrawems or large white cotton wrappers. One they put about their middle, which reaches down to their ankles; the other they cover the upper part of their body with, except the head. And they wear no other thing on their bodies but these wrappers; only a pair of gimgameea, ie. thin-sol'd shoes, like sandals, the over-leather of which covers only the toes, their insteps being all naked. In this manner, like humble penitents, they go from Rabbock till they come to Mecca to approach the temple; many times enduring the scorching heat of the sun till their very skin is burnt off their backs and arms . . . Yet when any man's health is by such austerities in danger and like to be impaired, they may lawfully put on their clothes, on condition still that, when they come to Mecca, they sacrifice a sheep and give it to the poor . . . During this time . . . they will also be careful to be reconciled and at peace with all such as they had any difference with; accounting it a very shameful and sinful thing to bear the least malice against any.[51]

And so it went on for almost 200 pages, an uneducated working man's evocation of what this wide world so far removed from Exeter had once offered him: the bright sashes of the whores in Egypt, the cheapness of fresh eggs in Cairo, the sweet taste of good camel meat, the whorls of henna that decorated the hands and feet of women. How, on hot North African nights, you could freshen your bed linen by sprinkling it with cold water and wake up baked dry again come morning. And, interspersed among all this, long passages of thick description, like the one quoted above, on the seriousness of Muslim devotion. By the end of his book, Pitts seems to have realised something of its likely effect on British readers, without however wanting to change it. He did his best to extract an

J. Mynde fc.

The various gestures of the Mahometans in their prayers to God.

22. Muslim devotion: an illustration in Joseph Pitts' narrative.

orthodox moral of a kind: 'If they [Muslims] are so strict in their false worship, it must need be a reprimand to Christians who are so remiss in the True,' but he also struggled to find some kind of closure that might connect and not thrust apart the Islamic and Christian phases of his life. 'O merciful God,' he ends, '. . . have mercy upon all Jews, Turks, infidels, and heretics . . . and so fetch them home.'[52]

Some two hundred years earlier, an Italian miller called Menocchio had taken a roughly similar line when dragged before the Inquisition, insisting that a merciful God would surely save heretics, Turks and Jews as well as Christians.[53] To a degree, Joseph Pitts was much the same sort of man as Menocchio, a poor, thoughtful, autodidact whose life had been harsh, and who had struggled through to his own conclusions about important things. There was a vital difference however in the respective fates of these two extraordinary plebeians. Menocchio was burnt at the stake as a heretic for his ideas. By contrast, the book in which Pitts set out his personal cosmology was well received and regularly reprinted. In eighteenth-century Britain – and in nineteenth-century Britain – expressing sympathy for elements of Islam, and suggesting that it was a superior faith to Roman Catholicism, did not necessarily set you apart, still less invite fierce persecution. At all social levels, there were Britons who believed – as Pitts did – that the Crescent was far less alien and dangerous than the Cross on a Catholic's rosary.

Transitions?

So when, and to what extent, did all this richness and variety of response begin to change and harden? I have argued that Britain's disdain for Islam and the Eastern, which some have viewed as a vital motor for its subsequent rampant imperialism, was – before 1750 especially – more apparent, noisy, and ritualistic, than profound and formative. Islamic regimes were viciously othered at times, in speech, in texts, in art, and in government pronouncements, but the accusations and language levelled against them were very similar to those used against European Roman Catholic regimes. And hostility towards the Crescent always coexisted with very different trends and tendencies. Islam was certainly rated lower than Protestant Christianity (though not by all Britons), but it was also treated respectfully and even with awe in both polite and popular writings. Muslims' capacity for advanced civilisation was explicitly conceded, and their racial and physical similarities to Europeans often openly canvassed.

As far as relations with the Islamic powers of the Mediterranean were concerned, the British sense of difference and superiority – though present – was frequently offset by other considerations. It was offset by the power of the Ottoman empire, which long overshadowed Britain's own, and by the depredations of the Barbary corsairs. It was offset, too, by the constraints on Britain's military and naval power in this region, and by its need for North African aid to retain its white colonies in this sea among the lands, Gibraltar and Minorca. But, as the multiple testimonies of British actors caught up in the Mediterranean zone document, the sense of difference vis-à-vis Islam was also offset and problematised by divisions within the British state itself. Until Britain could become more assured of its working unity and its own stability – and less conscious of its inhibiting smallness – its capacity for real, as distinct from assumed arrogance towards other regimes, and its capacity for successful imperial aggression had marked limits.

Yet by the 1750s, circumstances were changing. The failure of the 1745–6 Jacobite rebellion marked the end – for well over two hundred years at least – of the spectre of Scotland and its precious manpower breaking away from the British Union. More significantly still, the destruction of Jacobitism ended forever fears of a takeover of the British throne by a Roman Catholic dynasty by force of arms, and this helped to smooth over the fierce divisions between Protestant and Catholic within the British state. These domestic resolutions, and the increased stability and internal cohesion they afforded, helped power the conspicuous take-off in British imperial enterprise in the second half of the eighteenth century. As always, the trajectory of British empire overseas has to be understood in connection with British internal developments, and *vice versa*. In the Mediterranean, as elsewhere, this heightened British power and imperial activism after the mid-eighteenth century showed itself in an increase in soldiers, ships, sieges and battles. Yet as far as the Islamic societies of this region were concerned, Britain's escalating imperial aggression after 1750 remained tempered and qualified in all sorts of ways. Looking through the highly specific but powerful lens offered by captivity and its writings helps to clarify why this was so.

Enter Captain Hyde Parker, RN, young, brave, fundamentally unintelligent and, tellingly, a man in uniform. He was dispatched in the spring of 1756 to negotiate a treaty with Morocco and to recover any British captives remaining there. Sidi Muhammad, the acting ruler and future Sultan, had asked that a British consul fluent in Arabic be based permanently in his country, and expected as well a substantial gift of naval stores. Parker had been instructed to reject both of these Moroccan demands, and was anyway a man tightly corseted in his belief in 'the providence of God and the terror of His Majesty's naval power'. Accordingly, the naval officer removed neither his tricorne hat nor his heavy boots on entering Sidi Muhammad's palace, and made a point of sitting down firmly in the latter's presence, thereby insulting him both as a ruler and as a lineal descendant of the Prophet. Parker and his crew managed to escape the resulting explosion of princely anger, but others of their compatriots did not. Morocco, like the rest of Barbary, had taken few British captives since 1735, bought off in its case by over £60,000 of protection money. Now, Sidi Muhammad reversed this policy of profitable restraint, and by 1758 had secured almost 400 British captives.[54]

This provoked the last substantial cache of British writings about captivity in North Africa, and one of the few full-length Barbary narratives written and published by a woman. Its author was Elizabeth Marsh, the daughter of a British naval dockyard official based in Gibraltar (again, note the heightened presence in the Mediterranean by this stage of agents of a more strongly armed and extrovert British state). Marsh and her fellow passengers were seized off the coast of North Africa by Moroccan corsairs in August 1756, and held captive in Salé and Marrakesh until late that year in retaliation for Captain Hyde Parker's diplomatic deficit. An enthusiastic though strictly amateur writer, Marsh went on to draft several versions of what had happened to her. Initially the plot-line she selected was stark and traditional. She presented herself overwhelmingly as a victim of Islam's historic antipathy and aggression towards the Christian West, even quoting from a popular play about the crusades, John Hughes's *Siege of Damascus*:

> Now in the name of Heav'n, what faith is this
> That stalks gigantick forth thus arm'd with terrors
> As if it meant to ruin, not to save?
> That leads embattel'd legions to the Field,
> And marks its progress out with blood and slaughter.[55]

In the immediate aftermath of her 1756 captivity, Barbary still signified for Marsh – as it had for many other Britons before her – terror, danger, and the alarming shadow of the Crescent.

By the time she came to publish her narrative as *The Female Captive* in 1769, however, her chosen emphasis and mode of writing had both shifted. In this two-volume work, completed more than a decade after her capture, Marsh omitted virtually all references to religious conflict between Christianity and Islam. She left out, too, much of the information she had garnered on North African topography and society, and on the complex inter-relationships that actually existed in Morocco between individual Europeans and Muslims. Traditional prejudice against Islam and close, empirical observation were alike downplayed. Instead, Marsh converted her captive experiences into high drama and romance. She claimed that, from the very beginning of her enforced residence in Morocco, she had trembled for her sexual virtue, and that these fears had reached their culmination in two interviews with Sidi Muhammad himself.

> The Prince was tall, finely shaped, of a good complexion, and appeared to be about five and twenty . . . His figure, all together, was rather agreeable, and his address polite and easy.

This eligible creature ('I was amazed at the elegant figure he made') tried to persuade her to join him in the splendours of his Marrakesh palace. As a result, Marsh wrote, she was forced to lie. She assured Sidi Muhammad that she was married in fact, and that she preferred this equal relationship with a man of her own kind to all the poisoned luxuries of the seraglio. She resisted the prince's subsequent anger as stoutly as his appeals, refused to convert to Islam, and at last obtained her release. 'The Prince, being asked if he would not see the fair Christian before her departure, after a pause, replied, "*No, lest I should be obliged to detain her.*"'[56]

Elizabeth Marsh was twenty-one and emphatically single when these Marrakesh encounters reportedly occurred, and Sidi Muhammad was indeed about five and twenty. If some version of them really did take place, there may have been a frisson of excitement on his part – and also on hers. It bears repeating, though, that the preliminary drafts of Marsh's narrative, composed soon after her capture, made less of the theme of sexual danger in general, and of these palace show-downs in particular. Nor does any of the considerable official British correspondence on Marsh's confinement in Morocco in 1756 raise the possibility of her virtue being at risk, or of her being swept into a harem. Some female British and Irish captives of Barbary had in the past disappeared into North African private and royal households, but such unfortunates had rarely been women of Marsh's comfortable social status, and there are no known examples of British women of any kind suffering this fate after the 1720s.[57] It seems likely, therefore, that Elizabeth Marsh's belated decision to give prominence in *The Female Captive* to issues of sexual danger and virile, importunate sultans stemmed from something more than just remembered terrors, or even the simple desire to write a quasi-novel and sell copy.

Representing Barbary as a place of sexual threat for captive British women had been unusual up to this point. Indeed, the experiences of British women in North Africa in general had rarely been touched on in any detail. Female captives in the North African powers were of course always very much a minority. None the less, they were sufficiently a presence over the years for dry, government documents regularly to make mention of them. Popular English writings in the seventeenth and earlier eighteenth centuries, by contrast, barely refer to women captives from these islands at all. Elizabeth Marsh's 1769 volumes were the first female Barbary captivity narrative to appear in Britain. There seem to be no popular ballads about British female Barbary captives; and British men's captivity narratives rarely discuss female experiences, even when the writers make it clear that women were taken alongside them. Instead, British captivity literature had traditionally been far more concerned to stress the sexual threat to male captives in Barbary. For every single reference to heterosexual sex I have seen in British discussions of Barbary and Ottoman captivity before 1750, there are at least five to sodomy: and this is true of polite as well as popular literature, public statements and the most private of writings.

The notion found its way into petitions. 'The said [Algerian] patrons' some captives' wives had complained in the 1670s, 'do frequently bugger the said captives, or most of them'. It was the stuff of parliamentary speeches. Algerian captivity, an MP had told the House of Commons in 1614, meant 'children taken, kept for buggery and made Turks'.[58] It informed diplomats' reactions to North African missions. The journal of Thomas Baker, England's consul in Tripoli after 1677, remarks its editor, is obsessed with 'homosexuality, which according to him, was quite acceptable in Tripoli, with homosexual rape . . . openly and violently practised'. Naturally the claim surfaced in captivity narratives. 'They are said to commit sodomy with all creatures,' wrote Francis Knight of his Algerian captors in 1640.[59] But it could equally well be found in more substantial texts, like Paul Rycaut's famous *Present State of the Ottoman Empire* (1668), where the Ottoman world's very need to import Christian captives from without was put down to its own internal failure to reproduce because of 'that abominable vice of sodomy'. And it circulated in all kinds of imaginary literature. Robinson Crusoe himself is kept as a slave by the Moroccan corsair who captures him because he is 'young and nimble, and fit for his business'. Defoe supplies his more sophisticated readers with ample clues as to just what this business is. The corsair's ship, Crusoe tells us, contains a 'cabin, which lay very snug and low, and had in it room for him to lie, with a slave or two'. The *double entendres* fairly jostle each other. William Chetwode's novel *The Voyages and Adventures of Captain Robert Boyle* (1726), reissued a dozen times over the century, dispensed with such wordplay. Sodomy, a Moroccan bluntly informs the properly appalled captive British hero, 'is so common here that 'tis reckon'd only a piece of gallantry'.[60]

For my purposes, it is immaterial how valid such accusations were.[61] Most of those who accused North African and Ottoman males of sodomy were not anyway seriously interested in delineating the sexuality of those they were denouncing. Nor were they using accusations of homosexuality merely as a way of 'othering' Islam and its adherents. Sodomy in the context of writings on Barbary and the Ottoman world before 1750 was rather a metaphor, a particularly acute expression of the fear and insecurity that Britons and other Western Europeans continued to feel in the face of Islamic power and, as they saw it, aggression. The claim sometimes made, that the West eroticised the Islamic world in order to feminise and dominate it, is therefore, as far as this portion of it is concerned, suspect. Indeed the claim can be reversed. Those who accused Muslims of sodomy in the context of discussions of corsairing and captivities were rarely primarily concerned with whether North African and Ottoman males allowed themselves to be sodomised. Rather, the burden of these expressed anxieties, was that captive British and other European males were the potential victims. It was *they* who might be penetrated and invaded. *They* who might be forced into the passive role. Accusing the Barbary powers, and the Ottoman empire in general, of practising sodomy on Christian captives was yet another way in which Britons gave vent to their insecurities and to ancient fears that Islam might in the end use its strength to reduce them to submission.

Only when Ottoman and North African power were broadly recognised as receding, did such accusations of sodomy become thoroughly drowned out by an emphasis instead on the supposed heterosexual lusts of Muslim men and on their harems of docile, scented females. Claiming that Turks, or Moroccans, or Algerians collected and domineered over sexually pliant women, both entrapped Europeans and non-Europeans, was a way also of saying that these peoples were no longer in a position seriously to threaten European males. This is the broader significance of Elizabeth Marsh's strange two-volume captivity narrative. Even more than Captain Hyde Parker's deliberate rudeness to the ruler of Morocco in 1756, it marks an important shift – though only a partial shift – in British perceptions and assumptions. For by the time *The Female Captive* was published, in 1769, global power relations had changed radically, and were still changing fast.

The Seven Years War, which began in the year of Elizabeth Marsh's capture, 1756, and ended in 1763, transformed global politics. Not only did Britain consolidate its position in North America through its conquest of Canada, but for the first time ever it also launched a major and successful military assault on territory governed by Islamic rulers by winning and retaining Bengal. The ghost of the fiasco at Tangier was finally laid, and from now on one of the world's great Islamic empires, Mughal India, would come under serious and escalating British pressure. By the time Elizabeth Marsh published, another Islamic empire was also coming under unparallelled European pressure. The Russo-Turkish Wars, which began in 1768, proved disastrous for the Ottoman empire and confirmed Western Europe's sense that this prime representative of Islam was fast becoming a rusting, antique titan. Confections full of scantily clad harems, Christian damsels in distress, and masterful and strangely attractive Sultans had circulated in Britain as elsewhere in Europe for some time. But, from the 1760s, this sort of 'oriental' literature and art, of which Elizabeth Marsh's *The Female Captive* was a minor example, became conspicuously more prolific, and more easily accepted, because the Islamic world was now seen to be losing much of its power to frighten.[62] References to the threat from Muslim sodomy receded, along with British and European fears of penetration from without. The preferred story-line was now more likely to be that which Mozart selected for his opera about captives, *The Abduction from the Seraglio* (1782), plucky English blondes resisting overweening sultans (had the composer read Miss Marsh?), titillation rather than terror.

In retrospect, then, *The Female Captive*, can be situated on the cusp of what would prove to be a long drawn-out, and never complete, shift away from residual British apprehension and awe of Islam to low regard for, and condescension towards at least some of the states associated with it. In Elizabeth Marsh's strictly amateur production, Morocco is indubitably orientalised, exoticised and downgraded. But all this said, the relationship between British literary and artistic representations of Islam on the one hand, and British coercive power and colonial intent on the other, was not a straightforward one even after 1750, any more than it had been before. It is certainly possible to discern changes in tone in British commentary on Islamic societies in the Mediterranean zone and elsewhere after the 1750s, and of course a quantum leap in British global power. But these shifts were not – repeat not – accompanied by a marked and immediate upsurge in British physical coercion and colonial power in the North African and Ottoman regions.

This point is crisply underlined by the quality of Britain's response to Sidi Muhammad's furious burst of captive-taking after 1756, or rather by the lack of it. No eighteenth-century precursors of gunboats were dispatched to punish the Moroccan ruler and force him back in line, and this was not simply because of the logistical difficulties involved in taking offensive action against the North African coastline. The British simply had no wish to employ force in this direction, and could not afford to do so. William Pitt, soon to be styled 'The Patriot Minister' for his warlike endeavours and public spirit, emphatically did not want to bluster or fight in this part of the Mediterranean world. Instead, he apologised to Sidi Muhammad for Captain Hyde Parker's atrocious manners, and quietly paid out 200,000 Spanish dollars in ransoms for the hundreds of British captives now detained in Morocco. Pitt also climbed down and agreed to station a British consul there. 'We have tested him and conversed with him,' wrote the sultan subsequently of this new official:

> At his appearance in our noble presence he addressed us politely and observed the courtesies incumbent upon him . . . It will not be unknown to you that you were servants of our noble ancestors and it was your

obligation to gladden us before any other nation. But then you fell back
. . . so that we became resentful of you. Despite this we have pardoned
you for the negligence emanating from you . . . and have returned to
peace with you.[63]

Sidi Muhammad dispatched this official communication to the elderly
George II in 1760, when British legions (and large numbers of non-British
auxiliaries) were conquering Canada, driving into Bengal, and helping
themselves to Caribbean islands like so many sugar lumps. Yet Britain's
monarch and its first minister still allowed themselves to be lectured to in
these unabashed terms by the ruler of Morocco, meekly complied with
his wishes, and paid up for the captives he had seized in a unilateral show
of force.

Nor was this at all surprising in the light of the distinctive politics and
practices of the Mediterranean zone, and the nature and familiar limitations of British power here. Britain's perceptions of Islam may have been
shifting by this stage, but it still relied on North African aid to hold its
vital Mediterranean colonies, Gibraltar and Minorca. Indeed, the temporary loss to France in 1756 of Minorca, made maintaining Gibraltar
even more essential. Neither Hyde Parker's stupidity, nor Sidi
Muhammad's retaliatory captive-taking, could be allowed to disrupt this
essential arrangement, especially since the British knew full well that if
they broke with the Barbary powers, the latter might commit themselves
entirely to France, the other prime contender for Mediterranean power.
North Africa could not be invaded, and neither could it be ignored. It
had to be negotiated with, and if need be appeased. After the 1750s, as
before, the British continued to do both.

This situation continued into the nineteenth century, and not simply
because of Britain's enduring need for supplies for its white Mediterranean
empire and ever-expanding Mediterranean fleet. Edward Said and others
are entirely right to stress the importance of investigating the minds and
myths of empire-makers, and not just their weaponry and economic
muscle. None the less, material factors did matter, and were bound to
matter; and in this zone the British capacity to deploy force, as well as its
will to do so, remained circumscribed. The most dramatic proof of this
lies, paradoxically, in an act of British aggression. In 1816, the Royal Navy
bombarded the city of Algiers from the sea in an attempt to put an end
to corsairing and white slavery. Large parts of the city were devastated,
but the corsairs soon returned to work, while Britain's naval casualties in
this action – as a proportion of the men involved – were heavier than at
the Battle of Trafalgar fighting the French and the Spanish. Britons might

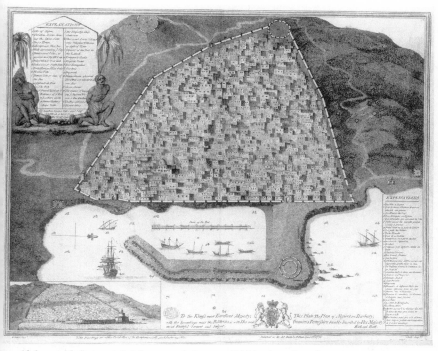

23. Algiers, with its coastal defences and slaves: a British plan of 1776.

choose (or not) to effeminise and belittle the Islamic, but – as in this case – doing so did not necessarily help them to invade or defeat it. The British government understood this very well. It pointedly refused to listen to siren voices at home and abroad urging it to convert this naval assault on Algiers into full-scale military occupation and colonisation. But the enduring constraints on the British sense of the possible in this zone are perhaps best evoked by a single remark. The Turks, wrote a Major Lowe worriedly in 1801, were 'invariably men of large stature who appeared to look down on us'.[64] In the Mediterranean, at the start of the nineteenth century, the Crescent and its powerful rays could still seem far from eclipsed to a people even now conscious of their own modest, indigenous size.

Here, in North Africa, and still more in the Ottoman heartland, were boundaries which Britain, even at its most vigorous and vainglorious, was reluctant to cross, and ill-equipped to cross, a sector of the Islamic world which – for all its physical proximity to western Europe – refused for a long time to buckle. Here, too, writ large in this Mediterranean zone, but often passing unnoticed, are persistent reminders of the compromises and

133

collusions that imperial appetite necessarily imposed on the British, a small people who could therefore be caught and caught out. There would be many other reminders of this combination of marked British aggression and inherent British vulnerability, in many other places.

For it is time to leave this sea between the lands and between competing faiths, and look instead across an ocean.

Part Two

AMERICA
Captives and Embarrassments

Different Americans, Different Britons

Looking beyond the Atlantic

The Native American crouching as if in ambush before the west front of St Paul's cathedral in London gazes stone-faced at the passers-by. Most are too intent on tourism or worship to glance in her direction, yet over the centuries the assemblage of statues of which she is a part has provoked individuals to anger and violence. In 1743, a reputed lunatic rudely divested Queen Anne of her orb and sceptre. In 1769, the sculptures were attacked again by a seaman from India, who interpreted them as an affront to his mother. Still more assaults followed, and in the 1880s the battered originals were replaced by the dim replicas existing today. Even they can arouse fury. The figure of Britannia was recently decapitated, while America has lost her bow, though her quiver of arrows remains. Behind some of these mutilations, in the more distant as in the recent past, may have been a half-conscious recognition that more is present here than just a jumble of royal and allegorical images, weighed down by fusty symbolism and the efforts of a second-rate sculptor. For this is quintessentially a monument about British power, and its extension by force and guile over other peoples.

The work of a Londoner called Francis Bird, the initial version was unveiled in readiness for a royal service of thanksgiving for the Treaty of Utrecht in 1713, the formal end of Britain's involvement in the War of Spanish Succession.[1] Imperially, there was a lot for its rulers, politicians and merchants to feel thankful for. The eleven-year-long conflict had gained them Minorca and Gibraltar in the Mediterranean, the right to ship black slaves to Spanish America, and additional territory in North America, Hudson Bay, Nova Scotia, and Newfoundland.[2] All this will have been in Bird's mind as he designed this, the first ever outdoor monument to connect Britain's monarchy explicitly with its extra-European empire. A somewhat stiff figure of Queen Anne, a deeply religious woman, whose back – as the wits commented at the time – is none the less turned uncompromisingly towards Christopher Wren's ecclesiastical masterpiece, surmounts four baroque statues each commemorating one of the

24. Francis Bird's Indian, Queen Anne statue, St Paul's Cathedral.

dominions claimed by her. There is Britannia. There is Hibernia or Ireland who is equipped with a harp. France is represented here too, since on paper it was still part of the British monarchy's inheritance. The fourth figure symbolises America. She is also what white people in Bird's era and long after commonly referred to as an Indian.

As such, she conveys ambivalence but also something more. Bird has given her the same classical features as her sister statues, but has also placed beneath one of her feet the severed head of a white male captive. Bare-breasted, such costume as she possesses is wildly inaccurate. Hers is the feathered skirt and straight-up feathered headdress once characteristic of the Tupinamba Indians of Brazil. Possessed of the notion that all Indians, whether South or North American, must somehow look the same, European artists had been portraying them in this fashion since Portugal's conquests in the New World in the sixteenth century. But it is this figure's inclusion and role in Bird's design that are striking and deserving of notice. Superficially, she is merely subordinate, trapped underfoot by a victorious British monarch. Yet she is also indispensable, for without her sculptural support, the figure of Anne could not remain standing in its elevated position.

25. The severed head of a captive: detail from Francis Bird's Indian.

And while Bird's vision of a Native American was distorted by ignorance and prejudice, in one sense at least he got it absolutely right. From the beginnings of settlement through to the Revolution of 1776 and beyond, the people called Indians were integral to how men and women in early modern Britain perceived that part of their empire that was America.

This essential fact has not always been evident from the history books. Until recently, most writers on Britain's empire in North America – particularly on the British side of the Atlantic – tended to leave out indigenous peoples altogether. Even now, the latter are often ghettoised.[3] They may be allocated a token chapter or two, but they can still appear marginal to the famous and familiar saga of how English, and ultimately Welsh, Scottish and Irish emigrants established themselves successfully on the eastern coastline of North America from the early 1600s onwards; and of how these incoming peoples continued for one and three-quarter centuries to share a monarch, language, secular culture, political ideologies, Protestantism, and abundant trade with their counterparts back in Britain, only for the majority of them to go their separate ways after 1775 in a revolution which also partook to some degree of a civil war. Yet different groups of Native Americans were tightly enmeshed within, and crucial to, the evolution of this story throughout, and so were different kinds of captivity.

This latter point, too, is usually missing from the history books. There has been a long tradition in the United States of scholarly and popular interest in the capture of whites over the centuries by Native Americans (though only recently a recognition of the degree to which whites in colonial America and the young Republic also captured and enslaved Indians), and this has been immeasurably deepened by the emergence of a more anthropologically, archaeologically and politically sensitive New Indian History.[4] But even this new work has tended to remain determinedly inward-looking. Indian captivities are still overwhelmingly scanned for the light they can throw on the evolution of *American* national identities and cultures, while the narratives produced by one-time captive whites are still normally approached as a uniquely American mode of writing.

It should now be clear that they were not. The 400,000 or so men and women from Scotland, Ireland, Wales and above all England who crossed the Atlantic in the course of the seventeenth century, almost certainly took with them – along with so much else – a knowledge of the kinds of stories related by and about those of their countrymen who were captured by the powers of Barbary and Islam. These stories of capture by the forces of the Crescent were then adapted to a new American environment and to very different dangers. The very first account of an Englishman held captive by Native Americans to become a publishing success in London, John Smith's famous description of his seizure in Virginia by the forces of Powhatan, and of his subsequent 'rescue' by Powhatan's daughter Pocahontas, was indeed the work of a man previously captured while fighting against Ottoman armies and sold as a slave in Constantinople.[5] As this suggests, Indian captivities in early modern America, and the stories they gave rise to, need examining through more than just a parochial and national lens. Above all, they need situating in a transatlantic and in an imperial context.

Throughout the seventeenth century, and for most of the eighteenth century, white captive bodies in North America were, among many other things, emblems of Britain's imperial ordeal as well as symptoms of the limits of its imperial reach, its besetting, anxiety-making smallness. In the American colonies, as in other zones of Britain's imperial enterprise, the bodies of its people held captive and in terror focused attention on and prompted discussion about much broader constraints, embarrassments and fears. This was the case despite the fact that the initial captors involved in this zone of imperial enterprise – Native Americans – were in some respects peoples in retreat, rolled back and diminished by the spread of British empire, even as they seemed to threaten it.

Taking captive

To begin with, relations between English incomers in mainland North America and its indigenous peoples were complex, mutually uncomprehending, but by no means automatically hostile.[6] The earliest settlers in Virginia and New England were necessarily highly dependent on local Indians for food and for advice on how to grow it, for trade, and for guidance on survival techniques in a new land. They were also initially small in number by comparison with their Indian neighbours. The famous story (at least in the United States) of Tomocomo, Pocahontas's brother-in-law, accompanying her to England in 1616, and bringing with him a 'long stick, whereon by notches he did think to have kept the number of all the men he could see', may be more than just a condescending fiction. As Tomocomo would have known, whites in Virginia at this time were still painfully thin on the ground. There would have been no way for people like him to foresee that the original homeland of these sparse, disruptive and hairy intruders would be any more populous, nor could English settlers themselves have foreseen at this stage that their numbers would burgeon at the rapid rate that they later did. Even in 1630, there were probably fewer than 10,000 English men and women scattered along the eastern shores of North America.[7]

Since they themselves were initially so small in number, and Native Americans had to be taken seriously, the English reacted to them as they nearly always did to overseas peoples. They did not simply 'other' them, but rather looked for and invented points of similarity and contact. They scanned Native American faces and bodies, and saw them – not as red or even tawny at this stage – but as almost as pale-skinned as themselves. They took note of the rituals and ornate possessions surrounding sachems or chiefs, and concluded that these individuals must be 'kings' or 'queens' or aristocratic hunter-warriors. That such wilderness patricians were surrounded by multitudes of lesser, unruly folk seemed only to mirror still further the scheme of things that the English were used to back home. 'You may save your labour if you please', wrote the poet Michael Drayton from London to a friend in Virginia in 1622:

> To write me ought of your savages,
> As savage slaves be in Great Britain here,
> As any one that you can shew me there.[8]

Because Indians were deemed rudely similar, and Indian chiefs incontestably more important than England's own impoverished multitudes, this emphatically did not mean that Indian modes of society and culture were viewed as being – in their current state – of equal worth. The perception of them as heathens, as stateless, and as nomadic precluded that. 'Bestow small crowns or coronets', the King of England, Charles II, was advised in 1677 in relation to some Indian 'kings' who needed wooing: '. . . to be made of thin silver plate, gilt, and adorned with false stones'.[9] The calibration of human significance in terms of glitter is precise. Indians, even their leaders, were not, in this view, people deserving of gold, silver and precious jewels. They could properly be fobbed off with plate, gilt and paste. Yet, for all that, these individuals were still to be crowned: still to be brought at some level within the English and European system of doing things. For their own self-interested reasons, but also sometimes for other reasons, this would always be the strategy favoured by governments in London and by the generality of royal officials in North America. As far as the men and women from Britain who settled here were concerned, however, an initial desire to improve and in some measure to incorporate the Indian easily came to be at odds with other imperatives, and was increasingly overborne by them. The urge to redeem and bring civility to the Indian retreated – albeit unevenly and at different rates in different regions of America – before the settlers' swiftly growing numbers and appetite for land. It faded too before the convenient discovery that Indians were people who could be surprisingly easy to kill.

Historians sometimes claim that, as relations began to sour, English settlers employed unusually lethal styles of warfare against Native Americans because they viewed them as inferior.[10] In fact, the intensity of these struggles proved deadly – and initially impossible for Indians to comprehend – precisely because the English made use of the same brutal strategies in North America as they and other Europeans routinely deployed against each other in their home continent. Thus Captain John Underhill's infamous massacre of Pequot men, women and children near the Mystic River, Connecticut, in 1637 has often been cited as exemplifying the settlers' peculiar bloodthirstiness in the face of Indian opponents. But this act of slaughter needs setting against the contemporaneous Thirty Years War in Europe, which annihilated perhaps a third of the population of the German states, including vast numbers of non-combatants. By the same token, what became a widespread practice of seizing defeated Indians, and selling them as slaves to the West Indies, represented an extension to North America of a penalty often employed against rebels within England itself. Oliver Cromwell enslaved hundreds of defeated Scots in the 1650s, dispatching them, too, to the West Indies. Those English West Country supporters of Monmouth's rebellion in 1685 who were not summarily executed experienced a similar fate. What was distinctive about English settler assaults on Native Americans as time went on was less the degree of violence employed, than the fact that it was not confined – as usually in Europe – to discrete periods of open, declared warfare or rebellion. There was another, far more conclusive characteristic of cross-cultural warfare here. English and other European emigrants to North America had unknowingly brought with them invincible storm troops, their own teeming microbes.

The full extent of the destruction these caused will never be known with any precision. There is no consensus even about the scale of North America's pre-contact indigenous population. Estimates range between two and eighteen million.[11] It is clear too that in some regions, the invisible immigrants of smallpox, diphtheria, influenza, cholera, measles and the like, against which Indians possessed no immunity, had only a blunted or very belated effect. In others, however, Indian communities exposed to these diseases – as well as to white settler violence – experienced mortality rates as high as 70, even 90 per cent. Nine out of every ten New England Indians seem to have died from the effects of European diseases in just the dozen years between 1608 and 1620; the 10,000 Indians still alive in *each* of the Carolinas in 1685 had been pared down to only 8000 in total by 1715.[12] English, Scottish, Welsh and Irish incomers quickly came to recognise, although they did not comprehend why, that death and disease haunted Indian settlements, while ever more impressive rates of fecundity, far higher than in the islands they had left behind them, came to grace their own.

The quality of the challenge posed to incoming whites by indigenous peoples in America – and consequently the quality of captivity panics here – was therefore very different from that in the other geographical zones explored in this book. In the Mediterranean region, and in South Asia, early modern Britons confronted societies that were partly urbanised like their own, and frequently far more populous and demographically buoyant. In these areas, large-scale English and British settlement either proved impossible (as at Tangier), or was never viewed as a feasible option in the first place (as in India). Accordingly, in the Mediterranean and Asia, the British intruded mainly as traders, soldiers, sailors, administrators and the like, but their overall numbers remained limited, often perilously so. In North America (as in Britain's Pacific colonies much later), it was altogether different. On the one hand, the English came here from the start with the definite intention of settling, and high birth-rates as well as migration subsequently boosted their numbers to more than 260,000 by 1700, and over a million by 1750. On the other hand, North America's own first peoples proved an ever more diminishing asset. None of this prevented various Indian groupings from launching attacks on the English, or from taking them captive, however, for it was often precisely these acute pressures on their numbers and increasing white incursions into their lands that impelled them to action.

Native Americans could not stem the flood of white incomers who multiplied at such a staggering rate, but they did strike back as well as try to secure some advantage from them. The potential for Indian anger to express itself in large-scale violence appeared early. In 1622, local Indians almost succeeded in wiping out the white settlement in Virginia. The conflict known as King Philip's or Metacom's war in southern New England (1675–6) eventually resulted in the destruction of effective Algonquian resistance to white expansion here, but in the process, about 10 per cent of the white colonists involved were killed, and an estimated 12,000 buildings and 8000 cattle were destroyed. In terms of mortality rates as a proportion of population, this was the most lethal war in American history.[13] The Yamasee War in South Carolina in 1715 was at times almost as intense. It forced a sixth of the colony's white males to take up arms, and killed about 7 per cent of the province's 6000 European inhabitants. In addition to these fierce, set-piece conflicts, there was also a perennial, even a daily risk of skirmish, ambush and slaughter for whites, and of course for Indians, in more exposed settlements. 'Every week, some or other is taken captive or killed,' complained the Lieutenant Governor of New Hampshire to London in 1724: 'so that your Lordships may judge how we are wasting.'[14]

To Britons on both sides of the Atlantic, but particularly to those directly affected, the forms of Indian violence easily seemed anarchic and mindlessly cruel, the mark of the savage. Cruel it was, as war always is: but it was less mindless than a message written in blood and flame and destruction of the nature of Indian grievances. When Indians slaughtered and maimed the white man's cattle, horses and pigs, they were also attacking his animal husbandry practices which consumed so much land, and stole pasturage from the wild animals they depended on for food.[15] When they stripped white captives naked and forced them to cover their genitals with pages ripped out of the Bible, they were making clear their opinion of Christianity, and of the white clergymen who sought to impose it on Indian bodies and souls. And when they raided colonial settlements, and systematically killed babies and infant children, as they sometimes did, this was perhaps a conscious strike at these invaders' capacity to reproduce themselves so abundantly, and in revenge for their own lost children.[16] In the same way, Indian captive-taking was rarely a random business, though it was never as overwhelmingly money-oriented as Barbary corsairing gradually came to be.

Indians did sometimes make use of British and other captives to extort ransoms. They also sold them on occasions for cash or kind to representatives of rival empires in America, to the French or Spanish.[17] But white captives might also be employed as slaves. Or they might – particularly if they were adult males taken in combat – be tortured to death, sometimes over many days, in order to appease the spirits of their captors' own dead or their grieving womenfolk. This was the fate of Thomas Nairne, a British Indian agent in Carolina. A man who had lived with the Chickasaws for several years and admired them, he was captured on the first day of the Yamasee war in 1715 and burnt at the stake, very slowly.[18] By contrast, some captives, particularly women and the healthy and malleable young, were adopted by and absorbed into Indian communities as a way of compensating for the losses they had sustained from disease and war. An awareness that white children could become targets for adoption in this way lies behind the most anguished passages in Jonathan Dickenson's *God's Protecting Providence, Man's Surest Help and Defence* (1700), one of the very few American captivity narratives to be a runaway publishing success in Britain before 1750.

Dickenson, his wife Mary, and their six-month-old baby son, were shipwrecked off the coast of Florida in 1696 while on a voyage from Jamaica to Pennsylvania. Together with the rest of the survivors, they were seized by a party of local Indians, and to the Dickensons' initial horror one of the women (whom they decided must be a chief's wife) insisted on holding and suckling their child, and 'viewing and feeling it from top to toe'. This happened first on 25 September. By the time another week had passed, the Dickensons had shifted to feeling profound relief whenever this same woman took an identical interest in their child, because:

> Its mother's milk was almost gone . . . And our child, which had been at death's door, from the time of its birth, until we were cast away, began now to be cheerful and have an appetite to food.

After another week had passed, the couple were actually 'begging' the woman (whose name we never learn) to feed their baby. By now, they themselves were having to subsist on the 'gills and guts of fish . . . and the water they [the Indians] boiled their fish in', and Mrs Dickenson was too malnourished, and too fatigued and frightened with the effort of keeping up with her captors, to be able to produce any milk of her own.[19]

Yet, in the days immediately before they were rescued by some Spanish soldiers based at St Augustine, the Dickensons' attitude to this woman who was bestowing such charity on them shifted once again. They continued to draw comfort from the restored health of their child, chubby and contented now on its borrowed milk, but only up to a point:

> One thing did seem more grievous to me and my wife, than any other thing; which was, that if it should so happen, that we should be put to death, we feared that our child would be kept alive, and bred up as one of those people: when these thoughts did arise, it wounded us deep.

What if the woman who so eagerly suckled their child were to become in time and in name its mother, and the child itself were to be reborn, as it were, as an Indian: no longer a Christian, no longer English, and no longer theirs? As this private captivity crisis suggests, whites who were seized in North America had to confront the possibility – to a greater degree than in the other zones of empire examined in this book – that they or their children might be coerced or coaxed into becoming something else.

To be sure, Indians sometimes made a point of selling Anglophone captives to those other Europeans who were contending for America, to the French authorities in Canada, or the Spanish in Florida, New Mexico, and Pensacola: but to ardent Protestants this fate could seem just as alarming as enforced or self-willed residence among Indians. Having been purchased from their captors, and brought to St Augustine late in 1696, the Dickensons encountered there a man called William Carr, a native of Ely in East Anglia. He had been shipwrecked in Florida *en route* to South Carolina back in the 1660s, lived as a captive among the local Indians for some years, and was then sold to the Spanish. Carr himself appeared contented enough with his situation. He had long since converted to Catholicism, married a Spanish woman, produced seven children, and was now gainfully employed as an interpreter, making full use of the many languages his disparate life had allowed him to acquire. But the Dickensons still shuddered whenever they saw him. What of Carr's English, Protestant soul? What of that?[20]

Ascertaining precisely how many English, Welsh, Scottish and Irish settlers, soldiers, and officials were made captives by Indians in North America during the colonial period is no easier than calculating the exact total of British captives of Barbary. But, once again, the numbers were substantial, and they remained so throughout. We know something of what happened, for instance, to over 1600 New Englanders who were seized by Indians and taken to New France between the mid-seventeenth century and 1763.[21] Fewer than half of these people seem to have returned home. Almost one in ten of the males involved, and close to a third of the females, opted or were compelled to stay with their Indian captors, or more commonly with the French. Of those aged between seven and fifteen when captured, almost 50 per cent remained in their new surroundings. In many cases however, the ultimate fate of captives, and even their existence, went unreported, especially if they were taken from isolated farmsteads, or while travelling alone, or if they disappeared in the course of battle. Only by surveying a mixture of newspaper reports, archives, and captivity narratives has one historian been able to calculate that some 2700 whites were seized in Indian raids on the frontiers of Pennsylvania, Maryland and Virginia alone between 1755 and 1765.[22] This kind of heroic body-count has not been attempted for all of Britain's American colonies, and would not anyway be possible for much of the colonial period.

There is a sense also in which it scarcely matters, because those who had to contend with these captivity panics had no accurate grasp of the total numbers that were involved either. What mattered to them, as so often with such panics, was a dimensionless fear. 'Think upon the miserable captives now in the hands of that brutish adversary,' thundered Boston's most prominent clergyman, Cotton Mather, in 1691:

> *Captives* that are every minute looking when they shall be roasted alive, to make a sport and a feast, for the most execrable cannibals; *Captives*, that must endure the most bitter frost and cold, without rags enough to cover their nakedness; *Captives*, that have scarce a bit of meat allow'd them to put into their mouths, but what a dog would hardly meddle with; *Captives*, that must see their nearest relations butchered before their eyes, and yet be afraid of letting those eyes drop a tear.

Or as one female victim of sudden Indian attack and subsequent captivity put it, less rhetorically but more movingly: 'I can remember the time, when I used to sleep quietly . . . but now it is other ways.'[23] Here was yet another aspect of the imperial ordeal.

Except that, in a crucial respect, these captivities in North America challenged the British in a unique and distinctive way. Here – as in other zones of imperial invasion and enterprise – captives taken from their ranks acted as catalysts of wider anxieties. But white captivities in North America also functioned over the years as a sword dividing the different varieties of British.

Before 1776, the majority of white inhabitants of what became Britain's Thirteen Colonies in America did not view themselves exclusively or even primarily as Americans. In their own minds, they were English, and ultimately Britons, free subjects of the monarch in London, albeit subjects on another shore. As Cotton Mather insisted, New England was also 'a part of the English nation'.[24] Consequently, when men and women from amongst them were seized by Native Americans, American colonists viewed these emergencies in more than just local terms. To them, Indian captivity also seemed an affront to their identity as Englishmen and, in due course, as Britons. But, on the other side of the Atlantic, in Britain itself, it could be otherwise. Many of *its* inhabitants came – for a variety of reasons – to perceive Native Americans, and the dangers posed by them, differently from the colonists and to differing degrees.

Early American captivity narratives usually make abundantly clear their writers' sense of being part of a wider imperial whole. Consider the most famous of them, *The Sovereignty and Goodness of God . . . being a Narrative of the Captivity and Restoration of Mrs. Mary Rowlandson*, published both in Cambridge, Massachusetts, and in London in 1682, but probably written before 1678.[25] Rowlandson was taken captive in the early morning of 10 February 1676, in the course of Metacom's War. Three of her children were also seized, as were nineteen other inhabitants of the small town of Lancaster in Massachusetts. Because of the absurd convention whereby writings by men and women who left Britain for imperial locations drop out of the canon of 'English' literature, Rowlandson's account of her subsequent experiences living as a captive for three months among different groups of New England Indians, Nipmucs, Narragansetts and Wampanoags, remains little known within Britain. Yet, at one level, this is a narrative that is fixated on the bonds of Englishness. Rowlandson had been born in Somerset in the early 1630s, and her family, who were farmers, took part in the 'Great Migration' of English settlers to New England that decade. So did the family of the man who ultimately became her husband, Joseph Rowlandson, who was Puritan minister of Lancaster. For Mary

Rowlandson, though, 'England' was far more than just a shadowy, infant memory, a name for a now distant land. As she tells us repeatedly in her narrative, England, together with her Protestant God, were the totems to which she clung fast throughout her ordeal.

On the first night of her captive journey, weary with scrambling along with 'one poor wounded babe' in her arms (the child would shortly perish), she begged to be allowed to sleep in a farm that had been deserted in terror by its former English occupants. 'What', she claims her Native American captors replied, 'will you love English men still?', for their aim was to wean her from such attachments and make her one of them. All she could do in the days that followed was look for signposts to who she was in the landscape she was gradually being forced to abandon. She saw a place where 'English cattle' had been, and this was a 'comfort to me, such as it was'. When she came across an 'English path' – for settlers like her marked and organised the land in distinctive ways – she yearned to lie down and die there, almost as if she were another Eve reluctant to be driven out of Eden. And when a company of thirty horsemen suddenly appeared on the horizon, and rode towards the line of bedraggled prisoners 'in English apparel, with hats, white neckcloths, and sashes about their waists', her heart skipped with relief and delight, only to sink again. They turned out to be yet more New England Indians, got up in purchased or pillaged items of English Puritan costume.[26] It was the first of many lessons on the possible unreliability of markers of identity.

The ways in which references to England – and ultimately to Britain – served early American colonists as anchors amidst the shipwrecks of Indian captivity emerge from many other narratives. The printed account of John Gyles, who had been seized when he was just nine years old by Maliseet warriors in what is now Maine in 1689, begins with an almost elegiac reminder of his settlement's roots: 'Our people went to their labour, some in one field to their English hay, the others to another field of English corn.' He goes on to describe how his mother, who was also captured, murmured to him in what was almost their last meeting:

O, my child! How joyful and pleasant it would be, if we were going to Old England, to see your uncle Chalker, and other friends there.[27]

Forced, as were most individuals taken captive in North America, not into a confined space, but to undertake a long journey on foot across rough country, this woman's reaction was at once to comfort and torture herself. She travelled in her imagination, not through forest and undergrowth, but across the wide ocean itself to what once had been. In reality, there would be no such journey of return. Instead, what lay before mother and son was the tramp to French Canada, final separation and, for John Gyles himself, a six-year captivity with different Indian groups, and a further three years' service with a French master.

The extreme pathos of many of these early American captivity narratives was partly calculated. Describing in detail touching last interviews, the death agonies of captured infants, storms of women's grief, and the torments of memory, helped to lend colour and attract readers, especially in early colonial America where home-produced fiction and drama were still rare. The pathos of these captivity narratives also worked to sharpen the line between Anglo settlers and Native Americans, as Mary Rowlandson at least seems to have understood and wanted. But this marked sentiment was also a function of a distinctive facet of these North American captivities. As far as the British were concerned, Barbary captivity was a fate usually befalling working individuals and men. To a lesser degree, the same would also be true of pre-1850 British captivities in South Asia. But the various North American provinces were not places of work and warfare merely: they were settlement colonies. So captivity here regularly engulfed whole families, all age-groups, and large numbers of women as well as men. This influenced both the content and the style of the narratives that emerged from them. Mary Rowlandson's was not the first captivity narrative to be a publishing success in the Anglophone world, nor even the first Anglo account of Indian captivity. But it was the first narrative by a settler to become an American bestseller. As such, it influenced how later writers in North America, both female and male, expected to tell their captive stories. American-produced captivity narratives are arguably more feminised, and certainly more domestic and personal, than the generality of their North African and Asian counterparts.[28]

But the frequent, haunting allusions in these early American texts to things English or British were informed by more than private sentiment. For early settlers, as Jill Lepore argues, the idea of the 3000 miles now separating them from England was both liberating and worrying.[29] How, they wondered, were they to preserve their Englishness now that their original homeland was so distant, and other, very different and increasingly despised peoples were so perilously near? How were they to guard against the wilderness changing and corrupting what they were in essence? The experience and even the idea of captivity brought such insecurities quickly to the surface, because – as we have seen – it could lead to assimilation into Native American societies, or into rival, Catholic empires. 'I dreaded going to Canada, to the French, for fear lest I should be overcome by them, to yield to their religion,' wrote Hannah Swarton. She was captured by Abenaki Indians at Casco Bay, Maine, in May 1690, and held for over five years before being redeemed. Her husband, a native of Jersey and an English army veteran, was killed, as was her eldest son; two more of her children were never recovered from the Indians. It was in this context that insisting on her Englishness in her printed narrative appeared crucial. It testified to any doubters, and also to herself, that she had success-fully preserved her national and religious identity. 'Came in two men', she recalled of one of her captive days in Canada, 'and one of them spake to me in English: I am glad to see you Countrywoman! This was exceed-ingly reviving, to hear the voice of an English man,' and so it was.[30]

Early American captivity narrators, then, dwelt on transatlantic ties. Out of loyalty, but also so as to reassure themselves and others, they insisted on their enduring Englishness, and all that this implied, and ultimately on their Britishness. So how were these particular captives' voices heard and reacted to within Britain itself? The answer, before 1750, is only intermittently.

This point can be easily made by looking at the publication histories of the narratives themselves. The first American edition of Mary Rowlandson's story sold out so quickly, and individual copies were passed around between so many people, that today no complete version survives, only a few stained and dog-eared pages. American-based printers brought out two more editions of the text in 1682, and yet another in 1720. But on the other side of the Atlantic the market was far less avid. The 1682 London edition of Rowlandson's tale appears to have been the only one published in Britain before 1900.

A similar pattern emerges in regard to other American captivity narra-tives. Some, such as John Gyles's belated publication of his experiences, which was published in Boston in 1736, were never issued in Britain at all. Others, such as the story of Elizabeth Hanson, who was captured in 1724 and held for five months, were published soon after the event in America, but had to wait until the second half of the century for a British edition, in this case until 1760. Such American captivity stories as did appear in London, or in provincial English, Scottish or Irish editions before 1750 were rarely commercial successes. In Boston in 1706, Cotton Mather published a highly influential omnibus of captive stories emerging from the colonists' involvement in what they called Queen Anne's War: *Good Fetched out of Evil: A Collection of Memorables relating to our Captives*. It sold 1000 copies in a week, this in a city of some 15,000 people. Again, its circulation was much wider than the sum of its purchasers. Individual copies of the work passed from hand to hand to such an extent that only four now survive. Yet this American bestseller seems never to have been issued in Britain at all.[31] Britons in the home country did have an opportunity to consult another of the prolific

Mather's collections of captivity stories, *Magnalia Christi Americana*, published in London in seven parts in 1702. But, as its format and latinate title suggest, this was an expensive book, take-up was slender, and no new edition ever proved necessary.[32]

In the early modern world, even more than now, publishers were not driven primarily by charity or idealism. Unless writers or subscribers could summon up sufficient resources to fund publication themselves, books were printed only if it was anticipated that they would sell. Manifestly, then, before 1750, printers and publishers in Britain reached the commercial decision that there was only limited domestic demand for tales of settler captivity at the hands of Native Americans, even though Britons in America and Britons at home were ostensibly one, united imperial people.

Why was this, and what does it tell us about the British empire in America at this stage?

Divisions

British domestic interest in and awareness of American captivity panics in the seventeenth and early eighteenth centuries were not limited because the colonial authorities themselves were unconcerned. As the superabundant archives of the Council (later the Board) of Trade and Plantations make clear, London regularly received information from officials and informants about the fate of North American captives, though such news only travelled as fast as a sailing ship could cross the Atlantic. Take the case of the famous attack on Deerfield. This settlement, which was situated on the furthest reaches of Massachusetts' north-western frontier, a short distance from the Connecticut River, had already been hit by Indians half a dozen times in the 1690s alone. But, on 29 February 1704, Abenaki warriors and their allies swept in again and killed forty-eight of Deerfield's 300 inhabitants, and captured 112 men, women and children. The news naturally took several months to reach London, and was not formally announced to Parliament until November. Ministers immediately authorised the dispatch of more firearms so that settlers and 'friendly Indians' in Massachusetts would be better able to defend themselves. When the Treaty of Utrecht was negotiated with France in 1712–13, British diplomats took care to include clauses demanding the return of all American colonists held captive in Canada, including any Deerfield victims still detained there. As late as 1721, British envoys in Paris were still putting pressure on French officials to organise the redemption of those few Deerfield captives who remained with Indian communities in Canada.[33]

In other words, politicians in London did all it was possible to do *indirectly and at an ocean's distance.* They read and digested the reports of the Deerfield 'massacre' dispatched by colonial officials and tormented eye-witnesses ('I shall give you an account of two young men who suffered the cruellest death that ever was thought of').[34] They shipped extra weapons over to America for the settlers to use. Their diplomats did what they could to put pressure on other European capitals to effect captive releases. But British-based politicians had neither the power nor the will at this stage to do much more. Nor was the bulk of their home population in a position to learn much about Deerfield, or the warfare in North America of which it formed only one incident. The major captivity narrative emerging from this disaster was a classic of its kind, *The Redeemed Captive Returning to Zion* written by John Williams, Minister of Deerfield. He lost his wife and two children in the 1704 attack and its aftermath, and subsequently had to wrestle with the grief and embarrassment of having another of his daughters, Eunice, both marry an Indian and turn Roman Catholic. Williams's 25,000-word story was published in Boston in 1707, and reprinted in America half a dozen times over the course of the century. It seems never to have been issued in Britain.

Some of the reasons for this limited British awareness of – and hence limited emotional involvement in – captivity panics in North America are clear enough. As John Elliott famously demonstrated, although the Spanish, Portuguese, French and English invasions of the Americas in the sixteenth and seventeenth centuries are in retrospect seminal episodes in global history, at the time many ordinary Europeans back home remained largely indifferent to these events. Even by the early eighteenth century, when Britain had evolved one of the most vibrant print cultures in the world, readers within its boundaries still found it easier and more to their taste to acquire books and in-depth newspaper reportage about domestic matters and about other European states, than copious, well-informed printed material about the colonies across the Atlantic.[35] Specific crises in North America could, to be sure, fire up British interest for a while. King Philip's War, for instance, led to the publication of at least fourteen narratives in London between 1675 and 1682, all of which had something to say about captivities; while the official broadsheet, the *London Gazette*, also printed several articles about the New England colonists' real and reputed sufferings. But, for most of the time, London's newspaper and book press devoted little sustained coverage to settler experiences in America, as distinct from details of transatlantic trade; while provincial publishers rarely tackled the subject before the 1740s.[36]

Uneven British coverage of American captivities prior to 1750 also reflected the fact that the mechanisms for responding to them differed significantly from those set up to cope with Barbary captive-taking. In the latter case, redemption money was raised time and time again by way of nationwide collections supervised by the churches, and this had the effect of informing English, Welsh, Scottish and Irish church-goers, whether they were literate or no, of the details of these captives' plight. Moreover, such collections occurred on both sides of the Atlantic. American colonial sailors and traders operating in the Mediterranean and Atlantic were regularly among the corsairs' victims. Cotton Mather, who built much of his ruthlessly successful clerical and publishing career on the backs of multifarious captives, devoted at least two sermons to the threat that Barbary and Islam represented to seamen in England and New England both.[37] Barbary captivity, in other words, was perceived and treated as an ordeal that Britons on both sides of the Atlantic had in common.

Indian captive-taking in North America was very different. Obviously, it never directly endangered men and women on the other side of the Atlantic. Nor did Indians always look to ransom their captives. When they did, the necessary cash seems generally to have been raised by the colonists themselves. The £20 needed to ransom Mary Rowlandson, for instance, came from a group of prosperous and devout Bostonians. There must have been some occasions when English, Welsh, Scottish and Irish individuals with kin in the colonies (and also Britain's dissenting churches), dispatched gifts in money and kind across the Atlantic to aid particular captives and their families. But no officially sponsored nationwide collection was ever organised in Britain or Ireland on behalf of settler victims of Native American captive-taking. Religious allegiances may have contributed to this failure. It was the Anglican Church that played the dominant role in synchronising relief for the Barbary captives, but most British settlers and captives in North America were not Anglicans, but Protestant dissenters. It seems very possible that one explanation for the limited take-up of early American captivity narratives within Britain itself was that – to mainstream Anglicans – the Puritan religiosity informing so many of these texts appeared alien and even uncongenial.[38]

Back in the early seventeenth century, an obscure Anglican clergymen had laboured to explain to his English provincial congregation why it was their duty to devote thought and charity to the victims of Barbary, confined and suffering so far from home. 'As for poor prisoners and captives', he told them:

> they (good souls) cannot come to us . . . Therefore it is our duty to visit them, either in person, if we may have access, or by provision, if we can send to them, or by prayers and supplications . . . *Make their bondage*

your thraldom, their suffering, your own smarting. Have a fellow-feeling with them, as being members of the same body.[39]

White settlers in British North America, and the inhabitants of the small islands three thousand miles away on the other side of the Atlantic, were by law and history members of the same imperial body, but before the mid-eighteenth century the captivities of the former did not – remotely as much as might have been expected – nurture fellow-feeling among the latter. This was not so much because men and women in Britain did not care, as because many of them never got to know, and could not properly understand.

Yet there was more behind the markedly different responses to Indian captivities on the two sides of the Atlantic than all this. There was also the matter of limited British imperial power, and – as always – limited British numbers.

From the very beginning, the role of the state in England's North American empire had been slender and enabling rather than interventionist. From Elizabeth I onwards, successive monarchs had authorised private investors to take the risk of establishing colonial outposts in America, and individual proprietors to claim title (on dubious legal grounds) to vast tracts of land there, and for a long time this was all. In some contrast to the Spanish monarchy's hands-on colonial policy in South America, England's rulers, in David Armitage's words, led 'from behind and allowed private enterprise to bear the burdens of conquest and settlement'.[40] One aspect of this cheap and indirect version of empire, was that London displayed only erratic enthusiasm for substantial military investment in its transatlantic colonies. The immediate consequences of this are writ large in early American captivity narratives. Contained within them are implicit (and sometimes explicit) criticisms of the imperial authorities' failure to defend settlers adequately against the threat of Indian and other attacks. Thus the preface to Mary Rowlandson's narrative attributes the Indians descending with such 'mighty force and fury upon Lancaster' to its 'not being garrisoned as it might'; while John Gyles reported that the Pemaquid settlement, in modern Maine, from which he was snatched in 1689, was defended only by an obsolete fort with just three cannon at its disposal and outworks barely nine foot high.[41] More dispassionate observers could be equally damning. When Colonel William Romer, the Crown's chief military engineer, toured New Jersey at the start of the eighteenth century, he found it 'without any forts, or places of defence'; such fortifications as existed in Pennsylvania and North and South Carolina appeared to his trained eyes scarcely more impressive.[42]

But Romer's survey of American defences signalled an important,

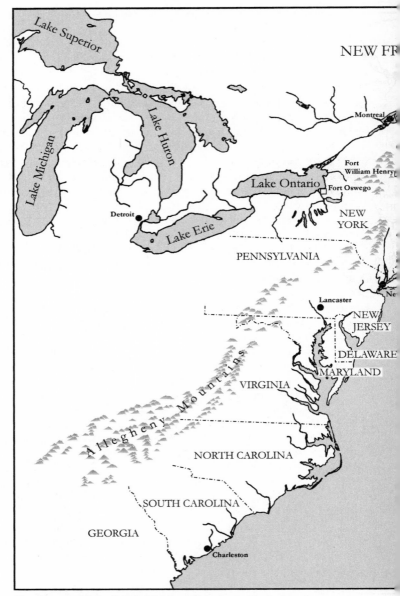

New France and the British Mainland Colonies in North America.

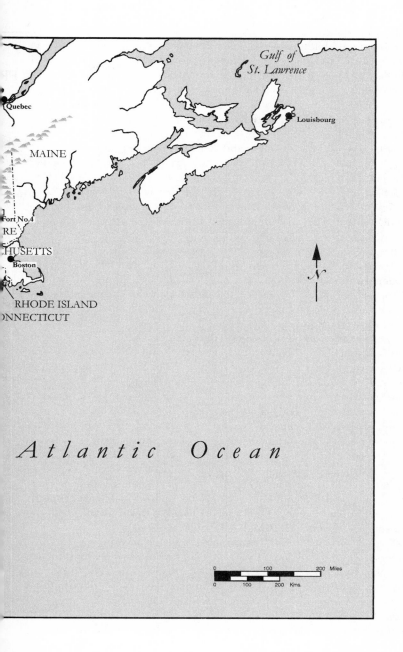

Gulf of
St. Lawrence

Quebec

Louisbourg

MAINE

Fort No.4

RE

HUSETTS

Boston

RHODE ISLAND

ONNECTICUT

N

Atlantic   Ocean

| 0 | | 100 | | 200 Miles |
| 0 | 100 | 200 | Kms. | |

157

though partial, shift in imperial policy. England's 'Glorious' Revolution of 1688 replaced a Catholic king, James II, with the Protestant William III and his wife Mary; it also inaugurated a series of Anglo-French wars which increasingly exploded beyond Europe's own battlefields into these rival powers' extra-European colonies. As far as Anglo settlers in North America were concerned, the so-called King William's War (1689–97), would be followed by Queen Anne's War (1702–13), King George I's War (1722–4), King George II's War (1740–48); and then by two more conflicts, that were fought out between 1756 and 1763, and 1775 to 1783, on an altogether different and larger scale. These serial contests between Britain and France and their respective allies progressively transformed the quality and seriousness of warfare in North America – and also intensified the threat of captivity there. They also transformed British official attentiveness to its American colonies, but in one conspicuous respect only slowly.

Beyond doubt, there was growing acceptance that, as the Commissioners of Trade and Plantations reported to William III in 1701: 'His Majesty has a dominion [in America] of a very large extent, which, at present, requires a more special care.'[43] In practice, this meant more fact-finding missions of the sort carried out by Colonel Romer, more subsidies and arms exports to colonial governors to help them defend themselves against the French and their Indian allies, and very occasional direct interventions in North America by British state forces. Thus in 1711, over fifty Royal Navy ships and 8000 men joined varieties of American colonial troops in an invasion attempt against French Canada, an expensive venture that failed dismally. Indicatively, however, even this rare initiative was based on Britain's sea-power, not on its land forces. Before 1750, there was no attempt to maintain large numbers of British troops in the American colonies to take the offensive – or to defend them from attack. The distribution of British army units over the years underlines the point. In 1726, a year of peace on both sides of the Atlantic, only one battalion of British foot soldiers was stationed in North America, as against seven in Minorca and Gibraltar. By 1742, when war with France was threatening both Britain and its colonists, the number of Crown battalions stationed in North America had risen to two, but this contrasted with the ten battalions guarding Britain's Mediterranean colonies.[44]

Behind this persistently constrained military investment in North America was the traditional British Achilles heel: a worrying insufficiency of manpower. Britain's army was just too small at this stage to play an effective global role. Thus in 1715, Carolina, then in the throes of the Yamassee War, petitioned Parliament for aid. The colony had only 'two thousand able men, and [was] in great want of arms', and believed itself confronted by an Indian confederation of 12,000 men, who were receiving assistance from both the French and the Spanish. London promptly dispatched arms and ammunition to the colonists, but not troops. Britain's army had been substantially demobilised after the Treaty of Utrecht in 1713, and what remained of it was now facing a Jacobite rising in the home islands. There were simply no British troops to spare for overseas ventures.[45] And there was another twist to the perennial problem of insufficient imperial cannon fodder. Rising Anglo-French antagonism after 1689 created for Britain a conflict of interest which for a long time it proved unable to resolve. On the one hand, its colonists in America and elsewhere were now threatened by French power and demanded more aid. On the other, Britain itself was now being repeatedly challenged by superior French legions *inside* Europe, and was often at acute risk of invasion. As a result, its already stretched land forces rarely had any slack to spare for military adventures in other continents.

Before 1750, British governments had little choice but to accept that, in any conflict between national and imperial imperatives, the former had to come first. They could not afford to denude themselves of large numbers of men for the sake of imperial commitments lest they themselves be invaded by the French and their Spanish allies. This was why, quite apart from the zone's intrinsic commercial and strategic importance, so many British army battalions were stationed in the Mediterranean at this stage, while so few were sent to America. Such troops as it possessed had to be where they could be ready to defend Britain in Europe, not dispersed across the Atlantic to defend those other Britons living there against Indian and French attack. The Secretary at War, Henry Fox, spelt out this policy in 1748, when it was finally beginning to change:

> In the wars ... both in King William's and Queen Anne's time, we did nothing but what we were obliged to do for our own safety ... Our ministers were reduced to the fatal necessity, that they must either neglect the war at land, or that at sea and in America, they must neglect the latter to take care of the former. And the reason is very plain: because our conquests at sea, or in America, would in the end signify nothing if, while we were busied about them, the French should make themselves masters of the continent of Europe.[46]

In North America, as elsewhere, the quality and the course of empire were determined, and sometimes distorted, by Britain's intrinsic smallness. Smallness – in this case, a paucity of military and official investment in the colonies – would come to matter crucially in the shaping of events and opinion on both sides of the Atlantic.

It mattered first and foremost because it nurtured division. After 1689, Anglo settlers in North America found themselves drawn into a succession of major wars with French forces in New France. There had been ample cause for many of them to fear Indian attacks before. But, now, particular Indian groupings acted as auxiliaries of the French (and sometimes also the Spanish) and were armed, supplied and incited by them. Captivities marked the escalating level of danger. New England lost at least 300 captives – and of course many dead – in each of the first three Anglo-French contests.[47] In the colonists' eyes, these were wars that sucked them in because of their connection to Britain. Hence the names they gave them: King William's War, Queen Anne's War, and so forth. The heightened risk these conflicts involved them in of fighting, dying, and being captured, stemmed – as the colonists saw it – from their position as subjects of the monarch over the water. Yet, before 1750, the king's horses and the king's men only rarely came to help them in their trouble. Instead, they had to help themselves. After King Philip's War ended in 1676, one historian writes, the colonists 'rejoiced that victory had been achieved without help from England, interpreting this as an affirmation of their longstanding autonomy within the Empire'. Such reactions became more pronounced after 1689. Part of the price the British state paid for being small – for having a modestly sized peacetime army that was unable, before 1750, to play a sustained role across the Atlantic – was increasingly self-reliant and uppity settlers in North America.[48]

The fact that their own troops were for so long uninvolved across the Atlantic also shaped attitudes among men and women in Britain itself, and helps to account for the restricted interest they initially displayed in tales of Indian captivity. As far as Britons at home were concerned, Native American attacks before 1750 almost exclusively affected colonists, people who increasingly were born in America, and who were unlikely ever to spend time in Britain itself. By contrast, since so few British-based soldiers were sent to America at this stage, *their* level of contact with Indians and risk of being killed or captured by them was naturally minimal. For these men and their friends and families, as for Britain's seamen, it was Europe, and the Islamic powers situated close to it, that were the primary zones of danger before the mid-eighteenth century – not North America. It is suggestive in this context that the British and their American settlers called these post-1689 wars that involved them both by different names. The latter, as we have seen, named them after the reigning British monarch, thereby affirming their ties across the Atlantic. People in Britain, by contrast, came to label these wars by reference to the European world that still dominated their thinking. For them, what happened between 1701 and 1713 was not Queen Anne's War, but the War of Spanish Succession; while the conflict which American colonists called George II's War, would become the War of Austrian Succession. For Britons at home at this stage, Europe and its environs remained the essential cockpit and testing ground; Europe was what had to matter most.

By mid-century, this was beginning to change. And once troops from Britain and their families began crossing the Atlantic in substantial numbers, after the outbreak of the Seven Years War in 1756, the metropolitan market for tales of Indian captivity, as for other information about North America, would sky-rocket. With large numbers of their own kind now flooding over to America – not to settle, but to fight and hopefully live to conquer and return – this vast territory and all its complex dangers came to seem to Britons at home infinitely more real and absorbing.

Yet, for all that it was now ending, the disparity that had for so long persisted between their experience of warfare, and that of their North American colonists had left an indelible mark, not least on this imperial but divided people's perceptions of the Indian. As far as the colonists were concerned, direct experience of danger from Indians in the case of some, a gut fear and dislike of Indians in many more, plus mass exposure to highly emotive captivity texts and sermons, encouraged a widespread though by no means universal belief that there was 'no such thing as a good Indian'. On the British side of the Atlantic, things were different. Overwhelmingly preoccupied for so long with European enemies, and substantially ignorant of Indians – as of much else about the land across the Atlantic – many Britons at home held understandably to a wider spectrum of attitudes.

Artefacts and images help to illustrate the difference. After 'King' Philip or Metacom was shot to death near his home in Mount Hope in August 1676, his ornaments and treasure were dispatched to the King of England in London. What the New Englanders kept for themselves was Philip's body. They hacked it to pieces, hung the joints on trees, and put the head on permanent display at Plymouth colony. Many years later, Cotton Mather – for once not busy penning sermons on captives – grabbed the Wampanoag leader's jaw bone 'from the blasphemous exposed skull of that Leviathan' and bore it away as a trophy.[49] Here, in Mather's gloating snatch of a macabre souvenir, was a hatred born out of fear, a hatred unsated even by the enemy's defeat and death. Here, too, was the disparity in transatlantic perspectives neatly displayed. To London went Philip's belt and gorge and emblems of rank, clean and elegant evidence of Indian artisanal skills and of the warrior's own distinction. Colonial New Englanders, by contrast, savoured the man's decaying carcass and admired his grisly skull. Let me be clear: both London and its politicians and merchants, and English settlers in America, contributed in their own ways to Philip's War, to his defeat, and to the gradual destruction of the way of life he represented. My point is that there were necessarily differences in how Britons on the two sides of the Atlantic tended to perceive these things.

Visual sources reinforce the point. Look, for instance, at the woodcut embellishing one of the many eighteenth-century American editions of Mary Rowlandson's captivity narrative. Its crude, over-exposed quality only makes it more effective as an image of horror. Transfixed lines of flame erupt from the roofs of the houses in Lancaster. Our heroine, Mary Rowlandson, rushes out of the burning buildings, arms raised, face frozen and contorted in a howl of terror almost as audible as Edvard Munch's *Scream*. Converging on her, half-hidden by the stylised undergrowth, are strange, skull-like faces with jagged hair. These are the monstrous instruments of pandemonium; these – as far as many settlers were concerned – were the faces of the Indian. Britons safe and snug at home were simply not in a position to see things in this fashion, or even in many cases to imagine them, any more of course than they were in a position to see what was being done by their settlers to the Indians themselves. The representations of Indians they were exposed to were usually of a very different kind.

Consider the most circulated images of Indians in Britain in the first half of the eighteenth century, those emerging from the famous visit of four Indian 'kings' to the court of Queen Anne in 1710. They were not kings of course, but young men linked to the powerful Iroquois confederacy – the loose union of Mohawk, Seneca, Onondaga, Cayuga and Oneida Indians – that dominated much of what is now upper New York state, the Lake Ontario region and the St Lawrence. They had been brought to London because the British were eager to secure Iroquois aid for their projected (and, as it turned out, abortive) invasion of French Canada. While in London, the men were feted, made much of – and abundantly painted and engraved. It is striking that most of their London hosts had no idea what the 'authentic' appearance of these men actually was (any more than Francis Bird knew what costume his imaginary Indian female should be sculpted in). It is striking too that the theatrical costumier who was ordered to outfit the four 'kings' in readiness for their presentation to the Queen supplied each of them with a turban and a pair of slippers. Naturally enough, given what we have seen of Britain's dangers and concentrated involvement in the Mediterranean, this Londoner's stereotypical non-European was not an Indian at all, but a Muslim, a Turk. Most striking of all, though, is how official Britain determined to see and commemorate these four visiting Native Americans.[50]

26. Mary Rowlandson runs out of her burning house, pursued by Indians: American woodcut.

The most remarkable surviving portraits of them are by John Verelst, who was commissioned by Queen Anne herself. They are remarkable, first, because in some respects they are so individualised. Verelst did not paint archetypal savages, even noble ones. He painted the Iroquois as comely, well-built dignitaries, each with different physiognomies and tattoo markings. Only in one sense are they standardised. The men are posed after the fashion which early modern European artists reserved for patrician males from their own continent, with one arrogant arm akimbo, one leg extended, and with tokens displaying their military prowess and rank. Thus the 'Emperor of the Six Nations' (as the British chose to call him) is accompanied by a wolf, which serves here as the equivalent of his heraldic beast, and a wampum belt, a sign of communication and statecraft. The 'King of the Maquas' is pictured by Verelst as a mighty hunter, while the 'King of the River Nation' is a warrior, with a European sword in a scabbard buckled to his waist and a brocaded cloak falling in folds to the forest floor. Twenty years later, in 1730, seven Cherokee 'chiefs' brought to London on a political mission would be portrayed by another artist in very similar fashion, posed in the grand manner against the background of a landscaped park 'just as if they were members of the English nobility or at least the landed gentry'.[51]

Comparing images such as these, which circulated widely in Britain, against American images like the woodcut of Mary Rowlandson's terror is to some degree unfair. White attitudes to, and relations with Indians in colonial America were at no time ever monolithic or unvaryingly hostile. By the same token, perceptions of Indians in Britain could be brutal and uncompromising, especially amongst those with close ties to the colonists. Thus Daniel Defoe, a Protestant dissenter who was deeply sympathetic to his co-religionists on the other side of the Atlantic, poured scorn on the Iroquois visit to London in 1710. 'When they took any prisoners', he raged: 'they always scalp'd them, which many of our poor *English* people have felt.'[52] None the less, the different emphases of these images reflected a real difference of experience, and also different imperatives. It was not simply that people in Britain – unlike their colonists in America – were immune to danger from Indians, and immune as well to personal hunger for their land. At the same time, British governments were also increasingly coming to see particular groups of Indians as positively useful. It was no accident that Verelst's portraits of the four Iroquois 'kings' were put on display at Kensington Palace right next to a room full of portraits of Royal Navy admirals. To the rulers of the British state, desperate as always for additional manpower, Indian warriors seemed less an unmitigated menace than potential armed auxiliaries in the business of empire. As one imperial official put it cheerfully – writing in this case of the Cherokees, Creeks and Chocktaws – 'while they are our friends, they are the cheapest and strongest barrier for the protection of our settlements'.[53] Gripped and confined by their own smallness, the British in their imperial phase sought out allies, all kinds of allies, everywhere. They could not afford to do otherwise.

Here were tensions then between the different Britons inhabiting the two sides of the Atlantic, and also between different Americans. These

27. Tee Yee Neen Ho Ga Row, Emperor of the Six Nations, by John Verelst.

Sa Ga Yeath Qua Pieth Ton King of the Maquas

28. Sa Ga Yeath Qua Pieth Ton, King of the Maquas, by John Verelst.

166

did not initially detract from the close linkages that existed between Britons on both sides of the Atlantic in other respects: indeed, it bears repeating that the emergence of the captivity narrative in British mainland North America was itself an indication of just how much its inhabitants continued to draw inspiration from, and share cultural forms with, their point of origin. But captivity panics in North America, and the texts that emerged from them, also illustrated the differences that nestled and grated within these transatlantic connections – differences of religion, differences of knowledge and of experience and, of course, massive differences of geography, uneased at this stage by anything more than sailing-power. Despite its enthusiastic advances into the extra-European world, early modern Britain remained pre-eminently a European power. Rival European powers were what it necessarily had to measure itself against; and before 1750 this meant that its modest armies and resources, its official minds, and its inhabitants' attention were concentrated – though never exclusively so – on events and conflicts within Europe and its immediate environs.

Because they were limited in number, dependent psychologically and in many other ways on the 'mother country', and threatened by French power in Canada and to a lesser extent by the Spanish in the South, Britain's American colonists tended to view these European rivalries as involving them as well. Yet geography progressively served to differentiate their outlook too. Sharply threatened in some cases by the actions and existence of Native Americans, and threatened still more widely in their imaginations, they yearned progressively for these peoples' lands, and for their disappearance. The politicians sitting tight and safe in London might be inclined to view Native Americans as potential, subaltern manpower, a palliative for their own besetting smallness of military numbers, but Britain's white settlers in America were more likely to see them as obstacles, peoples to be feared, or despised, and – as time went on – impatiently swept aside.

As the scale of imperial warfare widened after 1750, so would these divisions and differences between Britons at home and British colonists in America. And at the heart of these tensions, would be the battered figure of the Indian, and the figure of the captive.

SIX

War and a New World

Confrontations

29 August 1754: Number 4, New Hampshire. It is so new this place, it has a number, not a name. The sparse white inhabitants, who trickle in on horseback, by cart, and via the Connecticut River, are scattershot in isolated homesteads, and heavily dependent for trade on the local Indians. Most of the time, however, they see no one, neither of their own kind nor of any other. Yet on this high summer evening, at least, Susanna Johnson feels at ease with the harshness of her life. Her husband James has just returned from a long journey, bringing with him some of their far-flung neighbours, a supply of water melons, and bottles of what they call flip, but what Britons back home are more likely by now to style egg-nog. She cuts herself a wedge of the fruit, savouring its coolness against her taut belly, but barely touches the viscous, yellow alcohol. Like all the women of her family, like most of the women that she knows indeed, she falls pregnant easily. This is the last month of her sixth pregnancy, and there will be eight more pregnancies to follow. Enforcedly temperate and dazed with the heat, she enjoys the unaccustomed company while remaining all the while detached within herself. By the time they retire, the Johnsons and their three surviving children to their beds, and the guests to chairs or blankets on the floor, she is probably the only sober adult of the party. She is also too swollen for heavy slumber, and so is the first of them to hear.

When, just before dawn, the rustling outside gives way to a violent pounding, James Johnson too is jerked into wakefulness. Cursing, he pulls on his nightshirt and pads unsteadily but unworriedly towards the door. It is another settler come to join the merry-making, he thinks, but arrived too late. Or a guest has gone out to relieve himself, and is too drunk to find his way back. It is none of these things. The door is forced open: and he sees at once that these are Abenaki warriors, Indians who fight in alliance with the French. There are only twelve of them, but they are armed and alert, whereas Johnson and the other male settlers are neither.

The sounds of struggle and of voices they cannot understand propel the rest of the family out of their beds. At first, Susanna is too shocked to take in the invaders or what their coming may signify. Instead, she stares at the exposed nudity of her three terrified children, and shrieks at them for violating Protestant modesty. Only then does she think to look down: 'On viewing myself, I found that I too was naked.'

An Abenaki busy ransacking the house tosses her a skirt which she has been obliged to lay aside many months ago. She fastens it tremblingly around herself, and then she, James, the children, her younger sister, and two male settlers are driven shoeless and barely clothed into the open, into 'a wilderness where we must sojourn as long as the children of Israel did, for ought we knew'. They have gone barely a mile, before she collapses, winded, to the ground. One of her captors raises his knife – but only so as to slit her too-tight waistband. As a woman who can clearly breed, and who will soon give birth to another captive, she is too valuable to kill, as long as she does not delay them too often or too long. When her new daughter is born a few days later, a child who will become her favourite and whom she determines then and there to name 'Captive', there is no wait for post-partum recovery. Nine days later, travelling in a pallet made for her by the Abenaki, but also at times on the back of a horse (until they slaughter it for food), Susanna, the baby called Captive Johnson, and the rest, arrive with their Indian escort at the east bay of Lake Champlain, New France. They have journeyed over a hundred miles into a different empire and utterly different lives.[1]

Yet although the threads of the Johnsons' previous existence have been severed, never to be properly mended, in some respects what happens to them now follows long-established patterns and precedents.

Ever since 1689, hot and cold war between the French and the British had led the former's colonial authorities in New France to sponsor Indian raids for loot, captives, and destruction against the latter's American colonists, and especially against New Englanders. Susanna Johnson's narrative reveals the extent to which, by the 1750s, this kind of captive-taking possessed, for all its violence, an almost routine quality. When Susanna and her children entered the Abenaki village of St François late in 1754, they were not made to run the gauntlet between two rows of Indians, or undergo any other harsh initiation ceremony: its inhabitants merely lined up and gave them each a purely token pat. She discovered too that the senior chief who became her master at St François was himself a fore-runner and a countryman of sorts, the son of two New Englanders who had been part of a previous generation of white captives. As suggested by this man's progress from birth as an English colonial Protestant to adulthood as a high status Roman Catholic Abenaki warrior, it was entirely predictable that the Johnsons' captivity would have its greatest transforming impact not on Susanna or James but on their children. The younger the victim, the greater – always – the potential pliancy and adaptability. The baby, Captive Johnson, would learn French as her first language, and subsequently refuse for a long time to acquire English, while their eleven-year-old son spent almost four years on his own in an Abenaki village, lost his English altogether, and forgot what his father looked like. All this naturally grieved the Johnsons, making them feel bereft of their own children, but historically it was nothing new or remarkable.

But another aspect of Susanna's own captivity emphatically was. When Britain declared war on France in May 1756, the formal beginning of what became known as the Seven Years War, the treatment meted out to the Johnsons changed abruptly. The couple, together with the girls and Susanna's sister were transferred from their alarming but sometimes congenial Abenaki surroundings to a prison in Quebec. It was from this city, on 20 July 1757, that the female Johnsons boarded a cartel ship that bore them across the Atlantic to Plymouth, England: and this sea passage from captivity in North America to the imperial metropolis was something new. During the seventeenth and early eighteenth centuries, men and women in Britain had learnt about colonial captivities in North America only indirectly, intermittently, and with limited interest. Capture by Barbary corsairs, and the perils of Islam and the Mediterranean, they knew about, understood after a fashion, and feared in their gut: but this was not true, to anything like the same degree, of this other, very different species of captive-taking. Now, in the 1750s, British aloofness and widespread ignorance in this regard substantially altered. The Johnson women were only some of a great many colonial captives who found themselves – because of the circumstances of the Seven Years War – brought to Britain as a prelude to returning to their respective American homes. These men and women were now able to spend time in Britain itself and communicate their experiences to its inhabitants face to face. 'I received much attention,' Susanna remembered complacently of her six-month stay in Britain, 'and had to gratify many inquisitive friends with the history of my sufferings.'

She recorded something else about this British episode of her life. When she, her sister and the girls finally boarded the Royal Navy vessel in Portsmouth that would take them back across the Atlantic, its captain initially misinterpreted their strange and shabby appearance, and 'swore we were women of ill fame, who wished to follow the army' to America.[2] As this suggests, it was not just a case now of some American colonists being able to come to Britain and tell their tales of captivity; British-born soldiers were simultaneously being dispatched to fight in America in unprecedented numbers. Between 1757 and 1761, Parliament provided – at least on paper – for a British force of 30,000 men in North America, which would be joined at times by some 20,000 armed colonists. A minority of these British regulars and the family members accompanying them would themselves go on to experience captivity at the hands of Native Americans and the French; and all would contribute to a quantum rise in British knowledge about America and its inhabitants. Here were multiple transatlantic crossings and confrontations of a new type all brought about by the onset of seismic imperial warfare.

The war proved transforming as far as the British were concerned in the obvious sense that it was successful on a scale never previously experienced. They wrenched Florida from the Spanish, and Canada from the French, as well as Cape Breton Island, strategic key to control of the Gulf of St Lawrence, plus new territories in the Caribbean and West Africa, Grenada, Tobago, St Vincent and Senegal, and their first major administrative enclave in India, the rich province of Bengal. By the time the war officially ended in 1763, the British empire – as Britons now began calling *all* the lands they laid claim to in a way not customary before – was five times larger than it had been a century earlier.[3] More broadly, the war fostered a shift in attitudes in Britain and throughout the West. Before 1750, the major European powers and their overseas settlers had rarely viewed empire as something of which people of their sort, Christian, Western, and white, were uniquely capable. The persistence of the great Muslim empires, and the vast, impenetrable expanse of the Chinese empire, had prevented that. After 1760, however, both the Ottoman and the Mughal empires came to be viewed in the West as weakening as never before, while commentary on China also became less awed and respectful. It was as if the extraordinary global range of the Seven Years War, and the radical transformations it effected, revealed to Western states in a new way just what their fleets, manpower and precocious national cohesion might accomplish – if only they so willed. Adam Smith, emphatically no knee-jerk enthusiast for empire, none the less conveyed something of this heightened sense of Western omnipotence and arrogance. 'In ancient times the opulent and civilized found it difficult to defend themselves against the poor and barbarous nations,' he wrote, but 'in modern times the poor and barbarous find it difficult to defend themselves against the opulent and civilized.' The whole world, 'the great map of mankind' as Edmund Burke styled it, lay open and exposed to European appetites as never before – or so it now sometimes appeared.[4]

In the light of these territorial and attitudinal shifts, one might have expected issues of captivity and confinement to recede rapidly from British consciousness, yet this was not the case. Unprecedented British military involvement in North America brought with it a fresh spate of profoundly disturbing captivities, and a new burden of imperial knowledge. It was now, in the era of the Seven Years War, that the British learnt at first hand the sheer physical extent and complexity of the lands they and their settlers had so casually accumulated. It was now that they were made to realise how varied the peoples of North America were, and the degree to which their own white settlers were more than simply mirrors of themselves. And it was now that they came to understand far more vividly than before that, for all their dwindling numbers, Native Americans could still be highly dangerous as well as potentially useful, and had necessarily to be taken seriously.

The individual captivities Britons experienced in this conflict contributed in all sorts of ways to this fast learning curve about America, but it was the enhanced sense they evolved of their *collective* constraints and challenges in America that proved more important. In the wake of an astonishingly successful global war, the British were left with an inflated commitment to an imperial mission, with a far more informed sense of the dimensions and workings of their rich and populous transatlantic empire, but with a heightened awareness too of the problems it posed in the light of their own inescapable limitations.

Into the wilderness

Many Britons at home embarked on the transatlantic phase of the Seven Years War with a belief comfortably rooted in ignorance that Native Americans were by now finished business, or just simply finished. A government MP waxed typically dismissive when discussing French and British rivalry in North America in 1755: 'Here is a contest between two equals,' he informed the House of Commons suavely, 'about a country where both claim an undivided right . . . I think it is allowed on all hands that the natives have no right at all.'[5] In this strictly armchair view of things, America mattered much less in terms of its own complexities, than as one more theatre for the all-important and protracted duel for primacy between Europe's two most aggressive and competitive states.

In one very practical respect, however, such Eurocentricism actually worked to improve Britain's understanding of its American colonists and the captivities sometimes inflicted on them. After 1756, Britain and France committed themselves to successive treaties whereby all prisoners-of-war 'of whatever sort, wherever' were to be exchanged or ransomed 'in whatever part of the world the belligerent or auxiliary armies of the two nations may be'.[6] Here was an explicit recognition that Anglo-French conflict now spanned the continents in a new way, and an expression too on the part of these powers of a far greater degree of global hubris. All prisoners in this war, whether in Europe or outside it, were now declared to be potentially the business of Britain and France, and not just their respective nationals. As far as British North America was concerned, what this meant was that colonists seized by the French or their Indian allies, like Susanna Johnson, now became London's responsibility, and were often transported to Britain at some stage in the course of their release. In just two months, October and November 1758, over sixty American colonists captured in this fashion were shipped from New France to England, where they were fed and clothed for several months before finally being transported home. Captivity narratives published by colonials during the war regularly refer to these unprecedented transatlantic redemptions. Thus Jean Lowry, who was captured by Indians at Rocky-Spring, Pennsylvania, in April 1756, and lost her husband in the process, described how she was held in New France, then shipped from Quebec to Dartmouth, England, in the autumn of 1758, before being sent back to New York the following year.[7]

It was not unusual by this stage for individual American colonists to pay visits to what most still regarded as the mother-country, but those who did so were generally prosperous males: Southern gentlemen on their version of the Grand Tour, candidates for ordination, well-heeled merchants and lobbyists and the like. The influx into Britain during this war of substantial numbers of miscellaneous colonists (and some blacks) caught up in and damaged by the conflict was a very different phenomenon which has never been investigated.[8] It must have resulted in the oral transmission of abundant though selective information about different kinds of Native Americans and about North American life in general; indeed we know from Susanna Johnson's narrative that it did. But this was only one aspect of an explosion in Britain at this time of information about America. In addition, there were the official and informal letters flooding back to Britain from colonists, and from British soldiers, officials and families dispatched to America for the duration of the war. And, most of all, there was an outburst of print.

It was now that the British began to read about the lands and peoples they laid claim to across the Atlantic as never before. At one level, this was because there was so much more available for them to read. One in five of all works published in Britain about North America between 1640 and 1760 appeared in the last decade of this timespan, the 1750s.[9] To these discrete volumes was added the more widely scanned information now on offer about America in the London and provincial press. As John Brewer long ago pointed out, the middle of the eighteenth century witnessed a quickening in the size and complexity of Britain's press network. More newspapers were sold – an expansion of about 30 per cent over the 1750s alone. More titles were issued – the slaving port of Liverpool, for instance, acquired its first ever newspaper during the Seven Years War, because of the intense local interest it aroused. And this proliferation of different papers and magazines meant in turn that particularly arresting stories and news items could be reprinted many times over and transmitted far beyond the bounds of London and the major cities.[10] Yet the increase in the *volume* of American and other information was only part, and not the most interesting part of the story. There was also a qualitative change in the kinds of information on offer.

Before 1756, most of what British newspapers and magazines printed about America had been brief, factual and overwhelmingly commercial, often little more than a record of incoming and outgoing transatlantic vessels at specific ports. But as the war advanced, far more attention was devoted in papers, pamphlets and books to the American interior, to issues other than trade, and to human interest stories, understandably so, since individual Britons and different varieties of Americans were now encountering each other at a hitherto unknown rate and degree of intensity. 'The scene of action is now in America', wrote a young and very serious Arthur Young in 1758, desperately keen to kick-start his career as a writer and pundit:

> To understand perfectly what the advantage or disadvantage of any place being taken on either side, is to us, it is necessary not only to know the latitude and longitude of such a place (which is frequently the best part of the accounts some authors give) but its situation with regard to its neighbourhood; what nations of Indians it lies near to; whether those Indians are best affected to us, or our enemies; what French forts or settlements are nearest, and their distance; if they can be known, which is not always the case in that uninhabited and extensive country.

Literate and patriotic Britons now came to accept that in regard to North America they had seriously to raise their game, and broaden and deepen their knowledge. A greater emphasis on accounts of captivity and on Native American encounters generally were an integral part of this wider reportage and yearning to know. Captivity narratives written by or about

29. Learning Empire: a post-war British public lecture on physiognomy makes room for a loyal Native American.

colonists, and originally published in America, came now to stand a far better chance of being reprinted in Britain or extracted in its press.[11] And, for the first time on any significant scale, detailed accounts of captivity and other sufferings at the hands of Indians were written and published by individuals who were active in America on account of the war, but based in Britain and intent on returning there.

By colonial American standards, some of these pioneering British texts about Indian captivities were markedly elementary in quality. When Mary Rowlandson and her clerical mentors put together the first, famous full-length colonial captivity narrative in the 1670s, they had made clear how precious and totemic Englishness remained for them, but they also revealed – perhaps unconsciously – the degree to which New Englanders like themselves were already familiar with some of the material circumstances of Native American life. Words like 'canoe', 'wigwam', 'sagamore', and 'squaw' appear in Rowlandson's captivity story, *The Sovereignty and Goodness of God*, without any explanations being provided, because for her original Massachusetts readers none were required. Well before 1700, British colonists in America were adjusting to, and assimilating information about their new environment and its plural peoples, in a way that was neither possible nor necessary for men and women living in Britain itself.[12] This experiential and knowledge gap between the colonies and the mother-country was far wider by the 1750s. Consequently, British-based writers on captivity and other contacts with Indians during the Seven Years War, who had their own compatriots in mind as an audience, sometimes felt obliged to devote space to very rudimentary information.

Some, like Peter Williamson, whom we will encounter at length later, sought out British analogies so as to make his Indian experiences better understood. A tomahawk, he wrote, was 'something like our plasterer's hammers'. While Henry Grace, a deeply miserable English soldier, who was seized and used as a slave for over five years by various Indian group-ings in Nova Scotia and New France, padded out his bitter, self-published narrative with descriptions of snow shoes and wigwams ('a kind of hut made with the bark of birch trees . . . There is always a place left in the middle at top to let out the smoke') that would have seemed superfluous to most American colonists, but not necessarily so to his immediate audi-ence in Basingstoke, England. Even John Rutherfurd, a Yorkshire-born Scot who wrote his remarkable account of captivity at the hands of the Chippewas late in the war, when British knowledge about America had expanded dramatically, still thought it appropriate to interrupt his story with carefully observed explanations of scalps or breech-clouts:

a piece of blue cloth about a yard and a half long and a foot broad which they pass through betwixt their legs, bringing each end under a belt which is round the middle for that purpose.[13]

As always, then, British and colonial American treatments of Indian captivities were characterised by significant differences. But not in all respects. Most of these new British captivity narratives, like most colonial accounts, lingered on the pornography of real or invented Indian violence, in part because such lurid passages attracted readers even as they allowed them to feel properly repelled. Thomas Morris's account of his brief captivity with the Miamis as a British infantry captain in the early 1760s was generally curious and sympathetic. He made a point, for instance, of advocating intermarriage between whites and the 'innocent, much-abused, and once happy people' he called Indians. None the less, Morris still devoted space to the variety and duration of Indian torture techniques:

> The usual modes of torturing prisoners are applying hot stones to the soles of the feet, running hot needles into the eyes, which latter cruelty is generally performed by the women, and shooting arrows and running and pulling them out of the sufferer in order to shoot them again.

'These modes of torture I should not have mentioned', he confessed artlessly, 'if the gentleman who advised me to publish my journal had not thought it necessary.'[14] The main reason why writings by Britons began devoting more space to Indian violence was not however reader titillation. It was rather that people of their own sort were now being exposed to this violence in a new way. Indians no longer just endangered British colonists living 3000 miles away. Because of the way this war was being fought, some Indian peoples were a threat to Britain's own armed forces, and a formidable one.

Some of the reasons why this was so were all too familiar. Initially, many of the British troops dispatched to America were deficient in local knowledge, deficient in training and proper equipment, and above all, and with dismal predictability, deficient in numbers. The destruction of General Edward Braddock and his forces at Monongahela, Western Pennsylvania, in July 1755, is conventionally attributed to the Yorkshireman's personal arrogance and unwillingness to adapt to wilderness fighting. These failings did not help. But the French-led force of Huron, Shawnee, Ottawa and Algonquin warriors was able to slaughter 1000 of the British (including Braddock himself and three-quarters of his officers) in large part because his troops consisted of the unwanted leftovers of several British and Irish battalions, plus some poor-quality American recruits, while the maps he brought with him turned out to be grossly inaccurate.[15] By the same token, the Fall of Oswego, a major fort and trading post on Lake Ontario, in August 1756 – one of the biggest British military disasters in North America that year – owed less to individual incompetence than to insufficient numbers and resources. The mixed French and Indian force that overwhelmed Oswego consisted of over 3000 men. Against this, the British had less than 1500 soldiers and only 'poor [and] pittyful' fortifications.[16]

In other words, at the start of this ultimately very successful war the British were forced to pay in defeats, high casualty rates and captivities for the sort of American empire they had chosen to run – or rather not run – up to this point. French colonisers in North America had long been aware of their demographic inferiority to British settlers here, and had endeavoured to compensate for this with a high level of military preparedness. New France was an armed society, with its own military nobility and culture. There were close links between its extensive militia and the French regular army. Its secular and religious officials devoted constant attention and imagination to nurturing military alliances with local indigenous peoples; while French government investment in the defence of New France rose from some 300,000 livres in 1712, to over 500,000 livres in the 1730s, to millions of livres every year from the 1740s onwards.[17]

Before the Seven Years War, Britain behaved very differently. Possessed of a much smaller domestic population, revenue base and army than France, it had never fortified its colonies in America to the same degree, or maintained large numbers of regular troops here, or exhibited a sustained interest in wooing indigenous allies, or devoted much time or trouble to training up its colonists in the military arts.[18] Yet it needs stressing that even when the British and their American colonists did begin to get their military act together in 1758–9, and finally learnt how to exploit the potential of their combined numbers against the arms and allies of New France, different groups of Native Americans continued to be able to inflict periodic defeats on British regular troops. In 1760, the Cherokees defeated a large British force commanded by Archibald Montgomery and captured Fort Loudoun in the Allegheny Mountains; and between April and June 1763, the confederation of Ottawa, Chippewa, Delaware, Huron, Seneca, Shawnee and other Native American groupings involved in Pontiac's War managed to capture most of the poorly defended British posts in the Great Lakes–Ohio region. ·

So British-based commentators explored Native American violence more emotionally and at greater length after 1756 in large part because they had been given ample cause to fear it, and because for them this was something new. It is clear, indeed, that some British troops dispatched to North America, already disoriented by their transatlantic crossing, froze into 'a sort of torpor and insensibility' when confronted for the first time by hostile Indians, an enemy of a kind nothing in Europe had prepared them for. The way that Braddock's doomed infantry continued to stand for hours in line together in 1755 while their French and Indian opponents picked them off, instead of scattering for cover into the woods, is usually put down to their ignorance of guerrilla tactics. But these raw recruits may well have found their only, final comfort in huddling together in this fashion, and feared separating in the face of an enemy they did not understand and most of the time could barely see. The few British survivors testified that rarely more than five Indian warriors had been visible during the battle, so adept were the latter at camouflage, and so thick were the surrounding woods.[19] When hostile Native Americans did come into view, it might be still more alarming. Confronted by his soon-to-be Chippewa captors, 'naked, and painted black and red', John Rutherfurd, who had only arrived in America the year before, and was just eighteen, simply gave up 'all hope of being saved, and became in a manner resigned to the worst'. And if war-paint failed to petrify – which was its purpose – inexperienced regulars trained to regard advancing in tight-lipped silence as a mark of military professionalism might still be unmanned by the howls and screams Indians made as they attacked. 'The Indian war cry is represented as too dreadful to be endured', reported Samuel Johnson to his British readers in 1758:

> as a sound that will force the bravest veteran to drop his weapon, and desert his rank; that will deafen his ear, and chill his breast; that will neither suffer him to hear orders or to feel shame, or retain any sensibility but the dread of death.[20]

Yet, in this kind of warfare, death might seem preferable to captivity. It was probably the exception rather than the rule for adult white males seized by Indians during this war to be nurtured throughout a long captivity and live to be freed and tell their tales. Even in the waves of Indian raids on civilian settlers in Pennsylvania, Maryland and Virginia in the late 1750s and early '60s, which resulted in some 3000 captives, white males are estimated to have been nineteen times more likely to be slaughtered than their female counterparts. Men in uniform seized in battle could fare worse. Only twenty captives were taken by Indians from amongst the remnants of Braddock's force at Monongahela. Eight of these were female and allowed to live, because women and girls were deemed fertile, useful and unthreatening. Twelve were soldiers, and these men were tortured to death, to test their courage and appease the dead and bereaved among the Indians themselves. 'They stripped him quite naked', Henry Grace reported being told of one of these victims:

> and tying him to a tree, made two large fires on each side of him and perfectly roasted him alive, while they danced round him, paying no regard to his lamentations . . . one of the young Indians ran in between the two fires and cut off his private parts, and put them into his mouth to stop him crying.[21]

It was not just the extreme physicality of this sort of violence that horrified and alienated, the blood, the body parts, the ingenious mutilations, the deliberate prolongation of excruciating, unmanning pain. For Britons who devoted any thought to it, the sense that all this constituted a kind of language which they themselves could not understand might be just as unnerving. When Colonel John Littlehales was captured at Oswego in 1756 and taken to Montreal, it is likely that neither he, nor his regular army comrades captured alongside him, understood why seventy Abenakis promptly seized upon him there, dragged him along the city's walls, made him dance, and 'afterwards beat him with sticks . . . swearing in Indian, calling him a rascal, a son of a bitch, a dog, and a scoundrel, which lasted for about one hour'. It is only possible for us to decode this behaviour because for once there was a witness present who had some access to all the different cultures involved. Richard Williams had been a drummer with the 51st Regiment at Oswego, but was captured by Indians from La Galette in 1755 and taken to New France. By the time he came to witness Littlehales' ordeal, Williams had already passed successfully through his own. He wore a carved stick through the bridge of his nose, his ears were ritually cut, 'he could paint himself so as not to be known from an Indian', and he had acquired the languages of his different captors. So he was able to ask Littlehales' Indian tormentors 'why they used him . . . and none of the rest of the [British] officers in that manner'. They told him it was 'because Littlehales was a coward and behaved ill, otherwise they would not have beat him'. Littlehales had indeed visibly lost his nerve in the siege in which he was captured, but the significant point is that neither he, nor his comrades, were probably able – as Williams was – to connect this personal failure as a warrior with the protracted and vicious beatings afterwards inflicted on him. Instead, this assault will almost certainly have been interpreted by those Britons witnessing it as one more proof of innate and thoroughly arbitrary indigenous savagery.[22]

The belief that Indian violence was at once hideously cruel and unpredictable, explains why some British troops (including men who had faced other enemies with equanimity) deserted rather than do battle with them, or simply resigned themselves helplessly to death in the face of their attack. This was what happened at Fort William Henry, near the southern end of Lake George, on 9 August 1757, in one of the most controversial episodes of the war. The British garrison had already offered their surrender, and this had been formally accepted by their French opponents, but the British and colonial troops involved were then subsequently attacked by a large band of pro-French Indians and, as one observer reported, some of 'the English were seized with such an unaccountable stupor, that they submitted to the tomahawk without resistance'. Once again, this was a case of men being thrown off balance by a gulf between military cultures. According to western European (but not Indian) conventions, having surrendered, their lives should have been sacrosanct. When this turned out not to be the case, some did not know how to react and so failed to react at all. But, in addition, some of the 180 or so British soldiers and camp followers killed on this occasion may well have given themselves up to a quick death out of fear that the alternatives were bound to be worse. As it happened, at least half of all the white male captives seized at Fort William Henry seem to have survived, while forty more chose to stay with their Indian captors. But to submit to Indian captivity on the offchance that it would lead to these happier results required nerve as well as a level of experience that British troops new to America were often naturally without.[23]

Such wartime incidents, and the accounts of them dispatched back across the Atlantic, served at one level to bring Britons at home into greater harmony with the attitudes towards Native Americans displayed by many of their colonists. The romanticism with which many Britons had earlier viewed Native Americans – their sense that these peoples were potentially useful, assimilable, wild, noble savages of the woodlands – shuddered and sometimes shattered irretrievably under the shock of actual contact and conflict. For dramatic proof of this, one has only to compare John Verelst's flattering and chivalric images of the four Indian 'kings' who visited Queen Anne in 1710 with George Townshend's sketches of Ottawa and Algonquin warriors made while he and they were engaged in the military campaign against Quebec in 1759.

Townshend was the son of an English peer, an army general, and an amateur artist, who enjoyed producing vicious caricatures of white males of his own social class and nationality, so one should not read too much into the negativity of these drawings. In some ways, indeed, he represents his Indian subjects more accurately than Verelst attempted to do. A keen and increasingly expert collector of Indian artefacts, as his income allowed him to be, Townshend would even take an Indian boy child back home with him to his family's great house of Rainham in Norfolk, one more object to be displayed and scrutinised. So he was careful how he drew his subjects and their material life, just as he took pains to convey their physical impressiveness, their tallness, which (normally shorter) British males regularly commented on, the strength of their limbs, and their evident stamina and agility. But it is the particular scenes of Indian life Townshend selected to record, and the titles he gave his drawings, that are most revealing. There is 'An Indian dress'd for war with a scalp', as well as 'An Indian pursuing a wounded enemy with his Tomahawk', and 'An Indian of ye Outawas Tribe & his Family going to war', and several more images of a similar sort. But nowhere in any of these sketches is there evidence of warm humanity or humour on the Indians' part, or of empathy as distinct from fascination on Townshend's. Here are Indians, and Indians in this case acting alongside the British remember, represented as unalloyed creatures of menace, raw, single-minded hunters, utterly beyond civility and sentiment. Emphatically the Other.[24]

Those Britons who came to regard Native Americans in this light were not reacting simply to wartime events across the Atlantic. Part of western Europeans' heightened conceit about themselves at this stage stemmed from a sense that they were coming to conduct war more humanely, as well of course as on a much larger scale.[25] Captives played a vital part in these self-serving ideas as in so much else. By 1757, there were already more than 13,000 French prisoners-of-war being held in Britain and Ireland, and by 1762 over 26,000 Frenchmen were detained there. Never before, had Britons at home been able to see so many defeated and helpless foreign enemies detained on their own shores; and printed accounts of these prisoners and their sufferings, and civic subscriptions on their behalf increased with every year of the war. In 1759, there were charitable collections on behalf of the French prisoners in London, Edinburgh, Dublin and many other major towns. Thousands of pounds were raised, and mountains of shoes, clothes and medicines donated for their comfort. The pamphlet issued to commemorate this nationwide benevolence was prefaced by Samuel Johnson himself, and copies were 'deposited in the British Museum, and in the several universities of the British Empire'. Here was to be proof, preserved in print for all time, that Britain was not merely victorious globally – as by 1759 it very evidently was – but humane in its conduct of war, impressively merciful, quintessentially civilised. Britons, as one journalist glowed, felt 'for their captives as men, and cannot but pity enemies in distress'. Naturally, the French thought exactly the

An Indian who has un—
his Enemy & prepares with his
tomahawk to scalp him

30. Watercolour of an Ottawa warrior, by George Townshend.

31. Trumpeting British military mercy: Benjamin West's *General Johnson saving a wounded French officer from the tomahawk of a North American Indian*.

same about themselves, and organised similar charitable collections for British prisoners of war held on their soil.[26]

It is in the light of this more proactive concern on both sides of the Channel on behalf of (overwhelmingly white) captives that one must understand some of the emphases in Emeric de Vattel's *The Law of Nations* (1758), which became one the most influential Enlightenment texts about property, war and empire. In his sections on war, Vattel, a Swiss jurist, drew an absolute distinction between 'unlawful war for havoc and pillage' ('almost all the expeditions' of the Barbary corsairs, he remarked pointedly, came into this category), and 'the humanity with which most nations in Europe carry on wars at present'. It was unjust, Vattel argued, indeed it was savage to kill prisoners-of-war. The lustre of victory should not be tarnished 'by inhuman and brutal actions'. Consequently, he declared: 'We extol, we love the English and French at hearing the accounts of the treatment [they have] given to prisoners of war.'[27] At the same time as it was accelerating in global scope and aggressiveness, European warfare was coming to be presented more explicitly as distinctively humane and generous, especially in regard to the treatment of captives. And in this respect, Vattel put into systematic, intellectual prose what many military professionals already instinctively took for granted.

In the same year as the publication of Vattel's masterwork, 1758, Britain's commander-in-chief in America, General James Abercromby, assured his French opposite number, the marquis de Montcalm, that he wanted 'to carry on the war in this country with the same humanity and generosity it is in Europe, and ought to be everywhere'. Tellingly, Abercromby cited behaviour towards captives as the vital test of these civilised qualities: 'the good treatment of these persons that the state of war . . . throws into our hands'.[28] Here was an approach to the conduct of war that – on the face of it – situated America's indigenous peoples firmly outside the charmed circle of those from whom humanity was to be expected, and excluded them as well from those to whom humanity was due. Indians, as Britons now had much better cause to know, did not invariably exhibit pity to enemies in distress. They were known to torture and occasionally cannibalise prisoners-of-war, and more generally indulged in public and ritual assaults on the human body in a manner that Europeans were coming (unevenly) to have qualms about. They sometimes killed those who had already laid down their weapons and were defenceless; just as they sometimes attacked helpless women and children. Indians, wrote General Jeffrey Amherst, his pen dipped in loathing, were 'the only brutes and cowards in the creation . . . known to exercise their cruelties upon the [female] sex, and to scalp and mangle the poor sick soldiers'. Indians, agreed another British general, were 'assassins, not soldiers, therefore they have no quarter'.[29] In this straightforwardly manichean and vengeful vision, Native Americans were fair game. They could have no respectable part in Britain's fast expanding empire, or be drawn into civilisation as Europeans conceived of it. Their conduct towards the white captives in their hands proved them barbarians, predators and monsters, beyond understanding, and beyond the line.

Yet it needs stressing that this was by no means the only British vision of Native Americans fostered by the Seven Years War.

Because this conflict was followed, barely a dozen years later, by the outbreak of the American Revolution, it can be tempting – especially for American historians – to represent the British military and political classes as already in the 1750s and '60s hardening into uniformly ruthless and intransigent imperialists. Examples of British arrogance and impatient authority in North America are looked for and lingered on, in part because of the retrospective knowledge that massive and successful resistance to them was just around the corner. Exaggerating the degree to which British soldiers and administrators were invariably antipathetic to Indians is one aspect of this. Thus Jeffrey Amherst (who indisputably *was* an Indian-hater) has been described by one scholar as summing 'up British military attitudes toward the Indians', while another has claimed that the British were 'trapped within their understanding of the Indians as childlike, violent creatures'.[30] Many of them were of course; but some were not. At the one extreme, to be sure, there were the likes of Amherst, a man who certainly advocated genocide against Indians, even if the jury remains out on whether he actually implemented it. But at the other extreme, there were British Indian experts like John Stuart, a fellow army officer and no less committed imperialist than Amherst, who married a mixed-blood Cherokee, who befriended Chief Attakullakulla and was rescued by him during the Seven Years War, and who is on record as regarding Native American violence as no more outrageous than the level of street crime in London or Paris.[31] Between the utterly disparate ideas and behaviour of these two equally atypical individuals, there existed many different gradations of British response to Indians at official and military level.

Among ordinary Britons at home, attitudes were even more mixed and shifting. Some of them emerged from the war convinced that Native Americans were irredeemably bestial, cruel to captives and cruel in essence. But other Britons recognised – on the basis of what they read in letters or print – that their own regular troops in America (like French and colonial troops there) sometimes behaved not much differently. British soldiers, too, as private wartime correspondence and the Anglo-American press made abundantly clear, regularly scalped wounded and dying enemies, and were guilty at times of killing women and children, and wallowing in slaughter.[32] So, if Indians were bestial in their conduct of war, then, so, at times, were Britons from both sides of the Atlantic. The increased flow into Britain of information about North America complicated perceptions

Hendrick the Sachem, or Chief of the Mohawks.
Etched from an Original Drawing.
Publish'd according to the Act March 11 1756 by T.Jefferys at Charing Cross.

32 and 33. Different ways of seeing: two British portraits of an Iroquois ally, Hendrick, during the Seven Years War.

The brave old Hendrick the great SACHEM or Chief of the Mohawk Indians one of the Six Nations new in Alliance with Subject to the King of Great Britain.

of Native Americans in another respect. British officials in America regularly reported back to London that Indian violence was frequently the result of provocation on the part of white colonists and their inroads into indigenous lands. As a letter in a London newspaper put it in 1763: 'if we search into the beginning of some of the late Indian wars, we shall find they have taken rise from some of our colonists over-reaching them in their treaties, and getting possession of the hunting and fishing grounds, without which they [the Indians] cannot possibly subsist.'[33]

So, while at one level this war encouraged Britons at home to view Indians as brutal villains, at another it made it easier for the latter to be seen as misunderstood victims. One can see these contradictory impulses in English and Scottish novels published in the aftermath of the war, which gave far more space than before to Indians and Indian captivities. Tobias Smollett's *Expedition of Humphry Clinker*, written in the late 1760s, has the veteran and raconteur, Lieutenant Obadiah Lismahago, at once testifying to comic-strip Indian tortures ('an old lady, with a sharp knife, scooped out one of his eyes, and put a burning coal in the socket'), and recounting his fruitful marriage to a 'squaw'. Indians, Lismahago concludes, 'worship two contending principles; one the fountain of all good, the other the source of evil'. The soldier taken captive in Henry Mackenzie's *Man of the World* (1773) is no less riven. He is cruelly tortured by the Cherokees, but subsequently becomes entranced by their society: 'Scarce any inducement could have tempted me to leave.'[34] But this complex vision of the Indian, at once repelled and admiring, was conveyed most richly – and propagated – by the captivity narratives themselves. Superficially straightforward and ephemeral, they turn out on closer reading, as these sources invariably do, to be anything but.

Consider the narratives – the plural is important – of Peter Williamson. He has been described as 'one of the greatest liars who ever lived', but is much better regarded as someone who repeatedly re-invented himself and his life-story in response to a brief but eventful encounter with Indians, and a longer, enforced encounter with North America.[35] He was born to a family of small farmers in the village of Aboyne, Aberdeenshire, in 1730 and kidnapped by some unscrupulous traders while on a visit to Aberdeen when he was about twelve years old. As happened to many young, poor and unprotected Britons in the seventeenth and eighteenth centuries, he was then shipped across the Atlantic, and sold into indentured servitude. This was Williamson's first experience of captivity. His second occurred in 1754, when he had finished his time in service, and was established as a farmer himself in Berkshire county, Pennsylvania. Early in October that year, his house was raided by Indians, Delawares he claimed, who held on to him until he escaped in January 1755. He was then swept into the colonial forces and the Seven Years War, fighting against the French and their Indian allies, until being captured a final time at Oswego. A Royal Navy vessel shipped him home late in 1756, and it was then that his writing career began.

The initial version of *French and Indian Cruelty exemplified in the life . . . of Peter Williamson* was published a year later in York. From the very beginning, it was a substantial text – over 100 pages – and in some respects conventional enough. There was the usual quota of 'terrible and shocking' Indian cruelties, though Williamson described his reactions to these with a vividness that was not usual. On one of the first nights of his Indian captivity, he wrote, his Delaware captors tied him up, lit a fire, and then brought red hot coals and sticks close to his face. When he wept in terror, they only brought the kindling closer still, 'telling me my face was wet, and that they would dry it for me'. This first version of Williamson's multiple captivities also included enough details to convince me, at least, that he really did live at one stage in close proximity to Native American peoples. There are obvious inventions, and naïve exaggerations designed to inflate his own importance, but there is also a core of close, accurate observation and original insight. He described, for instance, how the Delawares were now dependent on certain Western consumer goods, but systematically worked at adapting them: 'The better sort have shirts of the finest linen they can get, and to those some wear ruffles; but these they never put on till they have painted them of various colours.' It was not these earnest anthropological gobbets however that made *French and Indian Cruelty* a bestseller in Britain for over a century, nor even its tantalising references to 'various and complicated' Indian atrocities.[36] What did was Williamson's genius for gauging changes over time in the British public mood, and for making the leap from narrative to polemic.

These gifts appeared to the full in the extended 1762 edition of his narrative. As the title *French and Indian Cruelty* suggests, from the very beginning Williamson stressed that brutality – like captivity – was not a uniquely Indian practice. He condemned the French for hiring and inciting indigenous mercenaries. He criticised Anglo traders for cheating Indians and selling them alcohol; and he attacked Aberdeen's merchant community for conniving in white slavery and selling vulnerable youths like himself into bondage across the Atlantic. By spreading blame across various national and ethnic groups in this fashion, Williamson effectively liberated the Indians in his text from the usual exceptionalist stereotypes. As he treated them, they were not out-of-the-ordinary monsters, any more than they were romantic, woodland nobles. They were violent, imperfect beings contending against other, different beings who were themselves often violent and imperfect. What Williamson added to this in the 1762 edition of his captivity narrative was political and imperial advocacy. North America's Indians, he now insisted, had been 'treated as a people of whom an advantage might be taken'. Yet unless 'some method' was taken 'to draw them into our interest', Britain's empire here would always remain an unstable one:

> Our late transactions in America testify, that the friendship of the Indians is to be desired, and the only way to maintain a friendly correspondence with them, is by making such propositions to them as will secure their liberties, and be agreeable to their expectations; and not only by keeping these propositions inviolable as well in time of war, but also renewing our treaties with them from time to time . . . They are very proud and love to be esteemed.[37]

French and Indian Cruelty reached, and went on reaching a very wide audience in Britain, though suggestively it was not published in America before independence. By the early 1800s, the text had passed through several London editions, half a dozen Edinburgh editions, and there were separate editions as well – sometimes more than one – issued in York, Dublin, Glasgow, Leith, Liverpool, Stirling, Aberdeen and other towns. If there was a popular British classic about Native Americans in this period, this was certainly it. Yet what did it mean exactly that Peter Williamson chose to write about his captivity and America's indigenous peoples in the ways that he did, and was able to achieve such a wide readership in Britain for so long?

As regards Peter Williamson's own motives, the answer seems clear. To an almost over-determined degree, he was exactly the sort of individual who might have been predicted to view captivity at the hands of non-Europeans in an open-minded and exploratory fashion. He was poor. He was alienated. And he was from the geographical peripheries of Britain, a Northern Scot. As we have seen in the Mediterranean world, and will see again in regard to India, low-status, marginal, and/or alienated whites of Williamson's type frequently did react more flexibly when forced across cultural and political boundaries in this way. Neither Britain nor white colonial America had done Williamson many favours in life, so why not empathise with Native Americans who were also put upon by various whites? By the end of his extraordinary life, by which time he had successively run a coffee-house in Edinburgh (decorated with 'Indian' antiques and costumes), invented agricultural machinery, and set himself up as a publisher, Williamson had persuaded himself that his Delaware captors had actually reared him from childhood, and endowed him with a special wisdom and philosophy.

It was this Native American upbringing, he assured his readers in his last autobiographical work, in 1789, that had made him what he was, a

PETER · WILLIAMSON
In the Dress of a Delaware Indian.

1 Tomohawk.
2 Scalping Knife.
3 Shot Bag.
4 Purse & Belt of Wampum

5 Powder horn.
6 Indian Canoe.
7 Bush Feighting.
8 War Dance.

34. Peter Williamson as a Delaware warrior: frontispiece of the 1762 edition of his narrative.

fully natural man, capable of rising by his own efforts in defiance of European hierarchies. He conceded that 'had I the education of Voltaire, Pope, or Addison', he might have chronicled his experiences in a more polished manner. But his education had been different, and acquired in a distant and less corrupted school:

> The reader will be here asking, what school I was brought up at? I shall only tell them, that the extent of it was upwards of four thousand miles, and the height thereof as high as the heavens, governed by Indians of many nations; and regular education is no where taught among them, but handed down from one generation to another, and their records are kept, marked with tomahawks on the outside of trees, and can be distinguished by themselves for centuries back.

When Williamson was finally laid to rest in Edinburgh in 1799, it was in a costume he had brought back with him from North America (or so he told his family), the moccasins, fringed leggings, blanket and feathered headdress of the Delaware warrior.[38]

Viewed in this way, Peter Williamson was essentially a rebel and an idealist of a distinct but recognisable type. He was not a conscious disciple of Rousseau, a gentleman embracing the forest and the furred while preserving all the while the comforts of his study, but something rawer and more plebeian. Williamson's ultimate heir as far as his own island was concerned would be Archie Belaney (1888–1938), a very ordinary Englishman who emigrated to Canada in 1906, and re-invented himself there as Wa-Sha-Quon-Asin, He-who-flies-by-night, or, as he came universally to be known, 'Grey Owl'. Belaney became an expert trapper and riverman, adopted buckskins and moccasins, and lived with a succession of authentically indigenous women. He also published bestsellers about his idyllic life in the Canadian wilderness, and drew vast crowds to public lectures on both sides of the Atlantic in which he passed on 'Indian' wisdoms (some of them excellent and far ahead of their time) on man's duty to protect wildlife and the environment.[39] Yet, while Williamson was clearly a man of a similar stamp to Belaney, it would be wrong and inadequate to interpret his captivity stories and their remarkable British success merely in this sort of individual, idiosyncratic light. Williamson and his texts should rather be seen as particularly picturesque examples of a much wider recognition in Britain in the wake of the Seven Years War that Native American societies were complex, possessed of valuable qualities as well as evils, and that whites held captive in them might find the experience attractive and even alluring.

It is striking that the best captivity narrative written by a Briton about

North America at this time makes all of these points, even though the author was of a far more assured social status than Williamson, and shared none of his romanticism. John Rutherfurd was born in Yorkshire in 1746, but had Scottish gentry connections. In 1762, he crossed the Atlantic to join a trading consortium set up in Detroit by his uncle, a former British army officer. Once there, Rutherfurd, who was an ambitious, intelligent, self-regarding man, began learning French as well as several Indian languages so as to equip himself to join in the commercial exploitation of Britain's brand new Canadian empire.[40] Then, in May 1763, he agreed to join a party of British army officers mapping the lakes and rivers between Detroit and Michilimackinac, and as a result got caught in the outbreak of Pontiac's rebellion, the extraordinary attempt by a confederation of Native American peoples, Ottawa, Chippewa, Delaware, Kickapoo, Miami, Seneca and more, to drive the British and their settlers back east of the Appalachians.

What followed horrified Rutherfurd while also entangling him, yet he was able throughout to recognise some of the nuances both of his captors' behaviour and his own. Ambushed by Chippewas, some of the British officers in the party resisted and were promptly killed and scalped, including a Captain Charles Robertson, a friend of Rutherfurd's. Robertson's corpse was subsequently hacked apart and its joints roasted over a fire. 'Small pieces' were then put on a stick and offered to Rutherfurd with the spoken inducement that 'Englishmen's flesh was very good to eat'. As he tells it, Rutherfurd succeeded in controlling himself in this crisis; and we can believe this more easily because he freely admits that, at the moment of capture, he froze in terror and made no effort to save either himself or his friends. Still a civilian at this stage, Rutherfurd did not know how to fight, and he did not want to die. So he used his brain, as well as the new languages he had recently acquired. He also drew on the greater reserves of knowledge about Native Americans that the war had allowed Britons like himself to acquire. He recognised that what appeared to be raw cannibalism on the part of his captors, was in fact a 'religious ceremony' of sorts, and that collops of his former friend were being offered him not as a gratuitous atrocity, but as a test. Rutherfurd was a healthy, personable, eighteen-year-old male. What he was being given in fact – apart from the prospect of a singularly grisly meal – was the chance to submit to an ordeal and become in time a Chippewa warrior himself.

Keeping his head, he assured the Indian in charge of him, a man he called Peewash, that:

> I would obey him in everything he desired me, and even in that if he insisted, but that it was very disagreeable to me, and that this was the

only command I would make the least hesitation to obey him in, and begged he would not insist upon it. Thus, by a seeming readiness to obey him I avoided eating the body of my friend; and I believe by showing a desire to please him rather gained upon his affections.

Rutherfurd was subsequently stripped of his British clothes and given a blanket and breech-clout. His head was shaved 'leaving only a small tuft of hair upon the crown and two small locks' which were plaited with silver brooches, and he was instructed how to paint his face. But these were only the externals. He also had to submit to hard labour, cutting wood, planting maize, skinning animals, and doing chores for Peewash's formidable wife. Only when he had shown he was both tractable and useful, did the next stage of his initiation begin. As Rutherfurd describes it (and of course his understanding of what he witnessed will have been limited), there was a feast in which a dog was consumed but he himself was not allowed to eat. Another dog was ritually drowned; and then he and his sponsors visited an Indian burial ground on an island, and every member of the party planted a few grains of maize around the grave of one of Peewash's dead sons. Then Peewash killed a bear, and this time Rutherfurd was allowed to join the feast.

The following dawn, they all returned to sit around the same grave, burnt some of the fat of the bear upon a fire, and Peewash made a long speech 'during which he often pointed to the grave and to me alternately, and at every pause we joined in a sort of chorus':

> This, I was told, was to appease the spirit of the deceased, who might be offended at my being adopted in his place, for he then told me I was as much their son as if I had sucked these breasts (showing me those of his wife), telling me at the same time to look upon the boys [Peewash's three surviving blood sons, Mayance, Quido and Quidabin in Rutherfurd's transliteration] as my brothers, and that my name should be no more Saganash, or Englishman, but Addick, which signified a white elk.[41]

Thus did John Rutherfurd, more Scot than Englishman in fact, come by way of captivity to be ritually re-born – as Peter Williamson had so wistfully yearned to be – as something else entirely, as an Indian, as one of them.

Except that this particular crossing was never consolidated. In August 1763, Rutherfurd managed to escape and promptly joined the 42nd Regiment, the Black Watch, throwing himself into fighting Indians and ultimately rebel Americans. Yet the fact that he was never properly absorbed into Indian society, and unlike Williamson had never wanted to be, made the narrative he wrote the year after his escape more revealing in some respects than not. It meant that he was detached enough to be able to analyse in retrospect the degree to which he had – and had not – been accepted by the Chippewas. Rutherfurd recognised that Peewash and his wife wanted him not out of sentiment primarily, which they could not afford, but for the sake of his labour, and the ransom they might obtain for him if times became desperate. And he was aware that many of the other Chippewas had found his white skin risible for all its paint, and regarded him as an apprentice at best. Few of them called him Addick after his re-naming ceremony, he noted. Instead, they referred to him by Peewash's own name, making clear that he, Rutherfurd, was still a lesser, dependent being, a menial on probation who had yet to prove himself.

Yet for all of Rutherfurd's intelligence, and his determination to prise open while rejecting this Indian interlude in his life (for why else did he abandon trade and join the British army, but to wreak vengeance and demonstrate that his birth identity remained intact?), his text reveals rather more than he wanted. After he has described his initiation ceremony, he ceases to refer to Peewash, his wife and sons by their Chippewa names. Instead, he calls them 'my father', 'my mother' and 'my family'. Despite all his efforts, something ineradicable had happened to Rutherfurd on that lost burial island, which he did not wish to acknowledge but could not entirely shake off. Moreover, his captivity narrative is littered with references to other whites who had come by choice or accident into the orbit of Indian societies and been partly or wholly assimilated. There was Sir Robert Davers, an English baronet no less, who was captured alongside Rutherfurd and killed, but who had previously lived for two years with the Hurons, 'adopting their native dress and manners' in the hope that this would free him from his family's curse of melancholy. There was Ensign Pauli, a British army officer captured in Pontiac's War, who, Rutherfurd recorded, promptly got himself involved in a love relationship with a Chippewa woman. And then there was an unnamed Virginian, who had married an Indian woman, and whom Rutherfurd encountered acting as an interpreter for Pontiac himself. This narrative, in other words, contains ample evidence of hate, violence, and prejudice on both sides of the Anglo-Indian divide. But it also documents how this division still remained permeable to the extent that it was regularly broken through by individuals from different backgrounds.[42]

By the 1760s, this permeability had come to be widely recognised both among agents of the British state, and among Britons in general. During the Seven Years War, as Peter Way remarks, desertions from among the lower ranks of British regiments based in North America to various indigenous communities proved so numerous that any redcoat discovered living alongside Indians and claiming to have been captured, risked being court martialled unless he could somehow prove that he really had been forced to cross the culture line against his will. At every stage of their wartime and post-war advance through the American continent, senior British officers found themselves having to claw back white 'captives', who were often nothing of the kind. Jeffrey Amherst was predictably appalled when he occupied Montreal, and found 'British subjects' living contentedly among the local Indians and coming 'into town in their Indian dresses'.[43] More experienced and relaxed officers simply took the fact that such things happened for granted, and routinely inserted demands that stray whites be returned in any treaty negotiated with Indians. 'That any English who are prisoners, or deserters . . . shall be delivered up immediately' required a British treaty with the Hurons in 1764. Indians should not 'shelter wicked & runaway men', the Creek and Choctaw were reminded the following year, but 'deliver up all deserters, whether blacks or whites'.[44]

In the eyes of most imperial administrators, British soldiers and colonists who lived alongside Native Americans, whether out of choice or as an end-result of captivity, were to be deplored. Such interminglings affronted British national, religious, and racial pride, now much enhanced by successful global war. But, in addition, they compromised imperial stability at a strictly practical level. Britain's army in North America, especially after 1763, was simply too small for its soldiers to be allowed to drift away into wilderness entanglements with impunity. And civilian colonists who became 'white indians' might be just as troublesome. The British did not want (though they often had to put up with it anyway) bands of armed colonists attacking Indian settlements or invading Indian land on the pretext that they were only seeking to recover white captives. Much better if imperial officials could nip these problems in the bud, and recover all 'white Indians' in a systematic fashion by way of treaties and negotiation.

As far as ordinary Britons at home were concerned, however, the much greater awareness, bequeathed to them by the Seven Years War and its writings, that individual whites sometimes *chose* to live with Native Americans and were made welcome by them, proved a revelation. For such conjunctures confirmed that Indians were not simply monstrous others. Some Indians at least were manifestly capable of inspiring intense loyalty and attachment among individual whites, and of feeling affection for them in return. Thoughtful and sentimental Britons pondered what had happened when Colonel Bouquet, a Swiss-born British officer and doughty Indian fighter, had come among the Seneca and Delaware late in 1764 and forced them to yield up their white 'captives'. Some of the white children thus 'liberated' had to be dragged screaming from their

35. *The Indians delivering up the English captives to Colonel Bouquet* by Benjamin West.

adoptive Indian parents, to be reunited with blood parents they no longer recognised, and whose language they no longer spoke. But it was how the Indians involved had themselves reacted to these violent, imperially imposed separations that provoked most comment in Britain:

> The Indians too, as if wholly forgetting their usual savageness, bore a capital part in heightening this most affecting scene. They delivered up their beloved captives with the utmost reluctance; shed torrents of tears

over them, recommended them to the care and protection of the commanding officers.[45]

'*As if wholly forgetting their usual savageness*': these words from an account of Bouquet's mission written by a Pennsylvanian Anglican, and published in London in 1766 by the king's geographer himself, alert us both to an important softening of attitude, and to its limits. In the wake of the Seven Years War, and as suggested by the popularity of works like this and Peter Williamson's narrative, some Britons came to view Native Americans as more sinned against than sinning, and even to regard them as better than Europeans in the sense of being freer, more natural, and more generous even. It was still very rare however for Native Americans to be regarded or represented as rational equals to whites. None the less, the resonance in Britain of ideas and writings of this kind was still significant. For if Indians could indeed 'forget' their savageness and deal in recognisable human sentiment in their relations with captives and others, then here was impressive proof that 'savagery' was not innate, and that the 'savages' themselves were capable of change and improvement. And if Indians could indeed change and improve, then a secure and protected space must surely be found for them in Britain's American empire:

> These qualities in [Indian] savages challenge our just esteem. They should make us charitably consider their barbarities as the effects of wrong education, and false notions of bravery and heroism; while we should look on their virtues as sure marks that nature has made them fit subjects of cultivation as well as us; and that we are called by our superior advantages to yield them all the help we can in this way.[46]

For pragmatic as well as humanitarian reasons, this was a point of view that Britain's post-war imperial establishment was increasingly coming to favour.

The spoils of victory, the toils of insular constraints

For, as was always the case, the captive's story was about much more than individuals. Shifting British attitudes towards captives and captivities – in this case whites in North America and the Native Americans who seized them – were intimately bound up with shifting British attitudes towards, and anxieties about empire, in this case empire in America. The ambivalence so clearly exhibited by Britons in their discussions and imaginings of Native Americans in the wake of the Seven Years War was a function of more thoroughgoing uncertainties about their American empire as a whole. The war had been an unparalleled British success here as elsewhere, but extraordinary victories gave rise almost immediately to new challenges and misgivings.

These were partly a product of British America's now greatly inflated size. After 1763, British dominion stretched formally from the frozen Labrador beaches of the far North to the wetlands of Florida in the South, penetrated inland some 200 miles, and included a much wider range of peoples, religions and culture than before 1756. Even while the war was still being fought, British officials and soldiers newly arrived in North America had been startled by the vast size of the terrain and the heterogeneity of its inhabitants. They had been forced to recognise, as we have seen, the variety and potential danger of Native American peoples, as well as how useful some of them could be as military auxiliaries. Mobilising men to fight in America had also taught the British the scale of its black population, larger as a proportion of the Thirteen Colonies' total number of inhabitants at this time than blacks are as a proportion of the population of the United States now. Britain 'did not look to colour, size, or age provided they are able bodied . . . and know the use of a gun', its commander-in-chief in America informed New Yorkers in 1756, and no other attitude had been feasible given the British authorities' usual desperate need for manpower, and the fact that blacks made up a fifth of this city's population.[47]

Now that the war was won, and Canada, Louisiana, and Florida were part of their empire, British officials in America also had to deal with an accession of substantial numbers of new, non-Anglophone white subjects who were Catholics, not Protestants, as well as with these regions' respective indigenous peoples.[48] Here, then, was one dimension of Britain's postwar imperial challenge. British mainland North America was far bigger than before, and demonstrably far less British. Even the Thirteen Colonies, which had been in existence before the Seven Years War, were now increasingly seen in London as heterogenous in terms of peoples, cultures and interests. The wartime presence of so many British soldiers and officials in the Thirteen Colonies, and the increased flow of information about them, not only made Britons more aware of their non-white populations, but also more sensitive to the degree to which their white colonists here were both similar to, and different from themselves. It is surely suggestive that, after 1763, the British seem regularly to have referred to their white American colonists as 'Americans' – a decade or more before white Americans themselves began habitually doing so. Those white men and women on the other side of the Atlantic who had once been carelessly assumed to be identical to Britons at home, now came to be perceived by many, though not by all Britons, as already distinctive, and potentially different.[49]

And this in turn made another of Britain's post-1763 imperial challenges profoundly troubling. During the war, British imperial officials in the Thirteen Colonies had tried, for military and administrative purposes, to count the number of their white and non-white populations. As they soon discovered, there were now a lot of the former as well as the latter to count. The high fertility levels of successive generations of settler women like Susanna Johnson had helped drive the colonies' white population from some 55,000 in 1650, to 265,000 in 1700, to 1.2 million in 1750. In just a hundred years, Anglo colonists in North America had risen from being a hundredth of *England*'s own current population, to being a fifth of its current population; and, by 1770, the ratio of American colonists to English men and women had shrunk yet again, to a mere one to three.[50] This faster rate of American demographic growth after 1750 was influenced, like so much else, by the Seven Years War. Once the British proved victorious, and French ambitions in the continent came to an end, migration to America from across the Atlantic accelerated. Between 1760 and 1776, some 55,000 Protestant Irish, 40,000 Scots, and 30,000 inhabitants of England and Wales left their homes for America, a territory about which they and their countrymen were now so much better informed. The majority of these transatlantic emigrants, as the politicians in London took trouble to establish, were young men under thirty, the very age and sex cohort upon which the agriculture, industry, army and navy of Britain itself most depended.[51]

What usually lay behind Britain's recurrent panics about its imperial enterprise thus came after 1763 to rankle and provoke enormous anxiety yet again: the smallness of its own size, resources and population. How was Britain, whose population was known to be growing far less quickly than that of its American colonies, to retain authority over the latter in the future? 'In twenty or thirty years', predicted one expert in 1767 (with an expert's usual capacity for getting things wrong) 'there will be as many people in them [the American colonies], if not more, than are in England.' As it was, this same writer warned, Britain's population was 'a very insufficient number to manage and conduct all the affairs of this nation, both at home and abroad; to people and secure all the British dominions'. If large numbers of its young men were to be regularly lost through emigration to the American colonies, how indeed was Britain to maintain its own national prosperity and defend itself in war, never mind keep hold of its vastly extended empire? 'We know, sir', George Grenville had warned the House of Commons even before the war:

that Spain . . . [has] been almost dispeopled, by too much encouraging their people to remove to their settlements in America; and therefore, however useful such settlements may be to this kingdom, this should be a warning to us not to allow them to dispeople their mother country.[52]

Britons' increased tendency after the war to see the American colonists as people who were subtly different from themselves made such concerns still more disturbing. In the past, Britons had felt able to rejoice unstintingly at their American colonists' evident fertility and profusion, viewing this as an automatic accession as well to their own strength and power. Now some Britons felt less confident that the rapidly rising numbers of their colonists across the Atlantic, what Benjamin Franklin called 'the American multiplication table', would always and necessarily redound to their own national and imperial advantage. 'If they should continue to double and double', wrote Samuel Johnson darkly, in a draft pamphlet on the American colonists in 1775, 'their own hemisphere would not contain them.' The prospect was so terrifying that Johnson scratched these lines out of his manuscript before submitting it to the printers.[53]

But what most concerned the authorities in Britain was less the thought of Americans assuming in time an all-powerful, imperial sway of their own – which still seemed very distant – than the strictly practical question of how their white colonists and the other peoples of British mainland North America were to be effectively governed, controlled, and kept tranquil in the immediate future. During the war, British army and civilian officials in North America had come to the conclusion that it was ceaseless settler intrusions into Native American lands that were often responsible for provoking Indian violence. The outbreak of Pontiac's Rising in 1763, in which Britons like John Rutherfurd and Thomas Morris and many others were captured, and large numbers of British troops were killed, further underlined to the men in London just how imperative it was to keep colonial settlers and Native Americans cordoned off from each other, mutually secure from each other, and alike peaceful and obedient to the Crown. It was in the hope of achieving this that the British sought after 1763 – so contentiously as far as their colonists were concerned – to maintain an army of 10,000 British troops in North America. A permanent and sizeable force of regular army troops, London optimistically believed, would be able to hold the line between the rising numbers of land-hungry white colonists, and those angry, eroded and retreating Indian peoples, who were still capable of being immensely dangerous and expensive to subdue.[54]

But since American colonists understandably refused to be taxed in order that they could be better policed, this army of 10,000 British regulars never materialised. By the early 1770s, Britain had fewer than 4500 men in uniform to enforce its rule over the immense expanses of Canada, the Thirteen Colonies, Florida and the western frontier, because its own standing army was as ever limited, and its domestic taxpayers could not and would not subsidise any more men in time of peace.[55] As was so often the case, Britain's own varieties of smallness compromised and qualified its imperial practice and pretensions.

All this said, one should not exaggerate the degree to which British empire in America was under unbearable pressure at this stage, any more than one should over-emphasise the extent of post-war British angst. There were many men and women on both sides of the Atlantic in the 1760s and early '70s who rejoiced unstintingly in the British empire's unprecedented global reach and riches, who continued to regard each other as Protestant brethren and fellow Britons, and who believed that this transatlantic union based on commerce, religion, and a single monarch would and should always be maintained. But there were also other Britons, on both sides of the Atlantic, who were more presciently aware that victory on a previously unimaginable scale in the Seven Years War had brought with it stunning territorial gains, administrative and military burdens, and popular expectations that would be very hard to sustain, and that in North America British imperial power was already coming under extreme strain, and even in some respects retreating.

And this was perhaps the ultimate reason why post-war British reactions and references to Native Americans were sometimes conspicuously sympathetic, and why texts like Peter Williamson's later, nuanced captivity narratives won so much sustained popularity. Paradoxically, but not as paradoxically as it appeared, Britons at home and the retreating indigenous peoples of North America now possessed certain things in common. Just like the British empire, Native Americans faced mounting pressures. And, just as some Britons at home now felt anxious about the size of their population, and threatened by the rising numbers and restlessness of their white colonists in America, so with far more cause did Native Americans. British imperialists and their one-time indigenous victims thus found themselves, in the wake of the Seven Years War, coming sometimes strangely together in the face of a common challenge: those growing ranks of white American colonists who were growing increasingly impatient by now both of the claims of Native Americans, and of the claims of George III, Parliament, and imperial power. In the coming crisis, neither Native Americans nor the British empire would escape.

SEVEN

Revolutions

Mistaken identities

Friday, September 22, 1780: His second captivity is destined to be short.

It is already night when he is rowed ashore, and the trees lining the western banks of the Hudson River are almost as swallowed up in darkness as his own glittering jacket, concealed beneath his cloak. He rides, unseeing and unseen, to the pre-arranged site near Haverstraw, but the encounter goes on for too long. The American, who is perhaps no longer an American, has put him at risk already by refusing to meet on board the British warship moored discreetly down river. Now, he is obliged to thrash out details of pensions, promotions and proper safeguards until suddenly it is dawn. Tense with fatigue, and sensitive to every sudden sound, the unregarding birds, small mammals rustling the undergrowth, a single cannon shot he cannot place, he lets himself be persuaded to ride to a nearby house and shelter there until it is night again. His refuge is within sight, when suddenly, at far too short a distance, he hears the sentry's voice, and understands. He, John André, aide-de-camp of Henry Clinton, His Majesty's commander-in-chief in America, has closed a deal with a leading Revolutionary general called Benedict Arnold, to defect and deliver up West Point to the British. But, in the process, he himself has been drawn across a crucial boundary. For him, the safe house is not safe at all. It is behind American lines.

He does his best: though, by now, his judgement and nerves are under extreme strain. He replaces the gold-embroidered jacket of a senior British staff-officer with a plain, crimson greatcoat lent him by his Loyalist host, stuffs Arnold's secret instructions into the feet of his white, silk stockings, and sets off that Saturday morning to find a road back to New York and his headquarters. Arnold has given him a pass, and since the American's defection is still some days away, this proves sufficient to take him safely past two sets of sentries and into neutral territory once more. It is perhaps the surge of relief he experiences at this point that undoes him. The three Revolutionary militiamen, in homespun, mud-spattered civilian dress, have been combing the woods for deserters from their own ranks, and they are initially as uncertain of the stranger's identity as he is of theirs. True, his accent is distinctive, and his beard stubble and ill-fitting coat seem at odds with his poise and physical arrogance, but these are troubled, makeshift times, and nobody looks or behaves any more in predictable ways. They are alert enough however to parry the man's anxious, supremely ill-judged question. 'Of which party are you?' asks John André. 'Yours', they reply. At which point, he lets himself relax, and tells them he is a British army officer in need of help. With these words, he puts the rope around his neck.

They hanged him as a spy at Tappan, near the boundary between New York state and New Jersey, on 2 October, five hundred American soldiers keeping back the crowds of men, women and children, who wept and moaned and watched as his body swayed for a full half hour before it was cut down. The sentimental mythologies which sprang up almost immediately around André and his fate lasted much longer, especially in the new United States. Throughout the nineteenth century and after, American

36. John André's pen-and-ink self-portrait the day before his execution.

collectors bid against each other for locks of the dead man's hair, for one of the sketches he completed during his final captivity, for chairs he had sat on, and for books he had owned. Any portrait of a young, handsome, but unknown redcoat officer was virtually certain to be relabelled 'Major John André', so his image was perpetually shifting and multiplying.

This American cult around an executed, twenty-nine-year-old British army major was not as odd as it seems. John André had, after all, lost out in every sense. West Point did not surrender in the Revolutionary War, whereas George III's legions in America ultimately did. So to his admirers, André could appear wrong but unfailingly romantic, a useful foil to his nemesis Benedict Arnold who seemed merely repulsive and renegade, the Judas Iscariot of a great revolution. And André himself had been so charming, so different seemingly from the stereotypes of British arrogance and imperial thuggery. Part French, part Swiss, multi-lingual, a keen artist, a keeper of diaries, a devotee – like so many British army officers – of amateur theatricals, he had possessed as well startlingly good looks and a happy, easy manner that enchanted his own sex as well as women. For all that he was decidedly mercantile in background and flamboyantly cosmopolitan in outlook, the stiff, titled upper reaches of the British army parted and gave way before André's personal appeal like a red sea. And on his last day, he did nothing wrong but die. He cheerfully consumed the breakfast George Washington sent him from his own table. He walked to the place of execution arm-in-arm with two young American officers who had become instantly his friends, and bowed to those other, more senior officers who had sentenced him to hang. The sight of the scaffold and the rope made him stumble and look down for a moment (he had hoped to be shot as a soldier), but he made himself recover. The sound of the American drums, he remarked before stepping lightly on the cart that would transport him to eternity, was more musical than he could ever have imagined.[1]

Yet such details, which drew tears from spectators at the time and nourished his posthumous reputation, can obscure what André was and what he believed. Cultivated, glamorous, sensitive and brave he undoubtedly was, but he was also an ambitious, experienced imperial warrior who fought and schemed out of deep patriotic conviction. As he wrote to a British army friend before his execution: 'I could not think an attempt to put an end to a *civil war* . . . a crime.' Just as Washington, for all his chivalry, never doubted that his graceful British captive must hang, so André, for all his pleasantness to his American captors, never doubted for a moment that they and their kind were rebels wantonly disrupting the good governance and interwoven destiny of the transatlantic empire he served. We

Hamilton delin.   Goldar sculp.

— The Unfortunate DEATH of MAJOR ANDRE —
(Adjutant General to the English Army) at Head Quarters in New York, Oct. 2. 1780,
who was found within the American Lines in the character of a Spy.

37. The execution of John André.

must also consider that beneath the impeccable manners lay probably a desire for revenge. For André had been captured before. He had surrendered with hundreds more of his comrades at Fort St John, Canada, in November 1775, and was held for months on parole in Lancaster and Carlisle, small, backwoods settlements in Pennsylvania, where the more republican inhabitants sometimes pelted him in the streets, intercepted his letters, threatened him with jail and worse, and 'meant to humiliate us and exalt themselves'.[2] Here was one context where all of André's charm and accomplishments counted for little. Personally contributing to a coup that would strip the Revolutionaries of West Point, in the same year that had seen them soundly defeated at Charleston and Camden, must have appeared a singularly attractive mode of retribution. And what better way to wipe out memories of his own captive mortifications than to entrap and bring over the line Benedict Arnold, the man chiefly responsible for capturing thousands of British troops at the Battle of Saratoga back in 1777?

In this imperial set-piece drama, as in so many others, issues of captivity played a critical part. As far as the British were concerned, captivities of different kinds proved crucial throughout the American Revolutionary War, for distinctive as well as for more customary reasons. It bears repeating that the British had never succeeded in forging a consensus on how to view their American colonists. For a substantial minority of Britons, the people across the Atlantic were always too distant to arouse much interest at all. And while awareness of North America had certainly increased dramatically in Britain with the onset of the Seven Years War, this had not led to unanimity of response. To some, the white inhabitants of the Thirteen Colonies who had contributed so much to victory after 1756 seemed more than ever extensions of themselves on another shore, fellow Protestants and freedom-loving Britons. But, for others in Britain, white settlers in America were first and foremost colonists, people to be governed benevolently but also firmly, just as other North American groupings – Francophone Canadians or Native Americans – were to be governed.

War between Britain and the one-time Thirteen Colonies after 1775 both stemmed from, and also exacerbated these fundamental disagreements and uncertainties. John André gave himself away and was destroyed, because – when it mattered most – he failed to identify Americans correctly, to distinguish those who were his enemies from those who were his friends. In much the same way, vacillation and division over how to *see* the peoples across the Atlantic meant that Britons in this conflict proved unable either to legitimise their own captive-taking effectively, or to agree among themselves over who was to be considered captive from among their own ranks.

Out of these persistent embarrassments was bred a propaganda and political defeat to match the military one.

Who is to count?

At the most straightforward level, the American War of Independence saw tens of thousands of soldiers and seamen on the British side being taken prisoner. The fundamental reasons for this were the by-now familiar ones: Britain was too small, too under-populated, with too restricted a standing army to conduct successful, large-scale land warfare on imperial or any other territory over a protracted period, unless it enjoyed the active support of very large numbers of the local inhabitants, or other, substantial allies. This point needs stressing because, as Stephen Conway remarks, 'the image of a near invincible British military machine' is often summoned up in relation to this conflict 'consciously or sub-consciously . . . to magnify the achievements of the amateurish Americans'.[3] Witness Mel Gibson's film *The Patriot*, with its ranks of red-coated automata, commanded by glittering, malign British officers, confronting scruffy, ill-supplied but sternly virtuous American citizen soldiers. This is the potent legend of American revolution: the battlefield reality was something else.

To be sure, Britain appeared initially a mighty Goliath set against the Revolutionaries' alert but anorexic David, a supremely aggressive state that had transformed the balance of global power in the Seven Years War: but that had been a very different conflict. The British had fought it with the aid of powerful allies in Europe, crucially Prussia, which effectively tied down substantial sectors of their enemies' armed forces in that continent. As far as North America was concerned, the British had also secured the aid eventually of some 20,000 colonial troops, and extensive civilian support among their colonists as well. Even so, it had still taken them several years to beat back France's much smaller colonial forces and move decisively into Canada.

In 1775, the situation was very different and far more dangerous. The major European powers were either hostile to Britain from the outset, like France, or neutral, like Russia. Many American colonists were openly in arms against it, and far more remained glumly uncommitted; while Britain's own armed forces were not what they had been back in the *annus mirabilis* of 1759, when nothing, it seemed, could stand against them. For reasons of economy, the Royal Navy had been run down after 1763, while in reality, as distinct from on paper, the army at the outbreak of this new war could muster less than 36,000 men. The British government's best chance to contain and crush what it regarded as a rebellion was to do so ruthlessly and rapidly, but in the vital first two years of this American war, London raised fewer than 18,000 extra troops. These numbers can still seem impressive when compared with Washington's forces at this time, but distance and geography also need taking into account. Revolutionary troops were on home ground, though not always among friends. By contrast, almost everything the British army in America consumed, wore or shot with had to be shipped 3000 miles across the ocean, or requisitioned from the local inhabitants, and thereby risk alienating them further.[4]

Then there was the sheer scale of this conflict, which for the British was bigger than any previous war they had ever fought. Americans tend naturally to focus only on what happened in the Thirteen Colonies, the germ of what became a new nation and (eventually) a new empire. But these comprised only half of the twenty-six colonies contained within Britain's Atlantic empire at this time, which also included Canada, Nova Scotia, the Floridas, islands in the Caribbean, and unofficial settlements in the Bay of Honduras and the Mosquito Shore. Most of the inhabitants in *these* regions did not revolt in 1775, but almost all of these territories witnessed battles or skirmishes of some kind; and all of them sucked in British troops and auxiliaries, rendering them vulnerable to capture, disease or death.[5] The situation worsened immeasurably after 1778 when France formally entered the war on the Revolutionaries' side, followed by Spain in 1779 and the Dutch in 1780. This not only amplified the military and – above all – the naval resources available to the Americans, but also ensured that the conflict spread to other continents. Every Dutch, Spanish or French colony, and every British possession in the Mediterranean, Africa and India, now became fair game for fighting, fresh sites for death and capture. By 1780, the land forces at Britain's command exceeded 100,000 men, but the geographical range of the war by this stage had widened to such a degree that less than 30 per cent of these troops were available to fight in North America itself.[6] This seeming Goliath haemorrhaged at every joint.

The scale and nature of this war go some way towards explaining why the number of British captives seized during it was at once very large and peculiarly open to dispute. From the very beginning, significant numbers of British combatants and civilians were captured both on land and at sea. At least 250 troops were seized alongside John André in just the single engagement at Fort St John in November 1775. Two years later, the chief American commissary of prisoners, Elias Boudinot, calculated that the British held almost 6500 American prisoners, but that his side had some 10,000 British troops under various kinds of duress.[7] In 1780, in the wake of the battles of Charleston and Camden, the advantage in terms of prisoners-of-war held swung strongly in favour of the British, but Yorktown, and other, less spectacular defeats, changed this decisively. In May 1782, General Clinton grimly informed the authorities in London that the enemy now controlled some 12,000 British prisoners-of-war 'to our 500'.[8]

Yet such figures were little more than rough estimates of certain categories of prisoner. As the British War Office admitted, at this time, it simply did not possess:

> the means of ascertaining the number of men lost by captivity, having no account of what the whole number of prisoners taken in any one year may be, or of the prisoners that may have been exchanged in the course of it.

The Revolutionary American authorities were even less capable of maintaining precise and comprehensive records of captives taken, in part because British prisoners in America were never concentrated in a few, easily-surveyed detention camps and centres, but were widely, even haphazardly scattered. The 2500-odd British soldiers taken at Saratoga, for instance, were subsequently split up between nine of the one-time Thirteen Colonies, and thirty different settlements.[9] Given this scatter-shot distribution, it was hard for officials, however conscientious they were, to keep track of how many men died or escaped during the course of imprisonment, or of how many changed sides, whether by attaching themselves to the American Continental army or local militias, or by marrying a local woman and melting quietly into the community.

Such prisoner totals as were bandied about were also selective in other ways. Estimates of British captives by army men, like those cited above, usually omitted the thousands of Royal Navy prisoners and British merchant seamen and passengers captured at sea by American privateers. David Sproat, the British Commissary responsible for naval prisoners, claimed after the war that, by 1779, 'British seamen lay (much neglected) . . . in almost every gaol in America', and that he himself had supervised exchanges for over 7700 of them.[10] These men represented only a fraction of the total number of Britons captured at sea during this conflict. Once France, Spain and the Dutch entered the war, their navies and privateer fleets also joined in the work of captive-taking, while American privateers operating in the Atlantic and the Channel became able to unload any British captives they seized in French, Spanish or Dutch ports, instead of having to go to the trouble of sailing home with them. In 1779, Benjamin Franklin claimed that there were now more Britons held as

38. Loyalists rescue a British prisoner of war in America. Conditions were usually much harsher than this.

prisoners-of-war in France, than there were countrymen of his in jail in Britain. This may have been no more than a propaganda ploy, a transparent attempt to encourage British ministers to concentrate their minds on future prisoner exchanges. Or it may have been a well-informed guess on Franklin's part. The British themselves calculated that, by the end of the war, at least 2000 of their seamen were imprisoned in Spain, many of them brought there by American privateers.[11]

It seems likely therefore that, in certain peak years in the American Revolutionary War, the number of British soldiers and naval and merchant seamen held captive was in excess of 20,000, particularly since we need to add to the total number of POWs held in America and Europe, men taken in connected battles in the West Indies, in Latin America, in coastal Africa and – as we shall see in a later chapter – in India. Global war resulted in a global pattern of captivities. Yet neither this, nor the poor quality of contemporary record-keeping, is the main obstacle to reconstructing what captivity in this lost imperial war signified for the British. The more intractable and distinctive challenge has to do with definitions.

Who, in this conflict, is to be included in an estimate of 'British captives'? Whom exactly do we count? History is still written overwhelmingly from the viewpoint of the victors, so most accounts of this war conform to the assertions contained in the Declaration of Independence. This means that, after 1775, the main combatants are customarily labelled either as British and pro-British, or as American and pro-American, as though these were distinct, understood and agreed upon polarities at the time. Yet this imposes a degree of clarity and homogeneity on allegiances in this war, and on individual captives, which was often conspicuously absent.

Consider some of the women involved. In 1775, they made up about an eighth of the personnel clustered in the various British army camps in North America. By the end of war, the proportion of women to soldiers in these units was nearer one to four. Inevitably, in the course of battle or in ambushes while on the march, some of these female camp followers and army wives were seized by Revolutionary troops, just as others were raped and/or killed. Just under a quarter of the 'British' taken prisoners alongside André in Canada in 1775 are known to have been women and children. Hundreds more women were seized after the British surrender at Saratoga. 'Such a sordid set of creatures', wrote one genteel female witness who watched appalled as they tramped past in the wake of their captive menfolk:

> great numbers of women, who seemed to be the beasts of burthen, having a bushel basket on their back, by which they were bent double, the contents seemed to be pots and kettles, various sorts of furniture, children peeping thro' gridirons and other utensils, some very young infants who were born on the road, the women bare feet [sic], cloathed in dirty rags, such effluvia filled the air . . . had they not been smoking at the time, I should have been apprehensive of being contaminated.[12]

Here was a very different face of British armed imperialism. As the war went on, a growing proportion of these women, who were indispensable to the army in terms of the nursing, cooking and laundrywork they provided, were actually American-born. This is why their prominence in British army encampments rose so markedly throughout the duration of the war. Many were refugees who had lost parents, husbands or other providers in the course of the fighting, and attached themselves to a passing British regiment in return for a share of rations and a modicum of shelter and companionship. Some had simply formed close attachments to particular British soldiers while their regiment was encamped nearby, and subsequently joined them on the march, perhaps coming to regard themselves as common-law wives. These armed 'invaders' spoke, after all, the same language as the women themselves, and shared similar customs and cultural references, so 'fraternization with the enemy' was scarcely an adequate description of what was going on here. The question arises then: how are women like this who were taken captive, to be classified? Should they be counted as Britons, like the men they catered to? Or should they be viewed as Americans captured by their own side? Almost certainly, many of those involved would have found neither definition appropriate to the complexities and raw imperatives of their position.

Nor is it easy to categorise some of Britain's male auxiliaries in this war. Like their opponents, the British themselves normally drew a distinction between their own regular forces, and those Hessians and other Germans who were hired to fight alongside them, who made up about a third of 'British' troops in North America by 1778. When a Revolutionary soldier called Joshua Pilsberry made his own head-count of the men who surrendered at Saratoga in October 1777, he, too, was very clear on this point, but also unconsciously eloquent about his own lingering confusions. There were 2242 'British Prisoners' among General Burgoyne's defeated army, he calculated; and, in addition, there were also 2390 'Foreigners'. For Pilsberry, evidently, the British, though incontestably the enemy, were not yet foreign.[13] The British themselves also distinguished between the European troops in their service on the one hand, and their Native American allies on the other. They drew even clearer distinctions, on paper and in their minds, between their various white supporters in America and the black slaves that flocked to their armies in such vast numbers in the Southern colonies. American Loyalists, however, were (and are) much harder to categorise.

Naturally enough, in the eyes of zealous Revolutionaries, Loyalists were traitors aiding and abetting a dangerous enemy, friends of corruption, oppression and unfreedom. In December 1777, Congress ruled that any individuals who voluntarily sided with the British in any way were to be confined and dealt with by their respective states, thereby treating them as criminals rather than as prisoners-of-war, and opening the way for significant numbers of Loyalists to be incarcerated, often for many years, deprived of their property, driven into exile, and in some cases tortured and even lynched. As in France after 1789, revolution in America was propagated at grassroots level in part through vigilantism and varieties of terror. John Maguire, a resident of Lancaster, Pennsylvania, took the risk of hiding some escaping British POWs in his own house, and found himself subsequently 'discovered, imprisoned and is now ruined'. Other men and women fell foul of local Revolutionary committees for uttering the wrong words in the wrong places, or for failing to celebrate the right victories unambiguously enough, or simply because they were suspected or disliked by their neighbours.[14]

Naturally enough, in their own eyes, Loyalists were not traitors at all, but very much the opposite. They viewed themselves as adhering faithfully to the allegiance in which they had been born, and many regarded themselves not merely as British subjects, but quite simply as British. So, once again the question arises: how are men and women of this type to be classified? Certainly, if every North American Loyalist who spent some time in prison or in other forms of confinement between 1775 and 1783 is to be included, the total number of Britons taken captive during this conflict would easily reach 50,000, and perhaps even approach 100,000 souls.

There was a further complexity, a further sense in which the ostensibly clear terms 'American' and 'British' proved slippery and contested in practice. By 1779, some 2000 American Revolutionary POWs were being held in different sites throughout Britain and Ireland, but overwhelmingly on the southern coast of England, most of them men taken at sea by the Royal Navy or by British privateers.[15] This was nothing new in that large numbers of POWs had been confined in Britain before. And it was nothing new either for such men to attract sympathy from the locals. During the Seven Years War – as we have seen – there had been public subscriptions to buy comforts for the thousands of French POWs who were confined in Britain, and after 1775 similar collections were organised to aid these new American prisoners. What *was* novel was the degree of uncertainty about how the latter were to be seen. Allan Ramsay, the Scottish artist, put it in a nutshell when he wrote in 1777 that war with the one-time Thirteen Colonies was neither a dispute with a clearly foreign enemy, nor one with a purely domestic opponent. Instead, he argued, there had 'lately started up to view in America a new class of men, who will be found upon examination to belong to neither of these two classes; who, for that reason, give great perplexity'.[16]

Were these ragged, angry men, confined in different English, Welsh, Scottish and Irish coastal towns, who spoke the same language as the British troops and jailers guarding them, simply enemy POWs? Or were they, too, captive Britons of a kind? Or were they perhaps something else besides? To anti-war Whigs and radicals in Britain, the answer was clear. For them, Revolutionary POWs, whether held in North America or in Britain itself, were martyrs in the cause of liberty, victims of George III's oppression, and above all fellow-Britons. But many other Britons viewed their American captives and opponents more ambivalently and more

39. *The Commissioners Interview with Congress*: a British print of 1778.

accurately. They perceived them as different from former enemies, to be sure, but they remained uncertain as to what these people were, or just how far they were like or unlike themselves.

This was a dilemma that British cartoonists of the time ventilated without being able to resolve. For much of the eighteenth century, American colonists had been represented in British graphic art in the guise of Indians. This was clearly inappropriate after 1775, since Native Americans were progressively Britain's allies in the war. How, then, to represent the 'disloyal' American white? It is striking how often during the Revolutionary War British artists resorted to different kinds of costume to demarcate these people without ever reaching a satisfactory and universally accepted stereotype. So Revolutionary Americans are shown in British wartime prints wearing absurd, ill-fitting uniforms that look like something borrowed out of a particularly cobwebbed attic. Or the revolutionary purity of the governor of Massachusetts, John Hancock, is at once trumpeted and slyly mocked by picturing him in strange, fur-trimmed garments, with bare, muscular legs as against Lord North's foppish brocade, silken hose and Garter ribbon. Or members of Congress are displayed in the shade of a clearly alien palm tree, gazing disapprovingly at the effete, stick-like earl of Carlisle, who unavailingly offers them a peace, their heads and bodies swathed in fashions that are unquestionably their own. Here, in such images, were glimmers of a growing British awareness that some Americans at least were inventing themselves anew. Yet, at the same time, it is suggestive that American difference in these prints remains largely confined to dress, to that which is put on, but can also be taken off again.

The fact that so much of this conflict had to do with issues of identity and allegiance – with how 'Americans' and 'Britons' were to see each other – meant that men and women taken captive in the course of it became invested, more even than was usual, with a significance greater than themselves. It was not simply that the large numbers of captives seized, like the rising toll of deaths, injuries and taxes, marked out over the years just how dangerous and expensive this war was becoming, though this was certainly the case with regard to both of the main protagonists. In this American war, to a unique degree, the question of how captives from the other side were to be seen and treated fed into and focused much wider debates about where the boundaries of nation and empire were to be situated.

In part, this was due to the combatants' shared literary inheritance. Both the British at home, and British colonists in North America, had evolved their own traditions of narrating and wrestling with captivity. The former had become accustomed to employing such narratives to mull over their national and imperial strengths and weaknesses, and the differences and degree of overlap between themselves and various enemies. In this imperial war, however, the significance of captivity tales was a special one, because the main protagonists shared a common language and a common obsession with print. As a result, men and women in Britain were not merely exposed to accounts of their own soldiers' and supporters' experiences of suffering and capture, but frequently as well to accounts written and printed by Americans attacking Britain's role as an aggressor and captor. In these unique circumstances, the business of writing and arguing about captivity became itself an aspect of war and a Revolutionary manoeuvre.

Catching the lion in the net

On 1 June 1781, a man called William Widger had a dream. A semi-literate Revolutionary privateersman from Marblehead, Massachusetts, Widger had been captured by the Royal Navy in 1779 with the rest of the crew of the brig *Phoenix*, brought back to England, and lodged with other American POWs in Mill Prison in Plymouth. As a place of confinement, this was more ramshackle than ruthless, with a low death-rate by the standards of the day, and a high number of escapees, and Widger seems to have experienced little difficulty in keeping and concealing a prison diary. It was in the pages of this that he set down and attempted to make sense of his vision. Transported instantly in sleep across the thousands of miles that separated him from America, he had imagined himself walking again along a familiar road in Marblehead, though – as is often the way with dreams – he had somehow understood even at the time that this was only an illusion, and that he was engaging with shadows. A one-time neighbour named Sylvester Stephens suddenly materialised out of the mists to greet him, and for a while they had seemed to talk:

> I said to him: 'Tis damd hard now I have got so near home and can't git there'. I thought he asked me: 'What the matter was?' I says: 'Why you see I am this side of the way.'

In Widger's dream, the wide Atlantic Ocean narrowed drastically to a single dusty New England street, to one side of which he was bound fast. Unable to reach out and make contact with his place of origin for real, it was as if he could still discern tantalizing images of it. In his grimy Plymouth jail, he seemed 'so near home', and yet was not there.[17]

The Unconscious can select its symbolism with dazzling aptness: and Widger's night-time imaginings caught very well the sense that many POWs on both sides of this conflict seem to have experienced, that they were at once divorced from their familiar surroundings and existence, yet because of the peculiar circumstances of this war, not entirely so. Whether British or American, they had to deal with opponents whose skin colour and clothing was often the same as their own, and who might well speak the same language, worship the same Protestant God, react and think for much of the time in very similar ways. So the imaginary wall that normally descends in war brutally separating one side from the other proved in this one sometimes markedly unstable. Men and women would glance at those who were in name and fact their enemies, and find themselves staring at a mirror.

Virtually every captivity narrative that survives from this war contains such ambiguous and equivocal epiphanies. For Thomas Hughes, English army officer and old Etonian, the moment came in Bennington, Vermont, late in 1777. Captured at Ticonderoga that year, and marched along at gunpoint, he was suddenly crowded around by the town's inhabitants, and recognised in their faces a degree of shock that may have registered too on his own features. They 'appear'd surpris'd', he wrote, 'to find us like themselves'.[18] For John Blatchford, a cabin boy on the Revolutionary vessel *Hancock*, who was captured at sea and brought to Portsmouth, the sense of boundaries between enemies giving way occurred amidst the bric-à-brac of an English parlour. He was ushered in:

> To satisfy the curiosity of some ladies, who had never seen a Yankee, as they called me. I went in, and they seemed greatly surprised to see me look like an Englishman; they said they were sure I was no Yankee, but like themselves.

Charles Herbert, a fellow Revolutionary sailor confined in another English seaport, recorded a very similar exchange in his captivity narrative. In his case, it was some curious Royal Navy seamen's wives who pointed out the obvious. 'What sort of people are they?' these women asked, before catching sight of the American prisoners for the first time. 'Are they white?'

> Upon being pointed to where some of them stood, 'Why!' exclaimed they, 'they look like our people, and they talk English!'[19]

Such moments of mutual recognition, between enemies who spoke and looked the same, must have occurred in this war often enough. Yet some of those describing such encounters in retrospect almost certainly did so with an ulterior purpose. Passages, like the ones quoted above, in which captive Revolutionary warriors brought back to Britain are judged by onlookers there to be 'just like themselves', are often followed in American captivity narratives by an incident or a conversation showing that in fact the reverse was true. Thus Charles Herbert's posthumous and heavily edited narrative follows the account of the British seamen's wives' seeming recognition of American POWs as being 'like our people' with an anecdote making clear that this was not the case at all. Herbert (or his editor) describes how he subsequently got hold of a list of rations kept by his British guards in Forton Prison, marked with the words 'For the Rebel Prisoners'. Herbert – we are told – immediately 'scratched out the word "rebel" and wrote "American"' instead. The captivity ordeal, in this version, muddies Herbert's patriot identity only to proclaim it more vigorously than ever.[20] The hardships of detention on enemy territory serve to reveal what he and his comrades truly are – free and independent Americans – as distinct from what they only appear to be. As this example suggests, writings on captivity in the American Revolutionary War carry a particularly heavy freight of conscious political intent. For both main protagonists, but especially for the Revolutionaries, writing and acting out captivity became an integral part of the war of ideas.

As far as the British were concerned, it appeared imperative from the outset to signal exactly what they viewed captive Americans as being. Not until 1782, when all was lost, would the Westminster Parliament grant these men the formal status of 'prisoners-of-war'. Doing so earlier would have been to concede that they were agents of a sovereign enemy state. Instead, the line officially taken was that American prisoners were 'the King's misguided subjects'. Since Britain was a humane state, the official argument went, these men would not be exposed to the savage penalties conventionally visited on rebels. None the less, rebels was precisely what they were.[21] Other ways were sought to treat Revolutionary captives in such a manner as to deny American claims to independence. General Gage initially refused to accommodate his commissioned American prisoners separately from American private soldiers in order to make clear that he recognised no army ranks approved of by George Washington, only those granted by order of King George III. As more and more British prisoners, including officers, were taken by the Americans and placed at their mercy, this particular piece of gesture politics was abandoned, but language was deployed to make analogous points throughout the war. In 1777, Sir William Howe, then British commander-in-chief in North America, advised an underling how an imminent exchange of prisoners was to be conducted:

One caution I beg leave to add: which is, that neither His Majesty's name on your part, or the Congress on the other, be permitted to appear in any of your transactions, as the agreement must be supposed to subsist between Mr Washington and myself.

Congress's authority over the self-proclaimed United States was not to be formally admitted in British official dealings, any more than was George Washington's right to his army title now that he was leading a rebellion.[22]

From the viewpoint of today, these can easily seem the futile niceties of a bunch of imperial fogeys seriously out of touch with reality. But of course in 1777 neither Howe nor the rest of the world could know that Washington's cause would eventually triumph. What members of the British political and military elites did know, all too well, was that any verbal slip on their part would be gleefully exploited by an enemy that shared the same language and the same delight in printed propaganda. Revolutionary elites were just as concerned not to make any slip that might appear to admit George III's authority over them, and just as calculating about words and gestures. In virtually every exchange of prisoners negotiated, the Americans made use of the formula 'officer for officer, soldier for soldier, citizen for citizen'.[23] Insisting that it was citizens who were being exchanged was one more way of proclaiming that they, as well as the British, possessed their own sovereign state. There were some respects, however, in which American Revolutionaries exploited captivity issues very differently from their British opponents. They were far more unabashed about doing so, and they were infinitely more successful.

One reason for this was Congress's resolution on 10 July 1776 that any cruelties committed by British forces or their allies in North America would be viewed as being done on George III's instructions. This gave Revolutionaries the strongest possible incentive to assemble, broadcast, and, if necessary, manufacture as much evidence of British wartime atrocities as they could possibly manage. There was often plenty of such evidence genuinely available. British as well as American sources make it clear that, on many occasions during this lost imperial war, individual Redcoats raped helpless women, sometimes with their officers' approval, wantonly destroyed civilian property, routinely killed the wounded on the field of battle, arbitrarily imprisoned known and suspected Revolutionary supporters, and sometimes tortured and strung them up.[24] American prisoners-of-war could also run the gauntlet of casual and sometimes deliberate British cruelty. It has become a cliché of patriotic American textbooks that some 11,500 captive Americans were allowed to die in the dank, microbe-infested holds of British prison ships moored in New York harbour: and this number was memorialised in stone when such bones as could be recovered were given formal interment in the city in 1808. In fact, the total number of American POWs who died on these rotting hulks will never be known. The British themselves kept no records; and the figure of 11,500 (11,644 to be precise) seems to have been invented by a New York newspaper in 1783, and to have been faithfully repeated ever since.[25]

But many American prisoners of the British did undoubtedly perish, in New York and elsewhere, of smallpox, of malnutrition, of dysentery, of neglect, of despair, and occasionally of the actions of sadists. There is however an obvious point that is generally forgotten. As is always the case in war, atrocities and sufferings were never the monopoly of one side. Considerable numbers of British soldiers and sailors, together with Loyalist troops and civilians and, still more, pro-British blacks and Native Americans, also found themselves on the receiving end of rape, pillage, torture, arbitrary arrest, lynchings, and casual slaughter; and this side's prisoners-of-war, too, died in very large numbers. For every British villain, like Provost Marshal Cunningham, who – allegedly – embezzled food, fuel and medicines intended for the relief of American POWs in New York, there was a Revolutionary villain like Colonel Henley who – allegedly – used British POWs in Cambridge, Massachusetts, for bayonet practice.[26] For every American Revolutionary sweating and sickening in the dank holds of British prison hulks in New York, there was a captive British naval or merchant seaman sweating and sickening in equally insalubrious American prison ships moored at Boston or off the coast of Connecticut. No one has ever troubled to find out how many of the latter perished while in American hands, but whether offshore or on land the lives of British POWs and Loyalist prisoners seem often to have been nasty, brutish and short. 'The poor wretches under my care are almost all sick and dead', scribbled an (in this case humane) American prison official in 1778.[27] As is the way with conflicts that shade into civil war, the fact that so many of those involved in the Revolutionary War had much in common, usually did less to restrain cruelty than make instances of it even nastier.

Take the case of Captain Joseph Huddy, one of the great Revolutionary *causes célèbres* of the dog-days of war in 1782. Huddy had been a prisoner of the British in New York, but was scheduled to be exchanged along with two of his comrades. Instead, the Loyalist corps appointed to escort the three men to the place of hand-over, stopped on the way, strung Huddy up, and hung a placard around the corpse's neck: 'Up goes Huddy for Philip White', an executed Loyalist. This, understandably, provoked a furious letter from George Washington to the British commander-in-chief, threatening retaliation against British POWs if the murderers of an unarmed American captive were not immediately apprehended and handed over. The papers and testimonies that General Clinton wearily assembled on this case offer depressing evidence not just of one famous atrocity, but of many, now forgotten atrocities. The pro-Revolutionary inhabitants of Monmouth County, where Huddy had been based, testified to his patriot qualities. But Monmouth County Loyalists told, predictably enough, a different story, a story – as the placard around Huddy's stretched and broken neck suggested – of serial outrages followed by bitter retaliation. Huddy and his vigilantes, they claimed, had snatched a local Loyalist from his bed, and hanged him. They had dug up the corpses of other Loyalists from their graves and made sport with them. They had broken a Loyalist captive's legs, put out his eyes, and then bid the man run away. But the most poignant testimony, which Clinton must have tossed aside in disgust, told a different story again. Yes, this Loyalist witness agreed, terrible acts had indeed been committed against his fellow sympathisers in Monmouth County, and the ringleader may have been Huddy. But he was not sure.[28]

If all this sounds drearily familiar, it is. Similar sagas of multiple atrocities, of mistaken identities having lethal consequences, of terrible violence against the helpless on the one side breeding the same against the innocent on the other, are acted out regularly in our own time in a dozen trouble-spots around the world. The American Revolutionary War has been dignified in retrospect because of the ideals associated with it and the good that ultimately emerged from it, but at the time it was just like any other protracted war – filthy, unfair, and indiscriminately deadly for large numbers of combatants and innocent civilians alike. So an obvious question arises. Since suffering and cruelty – like captives – were never the preserve of just one side in this war, why were American Revolutionaries able to make so much better capital out of these things than their opponents? When Thomas Anburey, a British officer who was captured at Saratoga and held for several years in various prison camps in America, published his two-volume captivity narrative in London in 1791, he did so – he wrote in its preface – because he was angry that so many appeared to view 'the favourers of [American] Independence as possessed of every amiable qualification, and those who espoused the rights of the Mother Country, as destitute of common feeling, and humanity itself'.[29] Anburey's exasperation was understandable, but his words were also effectively an admission that Britain had lost not just the Thirteen American colonies, but also the propaganda war.

In part, this was because the Revolutionaries tried harder – since they knew they had to. Right from the beginning, they kept the pressure on. Of course, in virtually every war known to history, each side has routinely accused its opponents of atrocities while claiming superior humanity and morality for itself. This said, however, American Revolutionaries consistently 'emphasized the enemy's cruelty and vindictiveness', especially towards prisoners, 'in a way [that was] altogether unusual in eighteenth-century wars'. They did so at many different levels, but always with an eye to print. Congress passed resolution after resolution condemning real and invented British cruelties, knowing that its words would feature in every sympathetic newspaper in North America and beyond.[30] Any official communication with the British was tailored in the same way. Thus after Yorktown, American treatment of some of the 8000 British prisoners seized there shocked the French auxiliary troops present. None the less, Washington's letter to the hapless Lord Cornwallis, which was broadcast around the world, was utterly uncompromising, referring pointedly to: 'the benevolent treatment of prisoners which is invariably observed by Americans'.[31]

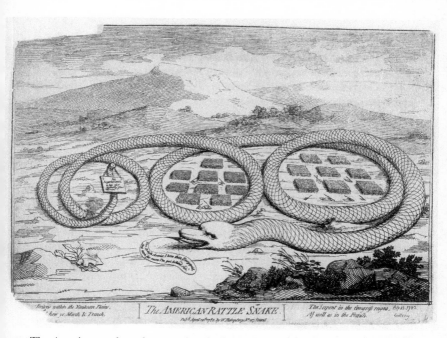

40. The American rattle snake capturing the British in its coils at Saratoga and Yorktown: a brilliant early print by James Gillray.

Along with this careful and calculated use of language by Revolutionary elites, there were hundreds of stories of suffering and captivity at the hands of the British contributed by ordinary men and occasionally women. Thus, in June 1777, the *Boston Gazette* devoted its front page to the tale of Philip Jones, taken captive, shot and bayoneted in the leg, it was claimed, by an arrogant British army colonel. This captivity story – which may or may not have been accurate – was subsequently reprinted in several Connecticut papers. Prison narratives, lists of American POWs, and affidavits from simple people caught and brutalised by the British enemy, became such standard Revolutionary newspaper fare in successive years that James Rivington, editor of the main Loyalist journal, the *New York Gazette*, attempted a spoof. In 1781, he printed a mock advertisement of a new book: *A New and Complete System of Cruelty: Containing a Variety of Modern Improvements in the Art. Embellished with an Elegant Frontispiece representing the Inside of a Prison Ship.* This was mildly amusing: but, again, a tacit acknowledgement that the Revolutionaries had achieved a propaganda walk-over.[32]

The British did sometimes publish their own captivity stories, their own tales of atrocities suffered and of soldiers and supporters brutally confined, but they were hampered in so doing in all kinds of ways. To begin with, they were disadvantaged – in this as in so many other respects – by operating at such a vast distance from their home base and without significant European allies. A Revolutionary soldier, sailor or citizen who was captured or mistreated in North America by the British, or wanted to seem so, was always likely to be within reach of a sympathetic printing press. With far fewer Loyalist papers in America than Revolutionary ones, and with London's print industry 3000 miles away, British and Loyalist victims found it far less easy to get their stories promptly into print.[33] Moreover, tales of Revolutionary captives enjoyed an international currency which equivalent British stories simply could not secure. Benjamin Franklin and other Americans resident in Europe made sure that a steady stream of appropriate material was fed to the French, Spanish, Dutch, and other European press networks. This included the British wartime press, which was far less rigorously censored than newspapers in Revolutionary America. In 1777, for instance, Franklin had an exchange of letters with the British Lord Stormont on the supposed treatment of American POWs in England. Doctored extracts of this correspondence were promptly leaked to the *London Chronicle*, an opposition journal opposed to the war.[34] This incessant print patter of tiny facts – and falsehoods – steadily wore away British resolve and British reputation.

Yet there was far more to the Revolutionaries' advantage than this. Telling tales of captivity catered to American imperatives in this war in ways that simply did not apply as far as the British were concerned. For the latter, complaining in luxuriant detail in print how one-time American colonists had inflicted defeat, imprisonment, and cruelties on their own soldiers, sailors and Loyalist supporters savoured too much of humiliation. 'Every gazette of Europe and America', chortled the anti-war radical John Wilkes to the House of Commons in 1778, 'has published the disgrace of our arms at Saratoga, the ignominious terms of the Convention.' But the British authorities themselves had no desire whatsoever to publish the stories of the thousands of prisoners taken from their army under the terms of the Convention, even though the treatment accorded these men was sometimes very harsh. Indeed, to this day, British historians have yet to investigate the multiple experiences of these prisoners.[35] Such things were simply not supposed to happen to the soldiers of a mighty empire at the hands of its own colonists. For American Revolutionaries, however, it was different. For them – as for Indian and Irish Nationalists much later – captives seized from their ranks were not grim emblems of humiliation, but exemplary figures. The sufferings and confinements of American POWs seemed almost providentially supplied as emblems in miniature of the chains and abuses inflicted on the Thirteen Colonies as a whole by monstrous British villains. For Revolutionaries, in other words, captives were useful, not least because they provided a means to stiffen the line between what was now being invented as America and what was now proclaimed to be foreign.

As we have seen, by its very nature, the American Revolutionary War had been characterised at the start by uncertain identities. The harsh divide between 'Us' and 'Them' that usually obtains in wars was conspicuously lacking in this one, and both main protagonists experienced instead frequent, jarring reminders of what they had in common. For the British, this was a problem throughout, but initially it was also a profound problem for their opponents. As was true in France after 1789, and in Russia after 1917, the outbreak of revolution in America was not remotely the act of a united people, but the work of substantial numbers of activists who had then to persuade and if necessary coerce the rest of their countrymen into thinking like they did. This was bound to be a challenge. Committed Loyalists, it is estimated, comprised at least one fifth of the white population of the one-time Thirteen Colonies, and may have come close at times to making up a third.[36] Moreover, and as the reactions of Joshua Pilsberry to the British captives at Saratoga demonstrated, even among the ranks of the Revolutionaries themselves there were many who found it hard to regard Great Britain unambiguously as a foreign power. This was why Congress and Revolutionary activists devoted so much energy throughout the war to making capital out of captivity stories and other real and invented British atrocities. They needed to construct a firm, unyielding wall between themselves and their opponents, to persuade their own supporters, as well as the uncommitted and as many Loyalists as they could, that the British were cruel *and therefore alien*.

The most famous captivity narrative published during the war illustrates this strategy very clearly. At one level, Ethan Allen was a tough and violent man, a natural democrat and as fiercely independent as only Vermonters can be. Before the war, he had functioned, in the words of one American historian, as 'a frontier ruffian', employing his band of vigilantes, the Green Mountain boys, to enforce supporters' land-claims and drive out rivals in those north-eastern stretches of New York colony that went on to become Vermont. But Allen was also a born actor who understood the potential of words as a means to reinvent himself and to fashion the world anew. As he remarked: 'One story is good till another is told.' When the Revolution came, he duly penned his own kind of story as a means of obliterating the old. Convinced that Canada was destined to form part of what he unabashedly styled 'the American empire', he joined the Revolutionary invasion of it in 1775 and was captured at Montreal. Had the British been prescient, they would either have shot him or let him go. Instead, they held on to him for over two years, sometimes in appalling conditions and sometimes in circumstances that allowed him a remarkable degree of licence.[37] Few such nuances informed Allen's subsequent narrative of his captivity experiences, which went through eight editions in two years, and was extracted in countless American, Continental European and British newspapers, and referred to approvingly in Parliament by Edmund Burke.

Allen's purpose in writing was twofold. He wanted to demonise the British as a 'haughty and cruel nation', and to show simultaneously how superior American virtue could defeat them. He accused Britain's leaders of nothing less than genocide: 'a premeditated and systematical plan . . . to destroy the youths of our land'. American POWs, he insisted, were routinely brutalised, killed outright, or deliberately infected with the smallpox. He, however, had defiantly held his own. Imprisoned for a while in Falmouth, England, he had resolved 'to keep up my spirits and behave in a daring soldier-like manner, that I might exhibit a good example of American fortitude'. He described how he had lectured his hapless guards and any Britons foolish enough to visit him in jail on the principles of the Revolution and on the futility of any attempts to repress it: 'Consider you are but an island! And that your power has been continued longer than the exercise of your humanity.' The bravura was tremendous and the apparent lack of fear or uncertainty was immensely cheering to wavering Revolutionaries and immensely effective.[38]

For political reasons, the British simply could not counter this kind of assault. It was not just that imperial conceit made them more reluctant than their opponents to admit to the thousands of prisoners taken from among their own supporters, and to the atrocities sometimes inflicted on them. Their real problem ran deeper. They could not properly retaliate in kind to Revolutionary atrocity accusations because of the nature of their war aims. Allen and his sort were out to alienate as many Americans as possible from Britain so that they would reject it utterly and commit themselves instead to independence. By contrast, the British military and political elites did not – and could not – want to stir up a thoroughgoing hate campaign against Americans, because their whole purpose in fighting this war was to keep as many of the latter as possible contained within the empire. As was so often the case, the British found themselves hog-tied by the numbers game. They knew, just as well as Allen, that they were 'but an island', and that therefore they could never retain their vast American empire by military means alone. They did not have sufficient manpower; they would never have sufficient manpower. They needed, as always in their imperial projects, the support at some level of substantial numbers of the people they sought to rule.

It was this consideration that sapped the British propaganda effort in this war of much of its potential force, just as it also hobbled their military strategy. British commanders and politicians were never able to make up their minds whether to seek to conciliate and go softly softly with those whom they deemed American rebels, or let loose the dogs of war against them as against any other enemy. By the same token, even on those occasions when the British lashed out in writing or print against their opponents, they often tried simultaneously to win them over. In August 1776, one month after the Declaration of Independence, Howe wrote sternly to Washington about a future exchange of POWs, but ended with a revealing appeal:

> I cannot close this letter without expressing the deepest concern that the unhappy state of the colonies, so different from what I had the honor of experiencing in the course of the last war, deprives me of the pleasure I should otherwise have had in a more personal communication.[39]

Engaged in launching his legions against American Revolutionaries, Howe sought simultaneously to appeal to his and their common cultural and political inheritance. Paradoxically, but not as paradoxically as it seems, he yearned for the Americans to love him and all that he stood for. Increasingly, the Revolutionaries experienced no such inner conflict. They did not care whether the British loved them or no. They did not want their love. They wanted to be free.

Blackening the empire, building empires anew

The bitterness of captivity, then, simultaneously linked the main protagonists in this conflict and drove them further apart. Thousands of American Revolutionaries spent some or all of this war in torment, in limbo, incarcerated; and so, too, did thousands of supporters of the British empire. But it was the former who derived by far the greatest political capital from all of this. The real and rumoured sufferings of confined individuals from among their ranks gave Revolutionaries useful and easily understood metaphors for those wider assaults on liberty they attributed to George

III and his ministers, while accusations of cruelty to captive Americans served to 'other' the British and mobilise support for a new republican nation. Yet while Britain secured far less propaganda advantage from its own individual captive supporters in this war, it remained dogged throughout by its more fundamental and collective brand of confinement, its deficiency of numbers, its irredeemable native smallness. The strategies it adopted in order to address this widened still further the divide between Britain and its former white colonists.

Just how is suggested by the tale of a captive and slaughtered virgin, a war propagandist's dream. In July 1777, Jane McCrea, who was in her early twenties and from Fort Edward, New York, left home under escort bound for Canada and her fiancé, one David Jones, a Loyalist officer who was serving there under Britain's General Burgoyne. What exactly happened on her brutally truncated journey will never be known for sure. According to one version, McCrea's party was ambushed in error by Native Americans in British military service and she was shot. Other sources suggest that it was two Algonquians from amongst the escort party itself who seized the woman, and that she was killed when they quarrelled over who was to take charge of her and of any subsequent ransom. What is rather more certain is that on 'the morning of her intended marriage' (or so Burke mournfully informed the House of Commons), a search party discovered McCrea's scalped and – according to some reports – naked body. After that, mere facts became of no importance whatsoever.[40]

In the ensuing propaganda storm, all that mattered was that an innocent civilian had been killed and mutilated by Indians in British pay. Moreover, McCrea had been from a largely Loyalist family and engaged to another Loyalist fighting manfully in support of the Crown. Her fate, insisted Revolutionary propagandists, offered terrible proof that British inhumanity threatened all of America's inhabitants, irrespective of their politics. Most crucially, McCrea had been a woman, and a white woman. Or as the American General, Horatio Gates, phrased it in a widely distributed public letter to Burgoyne: 'a young lady, lovely to the sight, of virtuous character and amiable disposition'.[41] In John Vanderlyn's painting, completed many years after the event, Jane McCrea is white-skinned to the point of pallor, clothed in blue, the colour of the Virgin's robes, and forced to her knees by two very brown and muscular Indians. One drags her head backwards by the long, unravelling black hair of which she had been naïvely proud. The other seizes her bare, outstretched arm, and raises his tomahawk. The woman's terror and pleas for mercy are plainly ineffectual; and the sinewy menace of her half-naked tormenters, together with the disarray of her own clothing, suggests that death is not the only

The Murder of Jane McCrea by John Vanderlyn.

violation intended for this captive. The Revolutionary press was careful to insist, with what degree of accuracy we do not know, that McCrea's body was found stripped.

At one level, this was another, particularly dramatic example of the highly successful Revolutionary propaganda tactic already touched on: a deliberate linking of British forces and auxiliaries with lurid instances of atrocity so as to de-nature them and make them into a thoroughly foreign enemy:

> Oh cruel savages! What hearts of steel!
> O cruel *Britons*! Who no pity feel!
> Where did they get the knife, the cruel blade?
> From *Britain* it was sent, where it was made.
> The tom'hawk and the murdering knife were sent
> To barb'rous savages for this intent.
> Yes, they were sent, e'en from the *British throne*.

Yet, as these lines by a pedestrian patriot poet suggest, the British were not just 'othered' on this occasion through being associated with acts of cruelty. In this and many other instances, Revolutionaries sought to blacken the British empire by conflating its cause with those who were not white. A great deal of McCrea propaganda not only reported that the Native Americans reputedly responsible were in British pay, but also collapsed the divide between them and the British themselves:

> Some *British* troops, combin'd with *Indian* bands,
> With swords, with knives and tom'hawks in their hands.
> They gave a shout and pass'd along the wood
> Like beasts of prey, in quest of human blood.[42]

New British imperial threat in this version became old Indian threat writ large and in very similar terms.

This idea, as John Adams put it, that George III was nothing less than a 'sceptred savage', that British imperialists were so vicious as no longer authentically to be white, also cropped up in American wartime captivity narratives.[43] John Dodge, whose story was published in Philadelphia in 1779, and reissued the following year, made a point of stressing the friendship and affinity between his British military captors and their indigenous allies: 'those British barbarians, who, on the first yell of the savages, flew to meet and hug them to their breasts'. 'The British', remembered another one-time American captive, '[furnished] the Indians with firearms, ammunition, the tomahawk and scalping-knife, to assist them against the whites of

America.' A similar point was made, indeed, courtesy of the most famous American captivity narrative of them all, Mary Rowlandson's. Her story, *The Sovereignty and Goodness of God*, that other tale of a lone white woman grievously beset by Indians, had been out of print in North America between 1720 and 1770. But in the 1770s, the decade of the Revolution, Rowlandson's story went through seven different American editions, some of which contained markedly novel illustrations. Traditionally, and if illustrated at all, Rowlandson's tale had been accompanied by an image of Indians surrounding and setting fire to her vulnerable cabin, reducing her and her neighbours to stark terror. In the 1770s, this familiar representational style shifted. Instead, Rowlandson was re-imagined as a plucky lady armed with a gun defending her home against lines of identical stick men who appeared to be wearing uniform jackets. Redcoats (and was this not perhaps an interesting choice of insult by American Revolutionaries?) were now being rendered stand-ins for those indigenous peoples who, by this time, were increasingly referred to as red-skinned.[44]

Nor was this all. To reinforce the argument that the British were so 'othered' by their misdeeds as no longer to be regarded as civilised and therefore white, some Revolutionary writers linked them with blacks as well as with Native Americans. The circumstances of the war made this very easy to do. Ebenezer Fletcher, who fought in the Continental army and was captured at Ticonderoga in 1777, dwelt on the poly-ethnic quality of the British army camp in which he was confined at one stage. 'Indians often came and abused us with their language,' he wrote, and what was worse: 'An old negro came and took my fife, which I considered as the greatest insult I had received while with the enemy.' The encounter with the imperial forces experienced by Benjamin Gilbert, a Quaker captured by pro-British Indians in 1780, was even more rich and strange. Taken under guard to Canada, he encountered there French guerrillas fighting on behalf of George III, pro-British Mohawks whom he rather admired, and various blacks:

These negroes had escaped from confinement, and were on their way to Niagara, when first discovered by the Indians. Being challenged by them, [they] answered '*They were for the King*', upon which they immediately received them into protection.[45]

They were for the King. As this suggests, the stereotypical view of British forces in the American Revolutionary War – homogeneous phalanxes of white, disciplined males in scarlet coats – is markedly inadequate. British army units in North America after 1775 sucked in Loyalists from different backgrounds and in a medley of uniforms, large numbers of Germans and other European immigrants, and a great many accompanying women. In addition, and of necessity, they operated over the years in alliance with substantial though always shifting numbers of people who were not white. To a degree, this was also true of their opponents. At least 5000 free blacks are known to have fought in the Revolutionary ranks, as did some indigenous warriors, like the Stockbridge Indians of Massachusetts.[46] But there was no comparison between the two sides in point of numbers of non-white auxiliaries. Initially, many Native Americans tried to remain neutral, but as Colin Calloway writes: 'in time and in general, most Indian peoples' who did commit themselves to fighting 'came round to siding with the British'. As for blacks, perhaps as many as 25,000 slaves in South Carolina fled their owners to seek refuge with British armies during the war. So did three-quarters of Georgia's black population and, if Thomas Jefferson was right, 30,000 slaves from Virginia, including many of his own. Blacks in the more northerly states often moved in the same partisan direction.[47]

In so far as the British exercised any control over all this, the immediate reason for their seeking out and accepting such conspicuously large numbers of non-white auxiliaries was straightforward enough: as ever, they had little choice. One of their propagandists wearily spelt it out:

> So small is the ordinary establishment of the British army, that there has never been a war . . . within the memory of us or our fathers, where foreign troops have not been employed.

Small was not beautiful. As far as imperial power under pressure was concerned, small was always desperate. The British had no choice but to mobilise support in America promiscuously: 'Since force is become necessary . . . it would make little difference, whether the instrument be a German or a Calmuck, a Russian or a Mohawk.' Yet, by so reasoning, by fighting in collusion with and in proximity to so many Native Americans and black slaves on the run, the British also made it easier for white American Revolutionaries to represent them as altogether alien in tendency, as un-white. Thus the McCrea incident was a propaganda disaster not simply because a young, helpless Loyalist female was (apparently) killed by Indians in British pay, but also because General Burgoyne was unable to take drastic retaliatory action against those responsible. All he could do was insist, probably correctly, that there had been 'no premeditated barbarity' on the part of the Indians involved.[48] But he was in no position to execute the supposed culprits, as Revolutionary propagandists demanded, even had he wanted to, because he desperately needed to retain the support of his Native American allies. As was so often the case, their own manpower limits – that fundamental captivity that never let them go – compelled the British into a kind of military multi-culturalism.

Yet, by itself, this is an insufficient explanation for the marked diversity of 'British' ranks in this war, because it tells us nothing about the motives of those Native Americans and free and unfree blacks who aligned themselves, for a time, with the forces of empire. Ideas and commitment in this conflict were never the monopoly of whites, any more than they were the exclusive preserve of Whigs. For some blacks, as for some Native Americans, joining the British after 1775 represented more than just a response to presents, bribes and varieties of coercion, and also more than simply a matter of not having anywhere else to go. Some made the choice, as Benjamin Gilbert's black guards did, to fight 'for the King'. Why?

We can dismiss right away any notion that the bulk of British-born officials and military men operating in North America were any less racist, in the modern sense of the term, than the majority of white American colonists who resisted their rule. Clearly they were not. As Thomas Jefferson trenchantly pointed out, it was at one level grossly hypocritical for a British imperialist like Lord Dunmore to proclaim 'Liberty to Slaves' in the American South, as he did in 1775, when it had been British slave-traders who had been responsible for shipping the majority of blacks into servitude there in the first place.[49] By the same token, Britain left its black and indigenous wartime allies in North America entirely out of the peace terms it negotiated with white Americans and with fellow European powers in 1783, though it did provide a post-war refuge for some of these now desperately exposed peoples in Canada, Africa, and elsewhere.

Admitting the evident limits of the British imperial authorities' solicitude for subaltern peoples in this case, however, only makes the original question the more pressing. Britain's own military and demographic reasons for seeking non-white support in the American Revolutionary War are clear enough, but why were its forces able to secure such support so abundantly if, in the end, unavailingly? Answering this takes us again to the very heart of this conflict which, as John André discovered, was always about different and shifting constructions of identity.

Behind all the many and different motives for Britain and its white colonists in America going to war after 1775 were two rival interpretations of what the empire involved. The interpretation favoured by most of those opting for Revolution, and by most of their supporters within Britain itself, was that the transatlantic empire was in essence no less – and no more – than 'two branches of the British nation' as Edmund Burke called it. Those holding this view believed that white British colonists in North America should enjoy the same rights, freedoms and privileges as Britons claimed at home (without however paying the same taxes). They also expected London to give them clearly preferential treatment to that bestowed on any other peoples in imperial North America, be they French Canadians, or Native Americans, or blacks. Hence the fury of James Otis, a Boston lawyer, when he discovered that, in the minds of some in Britain, all the inhabitants of imperial North America seemed much the same. The colonies, he wrote in 1764, were not settled 'as the common people of England foolishly imagine with a compound mongrel mixture of English, Indian and Negro, but with freeborn British white subjects'.[50] Implicit in Otis's words was an assumption that the only people who really mattered in America were its Anglo population and that other groupings were and should remain politically invisible. White, Protestant, Anglo-American colonists did not want to be first among equals. They wanted to be special, fellow and equal Britons on another shore.

For their own reasons, the British imperial authorities could not take such an exclusionist view. As we have seen, over the eighteenth century, and especially after the 1750s, they had evolved a more hybrid construction of their American empire. The growing scale and range of their conquests throughout the world forced this shift of policy and perception on them, but so too did considerations of self-interest and self-preservation. Britain's governing elites recognised, all too well, their state's territorial and demographic limits and the constraints on power and reach that followed from this. Consequently, absolutely to privilege and give free rein to its own fast-multiplying and persistently expanding British settlers in North America appeared unwise, possibly dangerous, and – to some in London – unjust. Far better to play the standard imperial game of divide and rule. Far better to extend a measure of protection and rewards to all the various different groupings in British North America, so that they might remain loyal and continue to coexist and balance each other. Hence London's attempt to seal off the American West from land-hungry white settlers after 1763 and so offer some protection to Native Americans, and hence the Quebec Act extending the legal privileges and territorial range of predominantly Catholic and Francophone Canada in 1774. To London, these initiatives represented both a pragmatic recognition of the diversity contained within its now vast American empire, and also a means of guarding against one particular set of potentially over-mighty subjects. To those American colonists who viewed themselves as fellow Britons, however, such policies savoured of betrayal.

It is against this background that we need to position those thousands of non-Anglos who chose to throw in their lot with the British empire after 1775. Only royal government, a British imperial agent had told the Creeks and Cherokee on the eve of the Revolution, could preserve Indian lands from acquisitive colonial frontiersmen; and many Native Americans decided that he and his kind were right, for what other options did they have? As for black slaves in America's South, the happy idea that Britain might – just – confer on them freedom as well as small-time favours, seems to have been nourished by news of the so-called Somerset legal decision in London in 1772. This was widely interpreted, on both sides of the Atlantic, as affirming that slavery was illegal on British soil. Hence, one historian writes, with some exaggeration, the 'almost universal belief in slave society that a British victory' in the Revolutionary war would lead to 'the eradication of slavery in America'.[51]

In other words, blacks and Native Americans sided with Britain in this conflict not just for the sake of bribes or because there appeared to be little alternative, but in some cases out of a measure of hope, realistic or no. Nor was it just blacks and Indians who decided that rule from distant

2. Strangely-dressed American revolutionaries trample on a black: a British print of 1778.

A VIEW IN AMERICA IN 1778

235

London woud be better for their sectional interests than a new independent America dominated by a highly self-conscious, fast-multiplying white Protestant majority. So, too – for broadly similar reasons – did other nervous minority groupings. Dutch and German immigrants who spoke only their cradle tongue and not English, French-speaking Huguenots in New Rochelle, Gaelic-speaking Highland Scottish settlers: all of these people, almost without exception, opted staunchly for the Loyalist side after 1775.[52] In many ways, support for Britain in the American Revolution was made up of a coalition of different minorities. This was one reason why it lost, but it was also one more demonstration of how empire, so often assumed now to be *necessarily* racist in operation and ethos, could sometimes be conspicuously poly-ethnic in quality and policy, because it had to be.

Many of these poly-ethnic American-based supporters of the British empire refused to hang around and risk the consequences of defeat. The number of people who fled the new United States after 1782, for Canada, for Britain, for the West Indies, and in some cases for Africa, was five times greater than the number of men and women who abandoned France after its revolution in 1789. As far as the miscellaneous whites involved in this exodus were concerned, such trepidation proved quite needless. For people like them, the new America would come to offer a degree of egalitarianism and opportunity that no other society in the world could or can match. Yet for a long time this wonderful, unprecedented American abundance would be paid for by others. Incomparably free and conspicuously idealistic, the new United States would also be firmly exclusionist and aggressively expansionist, an empire indeed, as Revolutionaries like Ethan Allen had prophesied. The fact that so many blacks and so many Native Americans had sided with the British during the Revolutionary war only made it easier for the new Republic to define citizenship in a way that excluded both of these groups completely.

The half-century after the American Revolution would be a critical era for empire globally, with massive transformations occurring in all of the major European maritime imperial powers, France, Spain, Portugal, Holland, and above all Britain. This self-same period – the 1780s to the 1830s – would also be a seminal era for land-based, contiguous empires. Some, like China and Ottoman Turkey, would weaken desperately; others, like the Russian empire, and the new American empire would be immeasurably strengthened. What he wanted, Thomas Jefferson would remark with regard to America's indigenous inhabitants, was 'the termination of their history', by which he meant an end to Native American land-holding patterns and migratory customs, so that successive generations of white farmers and families could migrate triumphantly ever westwards. And so in time it came to pass.[53]

For the British, the imperial consequences of the lost Revolutionary War were both traumatic and formative. What was involved was not a 'Fall of the First British Empire' (a truly Americo-centric coinage) because the empire had always been bigger than the Thirteen Colonies. Defeat in this war was rather a matter of bitter humiliation and of persistent anxieties being – apparently – proved right. Those who had argued that Britain was simply too small to sustain a substantial overseas empire successfully had, it seemed, been amply vindicated. And to a degree, this was a lesson that the British never forgot. Never again would they attempt to tax a major overseas colony directly from Westminster. Never again would they risk a really protracted full-scale war on several fronts – as distinct from long guerrilla campaigns – in the desperate hope of keeping hold of a segment of their empire determined to be free. To this extent, one might even argue that successful American Revolution in the eighteenth century helps to explain why the British submitted to such rapid decolonisation in the twentieth century. They had been taught by bitter experience to recognise their logistical and warlike limits.

In other respects, too, the American Revolution offered lessons on the strains and pains of empire. It showed the men in London, what Australia and New Zealand would only confirm in the nineteenth century: the extreme difficulties involved in an imperial power like Britain holding a balance between its land-hungry white settlers on the one hand, and halfway decent treatment of indigenous peoples on the other. The Revolution also illustrated the perils that empire could represent to national identity. In this conflict, for all sorts of reasons, the British had found themselves divided, their customary solidarities compromised, while their opponents had proved able to forge a much clearer sense of purpose and mission. The only way for the British to compensate for their smallness on the global stage was to be conspicuously coherent. In this imperial conflict, national and political coherence at home had faltered with disastrous consequences.

Yet for a while all these various failures would be recovered from to an astonishing degree, and so would the persistent fear of overseas disaster and embarrassments, of being too small to accomplish and consolidate great things. It was in 1821 that a British mission arrived at the site on the boundary between New York and New Jersey where some forty years earlier John André's body had been hurriedly buried. Excavating the remains so as to carry them back to his empty tomb at Westminster Abbey proved more difficult than was anticipated. André's skull had come apart from his fractured neck joints, and the roots of a nearby peach tree had wound themselves around it 'like a net'.[54] The small and subdued gathering of army men and officials staring down at this sad relic of imperial failure and ultimate confinement were not unduly dismayed however, for by now Britain's empire was growing at a more spectacular rate than ever before, albeit in different directions. And in this new imperial incarnation, the British would succeed in resolving the challenges of different kinds of captivity for much longer than their past experiences in the Mediterranean and America had given them any right to expect. It is time to turn east, and examine India.

Part Three

INDIA
Captives and Conquest

EIGHT

Another Passage to India

Sarah's story

London, 1801. It is barely twenty years since the hanging of Major John André, but the men sitting listening in this quiet backstreet room inhabit a world that is already utterly changed from his, and they know it. The speaker before them is as hardened a military and imperial actor as André was himself, but in more than just the obvious respect is otherwise a very different human being. We are in another country, and besides, this wench is determined to stay alive. Her name is Sarah Shade, and the story she tells is of India. Life has taught her how to read, and how to speak several languages, but not how to write, so her tale has to be reconstructed solely from memory. Accordingly, she stumbles over dates and the precise ordering of events; but she cannot afford to falter or give up. This is a year of high food prices and unemployment in Britain, as well as global war, so it is vital that she secures the attention and aid of these cautious, charitable gentlemen. All too familiar with tales of misery from the labouring poor, and wary of fraudsters seeking to extract money, the directors of the benevolent foundation are fortunately able to recognise gold when they hear it. Sarah's experiences are teased out from her at length, polished and amended as seems fit, and then published as a pamphlet in the hope that it will sell well enough to provide for her and her latest husband. This is the genesis of the first, reasonably authentic account by an English working-class woman of what it was like to attempt conquest in India and to be captured there.[1]

This is not the kind of text, or the sort of individual, with which conventional imperial histories – or even post-colonial histories – normally concern themselves. Looked at superficially, Shade seems indeed a purely idiosyncratic figure, inevitably marginalised in the broader scheme of things by virtue of her gender as well as her poverty. A worker for British imperial power in India, and therefore not even a conventional victim, she none the less possessed in her own right no power, no glamour, and no capacity for heroic endeavour; and may even have been unaware of the wider significance of the events in which she was caught up. The word 'empire' does not figure at all in the *Narrative of the Life of Sarah Shade*. Yet, for all this, Shade and her story are representative and repay close attention.

She herself was representative in that most Britons who worked in India from the 1740s to the winning of Independence in 1947, were in some respects exactly like her: lower-class and attached to the army. And – for all the peculiarities of its transmission – the tale she told derived from and draws attention to a major shift in British national mood and imperial direction at this time. Shade was not the first plebeian Englishwoman to testify in print to Indian adventures. The credit for that belongs to a Hannah Snell, whose ghost-written memoir *The Female Soldier* was a runaway publishing success in 1750. As her publisher told it, Snell had adopted male costume after being deserted by her husband. She joined the British army as a marine, and by 1748 was in an East India Company fort on India's southern (Coromandel) coast, subsequently taking part in a British assault on the French stronghold of Pondicherry. Wounded in the groin – where else? – Snell was none the less able to keep her identity secret until the regiment's return to England allowed her to dictate her tale at leisure. At the time, it seems to have been widely believed. Chelsea Hospital even awarded her an out-pension as a wounded veteran of imperial warfare. Yet it remains doubtful whether Snell's published Indian adventure contains more than a kernel of accuracy.[2] Certainly, reading it side by side with the *Narrative of the Life of Sarah Shade* is to experience an immediate sense both of disparity and of rapid change over time. It is not just that Hannah Snell's tale is probably bogus in the main, while the details of Sarah Shade's Indian life can be substantially verified in the archives.[3] These two accounts of semi-literate, impoverished women were also separated by a period of fifty years during which the pattern of global empire and of Britain's relations with India underwent a revolution.

In *The Female Soldier*, the Indian subcontinent, and the small European forces contending in the 1740s for a place on its southern shores, are little more than an exotic backdrop to a traditional tale of a bold, lower-class female driven into adventure and transvestism by lost love. Composed half a century later, Shade's narrative is utterly different. Her text is saturated with allusions to more than twenty years' exposure to southern India and Bengal. There are references to Indian cuisine, wild-life, scenery, shipping, languages, and Anglo-Indian sexual relations; and there are Indian place-names galore that Shade seems to have pronounced with facility to her cold, London auditors, and they have sometimes mistranscribed. Back in 1750, Hannah Snell's publishers had relied on episodes of cross-dressing and female transgression to sell her story. But for the men writing down

HANNAH SNELL,
the Female Soldier,
Who went by the Name of James Gray.

43. Hannah Snell as imperial warrior.

Sarah Shade's tale in 1801, it was its information on India that mattered, and understandably so. Now that the richest and oldest sector of Britain's empire in North America had broken away, political and public attention was shifting ever more markedly towards the Indian subcontinent. In the words of William Pitt the Younger, prime minister at the time that Shade's adventures were published: India's importance for the British 'had increased in proportion to the losses sustained by the dismemberment of other great possessions'.[4]

Sarah Shade and the story she related, then, emerged from and appealed to a sharper British awareness of India and appetite for it. Shade also typified the quality of British imperialism at this stage in a more intimate fashion. Not just her published story, but even her own body was a text of empire. While in India, she had been wounded twice in the face. A musket ball had passed through the calf of her right leg; and a sabre had slashed her right arm: 'the marks of which wounds are visible upon her'. Nor was this all. Shade had been scarred as well by powerful claws. She bore the marks of the tiger. She was thus, in her own riven and spoilt flesh, a fit representative of an extraordinarily violent phase of British overseas activity, both in India, and in every continent of the world. The geographical scope of warfare, and the rate at which Britain gained and lost territory in the course of it, had been increasing since the 1750s. From the 1780s, though, the global span of violence became even more pronounced, the stakes became higher, and the possible penalties for losing much greater. In the American Revolution, Spain, the Dutch, and above all France, had intervened to strip Britain of its Thirteen Colonies, and of other territory in the Caribbean, the Mediterranean, and Africa. By the time Sarah Shade dictated her story, at the start of the nineteenth century, Britain and France were caught up in a still bigger conflict that started formally in 1793 and lasted with scarcely a break until 1815. For much of this time, the British were at risk not merely of losing the war, but also of being invaded by Napoleon Bonaparte's numerically superior armies, and deprived of some or all of their overseas territories, a point often forgotten in conventional accounts of the relentless 'rise' of British empire. Britain, judged an experienced army officer in 1810, was 'menaced with destruction by a much superior force', and its 'empire of the seas' was unlikely to last for very much longer. Even now, the British had no way of knowing that unmatched global dominion would briefly be theirs.[5]

British aggression and expansion in India were bound up with the escalation in global warfare after the 1750s, but they also partook of this period's extreme uncertainty, anxiety and conspicuous vicissitudes. At the time, the 'swing to the east', as this shift towards India is often styled, seemed a far more close run and nervous thing than it came to appear in comfortable retrospect. How could it have been otherwise, given the besetting British dilemma: an excess of overseas ambition married to a serious deficiency of domestic size? In the context of India's geographical scale and its vast, indigenous population, Britain's smallness appeared particularly painful and exposed. The challenge for the latter, as always, was to find or manufacture ways around this: and doing so was difficult and fraught with risk. Sarah's mutilated body, like her narrative, evokes the high levels of violence and fear that swept over large parts of the subcontinent and its peoples at this time, and that also sometimes daunted and engulfed the British themselves.

Accompanying this woman on her strange but not atypical passage to and through India is, then, a way of exploring the quality of early British imperial activism in a place that always seemed too large, too crammed with life. It is a means, too, of establishing the essential background to British captivity panics in the subcontinent. Sarah's is a tale of the sea and of the East India Company, and of the constraints and collusions imposed by woefully limited British numbers. It is a tale of aggression and desperate improvisations, and – in the end – a tale of tigers.

Limits

As many of her compatriots would do, Sarah embarked for India because of very limited options at home and in the hope of making her fortune or at least making out. Born to an artisan family in Herefordshire in 1746, and christened Sarah Wall, she was orphaned in her early teens. By her own account, she then 'led the life of a slave' as an agricultural servant, before escaping to work in a button-manufacturer's in Birmingham. It was there that her stepfather, John Bolton, who may also have been her lover, caught up with her and made his proposal. 'Having lost her parents', he told her, 'and being, in short, very comely withal, she would do well to proceed [with him] to India'. And so they did.

It was on 20 January 1769 that they set sail for Madras on the three-decker East Indiaman, the *New Devonshire*. Its log-book, immaculately kept by Captain Matthew Hoare, confirms their embarkation at London, and shows that Sarah masqueraded for the trip as John Bolton's wife.[6] East India Company ships' logs of this sort are rich, still under-used sources that convey very powerfully the range, industry and audacity of 'the grandest society of merchants in the universe'. They document the intricacy of these ships' loading, the co-ordination, book-keeping and organisation required to stock a massive vessel like the *New Devonshire*, over several weeks and from different London dockyards, with the cargo, cannon, gunpowder, army and navy recruits, livestock and provisions needed for a protracted voyage in often dangerous waters. They demonstrate, too, the level of skill and hardship that was involved in navigating these heavily loaded, complex vessels from Britain to India and then on to China, a trip that in the 1760s still lasted close to a year, and for which an ordinary seaman got paid just £22.[7]

British marine artists loved painting East Indiamen. Obvious emblems of national reach and riches, they are represented in literally hundreds of canvases, sailing low in the water as they bring their precious commodities home, or setting out in convoy to keep privateers at bay, their red and white striped Company flags (which must surely have influenced the design of the Stars and Stripes), snapping and fluttering as the huge, drenched sails catch the breeze. Yet, looked at from another angle, these images convey not simply Britain's maritime and commercial reach, but also the quality and the limits of its power. The British delighted in pictures of the sea because – for two centuries or so – their merchant and naval vessels predominated there. Like the Dutch, however, they also relished marine art, because the sea afforded them a global ubiquity that compensated, but never entirely made up for, the restrictions inherent in their own constricted geography and demographic size. By means of the sea and ships, these puny people could and did go everywhere. Ships cannot operate on dry land, however; so after landfall things for the British were always very different, and usually far more difficult. This was emphatically the case as far as the East India Company was concerned.

The Company had been founded by a charter from Elizabeth I in 1600 and granted a monopoly on English trade with Asia. At this stage, neither the Crown, nor the Company's governor and twenty-four London-based directors, were in a position seriously to envisage an eastern empire. They aimed rather at making the English effective bit-players in one of the richest, most advanced, and most competitive manufacturing and commercial sectors in the world. The eight or so ships that the Company sent out every year during the first century of its existence concentrated initially on aromatic spices from the Indonesian archipelago, the cloves, nutmeg, pepper, cinnamon bark and cardamon that made unrefrigerated food and unwashed bodies more tolerable. But, by the second half of the seventeenth century, the Company had begun its work of transforming English lifestyles and consumer habits, importing an expanding range of fine Indian textiles, as well as coffee from Mokha in Yemen, and tea and porcelain from China. As far as the Indian subcontinent was concerned, the

44. English East Indiaman, by Paul Monamy, *c.* 1720.

Company came to operate out of three main coastal bases. The oldest and most southerly was Madras (now Chennai), established in 1639 and with an Indian population by 1700 of some 100,000 souls. On the western coastline was Bombay, acquired in 1661 along with Tangier as part of Catherine of Braganza's dowry. And to the north-east was Calcutta, founded in 1690 to take advantage of Bengal's expert weavers and trade along the Ganges and Jumna rivers. By way of this magic triangle – Madras, Bombay and Calcutta – the East India Company gradually became Britain's single biggest commercial enterprise, and secured a greater share of India's export business than the rival Dutch, Danish, Portuguese and French trading companies.[8]

But it continued for a long time to view its role and rationale mainly in private and commercial terms. Again, this is a point that can be made effectively through contemporary art. In 1731, the Company's directors commissioned George Lambert and Samuel Scott to paint six canvases for the walls of its newly-rebuilt headquarters in Leadenhall Street, London. The resulting works convey very well the Company's restricted image of itself at this time, and the limitations too of its vision of India. Two of the six Company bases chosen for commemoration were actually situated outside the subcontinent, on the Cape of South Africa (then under Dutch control), and at St Helena in the south Atlantic. As this suggests, at this stage, the Company saw itself as an intercontinental trader, rather than as having a unique commitment to India. Even the four Indian locations selected – Bombay, Madras, Calcutta, and Tellicherry on the Malabar coast – were represented from the perspective of the sea, from without. To be sure, Scott and Lambert were careful to foreground the incontestable sources of the Company's reach and power. Here, in their canvases, are the great masted East Indiamen, cannons booming, pennants flying, lying at anchor before the walls of Fort St George, Madras, and the Company's warehouse in Bombay. But these are still emphatically marine and coastal views. The Indian interior does not feature in them, and neither does the Indian population: for, even by the early decades of the eighteenth century, the East India Company possessed in regard to these minimal power and only intermittent interest.[9]

By the time of Sarah's passage to India in 1769, however, circumstances had changed: and, however unconsciously, she would participate in and witness still more violent and radical alterations. Behind all the changes lay the fluctuating fortunes of three different imperial systems. On the one hand, as the eighteenth century progressed, the power and grip of India's own Mughal emperors waned disastrously; on the other, the same Anglo-French competition that was responsible for convulsions and captivities in North America at this time also began impacting on the subcontinent.

After 1744, French and British traders on the Coromandel coast began recruiting small numbers of sepoys (indigenous soldiers), and raising extra levies of men from their respective home states, most of them paid for by the companies themselves, but some of them regular troops. This proved a dress-rehearsal for more extensive Anglo-French warfare in parts of India after 1750, and more ruthless interventions in local struggles and politics. In June 1756, the new young Nawab of Bengal, Siraj-ud-Daulah, seized

45. Bombay, by George Lambert and Samuel Scott.

the East India Company's settlement at Calcutta.The response was immediate and savage. A one-time Company civil servant at Madras turned soldier, Robert Clive, first recaptured Calcutta, and then destroyed Siraj-ud-Daulah at the battle of Plassey in June 1757. Subsequent skirmishes undermined the French and their indigenous allies, and culminated in a major Company victory at Buxar in northern India in 1764. The following year, Clive, by this stage Governor and Commander-in-Chief of the East India Company's forces, received the *diwani*, or land revenue rights, to Bengal, Bihar and Orissa as a (reluctant) grant from the Mughal emperor, Shah Alam II. A trading company once confined to the margins of India and of Mughal regard thus became responsible for some twenty million Indians, and also – and crucially – for the subcontinent's richest province. From now on, the Company had much less need to ship bullion from Britain in order to pay for the textiles, spices and saltpetre it had traditionally sought out in India. Instead, Indian land revenues could now be used to pay for the Company's purchases. Over time, these same revenues also came to pay for ever larger armies of Company soldiers and bureaucrats.[10]

Yet, even after securing the *diwani*, the East India Company's administrative power remained confined to Bengal and adjacent areas of Hyderabad, to the Northern Sarkars, and to its long-established coastal

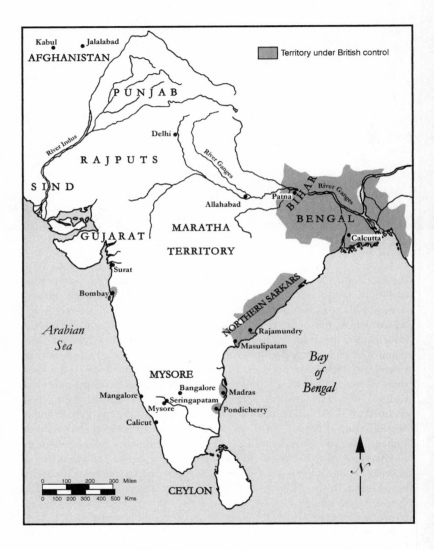

India after the battle of Buxar in 1764.

settlements at Bombay and Madras, while its British personnel continued to be perilously few.[11] Virtually the whole of Sarah's Indian career was shaped by just one aspect of this sparsity of British numbers. On her voyage out from England in 1769, she found herself 'the only woman on board' sailing with 185 men, most of them Company troops. A one-way passage from Britain to India at this time cost at least £30 (well over a thousand pounds in today's values), and the Company disliked laying out such sums on the wives of soldiers and menials. Moreover, Sarah was no wife. Three weeks into the voyage, 'in a fit of inebriety', her stepfather tried to exploit her rarity value by selling her to one of the soldiers on board. When the ship's captain halted the deal, the two men fought him in their fury and frustration. On Sarah's arrival at Madras, she was immediately taken under the protection and into the bed of a Company lieutenant who refused for a long time to release her to one of his subordinates, Sergeant John Cuff, who won her in the end by marrying her. As soon as Cuff died in southern India in the 1780s, she was immediately snapped up in marriage by an army corporal fighting there. One notes her pitiless descent through the ranks of the army as age, war, and the Indian sun stole away with her good looks.

Yet the sexual feeding-frenzy that Sarah Shade so spectacularly provoked in India had much less to do with whatever personal attractions she may have possessed, than with just one aspect of the crucial deficiency there in British numbers. Neither at this nor at any other time was the subcontinent viewed by the Company or London's politicians as a potential settlement colony. The rate at which British women arrived there increased after 1750, but even by comparison with the very limited numbers of their countrymen, they remained a tiny minority. The official intention was never that substantial numbers of Britons should settle there and reproduce themselves by sexual congress with their own kind. This was just as well since, in the eighteenth century and after, many who made the passage to India did not survive long enough to reproduce themselves at all. Of the 645 white male civilians who worked for the East India Company in Bengal between 1707 and 1775 (just 645!), close to 60 per cent are known to have died there, often in the early years of their appointment. Even at the end of the century, one in four British soldiers stationed in India perished every year.[12] Edmund Burke's famous accusation that India's indigenous inhabitants scarcely knew what it was like to see a grey-haired Briton was thus both partisan polemic and perversely accurate. Only a minority of high-level Company servants were able to do what Burke accused them all of doing: make vast, illicit profits in the subcontinent and return triumphantly to Britain as millionaire nabobs. The majority of Britons in India at this stage made limited fortunes or nothing at all, and simply did not survive long enough to go home. As a tour around the oldest Anglican church in India, St Mary's at Madras, demonstrates, one of the favoured epitaphs for memorials and gravestones of Britons perishing in India was necessarily: 'Wisdom is the grey hair unto men'. For many of those arriving in the subcontinent from Britain before and even after 1820, this was the only variety of grey hair that they had any chance of acquiring.[13]

Because their numbers in the Indian subcontinent were so modest and subject to severe attrition, the British always understood at some level that they could never satisfactorily and durably capture it, and that on their own they could not even try. India was too far away from their own islands. It was too big and too complex; and above all it was much too populous. India, calculated a Scottish politician and former military man in 1788, contained 'eleven times as many people' as Britain and Ireland put together, and this was probably an underestimate.[14] Even at the start of the eighteenth century, India's population may already have reached 180 million, which meant that then, as now, it contained a fifth of all the inhabitants of the globe. By contrast, the combined population of Britain and Ireland in the 1780s was under thirteen million souls. Of course, there is an obvious respect in which such a comparison between British and Indian population totals misleads. As Benjamin Disraeli remarked, eighteenth- and nineteenth-century Britons were nervously prone to imagining India as one mighty, unmanageable unit, but it was not one unit at all.[15] India at this stage was still a geographical expression, a collocation of states, kingdoms and sects, further subdivided by hundreds of thousands of intensely localist village communities. This in the end proved vital for British success. At their peak, the Mughal emperors had shown a capacity to tax efficiently, maintain stability, and monopolise force, and some of the successor states emerging in their wake proved highly sophisticated and resilient. But the subcontinent as a whole lacked impersonal, unifying state apparatus or national ideology. By contrast, the East India Company was increasingly bound up with a British state that was able to become precociously centralised and increasingly nationalistic in large part because it was also small and compact in territorial extent.

But for all this – for all the commercial success and financial muscle of the East India Company, for all its access through the British state to naval power on a scale that Indian rulers could only dream of, and for all its busy and highly successful exploitation of religious, cultural and political divisions within the subcontinent – the huge disparity in numbers between the British in India on the one hand, and its indigenous population on the other, meant that the former were of necessity always dependent upon the latter. As Om Prakash and K.N. Chaudhuri have shown, the East India Company – like its European rivals – only established itself to begin with through the aid of Indian bankers and shipping, by leasing land for its initially modest fortifications from Indian rulers, and by working closely with local merchants in the various regional economies, Gujaratis in the western Indian Ocean, Chettiyar and Muslim traders in the south. As late as the 1740s, close to half of the ships servicing the Company's base at Madras were still Indian-owned; and, when Siraj-ud-Daulah moved against Calcutta in 1756, almost all of its white inhabitants were in hock to Indian moneylenders.[16] The shift to military conquest over the next half-century only gave rise to fresh forms of British dependence. The Company increasingly relied on local rulers, agents and landowners to raise men and taxes, and employed a growing array of Indian informants, spies, suppliers, clerks and administrators of all kinds. Most of all, it was obliged to recruit from the same huge labour market of armed peasants that had traditionally served the Mughal emperors. In C.A. Bayly's words, these conquerors would always be 'strictly limited in what they could achieve, for to a great extent the British empire in India remained an empire run and garrisoned by Indians'.[17]

This dependence on those they increasingly strove to rule influenced both how Britons in India experienced captivity, and how the Company and its employees were regarded by their countrymen back home. In the Mediterranean region, and in North America, capture by non-Europeans usually signified, for the British settlers, soldiers, voyagers and traders involved, a sudden, traumatic exposure to alien customs, alien cultures, alien food, alien language and alien dress, and occasionally to cross-racial sex. In India, however, Britons were so thinly distributed and so dependent on the local population, that those who stayed here more than a short time usually had some experience of these things anyway. Indian food, languages and dress, and often Indian sexual partners, were things with which most Britons in the subcontinent before 1820 (especially male Britons) had at least some familiarity. Consequently, captivity here was often less of a cultural shock than in other zones of overseas enterprise, especially when the victims involved were poor whites.

The woman who became Sarah Shade is a case in point. When captured alongside her first husband, Sergeant Cuff, and imprisoned at Bangalore for eleven months by the forces of Haidar Ali, ruler of Mysore, she was able to derive comfort from more than just the companionship of her army spouse. She was aided too by the degree to which by this stage – the early 1780s – she had of necessity become assimilated. One of her Indian guards at Bangalore turned out to be a defector from the East

India Company's Madras army, and he 'interested himself for her on account of [her] speaking his language, and understanding cookery', by which was meant of course southern Indian cookery. This anecdote may seem too good to be true, but I suspect that there was some substance to it. Certainly we know that when Sarah returned to London and was widowed for a second time, in the mid-1790s, she kept herself going for some years by making vegetable curries and other Indian dishes. She would cook these meals to order and at a price for a network of 'different East India families' living in the capital, people, who – like her – had returned to what was nominally their home country, yet found themselves home-sick for the vast subcontinent they had left.

This points to another respect in which the meanings of British captivity in India were distinctive. In the eyes of many of their compatriots at home, *all* Britons who spent substantial time in India were at risk of becoming captive there in a fundamental, if not in a literal sense. Since Britons in India were so sparse, and dependent on the local population in so many ways, fears were regularly expressed back home – particularly at this early stage – that they would be taken over by their Indian surroundings, become entrapped by indigenous habits and values, cease to be authentically British, and go native.

As suggested by the enthusiasm for Sarah's curries among white veterans of the East India Company back in London in the 1790s, these anxieties were not entirely misplaced. But those who gave voice to them, believed that Britons in India were at risk of being suborned in far more serious ways than through their palates and taste buds. They accused the nabobs (and it is suggestive of course that this corruption of *nawab*, meaning a Muslim ruler, was applied to wealthy Britons returning from India) of succumbing to – and exacerbating – endemic Indian corruption and despotism, and of bringing these evils back home. 'They find themselves exotics, and that they have all along been considered as such,' complained one retired East India Company official of the reaction he and his kind encountered back in Britain:

> The honest, free-hearted Indian [and note the use of this term by a British Company servant about himself!] is ever considered as worse than a heathen and despising all religions – in short one of those miscreant delinquents, the produce of whose rapine and violence has poisoned and extirpated every genuine virtue of their native country.[18]

This was in 1797. In earlier decades, expressions of hostility within Britain to the East India Company's white employees, both civil and military, were still more pronounced and pervasive. This helps to explain why the published captivity narrative took so long to emerge as far as India was concerned. Before the 1740s, Britons there had rarely seemed dangerous or profitable enough for it to be worth indigenous regimes' bothering to capture them. But, even after this – when captivity for the British did become far more of a risk – printed captivity narratives from this zone of imperial enterprise remained for some time rare.[19] In part, I am sure, this was because, to those on the home front, Britons in India still seemed a long way away, the agents of a greedy, grasping Company rather than of the nation at large, alien in terms of their reputed behaviour, and altogether unworthy of much sympathy. If Britons in India sometimes suffered, Britons at home had no great desire – and would not have until the late 1780s – to read about or identify with their sufferings.

The seeming conspicuous exception to this, John Zephaniah Holwell's *A Genuine Narrative of the deaths . . . in the Black Hole* (1758), only serves to make the point more strongly. When Siraj-ud-Daulah seized Calcutta in June 1756, Holwell, a Dubliner by birth and a senior East India Company official, was imprisoned overnight along with, he claimed, 145 others in an eighteen-foot square punishment cell. By the morning, he tells us, all but twenty-three of them had suffocated, died of dehydration, or been trampled to death by fellow captives frantic to reach the only window, their only chance of air. The real body-count was probably closer to fifty people, not all of whom were British. Yet while Holwell clearly exaggerated what had happened so as to demonise Siraj-ud-Daulah, and revenge the damage done to his career and the death of several of his friends, this in itself was scarcely surprising. Much more striking was the limited impact that Holwell's narrative of the 'Black Hole', and the event itself, had at the time back in Britain. The Victorians would in due course convert 'the Black Hole of Calcutta' into a poignant foundation myth of British India: 'that great crime', as the future Lord Macaulay called it in 1840, 'memorable for its singular atrocity'. Holwell's British contemporaries reacted differently, and in many cases not at all. Extracts from his captivity narrative were, to be sure, reprinted in the English, Scottish and Irish newspaper and periodical press in 1758, but no new edition of it appeared in the English language after that year. Nor do British printmakers or painters seem to have devoted imagination to this episode before the nineteenth century. A monument to the 'victims' was only erected in Calcutta because Holwell commissioned and paid for it himself. It was quickly allowed to crumble into dust, and not replaced until Lord Curzon, Viceroy of India, intervened in the early 1900s.[20]

Some of the reasons why this emotive piece of partly bogus imperial history was neglected for so long have already been touched on. British public sympathy for, and patriotic indentification with the East India Company and its agents were limited at this stage, and remained so for some decades longer. 'I think the East India Company are greatly to blame for provoking the Moors' was how one British officer reacted to Calcutta's fall in 1756. By contrast, Holwell's vilification of Siraj-ud-Daulah was not generally accepted at this time. In 1772, a Parliamentary enquiry was firmly told by one witness that 'he did not believe the nabob had any intention of a massacre when he confined the English in the Black Hole'.[21] Even a careful reading of Holwell's own narrative reveals how removed we are at this point from a careful wrapping of the Company and its works in India in the Union Jack. Few of the Black Hole's victims are presented in heroic terms. Instead, they are described as desperately stripping off and sucking sweat from their clothes, or drinking their own urine until its concentrated acidity revolts them. We learn, too, how – as the night and the heat wore on, and oxygen became used up – those captives who were still living trampled on the dead and dying out of a sheer animal instinct to get to the one window and survive. 'All regards of compassion and affection were lost,' a British writer recalled with disgust in the early nineteenth century, 'no one would recede or give way for the relief of another.' This was not obviously the stuff of stirring imperial adventure, and nor was the immediate background to this episode. When Siraj-ud-Daulah's forces swept into Calcutta in 1756, there were just seventy Company soldiers to oppose them; there were no more than 500 British troops – perhaps less – in the whole of Bengal.[22]

The India in which Sarah arrived in the 1760s, then, was altered more in prospect than in substance. True, European powers had now succeeded, for the first time ever in global history, in disrupting the political order in India, and an armed, mercantile company from Britain was now entrenched in one of its richest regions, Bengal, governing ostensibly as a vassal of the Mughal emperor. But the degree to which the East India Company was able to penetrate the Indian interior at this stage – or that anybody expected it to do so – remained very limited, and so did British domestic interest in and sympathy with such a project. Most of all, and more conspicuously even than in other zones of overseas enterprise, British manpower in India was markedly circumscribed and highly vulnerable. In order to expand their power here, the British would require a quantum leap in military force and available personnel. During the course of Sarah's career in India, they learnt how to acquire it. The price was paid in money, but also in terrible violence, warfare, and captivities.

Almost all of Sarah's life in India, from the late 1760s to the 1790s, was spent in armed camps, or tramping after a succession of uniformed males in one military campaign after another. As the subtitle of her narrative put it: hers was a saga of a woman 'traversing that country in company with THE ARMY [sic], at the sieges of Pondicherry, Vellore, Negapatam', and more. Sustaining this rate of warfare in India required a more dramatic and distinctive augmentation in manpower than the British had ever previously experienced. Back in 1744, a year of war, the East India Company had employed only about 2500 European soldiers in Calcutta, Madras and Bombay combined. By 1765, there were 17,000 Company troops in Bengal alone, and this was just the beginning. In 1778, British army and Company forces in the subcontinent comprised – at least on paper – 67,000 men. When Sarah left India, in the 1790s, the total was in excess of 100,000. By 1815, the Company's armies in India had risen to a quarter of a million.[23]

The connections between this military build-up and the expansion of the Company's territorial reach in India are well known. At one level, sudden, shattering reverses like the loss of Calcutta became much less likely. Enhanced military power made it far easier for the Company to hang on to such territory as it had already secured. At another level, exploitation became easier. The sword proved a powerful argument when extracting land revenues and taxes, or squeezing protection money or treaties out of individual Indian rulers. At another level still, this expanding, turbulent army took the Company much further into the Indian interior than the politicians and directors in London ideally wanted to go. In the half-century after the battle of Plassey in 1757, debates in Parliament, and the reams of correspondence between India House in London and its civilian and military servants in India are full of variations on the theme of 'conquest is by no means our desire', but they got it anyway.[24] Yet escalating military might and violence did not make comprehensive British empire in India a foregone conclusion. In at least four respects, the East India Company's position after 1757 was more vulnerable than the rapidly expanding size of its armies appears to suggest.

To begin with, there were the enduring challenges of the subcontinent's distance from Britain and its population and geographical extent. One indicator of the degree to which Indian history remains 'othered' even today, is the reluctance to apply to it the sort of logic that is customarily employed in analyses of British power in North America. It is a commonplace that the British will to defeat revolution in America was tested by the sheer scale of its terrain, the buoyancy of its population, and the logistical difficulties of transporting war materiel 3000 miles across the Atlantic. Yet the British in India often viewed themselves as facing similar difficulties. Here, too, it could seem that – while occasional, brilliant victories were more than possible – these by themselves would never be enough. That indigenous opponents would simply withdraw temporarily, tap into inexhaustible reserves of local manpower, and regroup to fight another day, with French aid, and with weaponry increasingly comparable to the Company's own. 'We drive Hyder from the field', wrote a British army officer despairingly of a campaign against the southern Indian kingdom of Mysore that would shortly steal his life:

> but we can neither take his artillery, nor prevent his retreat. Every man we lose on these occasions is valuable to us, and though he should lose ten for one, it is a matter of no consequence to him.[25]

As this suggests, while one challenge confronting the British was always the overwhelming scale of India and its population, a second was their own, incurable limits. After 1756, the Company's forces seemed ever more impressive on paper, but maintaining adequate and effective *European* armies in the field was another matter. Even getting sufficient white soldiers to India in the first place was difficult. Company recruiters in Britain were no more popular than their regular army counterparts, and especially in summer when agricultural jobs were plentiful, plebeian volunteers were sparse. The globalisation of war in the six decades after Plassey made them far more so. In 1776, as war with America began sucking in British manpower, the Company calculated that its artillery in India, an indispensable part of its armoury, was at least 700 men short. In 1794, by which time Britain was at war with Revolutionary France, the number of unfilled vacancies in the Company's European regiments was estimated to be as large again as the number of its European infantrymen actually serving in the field.[26]

Men successfully recruited in Britain still had to survive the passage to India. Before 1790, mortality rates among white troops on East Indiamen and transport ships sometimes compared unfavourably with that of chained blacks on transatlantic slave-ships. In 1760, thirty-three of the fifty-three officers and men sailing to India on board the *Osterly* died before arrival; a third of the men on the *Pondicherry* in 1782 perished just on the stretch of voyage between the Cape of Good Hope and Johanna Island, the latter a familiar stop-over *en route* to Madras. Sometimes whole ships, with all their men and would-be memsahibs, were lost to rough seas, as happened to the East Indiaman *Halsewell* in 1786.[27] Those Company troops

46. *The Loss of an East Indiaman* by J.M.W. Turner.

who did survive the voyage out and make landfall still had to contend thereafter with persistent germ warfare, especially dysentery, waterborne cholera, and malaria. At all times, some 20 per cent of the Company's European troops in India are estimated to have been out of action because of illness. It was a commonplace among Company surgeons that a European soldier wounded in India was six times less likely to recover than a sepoy in a similar situation, because the former's immune system was more undermined by recurrent illness, made worse in many cases by too much drink.

The logic of all this was clear to the Company from early on, and created its third perennial problem. If it was ever to control substantial tracts of India, the bulk of its manpower would have to be Indian. The stupendous rise in 'British' forces in India after the 1750s was therefore something of an optical illusion. Both the Company and the British state dispatched more European males to the subcontinent after this point, but the rise in Company army size chiefly signified a growing British dependence on Indians. Even at Plassey, more than twice as many Indians as Europeans fought on the 'British' side. During the next half-century, the disparity between white and

47. East India company sepoys at Bombay.

Indian troops in the Company's pay became far more pronounced. In 1767, just 13 per cent of the Company's rank-and-file troops in the Coromandel region were classified as European: though in reality their numbers included Americans and Caribbean blacks, as well as Germans, Swiss, Portuguese, French and varieties of Britons. Ten years later, the Company employed just over 10,000 white soldiers in India. These men were outnumbered seven to one by the Company's sepoys.[28]

The incidence of disease among whites made these already stark disparities still more so, as did the isolation of some of the Company's outposts. At Fort Victoria, 60 miles south of Bombay, 160 Company sepoys, plus their Indian officers, were nominally supervised in the 1770s by just three white Company officials, none of whom was a military man. In some Company bases, there appear at intervals to have been no whites at all. In the 1780s, a British officer recorded stumbling into a 'British' fort in the south of India where there were no Britons left. Its sepoys had continued to be provisioned by the Company, and so had simply continued to man their post. They all assembled to have a look at him, not having 'seen a European for many years'.[29] This was an extreme case that points however to an enduring phenomenon. Estimates of so-called British military strength in India need always to take account of the fact that most of it was not British at all.

By the onset of the Victorian age, this system of exercising imperial rule overwhelmingly through the bodies, swords and guns of some of the ruled was broadly, though not universally taken for granted. Earlier, however, its intrinsic insecurity and audacity alarmed and even terrified. 'It will be allowed', wrote a Company army officer frankly in 1769: 'that it is a dangerous measure to place our chief dependence upon the very inhabitants of the country we mean to keep in subjection', and similar arguments were regularly advanced in Parliamentary debates and in correspondence between India House and its agents.[30] In part, such nervousness simply reflected the fact that, as far as the Company was concerned, a large-scale sepoy system was still something new, and no one could yet be confident it would endure, as distinct from melting away or turning against its paymasters. But some British officials were also fearful that sufficient cash might not always be forthcoming to pay and provision this ever-expanding Indian mercenary army.

This helps to explain why the Company's directors in London opposed what they perceived as irresponsible expansionism by elements in its army. Warfare in India was expensive in itself, but it also devastated local trade, agriculture, and tax-payers. And how were the Company's sepoys possibly to be paid for, if profits from Indian commerce, agriculture and land began drying up? As it was, a shortage of provisions triggered large-scale sepoy desertions from the Company's armies during the First Mysore War in 1768, and disruptions in supplies of food and cash contributed to serious sepoy mutinies in the early 1780s. To John Zephaniah Holwell and others, it seemed that the spiral of violence after Plassey could only end by swallowing up the East India Company itself:

New *temporary* victories stimulate and push us on to grasp at new acquisitions of territory; these call for a large increase of military force to defend them; and thus we shall go on, grasping and expending, until we cram our hands so full that they become cramped and numbed, and we shall be obliged to quit.[31]

There was a fourth and final respect in which the Company's expanding armies could seem counterproductive, and dangerous to the British themselves as well as to Indians. The East India Company never operated in a vacuum. In the half century after Plassey, it was one, alien, expanding power amidst other contending Indian powers. South Asian scholars now accept that the contraction of Mughal political and military authority in India after 1720 by no means resulted in general fragmentation and disorder. Powerful successor states emerged in certain regions, that sometimes exhibited a greater capacity and will to modernise than had the Mughal emperors. As far as military change was concerned, these renovated Indian states never relied solely on European models. In some, such as the Maratha Confederation, the shift away from feudal armies to greater military centralisation was already apparent in the seventeenth century; while Persian and Afghan invasions in the early eighteenth century, and conflict between the different Indian kingdoms, also helped to power military change in the subcontinent.[32] None the less, and as had been the case since the 1500s, European technologies, tactics, and mercenaries were systematically copied and adopted by some Indian rulers. The growing military machine sponsored in India by the East India Company helped to bring into being – and had to contend against – other very large armies, supplied with comparable weaponry and equipment.

It is easy enough to detect in post-Plassey, post-Buxar British writings a growing recognition of these changes. Ritualistic and reassuring remarks on innate Indian passivity and ductility are ever more intermixed, especially in confidential writings and high-level missives, with acknowledgements that the Indian scene was becoming more militarily dynamic and dangerous in fact. 'Every year brought with it an increase of military knowledge to the black powers,' wrote an East India Company colonel of his Mysore campaigns in the late 1760s.[33] 'The Indians have less terror of our arms,' conceded the British governor of Madras in 1781, 'we less contempt for their opposition.' 'The mass of the [British] people are . . . uninformed in regard to the changes that have taken place among the warlike tribes of India,' wrote a veteran looking back on the struggles of the early 1800s, '. . . which, *combined with their natural courage* and their numerical superiority, has rendered our conflicts with them sanguinary in the extreme.'[34]

Euphoric British assumptions, in the immediate aftermath of Plassey and Buxar, that fighting and winning in India were always going to be a pushover, thus gave way to more realistic and grimmer appraisals of Indian warfare. Again, Sarah Shade's narrative makes the point. Utterly lacking in any kind of triumphalism, it is not just a testimony to over two decades of British imperial advance in India, but also a story of pathos, loss and mixed military fortunes. Shade herself, as we have seen, was taken captive in Mysore and wounded several times. She also lost two husbands, and – in the span of a week – saw 'sixteen officers' wives being widowed' in the British regiment she marched alongside. The essential context of her narrative – and what makes it an arresting read even now – was both expanding British power in India, and British fears and recurrent reversals there. This is also the essential background to the rise in British captivity experiences in India, and to yet another rich seam of captivity writings.

Apprehension and astonishment in the face of the huge risks involved in what they were doing, can be seen among Britons at home, as well as in India, and were expressed indirectly as well as explicitly. From the 1750s onwards, tigers stalk the British imagination. Sarah herself was mauled by a tiger in the early years of her marriage to John Cuff. Her arms were permanently scarified by its claws. She had another confrontation with the animal, when she witnessed one devouring the pregnant Indian companion of a Company army officer. (Or was this perhaps an addition by her ghost-writers worried at what was known about levels of cross-racial sex in the Company's legions?) Building on the horror of these fierce encounters, Sarah's publishers inserted a special appendix in her captivity narrative describing the wild animals of India, of which the tiger, they insisted, was by far the worst:

A tiger is one of the most ferocious animals that Nature has produced; stately and majestic in appearance, yet cowardly and artfully cunning in his actions; never openly facing his prey, but springing upon it from ambush.

The tensions in this description are interesting and suggestive. The tiger, in this version, is at once a magnificent beast and lacking in courage, both dangerous and devious. Most of all, it is unpredictable, as India itself seemed unpredictable. By this stage, anthropomorphic tiger references of this sort had become common in British literature and art. Before the battle of Plassey, however, Britons had known little of tigers outside of wildly inaccurate images in ancient bestiaries and books of heraldry. It was the conquest of Bengal that brought these animals to their notice.

48. George Stubbs' tigress.

Company officials working there encountered them in the wild, in princely zoos, and on tiger-shoots. A few managed to export live examples back to Britain. The duke of Cumberland was given several of the beasts in the 1750s; and in 1762 Robert Clive, now governor of Bengal, presented a tigress to the duke of Marlborough. This was the animal that George Stubbs painted three times over. More even than his canvases of leopards and cheetahs, Stubbs's *Portrait of the Royal Tiger* (1769) became a much reproduced image.[35] There were good and bad copies, engravings, polygraphs, even versions in needlework. Stubbs's tiger also established an artistic fashion. In subsequent decades, James Ward, James Northcote and other artists also painted tiger canvases; while the north country artist Thomas Bewick and the young Edwin Landseer produced wonderful engravings of the beast in books ranging from fine art albums to children's literature.[36]

It was not simply a case, however, of the East India Company's conquests familiarising Britons back home with the subcontinent's most impressive animal. To a degree that was deeply revealing, the tiger became synonymous in British minds with India itself, and an image through which shifting ideas and apprehensions of the subcontinent could be expressed.

9. *Fight between a Lion and a Tiger* by James Ward.

'The tiger is peculiar to Asia', wrote Bewick, '[but] the greatest number are met with in India.'[37]

Tigers seemed appropriate metaphors at various levels. They were massive, magnificent and regal, just as India itself was vast, costly, and a land of multitudinous princes. Sleek and deadly, they were also, as Edmund Burke wrote in the very year of Plassey, creatures of the sublime:

> Look at . . . [an] animal of prodigious strength, and what is your idea before reflection? *Is it that this strength will be subservient to you? . . . No: the emotion you feel is, lest this enormous strength should be employed to the purposes of rapine and destruction* . . . The sublime . . . comes upon us in the gloomy forest, and in the howling wilderness, in the form of . . . the tiger, the panther, or rhinoceros.

As this suggests, for the British, the tiger evoked India most tellingly at this stage because it was dangerous, beyond knowing, and beyond control.

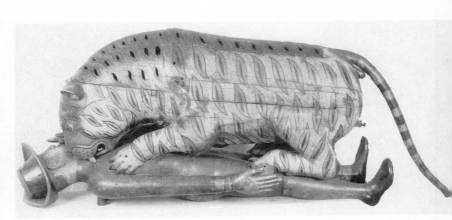

50. A tiger devours a British soldier: wood and clockwork effigy made for Tipu Sultan of Mysore

Stubbs painted his tigress recumbent and relaxed, but its immense musculature is easily apparent beneath the beautiful, striped pelt, and the lustrous eyes – which do not engage with the viewer – are entirely unhuman. As Judy Egerton puts it, we are left in no doubt that this superb beast possesses the power to 'spring to attack with one lithe and supremely co-ordinated bound'.[38]

The currency of tiger images after 1750 must be seen as one more expression of British wonder and uncertainty in the face of their own increasingly violent but still unpredictable involvement with the Indian subcontinent. It was an image both of obsession and fear. It was not long in fact before writers and artists began to play with the conceit of using encounters between a lion and a tiger to comment on the wider British–Indian encounter. One thinks of Stubbs's *Lion and Dead Tiger,* or of James Ward's vicious *Fight between a Lion and a Tiger,* both painted at times of sharp imperial conflict in India. As the nineteenth century advanced, imaginary animal contests of this sort became something of a source of complacency. 'The unanimous voice of ages', remarked Landseer in his *Twenty Engravings of Lions, Tigers, Panthers and Leopards* (1823), pronounced the lion 'to be the King of beasts'.[39] India and its tiger, it appeared, had been safely vanquished by a leonine Britannia. Hence, surely, the large numbers of Victorian British males who had themselves painted and later photographed with their feet firmly planted on the skin or the carcass of a dead tiger. What for Mughal princes had been an emblem of rule, a tiger caught and killed in the hunt or kept behind bars, became for the British an emblem of imperial supremacy over India. Before the early 1800s, however, this sense of confident, animal dominion in regard to the subcontinent was rare, because the tiger was still able to catch them unawares. 'They attack all sorts of animals, even the lion,' mused Thomas Pennant in his *History of Quadrupeds* in 1781, a year of terrible British defeats and captivities in southern India 'and it has been known that both have perished in their combats.'[40]

The tiger then was already established in British minds as an emblem for India *before* the reign of Tipu Sultan (1782–99), the Mysore ruler who employed tiger-symbolism for his own religious and ritual purposes in a systematic fashion, and who became the villain of a major British captivity panic in the 1780s and '90s, a captor indeed for several months of Sarah Shade herself. There was a sense in which, for the British, Tipu's tiger-ornamented court, the stylised tiger stripes on the uniforms of his soldiers, and the exquisite, jewelled tiger-heads snarling from the rings on his fingers and the pommel of his sword, only brought into focus more longstanding and inchoate fears that advancing into India was fraught with danger, that they were riding the tiger in fact. And tiger and lion imagery had another, less acknowledged significance for the British.

. A tiger-headed Mysore cannon at Madras.

If India often seemed to them a large, fierce, untameable, unknowable beast, then by the same token the British themselves appeared ever more dangerous, and ever more remorseless to the peoples of the subcontinent, and to many others across the entire globe. The half-century after the Battle of Buxar in 1764, that won them Bengal, would witness unprecedented levels of British military violence, much of it carried out – as in India – by *condottieri* of a sort, hard men with swords and guns and ships, fiercely on the make, and often operating substantially out of reach of London and its control. They would fall upon and tear out whole chunks of the world, like ravenous beasts unleashed:

'This I seize', says the lion, 'because I have got teeth; this, because I wear a mane on my neck; this, because I have claws; and this last morsel, not because I have either truth, reason, or justice to support me and justify my taking it, but because I am a lion.'[41]

Savage beasts preoccupied the British, then, even before their armies, with Sarah Shade trudging gamely in their wake, marched on to face the tiger-mouthed cannon of Mysore.

NINE

The Tiger and the Sword

Mysore and its meanings

10 September 1780. Pollilur: ten miles north-west of the temple town of Kanchipuram, and just several days' hard marching from Madras. It is imperial nightmare time. There are no Gatling guns to jam, and the one remaining British colonel still has some time to live, but the square of redcoats around him is diminishing in front of our eyes. Outside it, the stragglers are already being picked off, speared through the neck, or decapitated with vicious, curving sabres as they try to run. There is no refuge inside the square either. The men still have their muskets, but the ammunition wagon has just exploded, and soon they will be fighting with swords, pikes, bare hands. Converging on them from all sides is wave upon wave of Mysore cavalry, glittering in scarlet, and blue, and green. Colonel William Baillie lies wounded in a palanquin, sweats into his thick, braid-encrusted uniform, and gnaws at his fingernails in anguish. By contrast, Tipu Sultan Fath Ali Khan, eldest son and soon-to-be successor of Haidar Ali of Mysore, is in control and simply dressed in a silk tunic patterned with tiger stripes. He surveys the slaughter from his war elephant, savours the scent of a rose, and ponders how many of the British to kill, how many to capture.

Yet the thirty-foot-long mural of Pollilur that glows still from the walls of Tipu's elegant wooden summer palace just outside Seringapatam is more than a commemoration of Mysore victory. Looked at closely, this piece of courtly propaganda by an unknown artist in the service of Tipu is also a meditation on warrior masculinity and its absence. Without exception, Tipu and his turbaned armies are shown all sporting beards or moustaches. Even their French allies fighting alongside them bristle with facial hair. But their British opponents have been portrayed very differently. In reality, some of Baillie's men would have struggled and died that day wearing tartan kilts and motley colours.[1] Here, though, his white soldiers all appear in uniform jackets of red, a colour associated with blood, fertility and power, but also in India with eunuchs and with women. Baillie's men

52. The Battle of Pollilur: detail from an 1820 copy by an unknown Indian artist.

are also conspicuously and invariably clean-shaven. Neatly side-burned, with doe-like eyes, raised eyebrows, and pretty pink lips, they have been painted to look like girls, or at least creatures who are not fully male. This was not an atypical form of mockery in the subcontinent at this stage. The British were 'worse than women', another Indian ruler wrote in 1780, sly, fox-like traders who had been foolish enough to challenge tigers. And now the time for their destruction was come.[2]

British reactions at the time were not very different. When news of Pollilur, and other military reversals against Mysore's legions, reached London in 1781, it provoked 'universal consternation'. In rival European capitals, and in Revolutionary America, there was both astonishment and *schadenfreude*. This, after all, was the year of Yorktown, and the end of all of Britain's hopes of retaining the oldest, richest sector of its transatlantic empire. Now it seemed that Britain's newer, eastern empire was also coming under acute pressure. 'India and America are alike escaping,' predicted

Horace Walpole, an anti-imperial English Whig. This was over-euphoric:
but it was the case, as the prime minister, Lord North, admitted, that
defeat at Pollilur: 'had engaged the attention of the world . . . and had
given rise to so much public clamour and uneasiness'.[3] And although some
subsequent successes in southern India allowed this phase of conflict
between the East India Company and Mysore to end in a draw, imperial
confidence had been severely dented, and remained so for some time. In
1784, Parliament passed new legislation regulating the affairs of the
Company, and explicitly renouncing any prospect of future British expansion in India: 'schemes of conquest and extent of dominion . . . [were]
repugnant to the wish, the honour and the policy of this nation.' Doubts
about the feasibility – and desirability – of further advances in the subcontinent were still in evidence when war with Mysore resumed in 1790.
Political prints published in London at that time predicted almost without
exception that British forces would be defeated and humiliated there.[4]

53. A Victorian photograph of the original mural of Pollilur at the Darya Daulat Bagh, Seringapatam

The root cause of this mood of imperial recessional was at one level all too obvious: the lost war in America, and the ensuing global repercussions and domestic soul-searching. 'In Europe we have lost Minorca', catalogued one Member of Parliament drearily:

> In America thirteen provinces, and the two Pensacolas; in the West Indies, Tobago; and some settlements in Africa . . . In India . . . we have yielded up Chandanagore and all the French settlements in Bengal – We have yielded Pondicherry – Carical – and every settlement we had conquered from the French upon the coasts of Coromandel and Malabar.[5]

In retrospect, it seems clear that Britain's expulsion from the Thirteen Colonies allowed it to concentrate with more devastating effect on imperial projects in India and elsewhere. But most Britons at the time failed to anticipate that this would be the case. Instead, some of them interpreted these reverses in different parts of the globe as conclusive proof that their country was simply too small to engage in large-scale, territorial empire with any hope of durable success. Even those who did not take such a catastrophic view seem to have felt uneasy about post-American War prospects in India itself.

As we have seen, right from the start, the sheer extent of the subcontinent, and especially the scale of its population, had worked to daunt and disturb as well as attract and excite. Pollilur and other military failures inevitably reinforced anxiety that the British presence in India could never be anything more than 'a precarious dominion of a few over millions' which must by definition be short-lived. The experience of major military defeats here, unprecedented since 1700, also deepened pre-existing doubts about Britons in India in another respect. A parliamentary enquiry into these failures, which filled six, substantial volumes, together with investigations into the conduct of the former governor of Bengal, Warren Hastings, revealed levels of East India Company corruption and incompetence that some had previously suspected, but that had never before been so well or publicly documented.[6] Longstanding concerns about India's corrupting effects on the Britons exposed to it – and *vice versa* – seemed now to be fully vindicated. At least some of the pessimism in the 1780s about Britain's imperial prospects in general, and about its Indian enterprise in particular, stemmed from a sense that its civil and military agents had shown themselves unworthy, or at best irredeemably inept. They did not deserve to succeed. Moreover, succeeding in India might not any more be possible.

War with Mysore and its allies confirmed that some of the Indian successor states were evolving into major military players. Haidar Ali, a highly able though illiterate warlord, had usurped the throne of Mysore in 1761, and worked hard from the beginning of his makeshift reign at the modernisation of its armies. Tipu Sultan, who succeeded him in 1782, went further and converted Mysore into a formidable fiscal-military state.[7] The results were manifest on the battlefield. In its first extended confrontation with Mysore in 1767–9, the East India Company had come close to losing Madras and been forced to sue for peace. By 1780, the year of Pollilur, Mysore's war machine was bigger still, its fiscal, commercial and territorial resources stronger. Its intelligence networks were impressive. Its fortifications were generally agreed to be better than the Company's own, as were its supply chains. Its cavalry was easily superior. Two-thirds of Mysore's weaponry was European in manufacture; but it also possessed its own armouries, foundries and war technologies.[8] And its land forces outnumbered those at the disposal of the Company's Madras Presidency.

Haidar Ali commanded 90,000 men, one Company officer claimed in the early 1780s; 150,000 men ventured another British commentator; 200,000 reported a third. All these estimates are in fact suspect, but they suggest the level of British alarm at the scale and danger of Mysore's armies.[9] This was deepened by the fact that, in this second major conflict with Mysore, Britain came close to losing control of the sea. As had been true of Algiers and Morocco in an earlier period, Mysore under Haidar Ali and Tipu Sultan was an Islamic polity (although with a majority Hindu population) with little cause to fear European land forces on their own. Only substantial armies better ordered than in this conflict, effectively combined with sea-power, could render the British lethal here. 'I can defeat them on land,' Haidar is supposed to have remarked, 'but I cannot swallow the sea.'[10] But the French might: and, at one stage, seemed on the verge of doing so.

Even in the 1760s, Haidar had made adept and purposeful use of French and other European mercenaries, engineers, artisans, interpreters and doctors.[11] In the wars of 1779–84, he and Tipu had access to a formal French alliance. Busy undermining British imperial power in America, France was unable to supply Mysore with the men and finance both powers ideally would have liked. But over a quarter of France's war fleet, some twenty capital ships in all, were dispatched to patrol the Coromandel coast. Had this force under Admiral de Suffren succeeded not just in engaging the British, but also in stopping supplies of men, money, information, and provisions from reaching Madras, the Company's southern stronghold, it might well have fallen. Had this happened, the Company's sepoy legions in southern India would have gone unpaid and unfed, and surely have melted away. As it was, there were mutinies among the Company's sepoys in the early 1780s, as well as defections to Mysore.[12]

French sponsorship of Indian resistance, which persisted even after 1800, was one reason why Mysore and its Muslim warlords provoked such persistent British concern. Of course, France was hardly in a position by itself now to replace the British as prime European power in India; and the triangular Mysore state only dominated the southern part of the subcontinent. In 1791, Tipu's dominions extended for some 92,500 square miles, slightly smaller in extent than the Company's fiscal and agrarian base of Bengal.[13] But, even more than Haidar, Tipu showed himself adept at mobilising large numbers of peasant soldiers, at fostering trade, and raising money. If he were to have the additional aid of French warships and artillery, then his future success against the British came within the bounds of possibility. And this in turn might have a domino effect on other Indian powers. As both leading Company administrators and politicians in London realised, the smallness of the British presence in India meant that ultimately its power rested less on capital, or on force simply, than on opinion and imagination, on an *idea* of invulnerability sustained by sporadic bouts of efficient and successful violence on its part. The British had to be seen to win in India, because – bluntly – they could not

54. The British square at bay at Pollilur.

afford to be seen often to be losing. A senior Company army officer spelt it out in a speech to the House of Commons in 1781. The British purchase on India, he told them, was 'more imaginary than real, to hold that vast territory in subjection with such a disparity of numbers'. Defeats like Pollilur were therefore doubly dangerous because they resulted in a loss of face: 'I fear they [the Indians] will soon find out that we are but men like themselves, or very little better.' And, once that happened, what would happen to the British in India?[14] A powerful, expansionist Mysore, allied to Britain's prime European rival France, was therefore not just menacing in itself. In the aftermath of traumatic defeat in America, it also raised the spectre of a wider melt-down of British reputation – and therefore authority – in India as a whole.

And there was a particular, grating respect in which Mysore undermined Britain's imperial prestige. It captured large numbers of its warriors, some of whom it persuaded to change sides.

Just how many British captives were taken by Mysore in its successive wars with the Company will never be known. Pollilur alone resulted in over 200 Britons being seized (some 3000 'British' troops, white and Indian, were killed there). But there were many other defeats and skirmishes productive of captives. In 1782, for instance, the French handed over to Haidar 400 British sailors and more than sixty Royal Navy officers that their naval vessels had captured at sea. Many British captives in Mysore (there were far greater numbers of Company sepoy captives) did not survive to be freed, dying from disease, harsh treatment, or because they were already severely wounded when taken. But we know that over 1300 British troops and at least 2000 Company sepoys remained alive to be handed over when peace was signed in 1784. We also know that an additional 400 British-born captives stayed on in Mysore until the 1790s, some of them voluntarily as Muslim converts.[15]

In comparison with more recent captivity panics in Asia, with the 130,000 British soldiers seized by Japan after the fall of Singapore in 1942 for instance, these Mysore captives seem conspicuously modest in point of numbers. But they must be viewed in the light both of the smallness of the British-born military presence in India at this stage – no more than 10,000 men – and of earlier complacent notions that such paltry numbers of whites, plus a few regiments of Indian auxiliaries, were all that was necessary to carve a swathe through the subcontinent. At Plassey in 1757, the 'British' force of 600 white troops and 2400 Eurasian and Indian soldiers had routed a force some fifteen times larger in number. More dramatically than anything else could have done, the number of white as well as Indian captives seized by Mysore after 1779 – at least one in five of all Britons in arms in the subcontinent – signalled that the days of clear European supremacy in India in terms of military technology, tactics and discipline were well and truly over. As one captive British officer wrote in 1784 of his comrades seized by Mysore: 'Such a force as this twenty years ago would have marched through all India.'[16] But no longer. In Britain, too, the number of Mysore captives was of less importance than what their existence was viewed as signifying. A belief that Mysore was somehow 'teeming with British captives' had an impact similar to post-Vietnam American anxieties about the fate of unknown but wildly inflated numbers of GIs captured by the Vietcong or missing in action. In both cases, the real and rumoured scale of captivity deepened the humiliation of an unsatisfactory imperial war and fostered hatred and apprehension of an insidious, too efficient non-Western enemy.[17]

But there is another important twist to this particular captivity panic, and it can be appreciated by looking again at the mural of Pollilur on the walls of Tipu's Darya Daulat palace at Seringapatam. As we have seen, this was Mysore propaganda as well as wonderfully vigorous art. Yet in spite of himself, the unknown Indian artist responsible for painting it hints at British strengths, even as he celebrates their near-annihilation and strives to un-man them. *In extremis*, the British square – at least in this version – remains conspicuous in its solidarity and almost eerily regimented. The spate of manuscript and published writings on British captivities in Mysore, that started in the early 1780s and continued into the nineteenth century, is revealing about British imperial anxieties in the wake of massive global defeats, and uncertainties about India in particular. But these same texts also document the evolution of a tougher, profoundly military imperial style, and the emergence too of a more self-conscious and confident national and imperial culture within Britain itself. Out of unprecedented British defeat, first in America and now in India, would come something very different and infinitely more dangerous.

Fighters as writers

Mysore captivities spanned barely four decades in all; those we know most about barely two. Yet because many of the Britons detained there were highly literate, and – in contrast with most Barbary and Native American captives – substantial numbers of them had little to do with their time but endure, the captivity texts they produced were abundant and diverse in content and form. There is one characteristic, however, that distinguishes them. Most of the writers were men-at-arms.

At least two women produced Mysore captivity narratives, Sarah Shade whom we encountered in the last chapter, and Eliza Fay, a barrister's wife who was seized with nine other Europeans while journeying through Calicut in 1779. And there were male civilian narrators, like Henry Becher, a trader held captive in Mysore between 1790 and 1792, whose story became the first ever English-language text published in Bombay. Almost certainly, too, many more captivity narratives emerged from these wars than have survived. The Mysore authorities periodically searched prisons and prisoners for concealed paper and books; and captives themselves sometimes destroyed writings to prevent their discovery. Sometimes writers perished along with their texts. In July 1791, British troops invading a fort near Seringapatam, uncovered a 'little journal' in a storehouse there. The Indian storekeepers told them that the document had belonged to a British seaman called Hamilton, captured some nine years before and detained in Mysore because of his carpentry skills. Hamilton had recently been executed as punishment for his countrymen's renewed invasion; and the secret diary he had maintained so painstakingly during nine years of living as a Mysore artisan appears not to have survived either.[18]

But even if the Mysore captivity archive had been preserved intact, as far as the Britons involved were concerned, it seems likely that the same point would still have held true. The vast majority of writers there were men, and men who fought and killed for a living.

Historians of Britain have been less ready than some of their Continental European counterparts to integrate men of the sword into broad cultural and intellectual history. Military and naval historians still concentrate on their subjects' administrative, social and warlike roles; while historians of literature and ideas often write as if in tacit agreement with Aldous Huxley's view that military intelligence is a contradiction in terms.[19] Only rarely are men (or women) in uniform examined in tandem with civilians as creatures who argue, think, write about and react to the societies that contain them both. Yet, as Michel Foucault acknowledged, the 'men of the camps' (and, he might have added, men of the navy) were leading players in the European Enlightenment.[20] This was partly because their numbers and importance rose so conspicuously in all the major European states after 1740, but it was also because – especially, though not exclusively at officer level – these were people of considerable education who naturally participated in the intellectual curiosities and debates of their day. In France, as Robert Darnton shows, demand for Enlightenment literature in garrison towns like Metz or Montpellier was markedly high, as was the proportion of military subscribers to the *Encyclopédie*. And here, as in other European states, men at arms were sometimes highly active as producers of culture, as well as being avid consumers of it.[21]

Despite their lingering, stereotypical reputation as chinless wonders and/or mindless action men, there is no reason to believe that Britain's military in the eighteenth century, or after, was any less intellectually engaged. As in most other European states, British regular army and naval officers were recruited disproportionately from the younger sons of landed, moneyed, professional and clerical families. This did not necessarily make them intelligent, but it did ensure that most received some education. John Burgoyne, the British general whom we have encountered surrendering at Saratoga, was arguably much more successful as an amateur playwright with close connections to the London theatres, than he was on the battlefield. Nor was Burgoyne at all unique in his interest in the written word. Back in the 1750s, when still a lieutenant-colonel, he made it a rule that all army officers serving under him should be able to speak French, be numerate, spend a portion of each day reading, and write English 'with swiftness and accuracy'.[22]

As this suggests, writing was something that British officers were increasingly expected to do as part of their job. Keeping a journal or a detailed

55. Mrs Louisa Brown in 1841 with the military journal of her son, an officer of the East India Company.

log-book, like writing copious letters, was for men of this profession often a response to orders, and not merely a private, individually chosen pursuit. This was virtually always so in the case of senior officers. When Colonel Adlercron went with a royal regiment to India in 1754, he carried with him instructions to 'keep a regular diary of all your proceedings' from both the king, George II, and the commander-in-chief of the army, the duke of Cumberland. As British imperial ambition widened, the ceaseless hunger for intelligence meant that junior officers too, and occasionally even their men, were expected to observe alien surroundings and encounters closely, and commit their observations to paper. This was emphatically true of India, even though most army officers here were employed by the East India Company and not directly by the British state, and were usually of lower social origins than the generality of regular army officers. 'Those officers are deserving of your notice', the Company's historiographer Robert Orme advised in the 1760s, 'who in their marches through the country, make . . . remarks of whatever is worthy of observation, who in short keep a kind of journal.'[23] Men-at-arms not only fought for empire, they also played a prominent role in describing, analysing, and communicating it on paper.

The growing number of fighters who were also writers in this period was thus partly a function of growing military professionalism, and the demand by states for detailed, on-site reportage of the extra-European world. But men of the sword did not simply write in obedience to their superiors and because it was part of their job. Some also wrote for pleasure, and/or in the hope of making their name or at least making money. As a glance through any British newspaper or periodical from this time will demonstrate, military and naval officers regularly sold stories, memoirs, maps and drawings of European and extra-European campaigns and explorations to the press, as well as publishing discrete volumes on these topics. The young Winston Churchill was thus acting entirely in conformity with British army traditions when he wrote up and published his own imperial and military observations – and captivity experiences – on the north-west frontier and in the Boer War.[24] Just what men in uniform chose to publish or contribute to the press tended at all times to be varied. An officer who had retired from active service, or who nurtured some kind of grievance, might decide to publish controversial or embarrassing material and be damned, but paid for his trouble, rather than confining himself to the official line. As for common soldiers and seamen, the constraints on what they wrote and published could be sparser still. So to say that most Mysore captivity writings were by men in uniform is not to say that these texts were uniform as well. Many of the authors involved had been taught ways of writing and techniques of close observation by their profession. Some were conventional patriots, warriors, and careerists, anxious to serve their country, the East India Company, and the politicians. Others were not. Theirs was a distinctive but also a mixed genre.

Initially, however, most of those who wrote while they were still captives in Mysore did so as a strategy of resistance and survival. There were two reasons why Haidar Ali and Tipu Sultan went to the trouble of taking and feeding large numbers of British prisoners. First, these men and the

56 and 57. Exterior and interior of the officers' dungeon at Seringapatam.

occasional woman were counters in the diplomatic game, means whereby the Company might be brought more quickly to terms, and pressured into yielding up territory and concessions. Second, both Haidar and Tipu viewed select Britons and other Europeans as useful and exploitable. Highly ambitious and expansionist rulers themselves, they were understandably suspicious of the Company's territorial intentions in India. But both men accepted – as Indian rulers had persistently done since the 1500s – that individual Europeans could supply useful skills, and might potentially be incorporated in their state.[25] Consequently, both men sought to divide their British prisoners in order better to control and make use of them.

As a result, there was never one Mysore captivity experience, any more than there was ever a single Barbary or Native American captivity experience. Even when men from the same regiment, company, garrison or ship were seized as a group, Mysore tactics were speedily to fragment them. Captives held in the same fort or city were usually housed in different parts of it. Even now, if you visit the massive, ruined fortress-city of Seringapatam, badly overgrown and crumbling, but still profoundly impressive on its island site on the Cauvery River, your tour guide will probably show you a large vaulted prison where some 300 British officers were reputedly incarcerated in the early 1780s. This particular prison was carefully preserved by Victorian imperialists, and has been rendered and whitewashed so often that it now resembles a rather elegant, subterranean wine-bar, and not a place of pain, squalor, and fear. Break free from the standard tourist route and explore Seringapatam on foot or by bike, however, and you quickly come across other, less well-signposted, less salubrious prison sites where non-commissioned Britons along with Company sepoys and other Indians were detained.[26] Confining the non-commissioned away from their officers was the norm in most, though not all Mysore forts. But both captive officers and captive men could expect to be split up, sometimes repeatedly so, and allotted different kinds of treatment during their detention. James Scurry, a boy serving aboard HMS *Hannibal*, was captured by the French at sea, handed over to Mysore, and taken with his comrades initially to Bangalore. Once there, this batch of captives was split into three. His group was marched to another settlement where it was then further subdivided according to age. Scurry ended up back in Bangalore along with some fifty other British boy soldiers and sailors, the oldest of whom was seventeen years of age, the youngest twelve.[27]

Mysore captivity involved then a deliberate assault on the cohesion of those British individuals experiencing it. It was also physically harsh, though not uniquely so. As we have seen, European writers at this time were agreed that the treatment of prisoners-of-war was a significant measure of a nation's level of civilisation. Yet, as in the American Revolutionary War, peacetime scruples on this score were often abandoned in practice under pressure of actual conflict. The penal reformer, John Howard, claimed it was the 'barbarity' of French treatment of some British prisoners during the Seven Years War that first aroused his interest in prisoner welfare. Conversely, Admiral de Suffren justified handing over British prisoners to Mysore in the early 1780s by reference to the sufferings their countrymen were allegedly inflicting on French POWs in North America and India.[28] Whether in Europe, or outside it, the life of a POW, especially if he came from the lower ranks, was fraught with risk and sometimes very brief. The sufferings of British captives in Mysore were not exceptional, then, so much as of a particular kind.

There was the year-long exposure to southern India's tropical climate, the chill nights followed by burning sunshine, the devastating monsoons, the millions of biting insects, and the persistent disease, made worse in the case of non-commissioned soldiers by their being forced to labour outdoors digging trenches or repairing fortifications. There was the lack of proper medical attention, which meant that those wounded when seized died in very large numbers, or only semi-healed with broken bones or internal organs still protruding from their flesh.[29] There were the 9lb irons and chains linking the captives' ankles, which made anything more than hobbled walking impossible, and deformed some of them for life. There was the regular verbal and sometimes physical abuse of guards, many of whom had no cause at all to love the Company or the British. And there were the humdrum mortifications of having to carry out all bodily functions in public, of rarely or never being able to bathe, of being deprived of adequate or familiar food and the cutlery to eat it with. There was a lack often of books, a lack always of liberty, and a lack too of alcohol. Many British males in India drank to excess. But captives supervised by strict Muslim or Hindu guards might be deprived even of this means of escape. When the British peace commissioners travelled to Mysore in 1784, they came equipped with all kinds of comforts for the captives there, medicines, hats, shoes, preserved meat, familiar British condiments like mustard. But above all they brought along drink: one hundred dozen bottles of Madeira alone.[30]

And as it always does, captivity preyed on minds. One of the reasons why few British POWs in Mysore in the early 1780s attempted to escape was because it was desperately unclear to them at this stage *where* exactly they should try to escape to. Seringapatam was only some 250 miles of harsh terrain away from the Company's stronghold of Madras. But what if Madras itself should fall? The captives knew, none better, that Mysore's armies could be formidable. Cut off and incarcerated, they had no means of telling how far those armies would eventually advance. Mysore captivity narratives testify to the debilitating effect of rumour in this situation. Newly arrived prisoners would pass on reports of fresh British defeats or, even worse, news of British victories that turned out to be false. Sometimes Mysore guards fed prisoners reports designed to sap their morale. Thus on 27 February 1782, officers held at Seringapatam learned that the British commander in southern India, Eyre Coote, was now a captive like them; the next day they were told that '15 Battalions of ours are taken', and that 7000 Frenchmen together with Haidar Ali's forces were laying siege to Madras.[31] None of these reports was true, but British captives could not be certain of this – any more than they could be sure of ultimately being set free. Britons captured by Mysore forces in the early 1780s encountered in its prisons countrymen who had been seized during the 1767–69 Anglo-Mysore wars. 'They have guards over them, and appear quite dejected,' an officer recorded of these veteran captives: 'They are allowed to dress in the European style, but are very dirty.'[32] By this stage, these men had been POWs in Mysore for over a dozen years. So what chance did the rest of them have of ever getting out?

The need to counter the corrosive effects of uncertainty, fear, physical hardship, and being separated from comrades helps to explain why so many of these captives resorted to writing. Not all of them could write. Some British soldiers and sailors held in Mysore were illiterate. Moreover, paper was a sparse and costly commodity in the prison economy. Indian guards and servants had to be bribed to smuggle it in; or a dead officer's few precious books had to be cannibalised for blank pages; or a prisoner had to have enough free time to improvise his own paper and ink from material around him. Captives also needed sufficient time and space to be able to write safely removed from the guards' surveillance. All these things worked against members of the other ranks, who were generally worked harder and held in more crowded cells, keeping prison notebooks during their captivity. Letter-writing, though, was another matter. Writing to each other was what most kept the captives together. Brief, scrawled messages were constantly circulating among them, rolled up and concealed in rice cakes, in cheroots, in bricks, or behind loose tiles. On at least one occasion, a captive officer wrote his message on a tiny strip of paper, and rolled it up tightly so that it would fit into the quill of a pen. The pen and its contents then disappeared into the anus of an Indian servant who walked it out of the fort and to its intended recipient.[33]

This ploy, which manifestly relied on the consent at some level of the messenger, was a particularly dramatic instance of a widespread pattern. In Mysore captivity in the 1780s, as in all other parts of India and at all other times, the British remained profoundly dependent on indigenous auxiliaries. It seems overwhelmingly to have been British captives who wrote messages (though at least one sepoy message survives). But it was Indian servants, washermen, guards and workers who necessarily carried these messages between the different prisons in the various Mysore cities and forts.[34] Their motives for acting in a way that inevitably put their own safety at risk were various. Some of these Indian messengers were bribed. Some were sepoy deserters from the Company's service, who perhaps chose to aid white representatives of their former employer out of residual loyalty, or because they could not know at this stage who would finally triumph in southern India. A few message-carriers may have been Hindus who regarded Haidar and Tipu as Muslim usurpers. And some, on the basis of the accounts we have, simply acted as they did out of charity.

Whatever the motive, these intermediaries have a broader significance. Superficially, the message networks that evolved to service the Mysore captives have an almost *Boys' Own* quality to them. Some later published captivity narratives certainly made the most of how British pluck and ingenuity had overcome Mysore attempts to divide and demoralise. Yet, as we have seen, communication between the captives actually relied substantially on *Indian* pluck and ingenuity. Moreover, not all Mysore attempts to divide and demoralise British captives failed. If some individual Indians crossed religious and racial lines during this captivity crisis and helped the British, the reverse was also true. Some of the latter also crossed the line and helped Mysore.

This was what lay behind some of the incessant message writing and smuggling. British captives in Mysore wrote to each other covertly for various reasons, to send words of comfort, to pass on the latest rumour, to ask for medical advice, to inform each other who among their ranks had died that day, to maintain – if they were officers – some contact with and influence over those of their men imprisoned in other places. But captives also used the message system to establish who among their number was still to be relied on, and who by contrast was showing signs of shifting loyalty.

One of the most extraordinary Mysore captivity narratives to have survived was kept by an Irish Company officer called Cromwell Massey (with that first name, we may safely assume he was a Protestant), imprisoned at Seringapatam from 1780 to 1784. Now in the British Library in London, the original is just over four inches high and barely two inches wide.[35] Massey sewed its makeshift pages together himself, just as he manufactured his own ink, scribbling his daily entries in microscopic script, and concealing the document in his clothing at night. But this tersely written journal, which is partly in code, was not just a personal record. Massey also used some of its pages to write to other captives in different parts of

58. Cromwell Massey's prison journal.

the fort. These miniature letters were then smuggled out and delivered by Indian guards and servants. Replies were smuggled back – also via Indian intermediaries – and then carefully sewn or transcribed into Massey's journal. The end-result is a testament to how protracted, harsh captivity tests and transforms individuals.

At some point in 1781 (Massey's dating is unclear), he and other Seringapatam captives noticed out of their cell windows companies of

Mysore troops being drilled in accordance with British army regulations by white men. Over the months, these white drill-sergeants and other whites in Mysore uniform reached more than a hundred in number.[36] Massey monitored the rot. In October, a sergeant smuggled a letter to him describing how fifteen 'healthy looking young men' from among the British private soldiers confined in the fort had been pressured to join Mysore's armies. On their refusal, they had been 'taken from thence one by one to an apartment', body-shaved, stretched naked on their backs over a large bowl with their legs and arms firmly held down by guards, and then 'circumcised . . . by force'. Massey soon learnt, however, that not every British defector who had undergone this conversion ordeal had been coerced. 'To be candid,' a young officer who had been circumcised wrote to him, 'when the Brahmin came to select young men for their diabolical purposes, I voluntarily offered myself and was accepted.' Massey learnt too that these crossings-over were not confined to Seringapatam. 'Fifty-one boys and young men . . . are now in the fort', wrote an informant from Bangalore, '. . . all circumcised, among them are 5 midshipmen.'[37]

This was perhaps the most dramatic, though not the most important example of overlap between the British on the one hand, and the Mysore of Haidar Ali and Tipu Sultan on the other. Having captured large numbers of officers and men, Mysore's warrior rulers were not only incorporating some of them in their own state, but also experimenting with British styles of military drill. As for the British captives themselves, some of them were voluntarily or involuntarily crossing frontiers of political and religious allegiance and being recruited into Mysore's service, their very bodies becoming marked forever in the process.

Adjusting to defeat

I stress the scale, quality and complexity of Mysore captivities because they are sometimes interpreted as a straightforward propaganda gift to the British, obvious material with which a striving imperial power could vilify a dangerous indigenous opponent. Yet Mysore captivities lent themselves to many kinds of interpretations, by no means all flattering to or convenient for the British. This was the first time since the East India Company's move away from a primarily commercial role that an Indian power had been strong enough to seize large numbers of its white and Indian soldiers, and members of the Crown's forces, and retain them for several years. In this context, captive British bodies easily appeared embarrassing emblems of defeat and disgrace. Especially as – when this war with Mysore ended in 1784 – it was with no triumphant treaty or territorial gain of importance on Britain's part. Those of its captives who were freed simply returned to their duties in India or limped home. 'The Government received us with every mark of inattention and incivility,' wrote a British ensign bitterly of his return to Madras.[38] This man had been captured at Bednur, and subsequently watched over a quarter of the ninety-three officers taken alongside him, die in a Mysore prison. Now he was free again, but found himself unwelcome among his own people, who seemed only to want to forget about former captives like him and what they represented. Not surprisingly, in the short term, none of these released military captives of Mysore published his story. Indeed, no British officer who kept a captivity narrative while being held in Mysore ever subsequently published his text directly and under his own name. When these writings did begin appearing in print, they did so only anonymously or posthumously, and invariably after heavy editing.

Some of the reasons for this initial reluctance to publish Mysore captivity accounts should be apparent. In this emergency, British solidarities had not been comprehensively maintained. According to contemporary estimates, some 1700 British-born male captives remained alive in Mysore in 1784. Almost a quarter of these men were either forced or chose to go over to their captors. That many of these individuals were circumcised only made their defection worse as far as their countrymen were concerned. As some British captives understood, circumcision for Muslims has far more of a social than a sacral significance. It is not one of the Five Pillars of Islam – prayer, the profession of faith, alms-giving, fasting, and the pilgrimage to Mecca – but is rather a practice signifying membership of the group.[39] Consequently, for British captives in Mysore to have undergone circumcision seemed a particularly indelible assault on their identity, an irreversible 'othering'. In the words of one ensign: 'I lost with the foreskin of my yard all those benefits of a Christian and Englishman which were and ever shall be my greatest glory.'[40] This is at once comic, tortured and eloquent. The man insists on his original religion and nationality, but at the same time presents these things as having been irretrievably taken away from him along with a small notch of flesh.

But it was of course the flesh in question that most provoked anger and anxiety. Exactly why the Mysore authorities ordered these circumcisions of British captives is unclear. British attempts at the time to explain them by reference to Tipu's 'bigotry to his religion' were expressions again of those ancient fears of Islam's proselytism by force that had influenced responses to Barbary captive-taking in an earlier period, but they do not convince. Just how strict either Tipu Sultan or Haidar Ali were as Muslims is still a matter of controversy. What is clear is that Tipu, like his father, was a pragmatist, accustomed both to ruling over Hindus, and working with uncircumcised French and Portuguese mercenaries and auxiliaries.[41] There seems little reason to suppose that either he or his officials wanted or expected a few hundred ragged Britons to become genuine co-religionists. In their case, circumcision was probably intended rather as a mark of new ownership, as an indelible symbol of these men's incorporation into the Mysore state. There may also have been an element of humiliation and even punishment involved. In Mysore, it was traditional for convicted felons to be cut in some way, to have their ear lobes removed, or their noses slit as permanent and shameful markers of their crimes. Were some British POWs also cut and marked after a fashion as punishment for perceived crimes? It seems possible.[42]

Certainly the British viewed what had happened to the bodies of some of their number in terms of shame, degradation and terror. As Freud observed, to the unsophisticated whose religion does not involve the practice, circumcision can appear akin to castration. Mysore prison narratives make it clear that the circumcision imposed on some of their number was perceived by British captives not just as a violent affront to who they were in terms of nationality and religion, but also as an assault on their manhood. 'Terribly alarmed this morning for our foreskins,' scribbled Cromwell Massey at one stage.[43] Fear that the Mysore authorities were seeking to unman them may have been sharpened by the fact – subsequently reported in the British press – that Tipu recruited some of the youngest captives, drummers, cabin boys and the like, to serve as *ramzanis* in his court, dancing boys who traditionally wore female costume.[44] In this sense too, then, the British bodies involved in this Mysore captivity panic could be viewed in terms of national humiliation: not just emblems of defeat and lapses in solidarity in India, but of emasculation as well.

Initial British uncertainty about how properly to see the Mysore captives, and how to tell their story, was also a function of there being so many army and naval officers involved, some of whom were of senior rank and considerable social status. Many of the captives examined in this book have been poor, mundane and miscellaneous, or private civilians from only modest backgrounds, merchant seamen, private soldiers, traders, male and female settlers, farmers, stray travellers and the like, typical representatives of the bulk of early modern humanity. The Mysore captives, like British captives in uniform during the American Revolution, were very different. The vast majority were military or naval men who had been captured in action, so what happened to them was a matter of national prestige. Moreover, their leaders viewed themselves as officers and gentlemen, and consequently

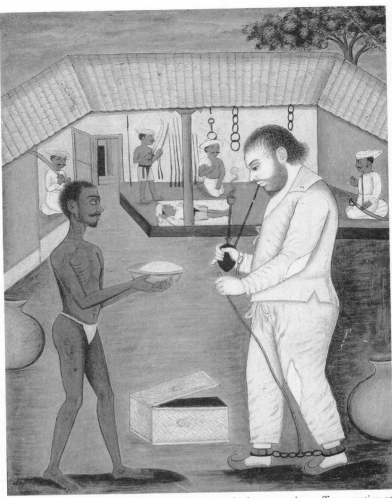

59. A portrait commissioned from an Indian artist by a one-time officer captive at Seringapatam. Is the servant included to offset the shame?

possessed a highly developed sense of individual and professional honour. These were emphatically not men used to posing as victims, or easily or appropriately represented as such in captivity narratives.

For individuals of this type, virtually any protracted captivity experience anywhere would have been a challenge. Accustomed to commanding obedience and prizing physical courage, they now had to learn to obey and submit to insult if they wanted to remain alive. Once men of status with a share of power over others, they now had to accustom themselves to insignificance and powerlessness in an alien society. John Lindsay, an army lieutenant captured at Pollilur when he was just nineteen, recorded being 'much hurt' when a Mysore official asked him if he possessed any skills as a blacksmith. Back home, Lindsay was the son of a Scottish earl: but who cared about that in Seringapatam? Lindsay was also resilient and intelligent, however, and in time came to derive a certain amusement from the metamorphosis that captivity was effecting in him and his fellows:

> Am tormented every day by a parcel of gentlemen coming to the end of my berth to talk politics and smoke cheroots. Advise them rather to think of mending the holes in their old shirts, like me, than trouble themselves about settling the balance of power in India and in Europe.[45]

As Lindsay recognised, these captive warriors could no longer strut upon the world's stage, much less determine how the world turned. They had been reduced to a peculiarly harsh and narrow private sphere, and those captives coped best who occupied themselves busily in the sort of minor, interior pursuits they would normally have consigned to their womenfolk or servants.

In Lindsay's case, this meant regularly dislodging a loose tile high on the outside wall of his prison cell in Seringapatam, and gazing through the resulting chink of light at the Mysore street life from which he was excluded:

> See a vast number of Brahmin girls going down to the river to wash – Four or five hundred horse pass by, guarding a multitude of the Carnatic inhabitants – A Moorman of high family, celebrating his marriage, passes by in great state, and his wife in a covered palanquin – Two old Moorwomen under the house scolding – a crowd of people around them, to whom they are telling their story. Shut my tile, for fear they should look up and observe me.

It was as if he were an inmate of a nunnery or a seraglio, reduced to passivity and enforced seclusion, and only able to sneak stolen glances at life outside that was literally passing him by. But Lindsay was armoured by the optimism of youth, and the confidence of his social class. He made himself take careful note of everything he observed, and then went back to his sewing. As his prison diary shows, he became immensely proud of a newly discovered ability to make and repair clothes.[46] Cromwell Massey, too, who survived his four years' in Seringapatam and lived to be over a hundred, kept fear and boredom at bay by domesticity as well as writing. Anticipating in this regard at least the most famous prisoner of the twentieth century,

Nelson Mandela, he found an unwanted patch of ground outside his cell and cultivated a garden. Some British officer-captives however found the transition to captive helplessness at the hands of non-Europeans unbearable. The prison notebooks of Richard Runwa Bowyer, a Royal Navy lieutenant held in Bangalore from late 1781 to 1784, were never published or extracted from, even posthumously.[47] To read them is to understand why. They are an almost unmitigated howl of pain and confusion.

A devout Protestant dissenter from a modest background, and younger even than his years, Bowyer was far more thin-skinned than Lindsay. But the depth of his trauma was primarily due to his being captured at sea off the coast of southern India, on his very first trip from England to the subcontinent. So, at one and the same time, he was obliged to adjust to a country, climate and cultures that he had never been exposed to before, and to the experience of having non-whites and non-Christians exercising absolute power over him, without ever having been in a position himself to exert power over Indians. As a result, Bowyer flailed about in panic, constantly trying to find some firm ground on which to moor his sense of his own religious, national and racial superiority, and frequently failing. The naïvety with which he recorded these struggles makes his narrative one of the rawest documents on cross-cultural shock that I know.

He found the cruder inversions and abuses of captivity – the fact, for instance, that in Bangalore he and his comrades were mustered daily by a 'black' officer armed with a whip – less dismaying than more mundane, seemingly innocuous encounters. He was troubled by the recognition that some of his Mysore captors were kind ('I must own this usage is more Christian-like, than any we experienced from the French'). He was also deeply hurt when some hungry Mysore criminals imprisoned alongside him rejected the food that he, in a conscious display of Christian charity, had offered them ('they would not accept . . . imagining the making use of any thing given them by us would defile them'). Unable himself to hold aloof – captivity, he wrote bitterly, meant being 'entirely dependent on the blacks' – he was never sure how to interact with his captors in such a way as to protect and assert his own precious distinctiveness:

> The black people take great pleasure in fighting cocks, and it is become quite modish in our prison. I bought a cock, as did some of my companions, and as the blacks often challenged us, and we in hopes of getting a *fanam* bet with them . . . I was fortunate enough to win 8 shillings by one cock, and after that refrained as I considered it brutish.

Yet, again, Bowyer had got it wrong.

The tensions in his mind emerged most sharply in an encounter that seems so strange, it may have arisen only from his own extreme disorientation. He claimed that in 1783, Bangalore's Muslim governor, with whom Bowyer established a kind of friendship, asked for the loan of some of his Western clothes, so that garments of a similar design could be made for one of Mysore's visiting French allies. 'At night', he writes, 'the Governor, attended by this pretended Frenchman, with music playing and a great concourse of the rabble, came to our prison.' Only then, Bowyer remarks, did he notice that the 'Frenchman's' hands and face were only painted white, and that between the man's new waistcoat and clinging breeches, it was possible to detect 'the genuine black colour of his skin'. Was this all or mainly a creation of Bowyer's tormented imagination, the effect of fear, extreme heat, imprisonment, and assumptions about race, power and virtue coming under strain? Or had Bangalore's governor detected Bowyer's prejudices and deep uneasiness and decided to pluck at them by this masquerade? Back home, Bowyer could easily have seen in the London and provincial theatres white actors playing blacks on the stage. But now he believed himself confronted by a 'black' imitating and mocking his own whiteness, and he could not bear it. Who gets to laugh, and conversely who gets habitually laughed at, are some of the best indicators in any time or place of where power and confidence reside. Those who laughed at Bowyer on this occasion, as he understood all too well, were really laughing at the extreme powerlessness he and his comrades had temporarily been reduced to.[48]

Bowyer was freed in 1784, and almost immediately returned home and sought refuge in the familiar, promptly marrying a woman from his own English county of Hampshire. But he never published his prison story; and neither in the short term did any of his fellow-captives. Their reticence must partly be attributed to the particular nature of this captivity ordeal. It was linked with British defeats in a subcontinent where winning had once appeared easy. It involved physical mutilations that could be interpreted as affronts to British masculinity. Some captives in Mysore had been high-ranking army and navy officers, and looked back at the fear, squalor and compromises involved with embarrassment and shame; and some British captives had defected to Mysore, and were consequently embarrassing and shameful. But the biggest obstacle to writing up these captivities was that few in Britain in the 1780s could feel certain that the military and imperial setbacks they had experienced in India and in other parts of the globe were reversible. Endurance in defeat only becomes something that nations can celebrate once they have regained a measure of confidence and success. Thus returning Vietnam veterans only became

Within the image: *Come if my Girls will Comply in Place with!* · *Terrah my Honey now for the Black Joke.* · *The Death of Tippoo or Besieging the Haram!!!*

60. *The Death of Tippoo or Besieging a Haram!!!* by Thomas Rowlandson.

personae gratae in the United States once its capacity for global intervention and dominion had been effectively reasserted. With the Mysore captives, too, vindication proved elusive until imperial momentum and national confidence revived. Nothing succeeded for them until there was once again evidence of a wider British success.

In the interim – and again just like US veterans of Vietnam – the Mysore captives found themselves castigated not just as losers, but as aggressors complicit in atrocity. In 1783, the year before most of the captives were freed, the *Annual Register*, a periodical associated with Edmund Burke, printed both a flattering obituary of Haidar Ali and a letter from an East India Company ensign accusing his comrades in southern India of pillage, rape and massacre. This letter, which was reprinted in other periodicals in 1784 and 1785, claimed that in just one British attack on a single Mysore settlement, Anantpur, 'four hundred beautiful women' had been killed and injured, '. . . while the private soldiers were committing every kind of outrage'. Other atrocity accusations were levelled against the Company at this time in the French press, and by British politicians intent on prosecuting Warren Hastings, the former governor-general of Bengal, in

Parliament.[49] But it was accusations of an Anantpur massacre against women that critics returned to again and again, and which stuck. As a result, when the earliest Mysore captivity narratives did begin to emerge from the press, their tone was markedly defensive. A bleak, retrospective account written by Harry Oakes, an officer captured at Bednur, came prefaced with an apologetic statement from its London publisher to the effect that Tipu Sultan's treatment of his British captives 'was evidently founded upon principles of retaliation . . . the unjustifiable behaviour of the Company's army goes a considerable way in justification of that of the enemy'.[50] Two years later, in 1787, a group of Company and regular army officers, again including Oakes, dispatched a formal letter from Bombay to East India House in London, insisting that the Anantpur accusations were fabricated, and expressing astonishment that the British press continued to repeat them:

> We will not pretend to assert, that the army was totally immaculate . . . [but] our present aim, is to convince the world, that during our residence in this distant clime, we have not forfeited every title to the feelings of humanity.[51]

The East India Company ordered this letter to be printed, and the House of Commons repeated the order in 1791, but to limited effect. Accusations that Company and regular army officers invading southern India had abused and slaughtered its women continued to be levelled. They surface yet again in a print issued in London in 1799 after the destruction of Tipu Sultan. Marauding Britons, their braid, epaulettes and tricorne hats marking them out as officers, are in every sense invading Tipu's harem. The balloons issuing from the officers' mouths ('Hurrah my Honey: Now for the *Black Joke*') make this undeniably what we would now call a racist print. But such racism as is present here is complex and broadly distributed. The women are shown with brown skins, but also wearing European fashions and features. White plumes ornament their curling hair; white stockings are chastely gartered above their knees. Tipu's bereft womenfolk in this purely imaginary scene become distraught ladies of fashion, undoubtedly so that their plight will more easily attract sympathy from a British audience. But the officers have also been re-imagined in this print, and far less flatteringly so. Their faces are disfigured by lust; their noses in particular are wildly elongated by the artist so as to suggest phallic urgency. Any restraint, like chivalry, is conspicuously absent. One British officer lies helpless beneath his ravished, half-naked Mysore victim, a rapist who has become a captive, and is even ridiculous.

Rewriting to win

So how did it change? How did these Mysore captivities shift from being emblems of anxiety, defeat and shame to becoming instead a profoundly influential component of British imperial story-telling? Part of the answer has to do with the French Revolution that broke out in 1789, and the world crisis it precipitated, that lasted until the second decade of the nineteenth century. At its outset, this Revolutionary crisis was a libertarian, egalitarian, and in some respects even an anti-imperial force, yet its end-result was paradoxically a strengthening of the power of many nation states, and a conspicuous strengthening too of some – though only some – of the world's overland and maritime empires. The Spanish and Portuguese empires in South America were terminally weakened by this crisis, and the Dutch and ultimately the French empires were also rolled back. But partly as a result of energising themselves so as to cope with the ideological and military ferment that followed on from the French Revolution, other states acquired in the process the momentum, organisation and opportunities to expand their territories at an unprecedented rate. This was true of Russia, which swallowed up Georgia in 1801 and Finland in 1809. It was true, too, of the new empire of the United States, that doubled its size by way of the Louisiana purchase from France in 1803. But, most dramatically, it was true of the British.[52]

After 1789, the British governing and military establishments went on the offensive, not just in terms of warfare on a massive and eventually highly successful scale, but also in terms of political argument and propaganda. India, like other parts of the world, felt the impact. In 1792, after three years of hard fighting, Tipu was forced to concede parts of Mysore's territory to the Company, though not the richest or most important sectors. Seven years and yet more savage fighting later, the walls of his capital Seringapatam shattered, Tipu was killed, and Mysore was restored – on terms – to its former Hindu dynasty, the Wodeyars. As had been the case in its previous conflicts with the British, Mysore received assistance from France. But this time, French aid did more in the end to ensure Tipu's destruction than to damage the British.[53]

True, in the course of the 1790s, French corsairs based in the Isle de France took out thousands of British ships and boats operating in the Indian Ocean; and, in 1798, Napoleon invaded Egypt arguably with the intention of using it as a springboard for a military invasion of India.[54] But this project proved a glamorous distraction, and when Tipu most required substantial French support, it was not available. Cornwallis's invasion of Mysore in the early 1790s was initially neither impressive nor successful.

Had France intervened at that point, it might have proved decisive, but it was still engulfed in its own revolution. Its known connections with Mysore ensured however that when a loyalist reaction emerged in Britain in opposition to the threat from Revolutionary and Napoleonic France, it also became directed against Tipu himself. There could be little sympathy for an Indian state that was linked to the European power planning to invade Britain itself. In the 1790s, as in the 1780s, British propaganda never focused exclusively on Tipu as 'Other', as an Asian prince and a proponent of Islam. It also aligned him with the prime Christian, European enemy. Tipu and Napoleon, in this version, became two sides of the same coin.

Thus despotism was not a characteristic attributed to Tipu solely or even primarily because he was an Indian or Muslim ruler. It was rather – in the British propaganda version – something he shared with Napoleon, yet another usurper.[55] This was just one respect in which the former Mysore captives now became a valuable component of British imperial argument. The harshness with which both captive Britons *and captive sepoys* had reputedly been treated in the 1780s ('worse than the slaves of Barbary') was now, some ten years later, disinterred and used to buttress assertions that Tipu was an oppressor of whites and Indians both. For the first time ever, the British state and the East India Company began orchestrating the writing and publication of captivity narratives about India. The Company now made a point of interviewing all escapees from Mysore imprisonment, both for any information they could provide, and for suitably emotive stories. The best were dispatched to East India House in London which promptly arranged for their publication in the official *London Gazette*. Thus in August 1791, Madras learnt that five British captives had escaped from Seringapatam, including a William Drake, a Royal Navy midshipman. An army officer was promptly instructed to 'collect from them all the information in his power'. Before the end of the year, Madras was able to send London 'a copy of a narrative delivered by Mr William Drake . . . and other prisoners . . . containing an account of the treatment they experienced'. Published the following April in the *London Gazette* (it also featured in the *Calcutta Gazette*), Drake's story was promptly reprinted in the London *Times* and other commercial papers and referred to in editorials on 'the Tyrant Tippoo': 'Perhaps a more interesting narrative than the following never appeared.'[56]

But Tipu, in the British imagination, was not just an Asian Napoleon. He was also – as his own court rituals and chosen symbolism proclaimed – a tiger prince, the personification of all that seemed to the British dangerous and unpredictable about India. And it was partly as a tiger, 'tearing in pieces the helpless victims of his craft, or his rapacity', that British propagandists now began describing him. This was something of a departure. Back in the 1780s, even captive Britons had generally described Tipu in moderate or even respectful terms. 'He bore his success like a man accustomed to victory,' wrote a colonel who had been captured at Tanjore: 'nothing haughty or imperious about him.' 'His manners were easy and affable; his address and behaviour agreeable,' recorded another British officer who was brought face to face with Tipu after the fall of Mangalore.[57] 'Easy', 'affable', 'agreeable': these are the sort of words that Jane Austen employed in her novels to alert readers to one of her more acceptable gentlemanly characters. And the use of code terms denoting an English gentleman in these early British descriptions of Tipu is surely no accident. Nor was it accidental that – like his father – Tipu was often described as pale-skinned. Robert Cameron, an army lieutenant captured at Pollilur in 1780, customarily referred to the guards in his prison as 'blacks'. Brought before Tipu, however, he saw him as 'fair, with a pleasing countenance'. Another Scottish officer-captive of Mysore, Innes Munro, was critical in his narrative of miscegenation in India lest it 'give a sallow tinge to the complexion of Britons', but thought nothing of comparing Haidar Ali approvingly to Frederick the Great of Prussia.[58] Even in 1790, an English observer could liken Tipu to Achilles, with all that this implied in terms of martial valour and classical physique.[59] As would always be the case, non-Europeans of power, rank, and – in the case of Haidar and Tipu proven military success – could deflect and correct a racially hostile European gaze (and *vice versa*).

By the end of the eighteenth century, however, private and public British descriptions of Tipu had darkened in every sense. A senior Scottish army officer who viewed his naked corpse in the ruins of Seringapatam in 1799 remembered it in these terms:

> The outlines of his person had that general shape which is common to the Musselman of India. His bust was corpulent, his thighs rather short ... *His complexion was swarthy and much darker than that of men of high family in the east.* The colour of his face appeared probably a shade fairer in death ... A promiscuous intercourse with the [female] sex had left its effects on the Sultan's body.

No longer a powerful southern Indian ruler able to inflict damage on the British, but dead and at their mercy, Tipu here is both blackened and orientalised. His corpse no longer evokes Achilles, but is rather feminised to the extent that it is even given breasts and foreshortened thighs. The fair skin that Cameron had admired back in 1782 is now dark – despite the pallor of death. And the writer's blatant accusation of Tipu's sexual

. The defensive walls of Seringapatam, drawn by a British artist in 1792.

excesses contains a hint of physical damage, even perhaps of impotence. Yet even this singularly unpleasant passage is a warning against selective quotation and facile assumptions about human consistency. The writer ends by conceding that Tipu's expression in death was 'gentle and contented . . . a tranquil and courteous air for which he was distinguished when alive'. He also concludes by urging that Britain should now consolidate its existing territorial gains in India 'without looking for objects of further aggrandisement'.[60]

The fall of Tipu and Seringapatam in 1799 was undeniably a seismic event, a vital component of Britain's progress towards hegemony in India, and something that attracted mass excitement and attention at home. Yet the surviving evidence confirms what the British government conceded in print at the time: attitudes towards Tipu certainly became more negative, but they remained complex and continued to fluctuate after his death as they had during his life. There was no new consensus either on the desirability or feasibility of continued British advance in India. This did not stop the advance from proceeding, though the scale of its success remained in question until the destruction of the Maratha Confederacy in 1803–4.[61] But British qualms persisted. They surface in high-level correspondence, as in the governor of Bombay's protest at the scale of British violence after the fall of Seringapatam ('a national blot exceeding in turpitude anything that our annals can probably furnish in any part of the world'). They surface too in the early decades of the nineteenth century in all kinds of low-level as well as polite culture. Patriotic parents who purchased *Tippoo Saib; or the storming of Seringapatam* from Hodgson's Juvenile Drama Series for the benefit of their children in the 1820s must have been somewhat taken aback by the opening speech allocated to Tipu himself:

> Tis well, my brave people! I know your loyalty, and dread not the tyrannic power that even now threatens us with destruction!

The argument that oriental despotism, if it ever existed, was now being matched in some respects by the East India Company's military despotism in India was expressed with greater sophistication in other private and public British writings at this time.[62]

And this was where a new generation of Mysore captivity narratives had, for conformists, their greatest value. They helped to humanise Britain's armed forces in the public imagination even as those forces grew in scale and global aggressiveness to an unprecedented degree.

An early but influential work in this regard was William Thomson's *Memoirs of the Late War in Asia* published in 1788, and reissued 'after a rapid sale of a large impression' in amplified form the following year.[63] It was significant that Thomson was not a soldier, but a one-time clergyman turned professional writer. Moreover he was a Scot, and this too was significant. As Tipu himself recognised, the Company and regular army regiments that invaded Mysore in the 1780s and 90s contained a disproportionate number of Scottish officers and men.[64] The government minister responsible at this time for India was also a Scot, Henry Dundas, who had chaired the parliamentary enquiry into Pollilur and other military failures in southern India. For Dundas, India was vital, while the mood of imperial recessional and disillusionment that had followed the lost war with America was anathema. Empire must continue to advance, as he saw it, because Britain's power in general, and Scotland and its talented, hungry males in particular, depended upon its doing so. There is no evidence that Thomson wrote his two-volume work on the Mysore captives on the instructions of the government or the East India Company, but he enjoyed close links with members of the Scottish elite and senior Scottish army officers, and this was crucial to the format of his book.[65]

Despite its title, *Memoirs of the Late War* is less a work of military history than martyrology. As the preface 'To the Reader' declares, it is 'a narrative of what happened to our men under confinement with the barbarians', and as such dwells not on empire or the field of battle but rather on 'the fate of individuals'. Thomson did not shrink from recording British defeats in southern India because he knew how to transmute them into something else. The remnants of the Company's forces after Pollilur became in his prose, for example, the 'gallant remains of our little army', a source of pride. Nor was Thomson afraid of the less dignified aspects of Mysore captivity. Squalor, pain, fear, grief, forcible circumcision, the strains that captivity placed on composure, allegiance and morale were all included in his volumes. As they were bound to be, since he drew heavily – as he admitted – on interviews with former officer-captives and on their prison writings. But by absorbing their stories and memories into his text without at any point naming his sources, he was able to bring out the full agony and pathos of captivity without outraging the masculine, gentlemanly or professional pride of his particular informants. In the process, what was ostensibly a chronicle of imperial warfare became instead:

A tragedy . . . of *suffering* not of *action* . . . It is hoped that no reader of humanity will be offended at the mention of many facts and circumstances, at first sight of no consideration . . . Violent moral situations tear up and display the passions and powers of the human soul. The sensibility of our captive countrymen . . . The strength of their sympathy with one another; the relief they found under strong agitation, in pouring forth, or in adopting strains of affecting though unpolished poetry.[66]

By means of this literary strategy and highly literary style, Thomson's book began the work of transforming the warriors of the East India Company and the British state into new men or, less anachronistically, into men of feeling. The focus was shifted, quite deliberately, from chronicling military action in southern India with all its controversial episodes and violence, to a moving evocation of British soldiers' emotional stress, torment, and resilience in a situation of extreme pressure.

Thomson was a highly professional hack, but not an original writer. He did not invent this literary method and style, but borrowed it, and his source is very clear: Samuel Richardson's three, immensely influential novels of sentiment, *Pamela* (1740–1), *Clarissa* (1747–8), and *The History of Sir Charles Grandison* (1753–4). Thomson constructed his supposedly factual history, just as Richardson does in his fictions, by linking together letters and narratives by different characters, in his case the writings of various Mysore captives. He also emulated Richardson's immense moral earnestness, his taste for minute detail, and – most of all – his concern with how individuals are tested and redeemed through suffering.

Even before Thomson's book appeared, some of the more educated Mysore captives had recognised the 'fit' between Clarissa Harlowe's predicament as evoked by Richardson, and their own far more distant, masculine ordeals. In the novel, Clarissa is imprisoned in a brothel, persecuted and tested relentlessly, and then drugged so that the villain Lovelace may finally prevail against her closely guarded virginity. But not having consented to her own violation, she retains her essential virtue. She escapes, fades away and embraces her own death, but is posthumously redeemed, while her tormenter is finally destroyed by his own violence. *Clarissa*, in other words, is itself a fictional captivity narrative; and after the appearance of Thomson's book, its influence, and that of other novels of sentiment on the writing of British imperial captivity narratives became increasingly marked.[67] As far as the Mysore captives were concerned, Clarissa's story seemed particularly apt. They too had suffered and been imprisoned; and some of them had been drugged as a prelude to physical violation, in their case circumcision. But, by implication, these men's essential virtue and identity also remained untouched because what had been done to their bodies had been carried out by force and against their will. And now these one-time captive sufferers were free and vindicated, while the chief villain of their story, Tipu Sultan, was set for violent and deserved destruction.

In part, then, because of global war, reviving imperial fortunes, and the emergence of a more conservative brand of British nationalism, but also because of these vital shifts in writing about Mysore captivity, what had previously savoured of humiliation, squalor and defeat came to seem deeply interesting and touched with moral fervour and pathos. One can see this shift at work in many of the Mysore captivity narratives published in the wake of Thomson's bestseller. In 1792, for instance, the Company's press in Calcutta financed the publication of the *Narrative of the Sufferings of James Bristow*. As its preface pointed out, this was designed to be read in conjunction with the *Memoirs of the Late War in Asia*. Thomson's volumes had focused on the British officer class. But Bristow's story was that of a humble Company private soldier captured, forcibly circumcised, and driven into one of Mysore's slave regiments, but who – in this dictated account at least – remains faithful at heart and eventually escapes the clutches of Tipu and returns to his own kind. Again, this was a deeply serious and highly detailed account, which concentrated not on military action or southern India, but on the agonies and determination of an embattled individual. Like Thomson's work, it remains moving to read, and at the time was commercially an immense success, going through at least two London editions in 1793 and a third in 1794, and continuing to be reissued until the 1820s.[68]

What I am suggesting therefore is that to explain British imperial resurgence and successful aggression in India and elsewhere after 1790 in terms of expansion of manpower, military and naval prowess, economic, technological and industrial power, and a hardening of conservative and nationalistic ideologies, is correct up to a point, but also insufficient. Teetering on the verge of unprecedented global intervention, the British then – rather like Americans now – needed to be persuaded that they were not only a superpower, but also a virtuous, striving and devoted people. Successful military machismo and conquests were never enough. Indeed, given the long tradition in Britain of suspicion of standing armies, military machismo by itself could prove immensely unpopular, as the outcry over the Anantpur massacre and other reputed Company excesses in the 1780s clearly demonstrated. Redcoats let loose upon forts, towns and villages in the Indian subcontinent, like those who had ranged themselves against American rebels after 1775, could not be certain of winning support back in Britain just because they were redcoats. They had first to be viewed as good men, and consequently as incapable of bad deeds. The rewriting of Mysore captivity ordeals from the 1780s onwards was one of the ways in which – very much with official sponsorship – the British military overseas was repackaged for improved domestic consumption.[69]

There were other manifestations of the same trend. It is striking, for instance, that – as far as British opinion at home was concerned – the most celebrated incident in these wars with Mysore, apart from the captivities, was Lord Cornwallis's 'kind' reception of two sons of Tipu Sultan, who were taken hostage in 1792 as a guarantee that their father would cede the Company both territory and a substantial cash payment. As Mildred Archer long ago pointed out, this was the most illustrated episode in this series of Mysore wars. There were umpteen paintings, engravings, prints, souvenirs, and even embroideries of it, as well as books, poems, and newspaper accounts. Indeed, almost as much artistic attention was devoted to this episode of apparent British clemency as to Tipu's death and the fall of Seringapatam.[70] In reality, there was of course limited kindness involved in the British taking two young boy children away from their home and father to be used as diplomatic counters. But most of those who recorded this scene in words or images for a domestic audience drew a straightforward moral from it, and one that explicitly contrasted British military virtue with Tipu's reputed systematic cruelty. When the latter had been powerful enough to take thousands of Britons and Company sepoys captive, they pointed out, he had made them suffer. Now, however, the British were not only powerful enough to take Tipu's own sons captive, but also showed their superior humanity by treating the boys well, for indeed these young princes were subsequently cosseted and made much of.

These goings-on can be understood at various levels. One was outlined with spectacular percipience by Edmund Burke in 1784:

> The main drift of their policy was to keep the natives totally out of sight. We might hear enough about what great and illustrious exploits were daily performing on that great conspicuous theatre [India] by Britons. But . . . we were never to hear of any of the natives being actors.[71]

By focusing attention on the incontestable qualities of the British armed forces, their courage, discipline, endurance, self-sacrifice, comradeship and the like, a new generation of military and imperial publicists was effectively distracting attention from the more controversial issue of what these men and their kind were actually doing in India and other parts of the globe. The casualty-levels, pillage, and destruction inevitably attendant on a policy of extending empire by force of arms were sidelined. Instead, Britons were encouraged to concentrate their emotional and moral gaze upon British officers and soldiers in their roles as suffering, valiant, and exemplary men and individuals. Thus when one of John Lindsay's descendants finally published his Mysore prison notebook in 1840, he not only omitted some of its original bleak, mundane and ironic material, but also inserted a preface:

> Deep moral lessons are unconsciously conveyed in every page of this Journal. The eye may be moistened, the heart saddened, but I am sure the reader will rise up a wiser and better man [sic] from its perusal.[72]

But it is also possible to look at these shifts in British representation of empire, armies and captivity in a rather different way. When the unknown Indian artist responsible for the mural of Pollilur in Tipu's palace had sought deliberately to feminise Colonel Baillie's embattled troops, it had obviously been with the intention of mocking and diminishing them. Yet, paradoxically, this successful British repackaging of the military in India and elsewhere also involved an element of feminisation, even to the extent of drawing inspiration from Samuel Richardson's novels of put-upon women. What happened was what Terry Eagleton has called the 'domestication of heroism' in which 'the barbarous values of militarism, naked dominance and male *hauteur*' were concealed or at least offset by the more 'fashionable virtues of . . . sensibility, civility and tendresse'.[73] British imperial warriors in this new and revised version became not just gentlemen, but strangely gentle – at least with each other. 'It is one of the most remarkable and beautiful features of this dreadful captivity', wrote the biographer of General Sir David Baird, a one-time captive in Mysore and subsequently a destroyer of Tipu, in 1832, 'that every man during its continuation seemed more anxious for his fellow-sufferers than for himself.'[74]

This highly effective formula of focusing attention on the emotional and moral development of Westerners caught up in extra-European conflicts has persisted to this day and has long since ceased to be confined to the British. Just think of how many Hollywood films of the Vietnam War, even some critical ones, confine the Vietnamese themselves to the role of extras while placing at their centre the bravery, torment and emotional struggles of all-American heroes. Here, too, in the cinema version of American global ventures, the natives are usually kept firmly out of sight, while the emotional spotlight focuses on the Western intruders. But there were particular reasons why it was the British who pioneered and worked on this shift in representing their armed forces overseas. Increasingly aggressive as the eighteenth century drew to its close, they remained demographically limited, though by now – as we shall see – far less anxiously so. After 1800, as before, British imperial warriors were always going to be at risk of defeat and capture and suffering, because their numbers and the size of their resource base never remotely matched the scale of their global ambitions. It was therefore vital, as far as the British were concerned, to evolve a way of writing about imperial warfare in which sporadic failures and disasters could be represented as being themselves a form of heroic virtue, moral improvement and patriotic service – a victory of sorts.

There is a final point. The East India Company's successive wars with Mysore illuminate the conspicuously shifting fortunes of a small country attempting empire at a faraway distance and on an unprecedented scale. The first and second of these wars, that lasted respectively from 1767 to 1769, and 1779 to 1784, reveal how the East India Company's advance into India became far harder than it had initially anticipated, and the depths of disillusionment and even despair that gripped Britain in the wake of defeat in the subcontinent, in America, and elsewhere. For pessimists, as we have seen, the circumcision inflicted on some British captives in Mysore seemed an ultimate and definitive emblem of national castration and unmanning. Britain, it appeared, was no longer the automatic winner that the Seven Years War had seemed to suggest, but a nation in retreat and an empire in decline. Had an opinion poll been conducted in the 1780s, many Britons, perhaps the majority, would have predicted that the nineteenth century could not possibly be their century. They had peaked, and were now on the way down. In much the same way, but with far less cause, many Americans in the 1980s believed that losing the Vietnam War had demonstrated that their empire too had peaked. The twenty-first century, they allowed themselves for a while to fear, would belong to some other power, not to them. These American pessimists were wrong. So, too, were disconsolate Britons in the 1780s.

For if the first two Mysore Wars, together with the lost American War, taught the British that acquiring overseas territory was not going to be the pushover some of them had foolishly allowed themselves to imagine, the last two Mysore Wars in the 1790s, like the concurrent European wars against Revolutionary France, demonstrated Britain's capacity to reassert and reconfigure itself in the wake of crushing global defeats. The British struck back, more violently than before, and with much more success. As we have seen, this imperial resurgence involved more than an escalation of military effort in India and in other parts of the globe. There was also a vital reconfiguring of both imperial and national ideology. The Mysore captives' transition from figures of national disgrace and embarrassment to gallant heroes whose sacrifice and sufferings exemplified the nation's manhood at its best demonstrates this ideological re-tooling at work. In much the same way, Vietnam veterans in America initially had to contend with the unconcern, embarrassed pity, and even open hostility of their own countrymen. Their subsequent transition to hero status has been so marked that US veteran organisations are now having to cope with an epidemic of American males claiming quite falsely that they saw combat in Vietnam.[75]

In the United States – as in Britain two centuries ago – the will to battle and the will to global dominance have been successfully re-tooled in the aftermath of traumatic defeat. But these comparisons should not be pushed too far. For, however much *in some respects* American empire now echoes earlier British empire, in terms of the size of the imperial metropolis there is an obvious and fundamental divergence. The USA spans a continent, whereas it was the very smallness of Britain's island dimensions that acted simultaneously as a spur to overseas empire, and as a persistent handicap in the process of achieving it. Yet, even in this respect, conflict with Mysore witnessed a significant transition. Initially, the British had been daunted by India's vast population and size, and some of them had also doubted whether the sepoys they necessarily recruited in large numbers to fight for them there would remain reliable under pressure. War with Mysore substantially eased these anxieties. British captives of Haidar Ali and Tipu Sultan were able to persuade individual Indians to take enormous risks carrying messages for them, and although a minority of Company sepoys mutinied or deserted in the wars against Mysore, the majority remained loyal. 'The fortitude and fidelity of our brave sepoys' is a theme touched upon by virtually every British captivity narrative that emerged from these wars.[76] For the British, this proved a vital revelation. They had never been able to recruit and incorporate Native Americans into their imperial war effort to the degree they would have liked, in part because of their relative paucity, and in part because of the objections of their own white settlers. But, in India – the British came to realise – it was very different. Here, they could compensate effectively for their own small numbers by recruiting indigenous manpower on a massive scale. Moreover, and as the Mysore wars demonstrated, men so recruited would in general fight bravely and if necessary die for the cause of Company and British dominion.

A secret memorandum written in 1805 by Lord Wellesley, Governor General of India, was tinged with all kinds of racist assumptions, but was in essence correct:

> As mercenary troops, the natives of India possess obedience, docility and fidelity beyond all others. These qualities are inherent in the people, as they are no less conspicuous in the British service than in that of the powers of the country. . . . [They] have assisted us in retaining their own country in subjection with a fidelity scarce less than our own countrymen.

This was one of the major steps on the British road to imperial resurgence after the lost American war. At the same time that Britain itself was evolving a more powerful and conservative brand of nationalism, its politicians and warriors came to realise as never before that – because of the lack of fully developed national ideologies in the zones where they were advancing – indigenous manpower could be recruited to make up for Britain's own smallness of numbers. The British could indeed capitalise on pre-existing divisions and so rule. By the time Wellesley wrote, there were almost 170,000 sepoys fighting on behalf of the East India Company, while on the other side of the world, black slave regiments were proving equally valuable fighting for the British in the Caribbean.[77]

Yet, for all this, the British still continued to wrestle with the problems posed by their own limitations. For all their growing reliance on indigenous warriors, they still needed a reliable core of their own. In the Mysore captivity panic of the 1780s, almost a quarter of the British troops seized, mostly men from the other ranks, had voluntarily or involuntarily crossed over to the other side. So as Britain entered on a new and far more dangerous and extensive phase of imperial expansion, it had to deal as well with the problems posed by the poor whites who manned its army and navy. How, and how far, could men like this be made into the reliable fodder of imperial legions? Let us see.

TEN

Captives in Uniform

Winning the numbers game

1798, the last full year in Western calendar time of Tipu Sultan's life, saw the publication of one of the most influential texts in imperial terms ever to appear in Britain. The work in question was not a novel, nor a piece of conventional political theory. It was a voluminous, uncompromising tract by a mild intellectual named Thomas Malthus, and its title was *An Essay on the Principle of Population*. Malthus went on to become the first Professor of Political Economy at Haileybury College, set up in 1805 to train civil servants for the East India Company, but his essay was not explicitly concerned with either India or Britain's empire in general. Nor, as an early editor conceded, was it initially widely read or generally understood. But it was one of those rare works that transforms attitudes beyond the bounds of its readership or the intentions of its author. 'When we speak of Mr. Malthus', declared William Hazlitt, who disliked the man and his arguments intensely, 'we mean the *Essay on Population*; and when we mention the *Essay on Population*, we mean a distinct leading proposition, that stands out intelligibly from all trashy pretence, and is a ground on which to fix the levers that may move the world.'[1]

The proposition involved was a blunt one. If left unrestrained, population would increase exponentially in advance of the supply of food: 'the power of population is indefinitely greater than the power in the earth to produce subsistence for man.' The *Essay*'s apocalyptic tone was more a result of Malthus's personal dread of the forces of the French Revolution (and perhaps of the raging toothache gripping him while he wrote it), than of any fear on his part that Britain was already suffering from over-population.[2] None the less, his book changed the terms of contemporary argument. Before this, Britons had often been fearful that their country possessed too few people. After the *Essay*'s publication, however, most came to believe that Britain's population was expanding at an accelerating, even uncontrollable rate. The challenge now appeared to be *too many* people, a revolutionary shift in perception that would be crucial to

Britain's growing involvement and investment in empire in the nineteenth century.

For most of the previous century, it had been widely though not unanimously believed that Britain's population was in free-fall. A rise in quantitative research in the second half of the eighteenth century failed to disperse this illusion. Richard Price, the most respected demographer of his day, drew meticulously on urban mortality rates and house tax figures seemingly to prove that the population of England and Wales had declined since 1688 to less than five million in the 1780s. (The real figure for England alone when Price wrote was actually well over seven million.)[3] This pervasive and perverse demographic gloom had profound imperial consequences. British politicians remained for a long time nervous of stationing substantial numbers of troops overseas, or of allowing large-scale emigration by the respectable labouring classes, in case an already diminishing home population became lethally depleted. 'The state of our population was not very flattering,' warned a member of Parliament in 1771, opposing an increase of troops for India: '. . . the species decreased, and . . . we ought to keep as many as possible for the defence of Britain'. As we have seen, such anxieties were reinforced by defeat in America and major setbacks in southern India. Britain, these reverses had seemed to confirm, was just too small and insufficiently populous to generate the taxes and the manpower that were necessary for major imperial conflict, while simultaneously maintaining prosperity at home. Large-scale territorial conquests, as distinct from global commerce, were indulgences the country could not and should not afford.[4] But Malthus's famous book signalled and quickened a transformation in the landscape of ideas.

His *Essay on Population,* as it was widely understood, together with the first ever census in Britain and Ireland in 1801 which showed that their combined population exceeded sixteen million, allowed Britons to feel infinitely more proactive about the demands of empire. Patrick Colquhoun, one of a new breed of political arithmeticians with close links to the government, spelt out the implications in his influential *Treatise on the Wealth, Power and Resources of the British Empire* (1814). His aim was to scotch any lingering 'gloomy apprehensions respecting the resources of the empire'. He printed copious population tables drawn from the second census of 1811, as well as statistics suggesting that the armed forces at Britain's disposal across the globe, including Indian and other foreign troops, now exceeded one million men: 'the most sanguine imagination could not have anticipated such an accession of population, territory and power.' In a suggestive early use of what became a famous phrase, he boasted that 'the sun never sets on the flag', and that successful global war against Napoleon had demonstrated once and for all 'the practicality of conquest'. There need be no more fears of imperial expansion draining Britain's economy and population. Properly regarded, empire was indispensable to both. Every five years, another polemicist suggested in 1817, Britain needed to shed 'at least one million of souls'. The new lands, opportunities, and combat involved in imperial enterprise were exactly the providential outlet required for Malthus's surplus population: 'colonizing . . . can only be looked to as the means of salvation.'[5]

Two other developments contributed to this rising confidence that Britain was now a big enough power for overseas diffusion and destiny: the retention of Ireland and the defeat of Napoleonic France. The year of Malthus's masterwork, 1798, saw a revolt by thousands of Protestant as well as Catholic Irishmen against rule from London. It was bloodily suppressed, and in 1800 an Act of Union brought Ireland into the United Kingdom. Irish manpower, growing at a faster rate even than Britain's own, was now secure, or so it seemed, within the imperial arsenal. This was vital because, without Irishmen, the rampant growth of Britain's empire at this stage would scarcely have been possible. By the 1830s they made up over 40 per cent of its legions. Before the Famine, more than half of all white soldiers in India were Irish: 'the Irish nursery seems inexhaustible', as one East India Company officer purred.[6] The proportion of Irishmen in the British regiments fighting at Waterloo in 1815 was almost as impressive: and this final, conclusive victory over France confirmed an already existing transformation in the scale of Britain's empire, and provided an essential precondition for its further massive growth.

War against Revolutionary and Napoleonic France (1793–1815) increased the number of Britain's colonies from twenty-six to forty-three. The Cape, Sierra Leone, Gambia and the Gold Coast were seized in Africa; Tobago, St Lucia, and Trinidad in the Caribbean; and Malta and the Ionian Islands in the Mediterranean. In addition, vast, additional swathes of Australia and India were conquered or annexed.[7] Dramatic though these new, blood-red splashes on the map were, in one sense the most crucial change in global power politics was within Europe itself. Stress is often laid now on how aggressive Europeans were in the past in relation to other continents. Yet this indictment, understandable though it may be, obscures what has always in fact been the prime focus of European aggression. In every century during the first and second millennium – with only one conspicuous exception – Europeans have devoted more energy to hating, fighting and invading each other, than to hating, fighting and invading peoples outside Europe. The dark continent, as Mark Mazower calls it, has persistently consumed itself, more even than it has encroached on others. The solitary, partial exception before 2000 to this pattern of obsessive intra-European warfare was the hundred years' comparative peace between the European powers from Waterloo to the outbreak of the First World War in 1914, a peace that as far as Britain was concerned was interrupted only briefly by the Crimean War (1854–6).

Victorian Britons would rarely feel completely assured about their continent's unprecedented tranquillity or their own European hegemony. They worried persistently about the old enemy France, about Russia and its possible designs on India, and ultimately about a newly unified Germany. None the less, between Waterloo and 1914, neither Britain nor any other European power experienced conflict on anything like the scale of the Seven Years War or the Napoleonic Wars. And never in this period was Britain confronted with a confederation of Western powers bent on attacking its colonial outposts, as it had been in the American Revolutionary War, and would be again after 1914. The profit and the price of this hundred-year partial European peace was unprecedented Western, and especially British freedom to concentrate on global empire. In 1800, the European powers, together with Russia and the United States, laid claim to some 35 per cent of the globe's total land area. By 1914, in large part because of their reduced tendency after Waterloo to war among themselves, the proportion of the globe claimed by western Europe, Russia and the United States had risen to 84 per cent.[8]

By 1815, therefore, anxiety over what had always been viewed as the main internal obstacles to Britain's indulgence in overseas empire – its demographic limits and its territorial smallness – was receding fast. Yet greater confidence on this score, together with an end to distracting European-wide warfare, and access to unprecedented levels of economic power, did not immediately bring a cessation of Britain's captivity panics. Rather what occurred was a shift in the nature of imperial captivities. Because it felt able to do so, but also because the scale of its empire gave it no choice, the British state now markedly increased the number of its own people who were exiled overseas for long periods of time. Many of these exiles were working-class men and women dispatched to imperial locations and set to labour there under a substantial degree of discipline, and with little say over when or whether they would ever return. In Australia before 1850, the bulk of these white, working-class British exiles were transported convicts. But in Asia, the majority were soldiers, the worker bees of the British empire, yet still men who, after a fashion, were captives of their own state, captives in uniform.

The last half of the eighteenth century and the first third of the nineteenth century witnessed a revolution in the extent and global distribution of British military manpower. In 1740, only three out of the forty-odd British army regiments had been stationed outside Europe. By the 1770s the position was already changing, and a spell of overseas duty was coming to be part of the normal expectations of every regiment of the line. By 1800, and still more after 1815, the situation was vastly different again. On the eve of Queen Victoria's accession in 1837, more than three-quarters of Britain's one hundred plus regular army regiments were based in the empire.[9] At least twenty of these were garrisoned in India, besides the East India Company's own army that now exceeded 200,000 men, the bulk of whom were sepoys.

These were dramatic transformations. Yet suggestions that they represented the construction of an essentially militarised empire need treating with some care.[10] The British military conspicuously expanded and globalised after 1750: yes. But while this expansion was impressive by previous *British* standards, it was less so when set against some contemporary European and non-European armies. By 1850, Britain's armed forces at home and in all of its overseas 'possessions', barring India, totalled just over 105,000 men. This was less than a third of the size of France's military at that time, less than an eighth of Russia's, and smaller even than the army of Prussia which possessed no colonies at all.[11] True: the East India Company's army needs adding to the equation. But the vast majority of its men were Indian not British; and, as one officer pointed out in 1833 – even here – the disparity between the number of British and Indian imperial troops on the one hand, and the subcontinent's size and population on the other, was a marked one. His estimate was one imperial soldier to every 450 Indian inhabitants. This contrasted poorly, for instance, with the situation in the United States, emphatically a second-rate power at this time, where the ratio of regular and militia troops to population was nearer one to a hundred:

> Casting the eyes over the map of British India, it seems incredible the long line of exposed frontier, frequently without a single regiment of the line, or even a scattered detachment of sepoys.[12]

In other words, the wider global distribution of British forces, and the emergence of a more relaxed domestic attitude towards the export of civilians and military men, were more striking developments in this period than an actual, sustained expansion in the sum-total of British imperial muscle. 'Imperial overstretch' was not something that Britain suddenly began to experience in the late Victorian era.[13] In terms of the gap between its military (and naval) manpower, and the territory it affected to govern, imperial Britain was always overstretched. The thin red line was more accurately anorexic. This helps to explain why, despite undoubted naval paramountcy at this time and a faster-expanding technological gap between the West and the rest, the armies of Victorian Britain continued to experience sporadic, savage humiliations in imperial locations – deaths, defeats, and occasionally conspicuous captivities.

But the shortfall between Britain's overseas manpower and its global pretensions also provided for another kind of overseas captivity. By 1815, virtually every British regular soldier could expect to spend half, and often two-thirds of his career in imperial postings. The persistent limits on the size of the army, and a consequent sparsity of replacement regiments, meant that before the 1850s especially these postings necessarily lasted for long periods of time, for ten, often twenty years without a break. In 1828, Viscount Palmerston, then secretary at war, told Parliament that two British regiments about to be dispatched overseas had, most unusually, been able to spend the previous six years at home. Before that, however, they 'had experienced seventeen years of uninterrupted foreign service, either in the East or West Indies, or at Ceylon'. Such extended periods of banishment meant that soldiers, superficially the most straightforward agents of British empire, became in practice rather more unpredictable actors. As the Army Quartermaster General admitted in 1836:

> Everybody who has seen the nature of colonial service must know . . . that it is exceedingly difficult, if not impossible, under the very best discipline, to prevent the soldiers acquiring directly, or through their wives, *a certain degree of locality*.[14]

From the authorities' perspective, it was the degree of locality that was the rub. Confined for years to non-European locations, without any provision for home leave, how were ordinary British soldiers to be prevented from becoming irremediably changed in the process? And what might follow from such changes? Were troops who spent virtually all their adult lives in other continents at risk of 'going native' to the extent that their original religious, political and national identities became compromised? Might some desert and go over entirely? How could British soldiers operating at vast distances from home, and in regions where communications might well be non-existent, be properly monitored and controlled?

Official anxieties on this score must be understood in the light of European as well as extra-European pressures. The period between 1770 and 1840 was an age of revolution and new republics in France and the Americas, and of accelerated growth in population, urbanisation, means of production, literacy, print culture, and consciousness of social class in

Britain itself. It is now generally accepted that there were parallels between the British state's reactions to this barrage of change at home, and the quality of its imperial exertion overseas. A more conservative and militaristic nationalism, a new emphasis on ceremonial display and religious seriousness, together with a proliferation of barracks and prisons, were cherished and fostered by those governing late Georgian Britain and Ireland; at the same time, a more rigorous policy of control and greater ideological assertiveness was practised by British imperial activists from Canada to the Cape and beyond.[15] Yet there was another side to this connection between accelerating change in Britain, and the quality of British empire at this time. Between the 1770s and the 1840s, Britain's own lower and middling orders became more turbulent, more politicised, more vocal in expressing complaints. In much the same way, and at the same time, those governing Britain's empire also faced growing disorder and protest from below. Not just from the indigenous populations they sought to rule, but also from their own poor whites, the captives in uniform.

These men were obviously not captives of empire in the same straightforward sense as the individuals we have encountered in earlier chapters. These were ostensibly free men, and they were armed warriors, not obvious victims. Yet the gulf between the growing numbers of British soldiers stationed overseas, sweltering (or freezing) in stinking, unsuitable red woollen uniforms in dingy barracks or insect-infested tents, and white and non-white colonial elites was a very wide one; and – in some respects – these white soldiers overseas shared levels of unfreedom with black slaves. As one British private soldier complained in his shaky grammar:

> In India the men of the army generally is looked upon as so many pieces of one great machine that is passive in the hands of the engineer: and as to sense or feeling, that is not thought of, the private soldier is looked upon as the lowest class of animals, and only fit to be ruled with the cat o' nine tails and the Provost Sergeant.[16]

Vulnerable to capture by non-Europeans because of where they worked and fought and what they represented, men like this could also feel in bondage to the British state. They were shipped abroad, often in foul conditions and sometimes against their will. They could be separated from their families, womenfolk and culture of origin for decades, often for ever. If judged disobedient or rebellious, they were likely to be flogged. If they tried to run away, they might be executed; and if they stayed and obeyed orders, they were apt to die prematurely anyway.

52. Depending on the Indian. Robert Clive receives a princely grant to aid the East India Company's poor white troops and their dependents back home: a painting by Edward Penny.

All imperial soldiers had to contend with these severities to some degree, but in India they registered with peculiar acuteness, for military service there and throughout Asia was arduous in particular ways. It was not just that tours of duty were long, and mortality and discomfort rates were high. Unlike British soldiers in Australia, or New Zealand, or Canada, or South Africa, ordinary soldiers in Asia had virtually no hope of being allowed a place to settle, a patch of their own land. Nor could the majority of white troops in India hope to marry while on service, or father children who would survive. But perhaps the biggest challenge they confronted was that, in the eyes of those in charge, these men were at once indispensable and of limited significance. In 1830, the 36,400 white officers and men of the East India Company and the regular army made up 90 per cent of all British males resident in India.[17] None the less, these white troops were outnumbered by Indian sepoys in British service five to one. As far as the Company and the British state were concerned, at least before 1857, the logic of this was clear. In times of pressure, it was the sepoys who most demanded consideration and conciliating, not their own working-class soldiery. It was on the sepoys, it was generally accepted, and not on the white soldiery, that Britain's empire in India perforce had to rely. As a result, and however accurately, British soldiers stationed here often perceived themselves as the lowest of the low. They were captives of an alien environment, captives of their own state, and captives of a situation where their sepoy counterparts were in some respects better treated because they were deemed more important.

Like the slaves some felt themselves to be, however, white imperial soldiers in India are hard to investigate outside of the archives compiled by their masters. Many of these men were unable to write; and there could be marked limits on what even fully literate soldiers were allowed to write, and on what they were prepared to write. But the biggest obstacles to investigating these men are the incuriosity and prejudices of posterity. Black slaves rightly command our retrospective sympathy. They are assumed to have suffered and often to have rebelled: and evidence is looked for accordingly. But, to modern eyes, the British or any other imperial soldiery easily appear uncongenial or at best predictable. It is assumed that they were violent (which they were), and that they were necessarily and inherently conformist (which they were not). Exploring these men, and their multiform experiences of imperial captivity, requires then a discarding of blinkers. Given the sparsity of their own writings, it also means drawing imaginatively on miscellaneous, less than satisfactory evidence, having recourse in Edward Said's words to 'unconventional or neglected sources', so as to construct 'an alternative history' of empire to the official one.[18] We need to probe beneath the lush proconsular and plutocratic chronicles of Indian empire and uncover different, more subterranean, less dignified stories, stories of renegades and deserters, stories told around punishment and resistance, stories of those majority of British soldiers who stayed loyal and outwardly obedient but sometimes with gritted teeth: the subalterns with white faces.

The ones that got away

Anyone curious about the last half millennium of global history should visit the National Army Museum in London. Yet few make the journey to Chelsea and walk past its famous hospital and gardens to the squat, charmless 1960s building concealing so much that is controversial, difficult and important. The catalogue of the Museum's library, still indexed on cards, is a painstaking guide through books, pamphlets, prints, maps and manuscripts on virtually every aspect of conflict in five continents in which the British participated as minor or major players. The changing face of battle, the meanings of fear, conquest, and slaughter, the fate of millions of war victims and victors, white and non-white, female and male, all await reconstruction here. Only in a very few areas is the Museum's catalogue stubbornly unrewarding. No amount of searching among its dog-eared cards will turn up references to 'renegades', any more than it will direct you to records of deserters. More even than most states, official Britain does not publicly admit to its warriors having changed sides or opted out.

Yet censorship is less of a problem in this regard than forgetfulness and myths. From the 1810s, at least, the British state compiled lists of known military deserters from all of its colonial outposts. It also published random statistics which confirm that the number of these men could be considerable. In 1815, an estimate based on seriously incomplete returns from India, South Africa, the Mediterranean colonies, and North America, still put the number of British deserters from those areas at 2400.[19] Yet no comprehensive study has been attempted of these figures, or of what they can tell us about the quality and attitudes of Britain's imperial manpower over time. At the height of Britain's cult of empire, it became almost unthinkable that its soldiery should ever have wavered in allegiance. 'A man of British nationality would not be suitable, because presumably he could not be trusted to oppose his own people,' pronounced a one-time governor of Bombay in 1907, introducing a book on white mercenaries in Indian service in the eighteenth and early nineteenth centuries. Thus, he suggested (quite inaccurately), 'the men available would [have been] of Continental origin'.[20] More recent histories can be almost as blinkered as Sir Richard Temple's sturdy Edwardian Euroscepticism. British renegades are either excised from the picture altogether, or treated as picaresque figures, cool, adroit white men on horseback astounding the natives. Yet the majority of renegades on imperial frontiers were more mundane beings. They were also a persistent minority whose experiences illumine more than just themselves.

Most military whites who turned renegade outside Europe did so because, as Braudel wrote of the Spanish troops shipped to North Africa in the sixteenth century, imperial service for the mass of men and women resembled deportation, and this was one variety of escape from it.[21] As far as India was concerned, English and British renegades of different kinds are known to have existed from the earliest commercial contacts, their numbers inversely proportionate to the power and geographical reach of the East India Company. In the seventeenth and early eighteenth centuries, as G.V. Scammell remarks, there is a 'huge fund' of information on renegades in the records of the Company because its position in the subcontinent was so marginal then. Once British soldiers, sailors, merchants and technicians passed beyond its coastal settlements into the rich expanse and employment prospects of Mughal India, they were equally beyond recall and retaliation. Both Charles II in 1680, and James II in 1686, issued proclamations ordering home subjects who had entered indigenous Indian service. Like similar proclamations by Portuguese, Dutch and French sovereigns, these had negligible effect.[22]

Patterns of renegade behaviour began to shift in the 1740s as the French and British became more active in local Indian wars. There was now a growing demand for military and technical manpower from contending white as well as indigenous regimes, and some Britons took advantage of this to change sides not just once, but several times with impunity. In May 1752, a French detachment surrendering to the Company on India's Coromandel coast was found to include thirty-five British deserters. Since healthy white soldiers were a scant resource, these men were pardoned and reabsorbed into the Company's ranks.[23] Indeed, the closer one looks at any military grouping in India in this early period (and much the same was true of armies in Europe), the more it becomes clear that overarching national and ethnic labels are frequently little more than that. Equipped in 1760 with a 'British' force of sepoys, Swiss, Germans, Americans, French, Caribbean blacks, Britons and Irishmen, and about to do battle in southern India with a no less miscellaneous 'French' army, Eyre Coote instructed all his men to wear 'a green branch of the Tamarind tree fixed in their hats and turbans' because this was the only way they could be confidently distinguished from their equally motley opponents. In such a swirling, multi-national, multi-racial military scene, turning renegade might be as simple as plucking a plant from one's hat.[24]

Losing men to other European powers in India remained a minor challenge to the Company until the end of the century. As late as 1785, when thirty of its white soldiers were deserting from Calcutta alone every month, the Company negotiated cartels with the French and the Dutch: British and Irish deserters were to be handed over in return for any French and Dutch nationals who had strayed into Company territory.[25] But it was British desertion to Indian regimes that was always the greatest anxiety. As a military lawyer wrote in 1825:

> When European soldiers desert there [in India], the consequences that may ensue rise in importance, for if they are enabled to conceal their flight, they enter, perhaps, into the service of one of the native princes . . . and thus give intelligence to our enemies.

The space devoted to curbing renegade tendencies in successive army general orders and parliamentary acts for punishing mutiny and desertion in India points to the longevity of official concern on this score. 'Notwithstanding the enemy's promises,' every white and sepoy regiment was pointedly told in 1813, 'those who have been guilty of it [changing sides] are employed only in services of the lowest and most laborious descriptions.'[26] In case such warnings proved insufficient, appeals were made to money, one of the imperial power's undoubted strengths. By 1810, any regular army or Company private or NCO taken prisoner in India lost six pence in pay daily until 'he should actually regain a British corps'. The intention was obviously to discourage soldiers from allowing themselves to be captured, or from remaining captive longer than was necessary. Forty years on, the rules were stricter still. Now, any soldier in British service 'absent as a prisoner of war' in Asia lost all pay and pension rights for the duration. Only if he returned and convinced a court martial he had not 'served with or under or in some manner aided the enemy' could he recover his arrears.[27]

Such legislation was partly aimed at Company sepoys. Yet by the early nineteenth century, desertion was becoming more a characteristic of *white* troops in India; and parliamentary speeches and officers' writings show that these controls were formulated very much with the white soldiery in mind and not just sepoys. The reasons are clear. By the early 1800s, it cost over £100 to recruit a soldier in Britain and ship him to India; training and equipping him cost yet more. So even men deserting with no intention of joining other armies represented a substantial waste of resources. British desertion to indigenous Indian forces was much worse, however, and not just because of the loss of face involved. It bears repeating that the British had cause to be worried about the growing military sophistication of some of the Indian regimes ranged against them, and this remained true after the conquest of Mysore. Hence the threat posed by the renegade. He might, it was believed, transmit to new, indigenous paymasters British military knowledge, information about emerging war technologies, and superior conventions of leadership and discipline.[28]

This was the official nightmare: what of the motives of the renegades themselves? Men who ran away and crossed over on imperial frontiers seldom hung around to tell, much less publish their stories; but on one occasion the British state did it for them. On 18 May 1792, an extraordinary edition of the official *London Gazette* was published, with a six-page account of over 200 Britons, most of them military and naval men, 'yet alive' in Tipu Sultan's Mysore. This information had been collected from a wave of recent British escapees from Tipu's fortresses who had made contact with Cornwallis's advancing armies. One wonders if any contemporaries speculated as to why these men, captive in the main since the early 1780s, had refrained from escaping until their countrymen were closing in on Mysore, for looked at in detail the *Gazette* report was an ambivalent one. It conveyed, as was intended, some of the undoubted horrors of this captivity, naming Britons held in Mysore who had committed suicide in desperation, or gone blind from malnutrition, or been executed. But the *Gazette* also documented how some captives had adapted and settled down. Over sixty were listed under new Muslim as well as their original British names, the confused spellings reflecting the printers' ragged attempts to deal with an unfamiliar language. Thus George Clark, a Madras Company ensign, appeared in the *Gazette* as 'Murtount Khan', while Sergeant James Snelling was listed as 'named in the country Sultaun Beg'. It was made clear too that most of these men were not in prison, but in some kind of paid employment in Mysore, and that some had deserted to Tipu rather than been captured by his armies. Information in the Company's archives, omitted from this published account, shows that officials were also aware that some of these men had assumed Indian dress, settled into relationships with local Hindu and Muslim women, and in some cases forgotten their cradle tongue.[29] What was ostensibly a list of captives of empire, then, serves as well as a guide to the kinds of men likely, if it seemed necessary or advantageous, to turn renegade.

Typically enough, most of them came from the other ranks. Only eleven of the men listed in the *Gazette* were army and naval officers, none of them senior figures. This does not mean that men holding British commissions were always averse to serving Indian employers as freelance warriors. About to launch a decisive assault on the Marathas in 1803, the future duke of Wellington chose first to detach all of their European mercenary officers. Sixty of these turned out to be British or Anglo-Indian.[30] But, as in this case, officer-class males usually felt that they had too much to lose in material and psychological terms to contemplate remaining mercenary if this involved fighting against their own kind. The exceptions to this rule tended to be men in dire financial straits. Company army officers in India were more eclectic in social origin than their counterparts in Britain's regular army, and some came unstuck. Alexander Dempster, who features in several British captivity narratives as one of the more flamboyant renegades in Mysore, clad 'in the Mohammedan dress, with a large red turban', was from 'a very respectable and ancient family'. He was also broke. He had been forced to sell his royal army commission, went to India, and was finally reduced to non-commissioned rank in the Madras artillery. From here he deserted to Mysore which made him an officer again. One of his fellow renegades, a man called Thompson, had also been obliged to sell out. He explained to a British captive in the 1790s how, after marrying a French woman from Pondicherry, he had found it impossible to support them both on half pay, and since 'he preferred a military life, and could not procure a commission in the English army . . . was come to Tipu to look for service'.[31]

Official accounts of British renegades tended to emphasise such mercenary motives as a means of downgrading the individuals involved. Greed or lack of cash were powerful incentives, of course, especially among the sparsely paid lower ranks; and so was a desire to escape the rigours of conventional military discipline. The mass of British private soldiers and ordinary seamen listed in the *Gazette* as having contrived a life for themselves in Mysore were men with low expectations and little hope of rescue, likely to take the easiest path open to them at any particular time, especially if it came strewn with rudimentary comforts. Back in 1783 some British soldiers who had already defected to Mysore, stood outside the walls of the southern Indian fortress of Mangalore, then under siege by their new masters, and harangued their former comrades inside on the compensations of a renegade existence: 'high wages, freedom from the restraints of discipline, food, women, and the means of intoxication'. As a result of these siren calls, at least seventeen more white British troops deserted from Mangalore, including the quarter master sergeant of the 42nd Regiment who slipped out of the city one night having first 'robbed one of the European women of what money she had'.[32]

It is suggestive, too, that many Britons who lingered on in Mysore were very young. In all places, and at all times, it is the young who find it easiest to forget past associations, learn new skills and adapt: the selfsame qualities that are required for successful defection. James Scurry, a former Royal Naval seaman who by his own account did not try escaping Mysore until Cornwallis's troops began closing in, was only sixteen when he was captured; one of his comrades in captivity, William Whiteway, a Company seaman, was just fourteen. Such boy-warriors were not unusual among British forces in India. Almost one in three of the East India Company's recruits in 1779 was sixteen or under. The proportion was much the same at intervals between 1793 and 1815, when once again the demands of warfare on a global scale led to fierce competition for men between the regular British and Company armies and the Royal Navy. Once the supply of qualified, mature recruits ran out, recruiting parties in Britain had no choice but to make do with second, even third best.[33] As so often, one comes back to the problems inescapably inherent in Britain's combination of limited human resources with inflated global ambition. The thin red line was not just anorexic. At certain times, and in certain locations, it was adolescent.

Whiteway's captivity narrative, which was published in London together with Scurry's in 1824, points to yet another reason why men from the lower echelons of Britain's armed and imperial forces might turn renegade: less out of simple greed, than from a desire to better themselves in other, more intangible ways.[34] When captured at sea by the French in 1782, Whiteway was a cabin boy on an East Indiaman. As a result of being handed over to Mysore, he received for the first time in his life an education. He was 'instructed in the Mahratta learning, and in Arabic, as preparatory to acquiring some knowledge of the Persian language . . . Of the masters, Mr Whiteway speaks in terms of high commendation.' This experience seems permanently to have shaped his mind. When he dictated his story in the 1820s, he broke away entirely from conventional imperial narratives. He admitted that the conditions Haidar Ali and Tipu Sultan had inflicted on their British captives were sometimes cruel, but this was 'not a fair criterion by which to estimate their characters', and anyway what could the British expect: 'Aggression provokes retaliation.' As Whiteway chose to remember him, Tipu had been no tyrant merely, but 'comely', 'noble', 'an encourager of learning in all its branches':

> With this view he endeavoured to secure the talents of such Europeans as the fortunes of war threw into his hands, and spared no pains to elicit their natural abilities, and extinguish in their breasts all attachments to their native home. With many of these he succeeded . . . He viewed them as incorporating with his subjects.

Confinement in Mysore seems to have released in Whiteway for the first and only time in his life a sense of wider possibilities: 'I was as happy as I could wish, I wanted for nothing, enjoyed good health, and was beloved by all.' Whether his ten-year renegade career was as unalloyedly fulfilling as this we may choose to doubt, but it is clear why he was desperate in retrospect to invest it with a rosy glow. Driven to escape in the early 1790s, almost certainly out of fright that the invading British would execute him as a traitor, Whiteway eventually returned, not so much home as to Britain. Having worked on an East Indiaman so briefly, he was not entitled to a pension or any arrears of pay. As a special concession, the Company gave him a labouring job in one of its London warehouses where his Persian proved of little use: 'His early acquirements have faded from his recollection, and he can now do little more than make the characters of words with which he was once familiar.'

Whiteway's experience was at one level an unusual though not a unique one, his adolescence burnished by alien captivity, his maturity impoverished by return. Yet his pitiful story also indicates why men such as this are more broadly significant. Renegades were not just marginal folk, idiosyncratic rebels, losers, and deviant careerists. They were usually extreme manifestations of more widespread patterns of weakness and unreliability in the societies and military forces from which they came. Thus the immaturity in terms of age of many Mysore renegades reflected the excessive youthfulness of the East India Company's white legions in general before 1815, which was widely acknowledged to be a source of instability. By the same token, experiences such as Whiteway's vividly confirm what many radicals and military reformers contended in this period: namely, that unreformed Britain's armed forces, both at home and abroad, offered poor chances of advancement or reward to men from the lower ranks.[35] Ordinary, low-grade British warriors with no hope of finding a marshall's baton in their knapsacks, might desert and cross over in imperial locations (or merely decide to remain captives) out of a conviction, justified or no, that the grass could only be greener on the other side.

There is another respect in which renegades and deserters from British forces overseas drew attention to a more broadly significant fracture. Many of them were Irish.

That Irishmen were prone to desert was an Anglophone commonplace in the eighteenth century, and it is easy enough to find seeming anecdotal corroboration as far as India is concerned.[36] Dempster, the Mysore renegade, was Irish. So was George Thomas, whom we will soon encounter, the only British renegade to be accorded a full-scale biography. But until an exhaustive analysis of deserters on this and other British imperial frontiers is attempted, we cannot know how far varieties of Irishmen were more likely to defect than their non-Irish comrades, or how far their prominence among these and other kinds of military trouble-makers merely reflects their preponderance in Britain's armed forces at this time.

Napoleonic France, like Bourbon France, certainly worked on the assumption that Catholic Irishmen in British uniform were potentially a weak link, and these expectations were sometimes validated in European theatres of war, and in colonial locations where the British were confronted by Catholic European forces.[37]

It is not clear, however, whether Catholic Irishmen in British service were less reliable than other groups in locations and contexts where the enemy was non-Christian and non-European. Many officers serving in India judged not. General Charles Napier, for instance, who was part Irish, and sympathised with Catholic Irish grievances, believed that Irish troops in colonial service were actually more tractable than their English or Scottish counterparts. 'There is a promptness to obey, a . . . willingness to act', another officer wrote of the Irish troops he had commanded in India, 'which I have rarely met with in any other body of men.'[38] Certainly, if even a bare majority of Catholic Irishmen in British uniform had rebelled, imperial enterprise in India and elsewhere might have foundered, since their numbers by this stage were so great. All this said, it seems likely that the long tradition, dating back to the Reformation, of Irishmen selling their swords to other powers, including Spain, France, Portugal, the Italian states, and Russia, allowed Irish soldiers who did change sides in colonial locations to inhabit their roles with greater fluency and conviction. This was emphatically the case with George Thomas.

Thomas kept his background deliberately obscure, but he was probably Catholic and born in Tipperary in 1756. He deserted from the Royal Navy in Madras in the early 1780s and went on to forge a successful mercenary career in Northern India. Agile as a verb, he worked in turn for the Poligars, for a remarkable female ruler, Begum Samru, in what is now the Indian district of Meerut, and for the Marathas. Then, 'about the middle of the year 1798', he 'formed the eccentric and arduous design of erecting an independent principality for himself'. Basing himself at Hansi, some ninety miles north-west of Delhi, he claimed overlordship of some 5000 inhabitants 'to whom I allowed every lawful indulgence'. He built fortifications, assembled his own mixed race mercenary army, set up a foundry to cast artillery, and a mint to coin rupees 'which I made current in my army and country'.[39]

At least some of this was true. Samples of Thomas rupees still survive. But Thomas's narrative of his Indian adventures, which he wrote or more likely dictated in 1802, and the biography of him published the following year by William Francklin, reveal not just an extraordinary career, but one that remains in large part concealed, and was ultimately a failure. As Rudyard Kipling's wonderful story makes clear, the white man 'who would

63. George Thomas: the frontispiece of William Francklin's biography.

be king' in a non-Western environment was always at the mercy of events beyond his control and comprehension.[40] Thomas's experiment in government at Hansi lasted barely a year. Then, his troops mutinied for lack of pay, his Indian 'subjects' began drifting away, and neighbouring warlords moved in. Early in 1802, 'as the only means of safety and escape from the persecution of numerous and inveterate foes', he crossed back into British-controlled territory. His subsequent narrative was compiled for the benefit of Richard Wellesley, governor general of India. Briefer and much less accomplished than that other apologia by a warrior crossing cultures, T.E. Lawrence's *The Seven Pillars of Wisdom*, Thomas's narrative resembles it in being at once selective and unintentionally revealing.

Desperately anxious to re-establish his credentials with the British, Thomas was unforthcoming about the circumstances of his desertion from the Royal Navy, and about his actions before 1793. It is possible that these included fighting at times against the forces of the East India Company. Instead, he concentrated on supplying Wellesley with erratic, strictly impersonal information about Northern Indian politics and princely armies, and on stressing his loyalty. His entrepreneurship at Hansi, he insisted, had been designed from the start to advance British imperium: 'I wished to put myself in a capacity . . . of planting the British standard on the banks of the Attock.' Since Thomas had deserted the British standard, and worked contentedly under different banners for two decades, this was audacious to say the least. But his rewriting of his renegade career was enormously assisted by Francklin, a lieutenant-colonel in the East India Company, a gifted orientalist and explorer, and a man utterly committed to empire. Francklin met Thomas just before he died at Berhampore in August 1802, and was captivated by the man. In the notes he compiled for his biography, Francklin describes Thomas as 'our friend and hero', 'an ancient Roman', a man, as the subtitle of his book puts it, 'who, by extraordinary talents and enterprise, rose from an obscure situation to the rank of a General'.[41] Francklin went on to place great emphasis on 'the wonderful and uncommon attachment generally exhibited towards his [Thomas's] person . . . by natives'. 'No man, perhaps,' he wrote, 'ever more thoroughly studied or more properly appreciated the Indian character.'[42] Here, in this tale of a charismatic, six-foot Irishman, often dressed in Indian costume, and fluent in Persian and Urdu, is a recognisably early variant of the kinds of legends that would later be constructed around Lawrence of Arabia. Thomas, as Francklin presents him, becomes the white man who knows non-whites better than they know themselves, and who can therefore lead them in battle, while all the time striving on the empire's behalf.

It was a sign of the tightening grip of empire on Britain's culture and self-image that this sort of mythologising of renegade experience was now being attempted, and not just in Thomas's case.[43] In reality, there were strict limits on the extent to which renegade Britons and other Europeans in non-Western environments were able to act as freelances. Thomas's own experiment at political autonomy in North India failed; and even highly valued European mercenary commanders and expert technicians in Indian princely service seem to have been kept on a close rein by their employers.[44] As for white renegade foot soldiers, they might sometimes win more freedom and rewards in indigenous service than were available to them in European armies, but most remained foot soldiers, low-grade human beings in societies that were different from their own but no less hierarchical. A Muslim account exists of the 400-odd Britons still hanging on in Tipu's capital, Seringapatam, in the 1790s. Most were working by then as soldiers in Tipu's *cheyla* or slave battalions, or as weavers making uniforms, or coining money in his mints, or labouring in his armouries and fortifications. For this, they received 'a rupee and a bottle of arrack a day'. Out of charity, whites who were unfit for work got 'an allowance of rice, ghee and curry stuff and fifteen gold fanams, about seven rupees per month', but they were not allowed to go outside the fortress walls.[45] Virtually all of these men were either executed on Tipu's orders as the British made their final advance on Seringapatam in 1799, or lost their lives in the chaos of its fall. It was a long way from the brilliant sagas of audacious white men on horseback ventured by George Thomas and William Francklin, but closer probably to majority white renegade experience in Asia.

Yet, just like T. E. Lawrence, Thomas gave more away than he intended even as he spun his calculated yarns of renegade adventure. For him, as for Lawrence, 'going native' was clearly never an option, but neither was it possible for either of these men to mimic and live within another society without becoming changed in the process:

> The effort for these years to live in the dress of Arabs, and to imitate their mental foundation, quitted me of my English self, and let me look at the West and its conventions with new eyes: they destroyed it all for me. At the same time I could not sincerely take on the Arab skin . . . I had dropped one form and not taken on the other.[46]

Lawrence's assessment of his own resulting schizophrenia and alienation must have applied as well to many earlier, less articulate Britons who crossed over into non-European societies. Only the very young sometimes managed this kind of transition decisively and satisfactorily. Thomas, for all his guts and energy, could not. He failed in the end both to construct the kind of Indian role he wanted for himself, and to reintegrate back into British imperial society, dying almost as soon as he tried to do so. 'What is to prevent the restless Indian from [rising up]', he enquires at one point in his narrative '. . . when a prospect offers of liberating themselves from our yoke?' Quickly, he recovers himself: 'Mr. Thomas observes that he purposely makes use of the word *yoke*, as he knows that the natives of India always consider the government they are under as such.' Perhaps so. But it seems more likely that, at this point in his tale, Thomas lost his narrative footing, and slipped into the crevices between his various identities and agendas. For just a moment, he seems to have faltered between the demands of British empire and self-interest on the one hand, and two decades of Indian coexistence and perhaps his own Irish origins on the other.[47]

George Thomas's fate points to something that was true of virtually all renegades. Superficially, these men were free spirits, rebels who kicked over the traces. Yet in reality their trade made them vulnerable figures who faced enormous risks, sometimes squalid compromises, and constraints. What they could do, and how long they remained alive to do it, always depended on state systems and rulers infinitely more powerful than they. This is why examining such men in the context of imperial frontiers becomes valuable. Far from being mere picturesque individuals, British renegades in India and elsewhere in Asia are a measure of indigenous regimes' ability and will to attract and employ British and other European strays, and of the imperial authorities' changing capacity over time to regulate their own manpower. As the British came closer to achieving hegemony in India, alternative options for white military careers and enterprise there were cut back, and regulations and restrictions increased. It is time to turn from this white renegade minority to the majority of white captives in uniform, the men who were kept in line.

Whipping the legions into line

Joseph Wall was hanged at Newgate on 28 January 1802. As he climbed the scaffold, his clothes were as elegantly understated as ever; and even without them, his six foot four inches of height would have proclaimed an affluent, unfailingly well nourished existence. Himself a former lieutenant-colonel in the East India Company, Wall had married the daughter of a Scottish peer. That money and position were perishing on a site normally given over to executing the underprivileged was, however, less remarkable than the size and behaviour of the crowd on this occasion. It took Wall twenty minutes to die, but the 60,000 spectators in front of Newgate prison and spilling over into the surrounding streets, many of them in red or blue uniforms, did not react with the usual voyeuristic pity, faintings and cries of shame. They howled in triumph and applauded. Yet Wall had been no standard bugbear, no child murderer, no killer or ravisher of helpless females. His chief victim had been a tough army sergeant, while his real crime had been to lay bare some of the more paradoxical captivities and costs involved in the expansion and exercise of British empire.[48]

Twenty years earlier, Wall had been governor of Goree, a slave-trading base on the west coast of Africa seized by the British in the Seven Years

GOVENER WALL.

Published Feb. 1. 1810. by Nuttall, Fisher & Dixon, Liverpool.

64. A cheap print of
Joseph Wall; note the
misspelling.

War. Lethal for so many blacks, the place also killed the majority of whites
who were dispatched there. Wall ran the risk of its climate, microbes, and
brutality, only because by this stage a reputation for violent temper, sexual
scandal and duelling to the death debarred him from more eligible imperial postings. Goree's British garrison was made up of 'regiments in
disgrace for mutiny, deserting . . . or some such cause', hard men with no
alternatives and no future. On the penultimate day of Wall's governor-
ship, sixty of these troops advanced on his quarters, demanding arrears
of pay that they claimed were due to them. Wall's response was to arrest
five of the ringleaders and, without a trial, order them 800 lashes apiece.
Three of the men, including a Sergeant Benjamin Armstrong, were
'whipped, not with the ordinary instrument, but with ropes; not by the

ordinary persons, but by black slaves'. The blacks in question, who spoke no English, had been assembled specially, and that day in July 1782 they took turns inflicting 25 lashes, till the number of 800 had been inflicted' on each soldier. 'Lay on you black bastards,' Wall called out repeatedly, and pointlessly, as he supervised the punishment, 'or else I will lay upon you!' Long before the end of his own ordeal, Armstrong was shitting and pissing blood, and choking as it flooded his lungs. The garrison's assistant surgeon who watched the man die over the next four days noted with interest that what was left of his back was almost 'as black as a new hat'.

After this episode, Wall went into hiding on the Continent, only returning to London at the beginning of the nineteenth century. He seems to have believed that with the passage of time, the distractions of the Napoleonic wars, and his wife's titled relations, he would be able to secure a pardon. As the Privy Council quickly resolved, this was out of the question. Wall was an embarrassment on every front. Britain was still effectively at war with the ideologies and armies of the French Revolution, and its rulers were desperate to sustain some kind of patriotic, cross-class consensus. Yet Wall was linked to the British aristocracy and guilty of murder and sadism against working-class soldiers. The Abolitionist movement had by now equipped Britons of all classes and both sexes with horrific images of West Indian overseers flogging black slaves. Yet Wall's case revealed how the whip was an integral part of Britain's own military culture. Wall had offended in another respect as well. The Attorney General at his trial, and virtually every published account and woodcut representation of it, dwelt on the point that Armstrong and his fellow-sufferers, white men in British uniform, had been flogged to death by men who were black.

Race and racial stereotypes were crucial and explicit ingredients of the Governor Wall affair. They were no less central to the growing debate at this time over the legitimacy of flogging as a form of discipline in Britain's armed forces. That the whip, the prime emblem of slavery, was deployed with sometimes lethal savagery against them, lay at the very heart of British soldiers' sense of themselves as captives of their own state, as white slaves.[49] These parallels between white soldiers and black slaves were laboured persistently, for their own purposes, by anti-Abolitionists. The polemic was already an established one when Edward Long compiled his unabashedly racialist *History of Jamaica* (1774). 'I need not *again* revive the comparison between them [plantation slaves], and the British sailors and soldiers,' he wrote:

> I need not urge that the ordinary punishment inflicted on these poor wretches for the most trivial offences against discipline, would, if inflicted

Governor Wall contemplating on his unhappy Fate, in the condemned Cell.

65. Joseph Wall awaiting
execution.

on a negro in Jamaica be condemned universally as a most detestable
act of barbarity.

Similar arguments were sometimes resorted to in courts of law by whites
seeking to legitimise physical assaults on non-whites in other parts of the
globe. In 1787, for instance, the Hon. Basil Cochrane, a senior East India
Company merchant and acting resident at Negapatam in southern India,
was put on trial for ordering one of his Indian servants a beating from
which the man subsequently died. Cochrane called as witnesses in his
defence a string of army officers who testified that in terms of severity

this flogging was 'not comparable to the punishments which are constantly inflicted on European soldiers'.[50]

Because such comparisons between floggings of blacks and floggings of white soldiers were regularly employed for contaminated purposes – to minimise the significance and iniquity of slavery and other abuses – they have generally been passed over by serious scholars. The Governor Wall affair, for instance, one of the great *causes célèbres* of class, race and empire, still awaits its historian; so, astonishingly, does corporal punishment and its shifting meanings in British imperial, military and masculine culture.[51] Yet because men like Long were bigots, this does not mean that the parallels they drew attention to were without foundation. As Seymour Drescher argues, one of the consequences of growing agitation over black slavery after 1770 was that discussion of the treatment of working people became globalised in a new way. Growing awareness of the sufferings of enslaved blacks in Britain's colonies worked to illumine as well the plight of its own white multitudes, and not least the plight of its common soldiers and sailors.[52] Those who were most active and risked most in defending and extending the bounds of the British empire – its plebeian warriors – were increasingly represented in this period, and increasingly viewed themselves, as being in some respects comparable to black slaves. The very vehemence with which spokesmen for the British state downplayed such comparisons testifies to their bite. The claim that a 'British soldier [was] . . . in a worse state than an African slave' was appalling, declared a government MP in 1812.[53] Any 'comparison . . . of the soldiers of England to negro slaves' should be met with indignation, Palmerston insisted in the same debate. There was nothing in common, wrote General Charles Napier, 'between the two cases of flogging soldiers and flogging black men'.[54] But, as the Governor Wall affair made damningly clear, there was. In both cases, the whip was deployed out of ruthlessness of control, and because of assumptions about the mentalities and limited worth of those enduring it.

As Robert Southey argued at the time, mass euphoria at Wall's execution was in a vital sense without foundation. Wall was found guilty not because three British soldiers had been flogged to death, but because he had not allowed them a trial first: 'Had he called a drum head court martial, the same sentence might have been inflicted and the same consequences have ensued, with perfect impunity to himself.'[55] Floggings in the British army (and Navy) remained common after 1802, and may even have increased in absolute terms, especially in imperial locations. In 1817, 692 British soldiers stationed in the Windward and Leeward Islands suffered the whip, as did 635 white troops in Jamaica. As these figures make clear, flogging was not reserved for a vicious minority. Like the branding-iron, sometimes inflicted on deserters, it was part and parcel of being in the lower ranks. In just one year, 1822, two out of every five white soldiers stationed in Bermuda suffered the lash.[56] The statistics for punishment in India are less comprehensive, but it seems likely that the Company's forces were no softer than the regular army in this regard, and may have been harsher. In 1836, a Bengal artilleryman claimed that thirty-one white troops in his Company had received on average 380 lashes each in the last six months. By this stage, it was rare for soldiers in the United Kingdom to be sentenced to more than 200 lashes.[57]

Behind these figures, so eagerly accumulated by early Victorian Britain's statisticians, lay the human reality, the scarified flesh, the spraying gobbets of clotted blood and skin, the split muscle, devastated spirits, and sickened stomachs characterising every ritual of military flogging. By 1815, corporal punishment in the armed forces had been abolished in France and the United States, and all but abandoned in Prussia. By the 1820s, even West Indian assemblies were prescribing severe limits, at least on paper, to the number of lashes overseers and owners were allowed to administer to black slaves. Why, then, did such physically violent, mutilating punishments continue to appear acceptable to the British state as a form of discipline against their own whites in military uniform, and especially against white troops in overseas locations?

One of the most common rationalisations would have been familiar as well to slave-owners. As James Walvin remarks, flogging slaves was regularly defended in the Caribbean and American South on the grounds that it was public and therefore exemplary, a means of keeping other blacks 'in awe and order'. This was exactly how the duke of Wellington also defended military flogging. The imprisonment of one of their own number, he argued, made no impact on men in the British ranks. The 'real meaning' of flogging, by contrast, was '. . . example'.[58] Whether it reformed the soldier victim was less important than its wider deterrent effect. There was also agreement that the condition of common soldiers made it hard to punish them effectively except through their own bodies. Like slaves, these men had too little money or property to be effectively subjected to fines. Imprisonment, if it released them from the everyday burdens of labour and discipline, might seem a reward rather than a penalty. Transportation certainly would. 'Was it likely', thundered a Member of Parliament in 1834, 'that a soldier smarting under the broiling sun of Middle India, would object to a trip to the cool and pleasant climate of Sydney.'[59] Australia offered the prospect of land for all and a place to settle, and some British troops stationed in Asia are known to have offended repeatedly in the hope of being dispatched there as convicts. A Private Forbes had to desert from Fort William at Calcutta seven times in 1820 before achieving his transportation; Private Ryder, who also served there, simply struck his sergeant full in the face in 1834, telling him 'it was intended to effect his transportation to New South Wales'.[60]

As this suggests, disorder and protest levels among the white soldiery in India were high. After 1809 – though not before – full-scale mutiny became virtually a monopoly of the Company's Indian soldiers; but less dramatic, everyday disobedience was much more a preserve of white troops. The latter were outnumbered by their sepoy counterparts five to one. Yet, in the 1820s and '30s, charges of desertion were brought against eleven times more white soldiers than against Company sepoys.[61] Although by now the opportunities to turn renegade in India were receding fast, other varieties of escape, be it desertion, absence without leave, self-mutilation as a means of securing discharge from service, and above all drunkenness, were abundantly practised by white captives in uniform. So, as court martial records show with weary regularity, were mutinous conduct, disobedience to superior officers, verbal sedition and riot. For disciplinarians, all this was proof positive of the low moral calibre of Britain's common soldiery, and consequently of the indispensability of the lash. They were 'fine fellows', Sir Henry Hardinge told Parliament smoothly in 1832, but the 'very irregularities' of their lives before recruitment dictated 'that strict degree of discipline which corporal punishment alone can give'.[62] Historians have sometimes acquiesced in this line of reasoning, forgetting perhaps that slave-owners also justified beating black slaves on the grounds that they too were congenitally idle or vicious. In the case of both of these groups, such rationalisations of corporal punishment were more often than not precisely that.

Thanks to the East India Company's own bureaucracy and the painstaking researches of Joel Mokyr and Cormac ó Gráda, we now know that the generality of white soldiers in India were not quasi-criminal, Foreign Legionnaire types, but broadly representative of their age and class cohorts within the home population.[63] Almost 10 per cent of Company recruits between 1802 and 1814, for instance, were weavers; another thousand were carpenters, cordwainers and tailors, standard artisanal trades. Such men were joined as recruits by very large numbers of agricultural and unskilled urban labourers and, in periods of high unemployment, by members of what might be styled the working-class aristocracy: petty clerks, failed printers, low-grade teachers and the like. These men were not in the main hardened desperados when recruited; and neither it seems were most regular army soldiers sent to India, though the latter were less likely to be literate. Granted that these were young, generally barely educated men who had been trained to violence, original sin forms an inadequate explanation as to why they protested and offended at the level and in the fashion that they did.

At least some of the disorder and disobedience that characterised British troops in Asia should rather be understood in terms of their society of origin. What E.P. Thompson styled the making of England's working class occurred much further afield, and not just in Ireland, Scotland and Wales. Because of the dimensions of British empire and emigration, this was a phenomenon acted out on a global scale, and urgently needs investigating as such. Since white soldiers in India were so representative of the British and Irish working populations at large, it was to be expected that their patterns of protest sometimes borrowed from those operating in the United Kingdom itself. In November 1816, for instance, a Corporal Kearnan in the Company's service was charged with 'entering a combination with several men of the horse artillery', administering oaths of secrecy, and then deserting with his weapons. He was caught and shot, and his fate read out to every regiment in India.[64] There were local explanations for this well-publicised punishment (artillery men were precisely the kind of white renegades indigenous rulers in India liked to attract), but there were also political reasons closer to home. Entering combinations, administering secret oaths, and collecting illicit weapons were common tactics in the United Kingdom at this time among illegal trade unions, among Luddites opposed to the new industrial machinery, and among secret societies like the United Irishmen.[65] Corporal Kearnan (who may well have been Irish) was executed in part because – just like these dissidents back home – he challenged the authority of the British state, but on another shore.

Yet customs of protest in common were only part of the story. White soldiers in Asia were also conspicuously unruly because of the particular circumstances of their jobs and lives. The East India Company army still behaved in many respects as a private, autonomous force. It was far more politicised than the regular British army, emphatically middle-class in terms of its officers, and often turbulent. In 1795, the year William Pitt the Younger rushed through parliamentary acts banning 'seditious' meetings of more than fifty people in Britain, Lord Cornwallis, governor-general in Bengal, also banned 'promiscuous meetings' within the Company army. This, be it noted, was a prohibition aimed at the commissioned ranks! As one high-ranking British officer remarked in 1832, when military men regularly met, as Company officers did in India, to 'form committees, appoint delegates, subscribe funds', and talked in terms of 'rights infringed', 'compacts broken', and the 'bad faith' of their rulers, it was 'idle to talk of military subordination' of a conventional kind. It is likely that at least some of the Company soldiery's unruliness and often highly literate protest was fostered by the politicised and sometimes truculent style of their own officers.[66] But both regular army and Company soldiers protested in India, and with reason.

There were, to be sure, compensations for the hardships they endured, enough for some men to be content, and even deeply committed. In wartime, there was pillage, the charge of combat, a reaffirming sense for some perhaps of national and racial superiority; and there was always comradeship, a reasonable certitude of employment and regular pay, the opportunity to see sights most of their compatriots never encountered, and the chance, as far as more literate Company privates were concerned, of promotion to sergeant. Against this, however, there was sporadic danger, unremitting heat and disease, protracted periods of boredom, savage discipline, and a sense often of terrible deracination and personal confinement. 'The irksomeness of the life of the European soldier is truly pitiable,' wrote the governor-general of India in 1834: '. . . his barrack with his check and roll-calls is converted into a sort of prison'.[67] The most demoralising circumstance of all was that these men were at one and the same time bound to stay in India, yet forced to remain in crucial respects rootless there. Until the 1840s, regular army soldiers commonly remained in India for up to twenty years without a break. Company soldiers were allowed to sign on for twelve years, but since they received a pension only after twenty-one years, most signed on for life: or rather death. In the 1830s, white soldiers in Bombay were more than twice as likely to die as soldiers based in Britain. In Madras, the death-rate among this group was over three times as high as among their counterparts in Britain, and in Bengal almost five times as high. Before mid-century, few private soldiers and NCOs in India could hope to live long enough to fulfil their term of service and return to Britain.[68] Yet these men were not allowed to make India their home either.

India was not a colony, and whites were discouraged by the Company from settling there. Those soldiers who did see out their time were promptly shipped back to Britain at the end of it, as were those who became too physically or mentally damaged to be of further service. Some eluded the net, but every official step was taken to gather up the maimed, the worn out, and the retirees, and prevent their establishing an Indian niche for themselves outside of the army. This policy also meant that British soldiers here were discouraged from marriage. Most were too young when recruited already to be married. Those with wives usually had to leave them behind in Britain, and in most cases never saw them again. Even in 1861, by which time the regulations had been much relaxed, only 12 per cent of men in each regiment dispatched to India were permitted to take wives along with them. What awaited these men on arrival in the subcontinent was predictably not celibacy, but close regulation of their sexuality and of any domestic urges they might cherish. This needs stressing, because attempts have sometimes been made to gauge soldiers' racial attitudes from the quality of their relationships with Indian women.[69] Yet these men were not free agents. They might be free to use the *lal bazar*, the regimental brothel. They were only occasionally free to marry Indian women and to have such alliances recognised by the British authorities.

By the 1820s, the East India Company leaned towards the view that 'only . . . Christians are capable of marriage'. Soldiers who married 'half-caste' women brought up in Christian orphanages might, it was thought, legitimately claim exactly half the marriage allowances granted to those few British wives who managed to accompany rank and file males to India, but this was all.[70] By this stage, soldiers' Indian wives and widows received no financial allowance whatsoever. Indian wives were not allowed to accompany soldiers who were sent back to Britain, and nor were any Eurasian children they might have. Indian families of white soldiers might even be forbidden to accompany their men when they were transferred to other postings in Asia. In 1817, for instance, the 66th Regiment was ordered from Bengal to St Helena. It left behind fifty-five unprovided for 'unmarried women' and fifty-one children.[71] Some of the British soldiers involved may have welcomed release from these commitments; others may have been distraught at being torn from the only families they were ever likely to have barring their regiments. As so often, the extant evidence shuts us out from the minds of this kind of men, and still more from the minds of this kind of women. The point is that the British state and the Company allowed these people no choice. The soldiers concerned could not take their non-white families with them to St Helena. They could not break their terms of service and stay on in Bengal. Had they deserted from the army, they would either have been hunted down, or remained precariously on the loose, unpaid, unpensioned, and at risk of starvation. As with slaves, the sexual and familial arrangements of men such as these remained substantially at the mercy of those with authority over them. 'The poorest labourer in England', scrawled a private soldier in India in the 1850s, 'when returning from his daily labour, finds someone to cheer his cares away, and participate in all his doubts and fears.'[72] So too did most of the Company's sepoy troops who could live with their wives while on service in their own accommodation. But the generality of British troops in India were allowed no such comforts.

66. Indian painting of a Company sepoy and his wife in the 1780s. Virtually no portraits exist of their poor white counterparts at this time.

There were some in positions of authority who believed that this was wrong. 'The discouragement to their [the soldiers'] marriage is unjust and impolitic,' a senior officer serving in India told a parliamentary committee in 1832:

> Where the European soldiers form connexions with local native women, and live out of barracks, they are generally remarkable for their good conduct, sobriety and attention to their duties. These women are faithful to them and are serviceable attendants in the field . . . These connexions would have a tendency to break down the prejudices of the European soldiery and would enable them, when superannuated, to become useful settlers.[73]

Yet, as this committee's final report makes clear, such a position as regards British soldiers' possible intermarriage and settlement in India was by this stage emphatically a minority one. The reasons for this hinged on attitudes to race and social class, but also on perceptions of the foundations of British imperial power in India, and the applicability of the lash.

Opposition to intermarriage in India certainly stemmed in part from racially driven xenophobia. It also turned, as so much else did, on a matter of numbers. Both the Company and London were concerned about the rising 'half caste population of India', by this stage larger at 20,000 than the total number of British civilians based there. To allow widespread marriages between white troops and Indian women would inevitably have led to this liminal grouping increasing at a still faster rate, and this – it was thought – might have significant and damaging political repercussions. The 1810s and '20s had witnessed successful creole and mixed-race revolutions in South America against Portuguese and Spanish imperial dominion. Some in Britain may have considered the possibility of a future dangerous alliance between an expanding contingent of Anglo-Indians on the one hand, and its own unruly white soldiery on the other, especially as most white troops in India at this stage were not employed directly by the British state, but by the Company.

Moreover, while some argued that soldiers' intermarriage with Indian women would serve to contaminate and enfeeble British males, at official level the emphasis was often on the reverse point: if allowed to settle and form permanent connections in India, the British soldiery would themselves be a contaminating influence. As Douglas Peers points out, there was a perception among British officers, not statistically impeccable but none the less powerful, that the majority of white common soldiers in India and elsewhere were in origin impoverished labourers, overwhelmingly from urban areas, dissolute, unteachable, godless, brave certainly, but brave because reckless and dangerous. By contrast, sepoys, especially those viewed as high-caste rural peasants, were praised for their zeal, honour, trustworthiness, temperance, physique, and above all for their obedience.[74] 'The moral character of the native', one British colonel told the parliamentary committee of 1832, 'is far superior to the European.' Were retired British common soldiers to be allowed to settle in India, agreed a major-general, it would be detrimental to the country: 'When control would be removed from them, they would become a very bad description of people.' The white soldiery, General, the Hon. Sir Edward Paget judged, were 'very drunken and dissolute people'. Or, as yet another senior officer had pronounced earlier: 'The English soldier exhibits to the natives of India a disgusting specimen.'[75]

Such comments must be understood in part in British domestic terms. Popular agitation in Britain and Ireland in the 1820s, '30s, and early '40s over parliamentary reform, Roman Catholic emancipation, trade unions, and ultimately Chartism inevitably shaped attitudes among the British elite in the empire as well. Expressions of alarm and revulsion by patrician officers and officials about British and Irish underprivileged elements in imperial locations cannot, and should not be disaggregated from similar responses by members of the British ruling order at this time to mass dissidence at home. In both cases, there was a heightened sensitivity to potential threats from those below, and a heightened determination to maintain control and discipline. Indeed, it is partly in this context of growing social polarization at home that one can understand the British state's continuing resort to the whip against its white soldiery. Slaves, observes Michael Bush, can be treated as such because they appear alien in some way.[76] They are black. Or in Islamic slave systems, they are non-Muslim; or they are Jews or gypsies perhaps. Whatever the source of their perceived difference, it allows them to be treated in a different and inferior fashion from individuals within the home society. By the same token, as a private soldier dispatched to fight for the empire complained, large numbers of affluent and powerful Britons did not 'consider a common soldier, as a fellow subject'.[77] And this made it possible for the British state, that prided itself on its superior freedoms, to deploy against these men the lash, the quintessential emblem of unfreedom. To be an effective common soldier, it was widely believed, a man needed to be tough, brutal and unthinking. And since British soldiers were tough, brutal and unthinking – and after a fashion alien – they could and must be whipped into line.

Yet there were also more pragmatic and entirely Indian factors involved here. In 1830, there were an estimated 36,400 British regular army and

Company officers and men stationed in India. But there were almost 190,000 sepoys in Company uniform, and these Indian warriors had proved their indispensability to the British not only in their own subcontinent, but also in the campaign against the French in Egypt in 1800–1, in the expedition to Mauritius and Java in 1810–11, and in other extra-Indian campaigns. The logic of all this was crystal clear to Britain's high command. British empire in India – and in other parts of the world – could never outlast the period of sepoy obedience. But since many Britons in positions of authority idealised the sepoy, they believed – as of course they had to – that a kind of perfect, enduring chemistry could be created between an expert and valiant British officer class and a noble, numerous but ultimately tractable Indian sepoy army. In this chemistry, the mass of ordinary British soldiers in India were seen as having little to do. 'There is no error more common', General Sir John Malcolm told the governor-general of India, Lord William Bentinck, in 1830:

> than that of considering [white troops] as a check upon the Native armies. They never have and never will prove such . . . The necessity of check implies distrust that degrades. It is by complete confidence alone that the Native army of India can be possessed in efficiency and attached to the Government.[78]

It was in absolute conformity to this line of reasoning that in 1835 Bentinck abolished the use of flogging against Indian troops, while permitting the lash to continue to be used on the backs of British troops in India. Indian soldiers, as he explained to Parliament, were much better behaved than the British variety. But, as Bentinck pointed out, there were also far more of them:

> He saw no reason why 150,000 men [sic] should . . . be subjected to corporal punishment in order that 20,000 [sic] other men, who might properly be subjected to the punishment, should not be displeased.[79]

For a small nation like Britain, engaged now in global empire on a scale that was unprecedented in history, numbers mattered and not just race.

Re-envisioning the imperial soldiery

In terms of opinion in Britain, Bentinck's reform proved decisive in a sense that he had not appreciated. A year later, in 1836, the Whig administration of the day conceded a parliamentary enquiry into military flogging. As one politician put it, Bentinck's initiative finally 'upset the system'. It had long been a commonplace that British soldiers were treated in some respects like African slaves. Now, it appeared, they were to fare worse than their Indian counterparts as well. Was there anything, an MP enquired,

in the character, habits, or disposition, of our fellow-countrymen to render them unworthy the consideration which the noble Lord felt justified in extending to the natives of India.

Or as the Irish radical Daniel O'Connell demanded, with an eye to his countrymen's massive representation in imperial legions, why should the lash be 'applied to the back of a British soldier, when it was discontinued even amongst the black men'.[80]

The racial assumptions behind such interjections are evident. O'Connell's phrasing '*even* amongst the black men' speaks volumes. Yet the paradox he and others identified was a real and jarring one. The early modern British state had never customarily employed the whip against its civilian labouring classes. In the last quarter of the eighteenth century, and the first quarter of the nineteenth century, its politicians and public developed growing qualms about the use of corporal punishment against black slaves. Yet during this same period, there was a growing recourse to the whip to discipline and terrorise Britain's own armed forces. This anomaly often passes unnoticed, perhaps because soldiers, and especially the imperial soldiery, still meet with something like the same condescension and contempt that was often bestowed on them in the past. These were violent, unlettered men. They were whipped. So what? Yet how these men were regarded and treated by their own state is crucial to an understanding of this most violent epoch of British imperial activity.

From the 1750s, but much more from the 1790s, a rising proportion of Britain's armed forces was active overseas transforming the geographical scale of its empire at an unprecedented rate. The political will providing for this later, particularly intense period of global aggression would not have been forthcoming had Britain's population not been expanding fast, and been recognised at the time as expanding fast. For the first time ever, it became widely accepted that Britain possessed a sufficiency of young males, and even a surfeit. War and empire could employ and winnow them, without fear of enfeebling Britain itself. Yet, in practice, it was not as straightforward as that. The United Kingdom was now more demographically buoyant than ever before, but its population and armed forces still remained smaller than those of other leading European powers. In order, therefore, to intrude as decisively into as many global zones as it did, the British state had to have recourse to extraordinary levels of determination and violence, not just with regard to European and non-European opponents, but also with regard to its own manpower. It is a commonplace that the classic era of Britain's pioneering industrialisation, c. 1770– c. 1840, was characterised by a more ruthless and systematic treatment of labour at home. By the same token, the contemporaneous surge in Britain's overseas empire was characterised by a more calculated, uncompromising and often brutal disciplining of its own white soldiery overseas. A thin red line kept ever more ruthlessly in line, these men were literally whipped to work and win.

They were also frequently looked down upon, denounced, and disapproved of for all their indispensability to the British imperial effort. The experiences of these captives in uniform demonstrates yet again that empire could disrupt racial notions and identities as much as it fostered them. Exposure to non-European otherness never straightforwardly and uniquely accentuated an assurance of British, still less European solidarities. It often served to throw into still sharper relief divisions and tensions already existing among the white incomers themselves. East India Company and British authorities treated Indian sepoys in some respects (and still more India's landed, mercantile and princely elites) more benevolently and more respectfully than they did their own white working-class soldiers, because they could not afford to do otherwise. At the same time, exposure to India, as to other imperial locations, tested, changed and sometimes alienated the white soldiery themselves. A minority turned renegade. More deserted. Still more perceived themselves as slaves, or lashed out in different ways at those with the power to lash them. The anonymous diary of an English private, stationed in India in the 1840s and '50s, devotes far more space to excoriating his own aloof, upper-class countrymen than to downgrading Indians. It was the 'aristocrats of our native isle' whom this man hated, together with Britain's middle-class reformers, 'talking gentlemen' as he called them, who seemed to care more about cruelty to dumb animals than about the treatment of ordinary red-coats like himself.[81]

This kind of anger on the part of discontented imperial soldiers rarely led them in the direction of anything approaching radical politics. Nor did men who thought like this necessarily feel any empathy with the indigenous peoples around them. A white soldier's sense that he was 'less thought of in India than a common *mheter* [sic] who looks after the officer's dogs' might indeed encourage festering racism on his part.[82] British captives in uniform overseas could not vent their fury, frustration and boredom on their own country's aristocracy or its comfortable middle classes, however much they might wish to do so. By contrast, it was all too easy to strike out physically, verbally, or only in their minds at those they presumed to call 'natives'.

Yet one should not fall into the trap of viewing these men in monolithic terms, or of taking on trust the characterisations of them supplied by their superiors. British officers regularly decried the unfortunate racial prejudices of the lower ranks, doubtless justifiably in many cases. But condemning the common soldiers as vulgarly racist was also a function of elite perceptions of these men as unlettered brutes. In this, as in other respects, it is vital to reconstruct the imperial soldiery, like other subalterns, from their own sources as much as possible, and to acknowledge their multiplicity.[83] It is imperative, too, to consider them in tandem with their civilian counterparts back home. Any assessment of the strengths and weaknesses of British empire abroad in the late eighteenth and early nineteenth centuries must take on board the fact that its white soldiers and seamen were recruited from the same social and occupational groupings that were becoming more literate, more disorderly, and in many cases more politically active at home. Controlling its white imperial soldiery was sometimes as troubling to the British state in this era as maintaining order at home, or ruling over indigenous populations overseas.

Yet, by the 1830s, there were signs that the imperial soldiery was coming to be re-envisioned both at home and abroad. A more active concern emerged for these men's physical and spiritual welfare, and there was growing provision of schools for soldiers' children, garrison hospitals, regimental libraries, recreational facilities, army chapels, and (relatively) clean accommodation. By the end of this decade, the mortality rate among British soldiers overseas, even in tropical locations like India, had fallen substantially; and by the late 1840s, limits began to be set on the number of years soldiers could be exiled overseas.[84] And there was another major change. Resort to the lash continued, but its use in the army (and the Royal Navy) much diminished, both overseas and in Britain itself. Back in 1822, two out of every five British soldiers stationed in Bermuda had been whipped. By 1836, the proportion of soldiers being flogged in this part of the empire was less than five in a thousand, and similar dramatic reductions occurred in other British colonies and overseas bases.[85] Despite Bentinck's ruling in 1835, flogging of white troops also declined sharply in India, though less rapidly in some areas than floggings of Company sepoys.

The amelioration in the condition of the British imperial soldiery after 1830, like their conspicuous disorderliness in previous decades, represented in part an extension of domestic social, political, religious and economic changes overseas. There were obvious connections between the growing concern to improve (and regulate) the conditions of the working classes in Britain's own sprawling industrial conurbations at this time, and efforts to improve the welfare (and good order) of its overseas legions. By the 1830s, for instance, the British government was providing annual grants to supply carefully chosen books and newspapers for its soldiers overseas, and so were the East India Company and various philanthropic associations. As a result of this campaign to 'inform their minds and to lessen licentious propensities', ordinary troops in Bengal, Bombay and Madras, and in other regions of British imperial enterprise, secured access to religious tracts in abundance, as well as to texts on geography and natural history, and stirring stories from Britain's past and present. They also received novels like *Robinson Crusoe*, and – as was only fitting – a volume entitled *Perils and Captivity*.[86]

In other respects, too, there were close links between Britain's domestic conditions at this time, and conditions in its empire. The improved living standards of the imperial soldiery evident by the end of the period covered by this book, 1850, owed much to the buoyancy of Britain's economy by that stage, which so transformed the welfare of its own domestic working classes. Now that job opportunities and income levels were rising, railway construction was booming, and large-scale factory production was becoming widespread, it was much harder to tempt labouring men into the armed services. As a result, the British state began to care for its servicemen more, not just because it wanted to, but also because it had no choice. The armed services had to be made more attractive, because civilian blue-collar job opportunities were rising, as was the rate of working-class emigration from the United Kingdom. The Irish Famine of 1845–9 only confirmed this trend. Together with the waves of Irish emigration that followed, this severely reduced – without ever eradicating – those bevies of Irish recruits, Catholic as well as Protestant, on which the imperial armed forces in India and elsewhere had previously been so dependent. Here was another reason why Britain had, perforce, to devote more attention and thought to those legions it still had left.

All of which goes to underline what I have argued throughout this book: namely, that the history of Britain and the histories of its various overseas ventures cannot be adequately approached separately. For good, and for ill, they were interlinked. On the one hand, the treatment of British soldiers in different continents, and indeed of the empire's indigenous troops, was influenced by circumstances within Britain itself. On the other, the working conditions of black slaves in Africa and the Caribbean, and of sepoys in India influenced – as we have seen – debates about Britain's own labouring population, both military and civilian. At plebeian level, as at other social levels, this was now an interconnected world.

It was also a world in which Britain was now the undisputed superpower. In 1839, Queen Victoria's geographer, James Wyld, published a map suggesting that the British empire was almost three million square miles in extent. Its dimensions, he claimed, made it twenty-eight times bigger than Spain's empire, and forty times bigger than the empire of France.[87] These measurements were questionable, and so – even more – was the degree to which a small set of islands could seriously exercise and sustain authority over such a vast expanse of the globe's surface. But the enhanced consciousness of Britain's astonishing imperial reach, of which Wyld's cartographic effort was merely one example, also contributed to the re-envisioning of the imperial soldiery. It now seemed far less appropriate to refer to these men – even casually – as brutes, rogues, immoral outcasts, the scum of the earth, for it was on them that this inflated empire substantially had to rely. Increasingly, as Victoria's reign wore on, Britain's captives in uniform came to be widely re-imagined by their civilian countrymen as 'an almost ostentatiously Christian army', our brave lads abroad.[88]

Yet, as Britons began to relax into a wholly unaccustomed level of global power, many of them nurtured the hope that the time of dangerous, unpredictable conflicts and collisions abroad was passing. They had finally escaped, or so it seemed, from the protracted constraints of their own territorial and demographic smallness. And surely, by now – many of them allowed themselves to believe – Britain was too strong to be seriously challenged, too formidable to be vulnerable anymore to captivity traumas overseas. In this respect, they were both right and wrong.

To Afghanistan and Beyond

More captives, more stories

It proved easy enough that autumn for the world's most powerful state to move against Afghanistan. Moving against Afghanistan usually has been easy. To be sure, the area that now goes under that name is protected by merciless winters that endure from November until April, by the great mountain ranges of the Hindu Kush, and by semi-desert conditions to the north, west and south of its heartland; but these harsh defences of climate and terrain have counted for little over the centuries by comparison with the curse and lure of its location. From the reign of Ashoka the Great, proximity to the subcontinent has exposed this region to the ambitions of successive Indian rulers; while, since the days of Alexander the Great, powers with designs against the Indian peninsula have regularly treated Afghanistan as a gateway and as a staging post for their legions. Poor, dusty, ethnically hybrid, and often startlingly beautiful, this is a place accustomed to invasion, less because of what it is itself, than because of where it is, and who its neighbours are.

The new intruders were a classic case in point. They were not, they insisted, at war with the Afghan people themselves, though thousands still died in the fighting, and from its disruption of food supplies and shelter. Nor, the intruders claimed – with a large measure of truth in this case – did they seek any permanent, large-scale annexation of Afghan territory. Their quarrel was with the current rulers of Kabul who threatened their own interests and security. Once a *coup d'état* had been forced, and new and better men governed securely at Kabul, the invaders would retreat back from whence they had come, well pleased. And so – initially – it came to pass: and the ease and speed with which the revolution was apparently effected only strengthened the invaders' belief that it was popular with the Afghan people at large.

The British had known little of Afghanistan or anywhere else in Central Asia before 1800, but as their grip on India increased, so, predictably, did their curiosity and their anxieties in this direction. During the Napoleonic

COLONEL STODDART AND CAPTAIN CONOLLY,
AT BOKHARA
FROM AN AUTHENTIC SKETCH, TAKEN BY OSMAN BURUKZYE

67. British officers captured in Afghanistan: a romanticised 1844 print based on an earlier Afghan sketch.

Wars, London had worried in case France invaded northern India through Afghanistan and so destabilised the richest and most populous sector of its empire. After Waterloo, British fears of a European rival using Afghanistan as a springboard into India became focused on another power with a far larger army than its own, Russia. In 1837, the year of Queen Victoria's accession, Persia besieged Herat in western Afghanistan with Russian encouragement. This was enough. Late the following year, the governor-general of India, Lord Auckland, ordered an expeditionary force of 21,000 men, the grandly named Army of the Indus, into Afghanistan. Its avowed aim was to restore the former shah, Shuja ul-Mulkh, who had been in exile for thirty years, and drive out the current amir, Dost Muhammad Khan, who was judged to be pro-Russian, or at least insufficiently pro-British. By August 1839, the *coup* had been accomplished, and

348

Shah Shuja was back in Kabul. Only belatedly was Britain made to realise what others would discover after its empire was dust and memory. Invading Afghanistan was relatively simple. Remaining there for any time, and imposing change was not.[1]

Wanting to cement Shah Shuja's patched-up regime, a portion of the expeditionary force lingered on in Kabul. The Indian troops who made up four-fifths of this force had already been allowed to bring their women and children along with them, though naturally most of the white working-class soldiery had not. Now, many of the British army officers who remained at Kabul, and who had families in India, summoned them to their side, and began making themselves at home. They organised a social calendar, set up a race-track, played cricket, indulged in amateur dramatics, held horticultural competitions, and competed against the locals at cock-fighting. They also constructed a cantonment in the city, but it was a weak and half-hearted affair. Money and manpower were stretched as usual, so fortifications at Kabul were skimped, and the storehouses of food and ammunition were allowed to remain outside the cantonment walls. And why not? From the start of this campaign in 1838, to 1840, just thirty-four British officers had perished in Afghanistan, and of these only five had been killed in action. Elaborate and expensive fortifications appeared superfluous. The invaders' recognised technological superiority, and the hospitality and tribal divisions of the Afghans themselves, seemed defences enough. But, in 1841, things began to change.[2]

What happened then has traditionally been interpreted as an extraordinary British humiliation, as a small imperial war that mushroomed astonishingly and unprecedentedly out of control because of local, individual and idiosyncratic factors.[3] Throughout 1841 relations between the expeditionary force and Afghan tribal groups deteriorated, and ambushes, assassinations and death-rates increased. In November, the month of Ramadan, an insurrection broke out at Kabul. The cantonment was besieged for over sixty days, and as its inadequate defences crumbled, so did the morale and discipline of its Indian and, still more, its British defenders. Late in December, the British capitulated; and in January 1842, some 4500 British and Indian troops and 12,000 camp followers began the 116-mile tramp from Kabul back to Jalalabad. By February, most of these men, women and children were dead, killed by exposure and frostbite, by starvation and disease, and by their desolate, snow-covered route that continually drove them along narrow valleys and ravines where Afghan tribesmen perched high above in the mountains could fire down on them with impunity. But some did not die. Some, famously, were taken captive.

This happened in various ways and at various stages. Having

announced in December 1841 that the British force 'was in their power and that they could completely destroy it whenever they thought fit', victorious Afghan warlords demanded that six of its married army officers and their womenfolk be handed over as hostages. Some of the British officers involved threatened to shoot their wives rather than entrust them to Muslim warriors (and consequently in their minds to the harem), so six bachelor officers were accepted in their stead.[4] Some women and children, both Indian and British, were subsequently snatched on the retreat to Jalalabad and disappeared for ever into various Afghan villages; while some Indian sepoys – and some British males – were seized and sold into slavery in the markets of Kabul.[5] Most dramatically, in terms of opinion in Britain itself, as those retreating through the snow, ice and bullets began to die in large numbers, Afghan proposals that British officers' wives be handed over, together with the husbands involved and some of the wounded, were agreed to, as the only way of possibly ensuring their survival. One Englishwoman subsequently described how she was taken with the rest to a fort:

> Three rooms were cleared out for us, having no outlets except a small door to each; and of course they were dark and dirty. The party to which I belonged consisted of Mrs Trevor and seven children, Lieut. and Mrs Waller and child, Mrs Sturt, Mr Mein, and myself, Mrs Smith and Mrs Burnes, two soldier's wives, and young Stoker, child of a soldier of the 13th, who was saved from people who were carrying him off to the hills, and came in covered, we fear, with his mother's blood . . . The dimensions of our room are at the utmost fourteen feet by ten.

How many captives were seized in total will never be known: but, as far as the British were concerned, thirty-two officers, over fifty soldiers, twenty-one children, and a dozen women remained alive to be handed back to their countrymen in September 1842.[6] Well before that, a remarkably high proportion of these captives had begun to write.

They did so for all the familiar reasons. Some of them wrote because, initially, survival seemed 'very doubtful indeed', and they wanted to leave some trace of themselves behind, as well of course as their own version of events.[7] Like others before them, these captives also wrote because they came from a profoundly Protestant culture that placed a high value on the written word, and that had endowed them with an expectation of peculiar and arduous trials, but also with a belief in ultimate redemption. 'It has pleased God to try us in the furnace of adversity for many years,' scribbled one of them:

68. Florentia Sale in captivity, a turban covering her lice-ridden hair.

But in every cloud that overhung our path, the rainbow of His mercy has shone conspicuously, forbidding us to despair, and reminding us that we are the object of His providential care.[8]

As the year advanced, and another army set out from India to Kabul, bent on rescue and revenge, still more of these captives wrote about their sufferings, emotions, and adventures because a return to Britain and its printing presses now appeared feasible again, and they clutched – as so many others had done – at the prospect of publication and momentary fame.

This was certainly true of Florentia, Lady Sale, wife of General Sir Robert Sale, whose captivity narrative *A Journal of the Disasters in Afghanistan* (1843) became a bestseller, and whose manuscript and printed words were studied by ministers, quoted in Parliament, and pored over by Queen Victoria.[9] She may have begun keeping a diary even before the British cantonment at Kabul came under siege. Once the situation deteriorated, she made notes whenever she could, keeping them in a bag tied around her waist under her clothes. An experienced imperial army wife, and tough as barbed-wire, Florentia Sale at least seems to have been confident that her virtue – and consequently her papers – were likely to remain safe even if she fell into Afghan hands. Her original intention in writing, she subsequently claimed, was to supply her military son-in-law (who died in the retreat) with material for a fully-fledged account of the war. But one suspects that this formidable, courageous, narrowly opinionated and immensely selfish woman, who was impatient of most males outside her family circle, also wanted her voice heard and her moment in the spotlight. To the early Victorian public, Florentia Sale would indeed become a heroine, the first British woman ever to achieve nationwide fame in connection with her own contribution to military action overseas, and as such a precursor of Florence Nightingale. But to her fellow-captives in Afghanistan, Florentia Sale and her relentless pursuit of copy were a pain and something of a joke. 'Lady Sale at Lawrence and the men for more particulars,' groaned Captain William Anderson in June 1842, after her Ladyship had wandered yet again, paper and pencil in hand, from her own loosely guarded room into theirs. 'I gave her a yarn yesterday.'[10]

Behind Anderson's tone lay not just personal exasperation and an element of masculine patronising, but also literary rivalry. Since many of these captives were educated, and since they were mewed up for months in moderately benign though unsanitary conditions, with nothing to do but kill lice, tolerate their own and each other's stench, and, in the case of some of the married women, give birth, writing narratives became a widespread habit amongst them and a highly competitive business. There are references to accounts by at least a dozen British army officers held captive in Afghanistan in 1841–2, though some of these texts seem not to have survived.[11] Anderson himself, like other East India Company men before him, showed how instinctively some imperial fighters turned in leisure or emergency to the business of writing. He had brought a notebook with him to Afghanistan in which he routinely jotted down pieces of information useful for a man of his trade: remedies for cholera and scorpion stings, instructions for preparing embrocation for weary horses, recipes for suet puddings and other nostalgic delicacies. Once captive, Anderson simply turned this home-made self-help manual back to front, wrote 'Private' on the cover, and began to pen his narrative, systematically keeping an illustrated diary on the right-hand pages, while inserting the more impersonal observations he was trained to make on the left-hand pages.

Several female captives, too, and not only Lady Sale, responded with pen, pencil and paper to the rare opportunity, for them, of being at the

69. A sketch of his cell in William Anderson's captivity narrative.

centre of imperial and military action: 'able to judge for themselves the actual state of affairs'. 'Our party', recorded one anonymous woman of those confined with her, 'were seized with a scribbling mania. Every one seemed occupied in composing "The only True and Particular Account" of the Kabul insurrection.' She noted too how some of the writers, like many captivity narrators before them, resorted to different modes of fabrication: 'Diaries were ante-dated, and made to assume the tone and character of memoranda written at the period. Those who had the most retentive memories, or fertile inventions, were likely to prove the most successful in this employment.'[12] The sheer number and variety of texts emerging from this expensive Afghanistan episode, by those in uniform and those not, and by women as well as men, form – at one level – a final, conclusive demonstration of how accustomed the British were by this stage to overseas captivity crises, and how automatically they converted them into different kinds of prose. They had been here before. And amidst all the anger, humiliation, tedium and terror, they knew what to do.

What remained the same, what was different

In some ways, indeed, what happened in Afghanistan was not an aberration in British imperial terms at all. As in every captivity crisis featured in this book, there were particular, contributing factors involved, like the frailties of the British commander, General Elphinstone, dispatched to Kabul in an heroic but on this occasion misconceived blow against ageism. But while such conspicuous idiocies attracted scorching criticism at the time, and have been satirised in novels and histories of this Afghan War ever since, to focus solely upon them is to neglect more significant and enduring problems, failures, and tendencies.

All too evident in this Afghanistan episode were certain constraints on British power that had existed in the 1600s, and could still prove problematic in some contexts a quarter of a millennium later. Even now, in the 1840s, the British could find themselves under pressure *vis-à-vis* numbers and availability of manpower and suffer militarily as a result. Since Afghanistan was landlocked, the Royal Navy's range and firepower signified little, and therefore the onus fell on land troops, Britain's besetting Achilles heel. 'The Russians were said to have an army of hundreds of thousands and untold wealth', a sepoy who fought for the British, Sita Ram, recorded hearing during the lead-up to this crisis. As a result, he wrote, some of his comrades and some of the British themselves anticipated the collapse of the East India Company's dominion: 'the end of the

Sirkar's rule was predicted. For how could they withstand their enemies with only twelve or thirteen regiments of Europeans, which were all that were then in India?'[13]

This was actually an underestimate of the number of white soldiers in India by this stage. But it was certainly the case that, of necessity, most troops in the Army of the Indus were not British at all, but Afghan supporters of Shah Shuja, and above all Indian cavalry and infantry from the Company's legions. When the crisis came, many of these 'loyal Afghans' proved unreliable, while some of the Indian troops succumbed very rapidly to freezing temperatures for which their own background left them utterly unprepared. None of this might have mattered had the British commanded the sort of overwhelming technological superiority still sometimes routinely attributed to nineteenth-century imperialists, but they did not. Afghanistan illustrates yet again what other captivity crises in this book have demonstrated: that before 1850, and in terms of land warfare, a technology gap between highly organised Western states and the rest could not always be relied upon, and – even when present – sometimes turned out not to be decisive. The British emphatically possessed far superior artillery at Kabul in 1841, but this was cancelled out by the Afghans' better rifles, and the fact that the latter were often more accurate shots.[14]

Then, again, the sort of collapse in morale and cohesion that occurred among the British at Kabul cantonment and on the subsequent retreat, would have been familiar to Tangier's reluctant garrison back in the 1670s and '80s. At Kabul, as in Tangier, regimental pay was sometimes badly in arrears, tensions surfaced between some of the English and some of the Irish troops, and some soldiers tried to desert or simply refused to do their job. It should come as no surprise to readers of this book that these defaulters were not in the main Indian troops, but poor British and Irish whites. 'The sepoys alone appear to have behaved steadily to the last,' thundered one English magazine on the Kabul débâcle, '. . . We have abundant evidence of a lamentable want of discipline and proper spirit in the European troops.' 'The native troops in our service', agreed a Scottish journalist, 'often behaved with more gallantry and devotedness than the Europeans.'[15] Afghanistan, indeed, confirmed some among the British political and military elite in the view that 'the brave sepoy . . . [held] a station quite on a par with our own excellent yeomanry', whereas the mass of British and Irish common soldiers were by contrast markedly inferior stock and by no means an invariable imperial asset.[16]

As this suggests, even now, those Britons engaged in implementing empire were far from monolithic. Compensated for their smallness by a remarkably strong state, and by a precocious and ever more assertive collective national ideology, the British none the less remained characterised by certain internal divisions that found ample expression in their overseas enterprise. Even now, at the start of the Victorian era, divisions amongst them, divisions of social class, divisions of religion, divisions of language and precise national background, and the gender division, proved *sometimes* more grating and more obtrusive than differences between Britons and particular non-Europeans.

In Afghanistan, as in Tangier in the 1680s, or Mysore in the 1780s, defeat and captivity could lead to these fault lines within the British ranks gaping open. When Afghan leaders demanded and received the officers' wives from the sad caravan retreating from Kabul in January 1842, the husbands concerned seem to have been content to go with them. By so doing, they left the lower ranks in their care and under their command – British as well as Indian – to their fate. As one NCO who survived grimly remembered:

> The men in front then said 'The officers seem to take care for themselves. Let them push on if they like, we will halt till our comrades in the rear come up.'[17]

And so these white subalterns waited, and most of them died. Captivity, and the writings spawned by it, exposed the gulf between imperial Britain's poor and privileged just as powerfully. Most manuscript and printed accounts from the time make a point of calling the officers' wives who were captured 'ladies', while referring to other captive British females as 'women' or merely by their surnames. Some of the other ranks' womenfolk were omitted from the record altogether. We know the names of at least two soldiers' wives, a Mrs Bourke and a Mrs Cunningham, who were taken by Afghan tribesmen on the retreat from Kabul and never handed back. Instead, these women remained in Afghanistan for the rest of their lives, embracing Islam and new, Afghan, husbands. Their memory endures in Afghan folklore, and is cherished as a demonstration of the triumph of Islam – and Afghan masculinity – over infidel invaders. But almost all British writings of the time (and since) ignore these women, and others of their sort who shared the same fate.[18]

Yet most contemporary accounts acknowledge how captivity in Afghanistan – like other captivity crises – sometimes strained and altered British identities. As always, it was the youngest captives who proved most susceptible. Captain Anderson and his wife lost their eleven-year-old daughter, 'Tootsey', to an Afghan family in Kabul for several months in 1841. When restored to the parents whom she now called infidels to their face, she was reported to have 'totally forgotten English . . . and could only chatter away in Persian'.[19] Some adults involved in these captivities also changed. It is often claimed that the British, and particularly the English, clung stoutly and ostentatiously to their own customs and company when exposed to foreign and imperial climes: stubbornly 'dining in the jungle' on roast beef, in black tie or pearls as it were. Yet this is a late and a very selective piece of national and imperial mythology. As countless episodes in this book have demonstrated, in the seventeenth, eighteenth, and early nineteenth centuries, some Britons reached accommodations with, and occasionally became amalgamated with the various non-European peoples amongst whom they found themselves. The same remained true to a degree in Afghanistan in the 1840s.

It is worth examining in this regard two very different images of captives. One is the work of Emily Eden, the highly intelligent sister and chatelaine of Lord Auckland, governor-general of India. In June 1841, she painted from life portrait heads of Dost Muhammad Khan, the ousted amir of Afghanistan, and three other male members of his family, who were then being held by the British in genteel imprisonment at Barrackpore. Dark-eyed, dignified, and austere, the men wear elaborate white turbans, rich robes and beards; and three of them gaze pointedly away from the unveiled female amateur who is so eagerly and – in terms of their culture – so inappropriately portraying them. These particular Afghan captives (who would soon return home in triumph) manifestly have little intention of adjusting to, or even acknowledging their surroundings, and are reluctant to compromise what they are. Compare this with some of the images of British prisoners in Kabul drawn from life by Lieutenant Vincent Eyre, with the intention (which he survived to carry out) of supplying his captivity narrative with illustrations should it ever reach the press. One heavily bearded British officer lounges cross-legged against a wooden chest, his hair bound up in a turban, a slippered foot protruding from his robe; another officer of the Queen stands barefoot, his long overdress slung over his shoulders, his hair done up in a striped cloth, and with an elaborate hookah in hand and in use. Without knowing, one would scarcely suspect that these men were British, or Christian, or professional agents of empire.

The disparity between these two sets of images was partly one of circumstance. Dost Muhammad Khan and his family were elite captives and ostensibly guests of the governor-general, at Barrackpore, so the conventions were observed. Servants were available to groom and oil their beards; and customary costumes were kept freshly laundered and in repair. British captives in Afghanistan on the other hand were a bedraggled lot coping

70. Emily Eden's water-colour of the four Afghan captives.

71. Captain Bygrave by Vincent Eyre.

with harsher conditions. Their skin was burnt brown from exposure, they had few razors or any other grooming aids to hand, and their original costumes had either rotted on their backs or been lost in the retreat. Yet the contrast between how these very different captives allowed themselves to be represented goes deeper than this. Evident in some of the British subjects drawn by Eyre is an active acceptance of new and different clothing and bodily postures. It would be wrong to interpret this as the swagger of confident imperialists moving coolly and assuredly in and out of different cultures, though Eyre himself may have added an element of flamboyance to his original drawings before publishing them. When he made his initial sketches, however, neither he nor his subjects knew if they would survive, never mind return home; though they did know, all too well, that they had lost. At some level, at least, these are drawings of individuals submitting to metamorphosis, ruefully adjusting to new surroundings, and in some cases even wilfully blending in. Such candour may have been one reason why, when Eyre did publish his text and illustrations in

72. Captive and artist: Lieutenant Vincent Eyre back in Britain.

London in 1843, they were roundly condemned by some senior British military figures.[20]

As this book has shown, such flexibility in the face of enforced exposure to alien surroundings had many precedents. Time and time again, British men and women taken captive in the Mediterranean, or in North America, or in India, changed their behaviour, their language, their outward appearance, and even their political and religious allegiance. Often this occurred under pressure and only temporarily; but in some cases it happened permanently and out of a measure of choice. Such adaptability in the face of other cultures was never confined merely to Britons taken captive. The cliché that Britons overseas clung to their peculiar, parochial habits ('Mad dogs and Englishmen go out in the midday sun', etc.) needs examining carefully and sceptically, like every other cliché, in the light of all, and not just some of the evidence. Always sparse in number, the British would scarcely have been able – or wanted – to attempt empire on the scale that they did, or be the avid emigrants that they remain today, had not some of them possessed in fact a markedly chameleon tendency.

In the case of the Britons held in Afghanistan, a measure of adjustment and mimicry may have been easier because their captors were Muslims. In this respect, too, what happened here in 1841 and 1842 was in keeping with other, earlier captivity crises. Once again, and as in Morocco and Mysore, British overseas enterprise was slowed down, embarrassed – and in this case defeated – by an Islamic power. Once again, Islam revealed its capacity to supply non-Western opponents of Western empire with a cohesion that was often otherwise lacking. This said, and as in other regions of the world, events in Afghanistan rarely revealed a clean and unambiguous gulf between Muslims on the one hand and British imperialists on the other. When the British invaded in 1838, they did so in alliance with an exiled Muslim ruler, and with the military support of other Muslims. And, as was usually the case, their own recorded reactions to contact with an Islamic culture were mixed and confused.

Britons caught up in this crisis regularly described the Afghans who fought them, defeated them, and captured them as barbarians, and as 'wild and savage men', cruel, primitive, treacherous, and all too susceptible to 'white-bearded mullahs'.[21] Simultaneously, however, and sometimes in the identical letter, narrative or report, Afghan Muslims were also described as 'gallant' defenders of their freedom, full of 'energy and activity', 'frank, open, and manly . . . brave and industrious', the very same adjectives that early Victorian Britons enjoyed applying to themselves.[22] It helped of course that Afghanistan was a cold, mountainous country full of warriors. It helped even more that it had resisted them successfully. None the less, this captivity crisis demonstrated yet again that, for the British, as for other Europeans, Islamic societies rarely appeared comprehensively and unalloyedly their own backward or malign antithesis. Those attached to the Crescent might often be the enemy; and were certainly often colonised. But they could not easily be merely despised or invariably and unmitigatedly othered, which was one reason why tough, angry and captive British army officers were willing to pose and be represented in Afghan dress.

Yet the most obvious respect in which events in Afghanistan in 1841 and 1842 form a fitting climax to, and summation of the themes treated in this book, is that they underline again just how central captivity was, both to the British experience of imperial conflict in this period, and to how Britons at home understood the business of empire. As critics of the war complained, before the Kabul insurrection in November 1841, Parliament and the media in Britain devoted scant attention to what its

73. Lieutenant Muir
by Vincent Eyre.

troops and their Afghan and Indian auxiliaries were doing in Afghanistan,
a place that most Britons would have been hard-pressed to identify on a
map. 'A few words written in the cabinet of England are like the sudden
removal of a tiny bolt, setting free the complex forces of a great engine!'
wrote the Whig colonial administrator and reformer, Henry Lushington:

> The vast machinery of oriental war stirs and works; armies march,
> artillery rolls, lands are wasted, cities are stormed, the thrones of Asia
> go down, half the human race is shaken with alarm. *And for all this —
> the nation does not care.*[23]

But the British nation began to care enormously once things went wrong and captives were seized. As had always been the case, Britons taken captive served to personalise overseas and imperial events and emergencies, making them seem far more immediate and engrossing to their countrymen at large. The fate of the captives, judged one British magazine in 1843, had 'excited more interest in the mother country than all the other events of the war'. 'The history of the world', declared the *Illustrated London News*, in an article that same year on the Kabul captives, 'barely contains scenes of more terrific interest.' So great was the public clamour, that the politicians were left with little choice but to act. In the wake of the disaster at Kabul, virtually the whole of British official and military actions became focused, as M.E. Yapp argues, on restoring national prestige and on recovering the captives, policy objectives that were seen as identical.[24]

If all this seems reminiscent of another international crisis over captives, then – in all sorts of ways – it is. The closest recent parallel to the British furore over its Afghan detainees in 1842 was the absorption of the White House and the American public in the fate of the Iranian hostages between 1979 and 1981. Both crises were prompted by the prime Western power of its day becoming linked with support for a highly unpopular Muslim ruler, Shah Shujah in the British case, the deposed Shah of Iran in the American case. And in both cases the number of individuals directly caught up in the hostage crisis was modest by the normal standards of global violence. Yet, for the British in 1842, as for Americans some 140 years later, this proved quite beside the point. Warren Christopher, the US Deputy Secretary of State who organised the release of the Iranian hostages, put it well:

> In the long sweep of history, the Iranian hostage crisis may occupy little more than a page. Yet it riveted the attention of the US government for more than fourteen months and preoccupied the country as an event rarely has.[25]

As Part Two of this book demonstrates, Britain, and what is now the United States, have long possessed an influential culture of captivity in common. That culture has usually expressed itself in different ways on the different sides of the Atlantic, but it stems from, and points to, these societies' linked pasts and joint Protestant tradition. This transatlantic culture of captivity arguably also points to a certain shared isolationism and insularity. Rather like the United States is now, Britain in its imperial phase was at once a power with vast global interests and influence, and simultaneously an often inwardly obsessed society whose citizens in general cared little for much of the time about events beyond their own borders. Overseas captivity crises and narratives of different kinds mattered over the centuries as far as imperial Britain was concerned – as they continue to matter in America – in part because of their bridging of the global on the one hand and the national and local on the other. It might be possible to disregard the outside world in normal circumstances, but not when Britons (or Americans) were dramatically caught fast or suffering there.

Yet the most significant parallel between British responses to the catastrophes in Afghanistan in 1842, and American responses to the hostage crisis in Iran in 1979–81, goes deeper than this.

For the British, overseas captivity crises in the seventeeth and eighteenth centuries, and even in the early 1800s, had often called forth more profound anxieties that winning and keeping territorial empire was too dangerous and might be beyond their capacity. Tales of captivity were not generated and scrutinised primarily because they deflected attention from Britons' own aggression, though this was sometimes part of their effect. They were scribbled and pored over as explorations of fear, risk and deeply felt constraints. But the Afghanistan captivity crisis was significantly different. To be sure, there were continuities between some of the weaknesses and divisions displayed in 1841–2 and earlier British imperial débâcles, but in terms of domestic responses there was also a crucial and perceptible change. The premier emotion displayed by the British in 1842 – as by Americans in 1979 – was not anger, or even humiliation, so much as shock and astonishment. By the 1840s, most prosperous Britons no longer expected to fail, or to be seriously constrained on the global stage. The domestic agitation over the Afghan captives, which was of a different and greater volume and scale than anything that had gone before, testified paradoxically to the degree that Victorian Britons had come to take for granted their nation's unique 'character of success'.[26] Like Americans at the time of the Iran crisis and since, they now viewed themselves as the most powerful nation in the world, and were consequently utterly taken aback, traumatised, and obsessed when a comparatively weak opponent damaged them and held their compatriots at its mercy.

To this extent, the Afghanistan captivity crisis marks both a summation of many of the themes treated in this book, and the onset of a different phase of British imperialism and imperial awareness. In the immediate aftermath of the crisis, some writers and politicians did hark back to earlier imperial traumas. British defeat in Afghanistan was occasionally likened to the humiliations of the lost war with Revolutionary America; and references were made to Tipu Sultan's tiger legions and to the captives of Mysore. Yet it is striking how – on this occasion – other, more imperturbable voices rapidly cut in and took charge of the post-mortem. Ancient history, wrote a singularly unexcited Dr Arnold, pondering the lessons of Kabul, was full of examples of individual Roman consuls and their legions being wiped out in stray imperial battles: 'but then the next year another Consul and his legions go out, just as before.' Arnold's use of a Roman parallel was eloquent, and his optimism entirely justified. The famous roll-call by Jack Gallagher and Ronald Robinson makes the point:

> Between 1841 and 1851 Great Britain occupied or annexed New Zealand, the Gold Coast, Labuan, Natal, the Punjab, Sind and Hong Kong. In the next twenty years, British control was asserted over Berar, Oudh, Lower Burma and Kowloon, over Lagos and the neighbourhood of Sierra Leone, over Basutoland, Griqualand and the Transvaal; and new colonies were established in Queensland and British Columbia.[27]

In the wake of a signal imperial and military calamity, the military, commercial, missionary and entrepreneurial legions of Victorian Britain were not simply going out just as before. They were going out faster still and even further.

The lack of sustained, worried introspection in the aftermath of a conspicuous defeat and a major captivity crisis, and the absence after 1841 of even a pause in the rate of Britain's global advance and aggression take us in many respects into a different imperial era. Back in 1600, when our story began, empire for the English had been something that the great Islamic powers, the Chinese, and some Catholic Europeans were adept at, but not them. As far as their own extra-European forays were concerned, reverses were for a long time as conspicuous as successes, and often resulted in definitive retreats. As Joyce Lorimer reminds us, the English frequently devoted far more thought, money and energy in the early decades of the seventeenth century to colonising Guiana, than they did to their settlements on the Atlantic seaboard of North America. But their numerous efforts in the former region miscarried, and they were forced to retire in the face of Dutch competition.[28] Tangier, as we have seen, captured the imagination as well as the unprecedented largesse of the English state. Yet it, too, had to be given up, and thereafter the English, and later the British, made no serious attempt at securing a permanent enclave in North Africa for almost two centuries. Instead, they tolerated for much of the time the existence of Barbary's corsairs, grimly paying ransoms and protection money, as the necessary price for a British presence in Gibraltar and Minorca. Even so, European rivals were still able on two occasions to expel them by force from the latter base.[29]

And while Britain's power expanded enormously both inside and outside Europe in the century after 1689, its politicians and public remained for a long while apprehensive and even incredulous. It still appeared possible that all their novel global reach, wealth and grandeur would vanish as rapidly and as embarrassingly as the Emperor's new clothes. So when a future prime minister, the earl of Shelburne, contemplated Britain's defeat against Revolutionary Americans, he was immediately fearful that this was only the start of the rot. 'Away goes the fishery and 20,000 seamen,' he predicted glumly: 'After this will follow the West Indian islands, and in the process of time, Ireland itself; so that we should not have a single foot of land beyond the limits of this island.'[30] By the same token, the defeats and captivities inflicted on the East India Company by Haidar Ali and Tipu Sultan frightened London into a formal declaration in 1784 that no further advance in India could be contemplated, and led some to predict that Asia, too, was a frontier much too far. It is easy to forget how stubborn such insecurities proved among men and women who naturally lacked our retrospective understanding of the 'Rise of the British Empire'. Even in the early 1800s, there were experienced and sensible soldiers, pundits and politicians, who believed that it was far more likely that Britain itself would soon be conquered and made part of Napoleon's empire in Europe than that its own extra-European empire would endure for very long.[31]

By the 1840s, however, the world looked very different, both to the British, and to those co-existing, competing and contending with them. True, the Afghanistan crisis provoked tremors even at the highest level. 'George', wrote Emily Eden in 1841 of her brother, the governor-general of India, 'wonders every day how we are allowed to keep this country a week.'[32] The perception, even at the acme of their power, that the British were being *allowed* to retain India, as distinct from thoroughly controlling it themselves, is well worth noting. But although expressions of imperial uncertainty and insecurity persisted – and with good reason always would – they were now more easily and quickly drowned out. The more representative British voice was not any more that of Lord Auckland, soon to be dismissed from the governor-generalship in disgrace. The more representative voice belonged to a deservedly obscure poet greeting the rescue by force of the captives in Afghanistan:

> *Io Triumphe*! Afghanistan's won!
> *Io Triumphe*! Our great task is done!
> Captivity!
> Thy thralls are free;
> Britons have nought to do with thee![33]

Yet how true could this be in fact? How and how far had these small islands been able finally to evade their intrinsic constraints?

The domestic underpinnings of Britain's national egotism and imperial reach by 1850 are by now well known, and in some cases have been touched on already. There was – as there had long been – its strong state and fiscal inventiveness. There was its unparalleled navy and merchant fleet, backed by a chain of dockyards and bases around the globe. There were the financial tentacles of the City of London, in which both Britain's older landed elites and its newer plutocrats were involved. There was the knowledge that Britain had formally freed its colonial slaves in 1838, after earlier pulling out of the slave trade, and that its navy and diplomats were actively coercing other powers to do the same. For many, these initiatives crowded out guilt about Britain's earlier, busy slave-trading, and offered irresistible proof that empire, modern liberty, and benevolence were fully compatible. And complementing all these sources of wealth, power and complacency, there was a widespread conviction that Britain was a chosen nation, morally serious and actively reforming, and reserved by God for great things. A striking aspect of the Afghanistan captivity literature is how often the authors involved – unlike many earlier British officer class captives – carefully record their Sunday rituals of worship and moments of private prayer.[34]

In addition, Britain's geographical smallness had paid off in a new and vital way. It was in large part because rich deposits of coal and iron, together with abundant water power, were situated so closely and so conveniently together within its narrow boundaries, that it was able to generate the world's first fully-fledged, mineral-based industrial revolution, although the full impact of this took longer to emerge than once was supposed. Even in 1800, Britain had still trailed behind both China and the Indian subcontinent in terms of its share of world manufacturing output; even then, by some economic criteria, it was possible to think of 'a polycentric world with no dominant centre'.[35] Not so by 1850. By then, a previously unknown level of industrial innovation and productivity, combined with Britain's older financial and commercial riches, had made the business of acquiring, running, and exploiting a vast overseas empire much easier – though never at any time easy.

Industrial and technological advance brought with them more powerful, efficient, and mass-produced weapons of control and coercion. Queen Victoria's iron-clad, steam-driven battleships, boasted Lord Macaulay, could have annihilated the ancient navies of 'Tyre, Athens, Carthage,

Venice and Genoa together' in 'a quarter of an hour'. Industrial and technological advance meant faster, cheaper, and more reliable communications, both within particular imperial zones, and between them and Britain. Trains and telegraphs spanned distances that had previously appeared unmanageable. Emigrants, soldiers, sailors, administrators, exports, and ideas travelled out to imperial destinations at a much faster rate and in far larger quantities; while information, imports and profits flowed back to Britain's shores as never before. 'A most powerful steam flotilla has been . . . created,' purred Sir John Hobhouse to the House of Commons in 1842:

> They have made the communications between India and England regular and quick – they have opened the Indus to British commerce – they have displayed the British flag, for the first time in history, on the Tigris and Euphrates.[36]

As this suggests, industrial and technological advance also fostered arrogance, a sense that Britain was in the vanguard of modernity, and consequently that its invasions overseas were both ineluctable and a motor of global progress. 'I tell them about steam-engines, armies, ships, medicine and all the wonders of Europe,' recorded a Scottish political agent of his interviews with Afghan leaders in the 1830s.[37] This did not save him from being subsequently hacked to pieces, but the assurance was unmistakable.

Better communications also made it easier for British governments to shape and regulate the imperial narrative at home. The English, Welsh, Scots, and (obviously but not exclusively) the Irish had never been unanimous in their reactions to overseas ventures. There had always been disagreements, doubts, and sharply discordant stories – as well as widespread indifference and profound ignorance. The invasion of Afghanistan in 1838, for instance, was condemned by *The Times* and the *Spectator* in London, and some more downmarket papers, as well as by most English-language newspapers in India.[38] The sheer volume and range of Britain's print culture made it almost impossible – at all times – to prevent dissenting voices and occasional, deeply embarrassing disclosures. But the more rapid transmission of information from imperial locations back to London, together with the faster circulation of news within the United Kingdom itself made possible by railways, by macadamed roads, by cheaper newsprint and by growing literacy, gave politicians and imperial officials means and opportunities to lead and shape opinion they had previously lacked.

Back in the 1770s and '80s, American Revolutionaries had sometimes contrived to have their versions of battles and controversies printed and circulated in London before any official British version was available. Compare this lack of grip and censorship with the imperial authorities' meticulous organisation and ordering of information during the Indian rebellion of 1857:

> At weekly or fortnightly intervals, official narratives of the latest occurences were compiled . . . by the Governments of Bengal, the North-Western provinces etc . . . The narratives were forwarded to the Governor-General and copies made and sent to London. In addition, a summary of military intelligence was prepared every fortnight by the Military Department for despatch by each mail steamer.[39]

Now that highly detailed, seemingly authoritative narratives of this sort reached London so much faster, and could be promptly distributed, after appropriate alterations, by way of the new national broadsheets, it became more difficult for men and women to remain uninfluenced by them, and harder too for more idiosyncratic, individual narratives of empire and encounter to find an audience, or even a publisher.

A closer monitoring of imperial writings, and a greater degree of homogeneity among those published, were already apparent during the Afghanistan crisis. The fact that the most successful and well-publicised captivity narrative to emerge from it was written by a woman does not disprove this point, rather the reverse. Waspish enough to entertain and savour of independence, Florentia Sale's was an essentially conformist, imperially zealous text: 'What are *our lives* when compared with the honour of our country?' – which was just what one would have expected from the wife of an army general, a favourite of Queen Victoria, and a correspondent of the prime minister. The fact that the author was female probably also made her tale of captivity and defeat more acceptable to conventional British patriots and imperialists. Any weakness and fear in its pages could be put down to her gender, while passages of self-sacrifice and courage appeared all the more impressive from a member of the weaker sex. There was another respect too in which printed accounts of this Afghanistan crisis revealed a greater conformity. No captivity text seems to have been published on this occasion by anyone outside the officer class. The likes of Sarah Shade, or William Whiteway, or Joseph Pitts, or Thomas Pellow, and certainly George Thomas would find it harder now to set their stories of empire free. Some disgruntled captives in uniform and other poor whites caught out in imperial situations continued to write, but they were less likely after 1850 to publish.[40]

But industrialisation's most crucial contribution to Victorian imperial confidence and aggression was not the factory chimney, the steamship, the mechanization of the press, or ultimately the Gatling gun, but its easing of former anxieties about population levels. On the one hand, the new jobs and greater agricultural productivity it made possible allowed Great Britain's population to come close to quadrupling over the nineteenth century, without any of the subsistence crises that Malthus had anticipated. (Though both Ireland's industrial and demographic experience were substantially and terribly different.)[41] On the other hand, this unprecedented population growth enabled Victorian Britons to regard the ceaseless outflow of soldiers, sailors, administrators and emigrants from their shores with greater equanimity. They no longer feared, to the extent that earlier generations had done, that there were far too few of them. Instead, the argument that Patrick Colquhoun had deployed now became a widely current one: that the sheer abundance of Britons rendered overseas empire logical and indispensable. By the late nineteenth century, even America's leading anti-imperialist, Carl Schurz, was allowing himself to think in these terms. '*Nothing could be more natural*', he wrote: 'than that, as the population pressed against its narrow boundaries, Englishmen should have swarmed all over the world.'[42] Before 1800, this version of cause and effect had rarely appeared natural at all.

Indeed, there were important ways in which – for all its new material wealth, technology and physical force by 1850, and the ingenuity of its actors – Britain's empire remained in fact deeply *un*natural, and even downright peculiar. The empire always seemed bitterly unnatural of course to many of the men and women ruled by it, though others supported it, or were simply too caught up in the business of survival to think much about it one way or another. But Britain's empire was also inherently unnatural for the familiar reason: the utter smallness at its core. Recovering the voices embedded in successive captivity crises has revealed – along with many other things – how different Britons coped over time with the challenges of smallness. But for all the expedients, the tremendous rate of change, and the growing, terrible power, Britain's domestic limits were ultimately non-negotiable. To this extent, Queen Victoria was precisely emblematic of her empire. Statues of her (invariably much larger than life and raised high on pedestals) preside over town squares around the world, while her name remains linked even now with huge tracts of land and mighty natural phenomena. Yet the reality behind this global ubiquity and the calculated evocations of tremendous size was actually a dumpy woman less than five feet tall. Victoria the Great was also Victoria the small.

An awareness of the disparities between Britain's domestic dimensions and its grand imperial frontage surfaces in even the most strident imperial propaganda. 'The British empire', explained a former royal geographer, G.H. Johnston, on a map of the world generously picked out in red and published in honour of the Third Imperial Conference in London in 1902:

> is fifty-five times the size of France, fifty-four times the size of Germany, three and a half times the size of the United States of America, with quadruple the population of all the Russias.

The studious number-crunching, like the points of comparison selected – all of them physically bigger powers than the United Kingdom itself – is eloquent both of tremendous pride and a certain trepidation. 'Greater Britain,' Johnston continued, 'that is the possessions of the British people over the sea, is one hundred and twenty-five times the size of Great Britain.'[43] So how was this extraordinary construct conceivably to be retained and kept together?

All empires and great powers suffer from insecurity and a sense of transience. This is the flip side of arrogance and aggression. But as those presiding over it sometimes acknowledged, Britain's imperium was peculiarly conditional upon circumstances beyond its control and auxiliaries outside itself. Much of its territory and influence were owing to the decline of the great eastern empires, and the weakening of the Spanish and Portuguese empires, processes that Britain had sometimes assisted but scarcely initiated. The inception of *Pax Britannica* had been contingent upon the post-Napoleonic exhaustion of France, which had always previously competed furiously for territory, while challenging and de-stabilising Britain's own colonies. *Pax Britannica*'s persistence relied upon the fact that, before 1870, no single German state existed. It relied too upon Russia continuing to concentrate, as China did, on its own internal demons and empire; just as it relied upon the United States not seeking a global role, for all that it was expanding and growing richer every year. Most of all perhaps, British imperium depended on those it ruled in Asia, Africa, the Pacific, North America, and Europe not developing the sort of fierce nationalist ideologies that the British themselves had forged so precociously. As more thoughtful Britons recognised, these external preconditions for their imperial pre-eminence were unlikely to endure for very long.

There was a further vital and vulnerable degree to which Britain's primacy was heavily dependent upon others. Of necessity, the so-called British empire had always been a cross-cultural enterprise in fact, relying in the Mediterranean upon the assistance of North African Islamic powers, drawing on various Native Americans for vital information and military support, and – in America as in the Caribbean – recruiting black soldiers

Lesson 1.—The British Empire, 1.

1. The British Empire is the largest empire on the face of the globe.

(i) The sun never sets on the British Empire, and never rises.

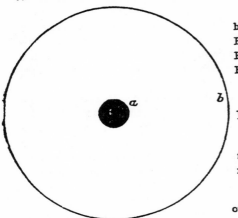

(ii) The British Empire is one hundred times as large as Great Britain. In this diagram, *a* is Great Britain; *b* represents the size of the British Empire.

2. It has an area of over 13,000,000 square miles.

(i) The British Empire is larger than the Russian Empire by above 4 millions of square miles.

(ii) The British Empire has about one-fourth of all the land on the globe.

3. It has a population of about 434,000,000.

(i) The British Empire has about one-fourth of all the people in the world.

(ii) The most thickly peopled part of it is the Valley of the Ganges.

74. Pride and insecurity: a 1913 textbook represents the disparity between British size and Briti empire.

in times of emergency. But in regard to imperial manpower and the money to pay them, Britain's dependence upon India was on an altogether different scale. To a very considerable degree, it was the Company's Indian troops – and Indian tax-payers – who supplied Britain with 'the rod of order, the shield of defence and the sword for further advance' that it wielded not just in the subcontinent itself, but increasingly as well in other parts of Asia, in the Middle East, and in Africa.[44] Awareness of this had been behind the cult of the brave and trusty Indian sepoy, and underlay much of the horror and hatred with which Britons reacted to the events they termed the Indian Mutiny in 1857–9.

It should come as no surprise by now that one of the most vivid expressions of this panic took the form of a captivity narrative, in this case a fictional one. In December 1857, Charles Dickens published a short story in his periodical *Household Words* entitled 'The Perils of Certain English Prisoners'. The story was set in South America in 1744, but what Dickens had in mind – as his readers recognised – were actually those Britons who had recently been killed, taken prisoner, or otherwise imperilled in the current rebellion in India. The story's hero is a private in the Royal Marines who is captured, along with other men, women and children, in an uprising against an English garrison. The rebels involved are described as 'niggers, savages, and pirates, hideous, filthy and ferocious in the last degree'. This careful selection of deviants (for the echoes of earlier captivity villains, Barbary *pirates* and Native American *savages* are clear) are led of course by a Roman Catholic, 'a hideous little Portuguese monkey'. There is also a spy in the English camp, a black called 'Christian George King', a sepoy-figure in other words, ostentatiously loyal, but secretly treacherous. After many hardships, heroic deeds and painful sacrifices, the marine and his English companions are rescued by 'good blue-jackets and red-coats . . . every man with his face on fire when he saw me, his countryman who had been taken prisoner'.

There are many things that might be said about this unpleasant tale. There is conspicuously its extreme anachronism: the way it reimagines the past to suit mid-Victorian imperial and nationalist expectations. A real-life English private soldier taken captive outside Europe in the eighteenth century (and after) would have had little expectation of a full-scale rescue party being dispatched to save him, and perhaps even little desire to be saved. As various captivity stories in this book suggest, such an individual – had he survived – might have been enslaved by the local population. On the other hand, he might have settled down placidly enough amongst them, abandoned his original identity, and found an indigenous wife. To modern readers, however, it is the overt racism of this tale that jars. 'I have stated myself to be a man of no learning', the marine is made to declare, 'and if I entertain prejudices, I hope allowance may be made . . . I never did like Natives, except in the form of oysters.'[45]

The shock of encountering this sort of language from a novelist normally associated with warm humanity can get in the way of recognising what lay at the root of Dickens's fury. He and many other Britons were certainly appalled by what they read about the 'Mutiny' and its white victims; but they were also more fundamentally dismayed. As they well knew, outside the realm of fiction, imperial Britain could not afford to rely only on 'good blue-jackets and red-coats' to fight on its behalf and rescue it in time of emergency, because there were not enough of these homegrown heroes available in a pre-conscription age. There never had been enough. Britain's own armed forces, and especially its army remained limited in size, absurdly so in terms of the global scale of its empire. Imperial defence, imperial enlargement, and imperial order had therefore to rely substantially on those whom Dickens presumed to style 'Natives'. And what would happen if these men were to prove unreliable like Christian George King, or rebelled *en masse* as tens of thousands of Indians formerly in imperial service were now doing? It was this fundamental manpower quandary – and not merely tales of massacre and rape – that made the British response to the events of 1857–9 so over-charged and emotional. Close, now, to the very apex of their global power and wealth, they thought they felt the cracks that always lay beneath them beginning to shift and widen.

Twenty-first-century issues

Those cracks have long since gaped open, swallowing up the British empire, together with those other European colonial empires it once competed against and ultimately surpassed in size. For many people in Britain now, the empire seems in retrospect embarrassing or anathema, or a subject of mild nostalgia and regret, or simply an irrelevance, in every sense a lost world. Either way, there is usually an assumption that the empire is a known quantity. It was about global power, which the British no longer have. For many people outside Britain, the empire also seems a known quantity. It was about global power, yes. But it was also about oppression, exploitation, violence, arrogance, slavery and racism, as indeed at different times and in different places it often was. For some, what the British and their miscellaneous auxiliaries once did represents no less than an early Holocaust, which demands apology and reparation, but requires no further investigation and no great effort to understand. Once again, the empire gets treated as a known quantity, as something that was uniform in character and *sui generis*.

The British empire is emphatically not a subject where the adage 'to understand all is to excuse all' should apply. But neither – and this must be my conclusion – is it yet sufficiently understood. In all sorts of ways, indeed, Britain's empire remains an unknown quantity. In part, this is a challenge for the historians. We still need to know far more than we do about the perspectives and actions of those whom the British sought to rule. We need to investigate far more thoroughly than we have how Britain's empire compared with other empires, both Western and non-Western, that influenced it throughout, and from which it regularly borrowed techniques and ideas of rule. In addition – and in two different respects – Britain and its overseas empire need approaching far more in tandem, and not separately as they generally have in the past.

At one level – and as writers as diverse as Sir John Seeley and Salman Rushdie have argued – this means treating Britain not as an Olympian initiator of empire elsewhere, but as a society that was itself caught up in, transformed, and sometimes traumatised by the business of empire, though never to the exclusion of other influences.[46] One of my purposes in *Captives* has been to demonstrate how wide and diverse the impress of empire was: how it affected Britain's economy, material life and politics, of course, but how it also impinged on private and public writings, religious and secular culture, polite and plebeian art, and on all sectors of society. Empire was never just the business of gentlemanly (or ungentlemanly) capitalists, of the politically influential, and the imperially grand and famous. As in every other part of the world, empire's impact on Britain and Ireland was directly and disproportionately felt by the unimportant and the poor, by the soldiers and sailors, by voluntary and involuntary emigrants and settlers, by small traders and fishermen, by multitudinous women and very many children. The history of empire has often been reconstructed as a grand and terrible saga of international and intercontinental rivalries, contacts and collisions, of epic initiatives and major acts of destruction and genocide: and it was indeed all of these things. But for the British, as for those they invaded, empire was also critically made up of small stories of small people whose lives were rendered utterly different and sometimes destroyed by it. This book has uncovered some of these individual stories: there are many thousands more, from these islands and beyond, that cry out for recovery and close analysis.

Insisting on the heterogeneity of the British experience of empire is important for more than just the British themselves. For while it is increasingly being argued – and I agree – that the British must come to terms with their imperial past, the logical corollary of this is often missed. The British need to understand more about their one-time empire: yes. But, by the same token, those concerned with this empire's impact on other parts of the world, require an accurate, comprehensive and nuanced understanding of Britain itself, the ways in which it was once powerful, but also the ways in which its power overseas was always constrained and sometimes faltered. In *Captives* I have insisted on complexity, drawing attention to the persistent divisions among 'the British', to the degree to which they were always dependent in their empire on those who were not British at all, and – above all – to the ways in which their limited population, limited geographical size and resources, and limited indigenous military power inflected and distorted their imperial enterprise throughout. My intention has not been to deny their devastating power and impact at particular times and in particular places, but to show how these people were not just warriors, but in different ways captives too.

Acknowledging both the power and the violence of Britain's one-time empire, and the degree to which it was always a miscellaneous and multi-stranded phenomenon, characterised at its core by insecurities and persistent constraints, is important for more than just historians. It is vital for a proper understanding of our twenty-first-century world. This is manifestly true for the British themselves, but it also applies far more generally.

It is often argued now that the British should learn more about their one-time empire so as to remind themselves of their debts to different parts of the world. Here too I am inclined to agree. But there are selfish reasons, too, why the British could profitably acquaint themselves with what their empire involved in fact, rather than assuming they already know. Acknowledging the degree to which it was not simply global and grasping, but also insecure, patchy, and dependent on others and causes outside itself, might mitigate the sense of decline and nostalgia: the persistent feeling that this empire ended because of some deep-rooted national malaise and a lack of grip. As Paul Kennedy suggests, it is the fact that this empire lasted as long as it did that is remarkable, not its ultimate and entirely predictable demise. British politicians, in particular, might usefully wean themselves away from the notion that a grand and intrinsic national destiny has somehow got lost along the way. Winston Churchill, who knew his geopolitics, once declared that: 'We in this small island have to make a supreme effort to keep our place and status, *the place and status to which our undying genius entitles us.*'[47] Churchill was absolutely right to see in British smallness an inherent challenge and obstacle: but the yearning revealed in his words for a special, global status in the wake of lost empire has sometimes distorted post-war British policy. In particular, it has encouraged a persistent inclination to pursue empire vicariously by clambering like a mouse on the American eagle's head. That great bird needs no assistance, and we should look to our own directions.

Then there is the urgent matter of race. There are those who argue, with the utmost sincerity, that were the British to remind themselves of their empire it would only further incite the racism inextinguishably associated with it. Others argue, with equal passion, that one of empire's legacies has been a rooted racism in Britain that will require massive work to extirpate. Both of these arguments seem to me not so much wrong, as overly simple and pessimistic. Empire, as this book has sought to show, was never a monochrome, predictable entity. British imperialists sometimes espoused what we would now regard as fiercely racist ideologies. But the practicalities of running a huge multi-ethnic global construct where they, the British, were so much in the minority, meant that these ideologies were always compromised and qualified in practice. For the British to familiarise themselves now with the racial mix and the ethnic messiness of their one-time empire, as well as with its intolerance, might be no bad thing. A wider knowledge, say, that 'British' rule in India relied in fact overwhelmingly on the bayonets of Catholic Irishmen on the one hand, and on Indian troops on the other, might open minds, not close them. To be sure, empire could and did deepen racial and cultural divides. But it also shook them up. Britain's current high level of racial violence *may* at some level be a legacy of empire, but the fact that this country now produces more mixed marriages and equivalent relationships per head of population than almost anywhere else in the world may also in some way be a legacy of empire. Either way, we should not assume that a past experience of global empire of itself makes racism inescapable in Britain. That way lies both complacency and despair.

Looking at the history of this empire questioningly, and with an appreciation of how it was impacted on by Britain's own varieties of smallness, is important, however, far more widely. It is important, obviously, for those countries that were formerly colonised by Britain. It is scarcely to be wondered at that their populations sometimes harbour resentment, and even hatred of the British and other past colonisers, and a feeling of debts owed. No one likes to be invaded. But it is possible to exaggerate the power and the durable impact of these one-time colonisers, to make them seem more important and formidable than in fact they were. In some contact situations, colonisers were unquestionably drastic and lethal. Certain Native American peoples, like certain Pacific peoples, were wiped out by the germs English, Welsh, Scottish and Irish intruders carried with them, or subsequently hunted to death by land-hungry settlers; while Africans transported as slaves across the Atlantic experienced an atrocity that was not peculiar to the British empire, but was certainly fostered by it. In other contexts, however, the impact of empire was more uneven, sometimes very shallow, and far more slow. Environments, economies, customs, power relations and lives were sometimes utterly devastated; but by no means always, because these intruders were frequently limited in number, and dependent often on a measure of indigenous tolerance. Minority languages, for instance, like many other forms of cultural diversity, have vanished at a much faster rate since 1945 than before, despite the disappearance of European empires. The enemy this time has not been arrogant colonial officials, but more insidious and ubiquitous invaders: television, Hollywood, cyberspace, and monster, multi-national corporations.

These are deeply controversial issues that arouse strong emotions, and about which no consensus will ever be possible. But, as this last example suggests, exploring what the British empire, and its European counterparts, were able to do in the past – and what they could not or did not do – matters for more than just academic reasons. We live in a post-colonial world, but we do not yet live in a post-imperial world. All of today's great powers, while eschewing the description 'empire', retain in fact an imperial component and quality, either because they still bear the impress of past European imperialisms, or because they possess an imperial tradition of their own, or both. India, that extraordinary experiment in democracy, none the less treats its Sikh and Kashmiri separatists/freedom-fighters with a ferocity that the Raj would scarcely have exceeded. Indonesia is a large, multi-ethnic polity dominated by the Javanese, whose control has often rested more on military force than on consent. The Chinese Republic rules over provinces that, in some cases, were conquered by former Chinese emperors long after the Spanish and Portuguese conquest of the New World, and – again – does not always do so with the conspicuous consent of the governed.[48] And then there is the United States, a fiercely anti-imperial, fiercely democratic republic that is also an empire like no other. It is an empire in the sense that much of its territory was originally acquired by force, purchase, and migration at the expense of other, weaker peoples. But it also possesses now a string of military bases across the globe, a paramount navy, and an air force that can strike anywhere. 'We are the first empire of the world to establish our sway without legions,' declared the American Reinhold Niebuhr in 1931. 'Our legions are dollars.' The dollar rules still: but now there are legions too.[49]

Is all this dangerous? Not necessarily. The sheer size of these twenty-first-century covert empires means that they are most unlikely to seize overseas territory as the old European empires once did. They have no need. It was Britain's very smallness that helped to drive – as well as constrain – its overseas enterprise, for without other peoples' land and resources it could not be powerful. Small can be aggressive; large can be confident and inward-looking. However, there is another side. Because its core was so constrained, and because it depended on maritime power, Britain's empire was always overstretched, often superficial, and likely to be limited in duration. The current behemoths, being in the main contiguous, land-based empires, are likely to prove far more enduring, and possess weapons of mass destruction of a kind that dead European empires never imagined.

And this is why looking intelligently, questioningly, and – above all – comparatively at Britain's empire is imperative, as is pondering the complex connections between size on the one hand, and levels of power and ambition on the other. The years between 1600 and 1850 saw a set of small islands acquiring astonishingly and at great cost the biggest global empire that the world has ever seen. The twentieth century witnessed this empire, and its fellow European empires, become one with Nineveh and Tyre, and the emergence in their stead of new nations in every continent. One of the challenges of the twenty-first century will be establishing how we can monitor, balance, and keep within bounds the vast, new multi-ethnic giants in our midst, that are both safer and more dangerous than the old maritime empires. Lest we fall captive.

The Captivity Archive

In the United States, captivity narratives have long been a familiar source for novelists, artists and film-makers, as well as for historians. On the other side of the Atlantic, these texts have been explored and exploited far less. Yet manuscript and published accounts of captivity overseas were produced regularly in England and its adjacent countries, and in other parts of Europe, from at least the sixteenth century, and have remained prolific to this day. As should now be clear, modes of writing about captivity were – and are – many and diverse; and it needs stressing that, as far as Britain was concerned, thousands of captivity narratives were produced over the centuries in response to conflicts *inside* Europe, as well as in response to extra-European encounters outside the three large geographical regions that feature in this book. What follows is therefore a very select list in terms of provenance, chronology, and locations of stories told.

This is also a select list in that it is confined to those prose narratives with a high autobiographical content that are referred to in this book. It omits the innumerable ballads, poems and novels that were produced about captives, as well as the reports of individual experiences to be found in official documents of different kinds, though all of these formed part of a broad culture of captivity. Nor have I included general works, like Increase Mather's *An Essay for the Recording of Illustrious Providences* (1684), which contain factual captivity tales alongside other material. I have also omitted many British narratives about captivity that are very slight in length or content, as well as narratives published only in North America during this period, which were not slight at all, but which attracted only minimal attention on the other side of the Atlantic. Readers curious about the whole range of North American captivity narratives, both before and after 1783, should consult Alden T. Vaughan, *Narratives of North American Indian Captivity: A Selective Bibliography* (New

York, 1983), and – better still – the hundreds of modern editions of these narratives published by Garland. Robert C. Doyle's *Voices from Captivity: Interpreting the American POW Narrative* (Kansas, 1994), takes the story of America's obsession with captives up to the Vietnam War. Those wanting to investigate British captivities in regions other than those covered here, might start with I. J. Niven, L. Russell and K. Schaffer (eds), *Constructions of Colonialism: Perspectives on Eliza Fraser's Shipwreck* (1998), a set of essays on one of the most famous nineteenth-century Australian captivity narratives. For two recent British and Irish narratives (both of which contain references to earlier captivity stories), see John McCarthy and Jill Morrell, *Some Other Rainbow* (1993), and Brian Keenan, *An Evil Cradling* (1992).

In the case of accounts of captivity in my three zones of concentration published between 1600 and 1850, I have given the dates of all British and Irish editions within this period known to me, because the content – and sometimes the title – of these texts often changed significantly over time. Many of these texts went through yet more editions after 1850 and continue to be re-issued even today. In the case of narratives published only in North America, but of broader British imperial significance, I cite the date and place of publication of the first known edition. For narratives that survive in manuscript, I have provided the archival location and reference where available, together with details of any printed edition.

I would be astonished if the manuscript originals of more of the printed text listed below, together with additional writings by English, Irish, Scottish and Welsh men and women who underwent captivity in the Mediterranean region, India and Afghanistan, and North America in this period, did not still await discovery in archives, libraries and private homes throughout the world.

Mediterranean

Anon: 'The manner of the slavish usage suffered by the English in Barbary written by one who by woeful experience endured the same', Bodleian Library, Oxford, MS Rawlinson. c. 695.

Anon: *An Account of South-West Barbary . . . by a Person who had been a Slave there*, 1713.

Hector Black: *A Narrative of the Shipwreck of the British Brig Surprise*, 1817.

Francis Brooks: *Barbarian Cruelty*, 1693, 1700.

Edward Coxere: *Adventures by Sea*, ed. E.H.W. Meyerstein (Oxford, 1945). Includes Coxere's memories of captivity in Tripoli.

Adam Elliott: *A Narrative of my Travels, Captivity and Escape from Salle*, 1682, 1731, 1770.

James Irving: Narrative. Beinecke Library, Yale University, Osborn shelves c. 399; version published in Suzanne Schwarz (ed.), *Slave Captain* (Wrexham, 1995).

Vincent Jukes: *A Recovery from Apostacy set out in a Sermon*, by William Gouge, 1639.

Francis Knight: *A Relation of Seven Years Slavery*, 1640, 1745.

Thomas Lurting: *The Fighting Sailor Turned Peaceable Christian*, 1680, 1710, 1766, 1770, 1813, 1816, 1821, 1832, 1842.

Elizabeth Marsh: 'Narrative of her Captivity in Barbary'. Charles E. Young Research Library, University of California, Los Angeles; version published as *The Female Captive*, 2 vols, 1769.

William Okeley: *Eben-ezer: or, a Small Monument of Great Mercy*, 1675, 1684, 1764.

Thomas Pellow: *The History of the Long Captivity . . . of Thomas Pellow*, 1739?, 1740?, 1751, 1755.

Thomas Phelps: *A True Account of the Captivity of T. Phelps*, 1685, 1745.

Joseph Pitts: *A True and Faithful Account of the Religion and Manners of the Mohammetans . . . with an Account of the Author's Being Taken Captive*, 1704, 1717, 1731, 1778, 1810.

Devereux Spratt: *Autobiography of the Rev. Devereux Spratt* (1886). Includes account of his captivity in Algiers.

James Sutherland: *A Narrative of the Loss of H.M.'s ship The Litchfield*, 1761, 1768, 1788.

Thomas Sweet: *Deare Friends*, 1646. Printed letter narrating his captivity in Algiers, BL, 669.f.11 (3).

T.S.: *Adventures of Mr. T.S. an English Merchant, Taken Prisoner*, 1670, 1707.

Thomas Troughton: *Barbarian Cruelty*, 1751, 1788, 1807.

John Whitehead: Narrative. BL, Sloane MS. 90.

America

Ethan Allen: *A Narrative of Colonel Ethan Allen's Captivity* (Philadelphia, PA, 1779).

Thomas Anburey: *Travels through the Interior Parts of America*, 2 vols, 1789, 1791.

John Blatchford: *Narrative of the Remarkable Occurrences in the Life of John Blatchford* (New London, CT, 1788).

Jonathan Dickenson: *God's Protecting Providence, Man's Surest Help and Defence,* 1700, 1720, 1759, 1787, 1790.

John Dodge: *A Narrative of the Capture and Treatment of John Dodge, by the English* (Philadelphia, PA, 1779); reprinted in *The Remembrancer,* London, 1779.

Ebenezer Fletcher: *Narrative of the Captivity* (Amherst, MA, 1798).

Benjamin Gilbert: *Sufferings of Benjamin Gilbert and his Family,* 1785, 1790.

Henry Grace: *The History of the Life and Sufferings,* 1764, 1765.

John Gyles: 'A Memorial of the Strange Adventures and Signal Deliverances'. New York Public Library; version published as *Memoirs of Odd Adventures, Strange Deliverances* (Boston, MA, 1736).

Elizabeth Hanson, *An Account of the Captivity,* 1760, 1782, 1787, 1791.

Charles Herbert: *A Relic of the Revolution* (Boston, MA, 1847).

Thomas Hughes: *A Journal by Thomas Hughes,* ed. E.A. Benians (Cambridge, 1947).

Susanna Johnson: *The Captive American, or, A Narrative of the Sufferings,* 1797, 1802, 1803.

John Leeth: *A Short Biography . . . with an Account of his Life among the Indians,* ed. R.G. Thwaites (Cleveland, OH, 1904).

Jean Lowry: *A Journal of the Captivity* (Philadelphia, PA, 1760).

Thomas Morris: 'Journal of Captain Thomas Morris', in R.G. Thwaites (ed.), *Early Western Travels 1748–1846* (32 vols, Cleveland, OH, 1904–7), I.

Mary Rowlandson: *A True History of the Captivity and Restoration,* 1682. The first American edition of this narrative is entitled *The Sovereignty and Goodness of God.*

John Rutherfurd: 'Relation of a Captivity among the Indians of North America', National Army Museum, London, Acc 6003/17 (transcript); version published in M.M. Quaife (ed.), *The Siege of Detroit in 1763* (Chicago, IL, 1958).

Captain John Smith: *The General Historie of Virginia* (1624): the first full account by Smith of his capture, and 'rescue' by Pocahontas.

Hannah Swarton: Narrative in Alden T. Vaughan and Edward W. Clark (eds), *Puritans among the Indians: Accounts of Captivity and Redemption 1676–1724* (Cambridge, MA, 1981).

William Widger: 'Diary of William Widger of Marblehead, kept at Mill Prison, England, 1781', *Essex Institute Historical Collections,* LXXIII (1937).

John Williams: *The Redeemed Captive, returning to Zion* (Boston, MA, 1707).

Peter Williamson: *French and Indian Cruelty, Exemplified in the Life and Various Vicissitudes,* 1757, 1758, 1759, 1762, 1766, 1787, 1792, 1794, 1801, 1803, 1806, 1807, 1812, 1826.

India and Afghanistan

Anon: 'Narrative of events following surrender of Bidnanore'. NLS, MS 8432.

Anon: 'The English Captives at Cabul, by One of the Female Prisoners', *Bentley's Miscellany*, XIV (1843).

William Anderson: Narrative. IOL, MSS Eur. c 703.

Henry Becher: *Remarks and Occurences of Mr Henry Becher during his imprisonment*, Bombay, 1793.

Richard Runwa Bowyer: Narrative. IOL, MSS Eur. A94 and MSS Eur. A141.

James Bristow: *A Narrative of the Sufferings of James Bristow*, 1792, 1793, 1794, 1828 (Calcutta).

Donald Campbell: *A Narrative of the Extraordinary Adventures and Sufferings by Shipwreck and Imprisonment*, 1796, 1797, 1798, 1801, 1808.

Robert Cameron: Narrative. Scottish Record Office, Edinburgh, RH/4/34.

Arthur Conolly: Narrative. IOL, MSS Eur. B29.

William Drake: Narrative. *Calcutta Gazette*, 8 December 1791; *Times* (London), 10 April 1792.

Vincent Eyre: Narrative. IOL, MSS Eur. A42. Version published as *The Military Operations at Cabul . . . with a Journal of Imprisonment*, 1843.

Eliza Fay: *Original Letters from India . . . and the Author's Imprisonment at Calicut*, 1817, 1821.

Robert Gordon: 'Narrative or Journal of the Misfortunes of the Army'. NAM, 6409–67–3.

J.Z. Holwell: *A Genuine Narrative of the Deplorable Deaths . . . in the Black Hole*, 1758, 1804.

John Kaye, *History of the War in Afghanistan. From the Unpublished Letters and Journals of Political and Military Officers* (2 vols, 1851). Includes selections from captivity narratives which have not otherwise survived.

John Lindsay: 'Prison Life in Seringapatam, 1780–84'. NLS, Acc 9769 (transcript); versions published in 1840, 1849.

Cromwell Massey: Narrative. IOL, MSS Eur B392; editions published in Bangalore in 1876 and 1912.

Innes Munro: *A Narrative of the Military Operations on the Coromandel Coast*, 1789. Includes references to his captivity in Mysore.

Henry Oakes: *An Authentic Narrative of the Treatment of the English*, 1785.

Francis Robson: *The Life of Hyder Aly* (1786). Includes references to his captivity in Mysore.

Florentia Sale: Narrative. IOL, MSS Eur B275; version published as *A Journal of the Disasters in Afghanistan*, 1843, 1846.

James Scurry: *The Captivity, Sufferings and Escape of James Scurry*, 1824, 1831.

Sarah Shade: *A Narrative of the Life*, 1801.

William Thomson: *Memoirs of the Late War in Asia*, 2 vols., 1788. Compilation of captivity narratives from Mysore.

Edward Arthur Henry Webb: Narrative. IOL, MSS Eur D160. This also contains captivity memories by his wife.

William Whiteway: Narrative. Printed in *James Scurry*, 1824.

Since the references to each chapter make up what is in effect a running bibliography, I have dispensed – with one exception – with a separate list of further reading. The exception is the Appendix which gives publication and provenance details of all the major captivity narratives drawn on in this volume, together with additional references. In the endnotes that follow, captivity narratives have been referred to throughout by the name of the captive involved: e.g,. *Edward Coxere*, followed by the relevant page numbers. In the case of published narratives that passed through several editions over time, I have also indicated the date of the edition quoted from in the text: e.g., *Thomas Pellow* (1740?). The endnotes also make clear when I am quoting from a manuscript rather than a published captivity narrative: e.g., *John Lindsay MS*. Interested readers should then turn to the Appendix for the full title reference and bibliographical and archival information on the narrative concerned.

The place of publication in these notes is London unless otherwise stated. The following abbreviations are used throughout:

Add. MS	Additional Manuscript
AHR	*American Historical Review*
BL	British Library, London
CSPD	R. Lemon *et al.* (eds), *Calendar of State Papers: Domestic Series*, 91 vols, (1856–1964)
CSPC	W. Noel Sainsbury *et al.* (eds), *Calendar of State Papers: Colonial Series*, 40 vols, (1860–1939)
DNB	*Dictionary of National Biography*
HMC	Reports of the Royal Commission on Historical Manuscripts
Hansard	*Hansard's Parliamentary Debates*
IOL	India Office Library, British Library, London
JSAHR	*Journal of the Society for Army Historical Research*
MAS	*Modern Asian Studies*
NLS	National Library of Scotland, Edinburgh
OHBE	W.R. Louis *et al.* (eds), *The Oxford History of the British Empire*, (5 vols, Oxford, 1998–9)
I	N. Canny (ed.), *The Origins of Empire*

II	P.J. Marshall (ed.), *The Eighteenth Century*
III	A.N. Porter (ed.), *The Nineteenth Century*
IV	J.M. Brown and W.R. Louis (eds), *The Twentieth Century*
V	R.W. Winks (ed.), *Historiography*
Parl. Hist.	W. Cobbett, *The Parliamentary History of England from the earliest period to 1803* (36 vols, 1806–20)
PP	*Parliamentary Papers*
PRO	Public Record Office, London
RO	Record Office
WMQ	*William and Mary Quarterly*

Introduction

1   Daniel Defoe, *Robinson Crusoe: An Authoritative Text, Contexts, and Criticism*, ed. Michael Shinagel (1994), 15, 100, 174. The quotation from Joyce is at p. 323 of this edition. Defoe's acute sensitivity to captivity stemmed in part, as Sir Leslie Stephen noted, from his own experience of prison.

2   A good modern edition of *Gulliver's Travels*, complete with critical essays and edited by Christopher Fox, was published in 1995.

3   *OHBE* 1, 77. The five volumes of this series, though controversial (how could they not be) supply an expert and broad-ranging survey of this extraordinary empire. For an interesting critique, see Dane Kennedy, 'The boundaries of Oxford's empire', *International History Review*, 23 (2001).

4   I have drawn these figures from *Whitaker's Almanac* for 2002.

5   Norman Davies, *Europe: A History* (Oxford, 1996), 1068–9.

6   E.A. Wrigley *et al.*, *English Population History from Family Reconstitution, 1580–1837* (Cambridge, 1997), 547.

7   On British population anxieties in the 1700s, see D.V. Glass, *Numbering the People* (1978).

8   Daniel A. Baugh, *British Naval Administration in the Age of Walpole* (Princeton, NJ, 1965), 147 *seq.*; N.A.M. Rodger, 'Guns and Sails in the First Phase of English Colonization, 1500–1650', and 'Sea-Power and Empire, 1688–1793', in *OHBE*, I, 79–98; II, 169–83.

9   John Brewer, *The Sinews of Power: War, Money and the English State 1688–1783* (1989). As one British politician complained in 1781: 'In every quarter of the world our forces were much more upon paper than they were in the field', *Parl. Hist.*, XII (1781–2), 833.

10 J.A. Houlding, *Fit for Service: The Training of the British Army 1715–1795* (Oxford, 1981), 7–8; Miles Taylor, 'The 1848 revolutions and the British empire', *Past and Present*, 166 (2000), 150–1.

11 On European versus non-European military technology on land and sea, see Michael Adas, *Machines as the Measure of Men: Science, Technology, and Ideologies of Western Dominance* (1989); Douglas M. Peers (ed.), *Warfare and Empires: Contact and Conflict between European and non-European Military and Maritime Forces and Cultures* (Aldershot, 1997).

12 Patrick O'Brien, 'The impact of the Revolutionary and Napoleonic Wars, 1793–1815, on the long-run growth of the British economy', *Review: Fernand Braudel Center*, XII (1989), 367–8.

13 C.W. Pasley, *Essay on the Military Policy and Institutions of the British Empire* (1810), 44; Edward Said, *Culture and Imperialism* (New York, 1993), 11.

14 J.H. Leslie (ed.), 'Letters of Captain Philip Browne, 1737–1746', in *JSAHR*, 5 (1925), 103. For Halifax, see David Armitage, *The Ideological Origins of the British Empire* (Cambridge, 2000), 142–3; Defoe is quoted in Daniel A. Baugh, 'Maritime Strength and Atlantic Commerce' in Lawrence Stone (ed.), *An Imperial State at War: Britain from 1689 to 1815* (1994), 201.

15 J.H. Stocqueler, *The Wellington Manual* (Calcutta, 1840), 195–6; Adam Smith, *An Inquiry into the Nature and Causes of the Wealth of Nations*, ed. R.H. Campbell and A.S. Skinner (2 vols, Oxford, 1976), II, 946.

16 Pasley, *Essay on the Military Policy*, 54.

17 On Britain's early state and national development and its limitations, see my *Britons: Forging the Nation 1707–1837* (1992); Brendan Bradshaw and John Morrill (eds), *The British Problem, c.1534–1707: State Formation in the Atlantic Archipelago* (1996); and Brewer, *Sinews of Power*.

18 I am indebted to Peter Gay for this glance at Adler.

19 Quoted in Jill Lepore, *The Name of War: King Philip's War and the Origins of American Identity* (New York, 1998), 74.

20 Mary Louise Pratt, 'Fieldwork in Common Places', in James Clifford and George E. Marcus (eds), *Writing Culture: The Poetics and Politics of Ethnography* (Los Angeles, CA, 1986), 38.

21 Mike Parker Pearson, 'Reassessing *Robert Drury's Journal* as a historical source for southern Madagascar', *History in Africa*, 23 (1996). I am most grateful to Dr Pearson for sending me this and other material on Drury.

22 *Ibid.*; Mike Parker Pearson *et al.*, *The Androy Project: Fifth Report* (1997), 40.

23 Brian Keenan, *An Evil Cradling* (1993), 58.

24 James S. Amelang, *The Flight of Icarus: Artisan Autobiography in Early Modern Europe* (Stanford, CA, 1998), 37.

25 Dominic Lieven, *Empire: The Russian Empire and its Rivals* (2000), 17; Anthony Pagden, *Peoples and Empires* (New York, 2001), xxi.

1 Tangier

1 Cholmley's letter-books and papers, which I have drawn on throughout this chapter, are in the North Yorkshire RO (ZCG). See also *The Memoirs of Sir Hugh Cholmley* (1787). The man deserves a modern biography.

2 On Tangier and the Navy, see Sari R. Hornstein, *The Restoration Navy and English Foreign Trade, 1674–1688* (Aldershot, 1991), a valuable study that neglects, however, the Moroccan contribution to the colony's fate. For Cholmley's contract, see 'A Short Account of the Progress of the Mole at Tangier', in *Tracts on Tangier*, BL, 583.i.3 (1–8); and PRO, CO 279/2, fols 18–19.

3 [Sir Henry Sheeres] *A Discourse touching Tanger* [sic] *in a letter to a person of quality* (1680), 7.

4 Robert Latham and William Matthews (eds), *The Diary of Samuel Pepys* (11 vols, 1970), IV, 299, 319.

5 Julian S. Corbett, *England in the Mediterranean* (2 vols, 1904), II, 17, 137.

6 E.M.G. Routh, *Tangier: England's Lost Atlantic Outpost 1661–1684* (1912), 38; Richard T. Godfrey, *Wenceslaus Hollar: A Bohemian Artist in England* (New Haven, CT, 1994), 27, 159–60.

7 For Tangier's colonial population, see Bodleian Library, MS Rawl. A185; 'A discourse of Tangier', BL, Lansdowne MS 192, fol. 164.

8 For the fabric of colonial life in Tangier, see the volumes of correspondence in PRO, CO 279; and *Memoirs of Sir Hugh Cholmley*, 103–296.

9 Routh, *Tangier*, 365–9; 'Reasons Touching the Demolishing Tangier', Beinecke Library, Yale University, Osborn MS, Fb. 190 vol. 4. The definitive work on English royal income and expenditure in this period – which, however and predictably, gives Tangier only limited attention – is C.D. Chandaman, *The English Public Revenue 1660–1688* (Oxford, 1975).

10 See the plans in PRO, MPH 1; and Cholmley's letter-book, *passim*.

11 Bodleian Library, MS Rawl. A342, fol. 151; MS Rawl. A191, fol. 44; Corbett, *England in the Mediterranean*, II, 137.

12 Frank H. Ellis (ed.), *Poems on Affairs of State: Augustan Satirical Verse, 1660–1714* (7 vols, New Haven, CT, 1975), III, 473–4; Edwin Chappell, *The Tangier Papers of Samuel Pepys* (1935), preface.

13 See *OHBE*, I. Atlanticist bias was already operative in Routh's day, as her subtitle suggests. At the time it was an English colony, Tangier was discussed overwhelmingly in terms of Mediterranean power and trade.

14 *The Mediterranean and the Mediterranean World in the Age of Philip II* (2 vols, 1995 edn), II, 1240. Scholarly interest in the Mediterranean is showing signs of reviving. In particular, the work of Professor Molly Greene of Princeton University promises much.

15　Hornstein, *The Restoration Navy*, 37–8. It bears repeating that England's European and extra-European trading interests were always interconnected. Colonial and extra-European re-exports contributed to its Mediterranean trade. Conversely, Mediterranean profits helped to offset the bullion it paid out for its East Indian commodities.

16　I owe this information on Ottoman population and army size to Professors Virginia Aksan and Sevket Pamuk.

17　I am grateful to Dr Simon Price for this example of Ottoman fiscal zeal.

18　Routh, *Tangier*, 264; P.G. Rogers, *A History of Anglo-Moroccan Relations to 1900* (1970), 232.

19　BL, Lansdowne MS 192, fols 123–9; *A Discourse touching Tanger* [sic] . . . *to which is added The Interest of Tanger, by Another Hand* (1680), 37.

20　*An Exact Journal of the Siege of Tangier* (1680).

21　For a useful discussion on these points, see Ann Laura Stoler, 'Rethinking colonial categories: European communities and the boundaries of rule', *Comparative Studies in Society and History*, 31 (1989).

22　See *OHBE*, I, 280.

23　Bodleian Library, MS Rawl. c. 423, fols 1, 127.

24　'Minutes of Courts Martial at Tangier 1663–67', BL, Sloane MS 1957, fols 45–6.

25　Rogers, *Anglo-Moroccan Relations*, 52–3.

26　See Colonel Percy Kirke's Tangier letter-book, Lewis Walpole Library, Farmington, CT, Hazen 2572.

27　HMC Dartmouth I, 96–7; PRO, CO 279/32, fols 184–9.

28　BL, Lansdowne MS 192, fols. 30 and 132.

2 *The Crescent and the Sea*

1　This was, Professor Shula Marks informs me, a common device for stressing the 'animality' of Hottentot women. It was also used to downgrade other subject or looked down upon females: Jennifer L. Morgan, 'Some could suckle over their shoulder', *WMQ*, 54 (1997).

2　Accounts of the 'Barbary' phenomenon are numerous but vary widely in quality. Some elderly, over-emotive books still contain valuable material: notably Godfrey Fisher, *Barbary Legend* (Oxford, 1957), and R.L. Playfair, *The Scourge of Christendom* (1884). M.S. Anderson, 'Great Britain and the Barbary states in the eighteenth century', *Bulletin of the Institute of Historical Research*, XXIX (1956), is a balanced overview of British diplomatic sources. John B. Wolf, *The Barbary Coast: Algiers under the Turks 1500–1830* (1979), and P.G. Rogers, *A History of Anglo-Moroccan Relations to*

1900 (1970) are useful accounts of the two main North African powers. Many of the best analyses though have come from scholars based in France or writing in French. Fernand Braudel, *The Mediterranean and the Mediterranean World in the Age of Philip II* (2 vols, 1995 edn) is essential. Bartolomé and Lucile Bennassar, *Les chrétiens d'Allah* (Paris, 1989), should be read for the European-wide context of captivity in Barbary. French-language journals like *Les cahiers de Tunisie*, *Le monde musulman* and *Revue d'histoire maghrebine* regularly contain valuable new research on the corsairs and their victims.

3   Jamil M. Abun-Nasr, *A History of the Maghrib in the Islamic Period* (Cambridge, 1987), 2.

4   Quoted in G.A. Starr, 'Escape from Barbary: a seventeenth-century genre', *Huntington Library Quarterly*, 29 (1965), 35.

5   On Muslim slaves in France and Italy, see Moulay Belhamissi, *Les captifs algériens et l'Europe chrétienne* (Algiers, 1988); Peter Earle, *Corsairs of Malta and Barbary* (1970). Christian corsairs in the Mediterranean – including English ones – also sometimes preyed on their co-religionists.

6   PRO, SP 71/16, fol. 135; Ellen G. Friedman, *Spanish Captives in North Africa in the Early Modern Age* (Madison, WI, 1983).

7   See, for instance, Admiral Herbert's letter-book, Beinecke Library, Yale University, Osborn Shelves, f.b.96.

8   Abdallah Laroui, *The History of the Maghrib: An Interpretive Essay* (Princeton, NJ, 1977), 244.

9   John Brewer, *The Sinews of Power: War, Money and the English State, 1688–1783* (New York, 1989), 198.

10 See David Armitage, *The Ideological Origins of the British Empire* (Cambridge, 2000), 100–24.

11 Russell King *et al.* (eds), *The Mediterranean: Environment and Society* (1997), 10, drawing on Braudel's arguments.

12 The following paragraphs draw heavily on Robert C. Davis, 'Counting European slaves on the Barbary coast', *Past and Present*, 172 (2001).

13 The earliest English language Barbary captivity narratives date from the 1570s: see Nabil Matar, *Turks, Moors and Englishmen in the Age of Discovery* (1999), 181.

14 William Laird Clowes, *The Royal Navy: A History from the Earliest Times to the Present* (7 vols, 1996 repr.), II, 22.

15 David Delison Hebb, *Piracy and the English Government 1616–1642* (Aldershot, 1994); Todd Gray, 'Turkish piracy and early Stuart Devon', *Report and Transactions Devonshire Association*, 121 (1989).

16 *A Relation of the Whole Proceedings concerning the Redemption of the Captives in Algier and Tunis* (1647).

17 Frank H. Ellis (ed.), *Poems on Affairs of State: Augustan Satirical Verse, 1660–1714* (7 vols, New Haven, CT, 1975), VII, 243. For the naval assault on Barbary, see Sari R. Hornstein, *The Restoration Navy and English Foreign Trade. 1674–1688* (Aldershot, 1991).

18 'Navy, state, trade, and empire', in *OHBE*, I, 473; Ralph Davis, *The Rise of the English Shipping Industry* (1962), 15.

19 'List of Ships and Men Taken', PRO, SP 71/18, fol. 25; Dominique Meunier, *Le Consulat anglais à Tétouan sous Anthony Hatfeild* (Tunis, 1980), 36–40.

20 W.E. Minchinton (ed.), *Politics and the Port of Bristol in the Eighteenth Century* (1963), 82–3.

21 Joseph Redington (ed.), *Calendar of Treasury Papers, 1556–1728* (7 vols, 1868–1889), III, 250–1.

22 Anderson, 'Great Britain and the Barbary states', 103.

23 Fisher, *Barbary Legend*, 227; *CSPD*, 1661–2, 285.

24 This is my estimate based on ransoming information scattered throughout the state papers and contemporary printed sources. As set out below, it rests on incomplete information and will err on the conservative side.

25 Meunier, *Le Consulat anglais à Tétouan*, 39.

26 PRO, SP, 102/1, fol. 53; *British and Foreign State Papers 1812–1814* (1841), 357, 363.

27 I am indebted here to Gillian Weiss of Stanford University who allowed me to consult her manuscript 'From Barbary to France: Processions of Redemption and Early Modern Cultural Identity'.

28 PRO, SP 71/16, fol. 256.

29 *An Exhortation to those Redeemed Slaves, who came in a Solemn Procession to St Paul's Cathedral* (1702), 17; *DNB*, 14, p. 775.

30 Gregory King placed seamen at the bottom of England's social structure in the 1680s alongside common soldiers and paupers. See Geoffrey Holmes, 'Gregory King and the social structure of pre-industrial England', *Transactions of the Royal Historical Society*, 27 (1977).

31 *CSPD*, 1700–1702, 470–1.

32 The 1714–19 list is printed in Meunier, *Le Consulat anglais à Tétouan*, 36–40; for the Tripoli estimate, see Michel Fontenay, 'Le maghreb barbaresque et l'esclavage Méditerranéen aux XVIè et XVIIè siècles', *Les cahiers de Tunisie*, XLIV (1991).

33 *John Whitehead*, 4–11; Abun-Nasr, *History of the Maghrib*, 161.

34 References to British captives in other parts of the Ottoman empire can be gleaned from Alfred C. Wood, *A History of the Levant Company* (1964).

35 'Petition of the Poor Seamen Captive in Algiers', 4 March 1641: I am

grateful to Professor Maija Jansson for referring me to this text, which she is editing. For the 1670s appeal, see Guildhall Library, London, Broadside 12.12.

36 Quoted in Christopher Lloyd, *English Corsairs on the Barbary Coast* (1981), 101.

37 For guidance on this inevitably contentious subject, see Joseph C. Miller, 'Muslim slavery and slaving: a bibliography', *Slavery & Abolition*, 13 (1992). I have also found useful J.R.Willis, *Slaves and Slavery in Muslim Africa* (2 vols, 1995); H.A.R. Gibb *et al.* (eds), *The Encyclopaedia of Islam* (8 vols, Leiden, 1960–97 edn): entries for '*Abd, Hab<u>sh</u>ī, Hartini, Ghulām*, and *Ma'dhūn*; Bernard Lewis, *Race and Slavery in the Middle East: An Historical Enquiry* (Oxford, 1990).

38 John Braithwaite, *The History of the Revolutions in the Empire of Morocco* (1969 reprint of 1729 edn), 67.

39 *Thomas Sweet* (1646); Braithwaite, *History of the Revolutions*, 185–6.

40 *Francis Knight* (1640), 29. On galley warfare and slavery, see Jan Glete, *Navies and Nations: Warships, Navies and State Building in Europe and America, 1500–1860* (2 vols, Stockholm, 1993), I, 114–46, 250–2.

41 *The Memoirs of Sir Hugh Cholmley* (1787), 137.

42 See *Thomas Phelps* (1685) for one Briton's involvement in Moulay Ismaïl's building works. For slaves and public works in Algiers, see Ellen G. Friedman, 'Christian captives at "hard labour" in Algiers, 16th–18th centuries', *International Journal of African Historical Studies*, 13 (1980).

43 *Thomas Troughton* (1751), 14–16 and *passim*.

44 See the discussion of these points in Davis, 'Counting European Slaves'.

45 *The Arabian Journey: Danish Connections with the Islamic World over a Thousand Years* (Århus, 1996), 87.

46 Orlando Patterson, *Slavery and Social Death: A Comparative Study* (1982), 7; Seymour Drescher and Stanley L. Engerman (eds), *A Historical Guide to World Slavery* (Oxford, 1998), 284–5.

47 A classic example is Samuel Pepys's account of how he strolled to London's Exchange at noon on February 8 1661 and encountered two former Barbary captives: 'and there we spent till 4 a-clock telling stories of Algier and the manner of the life of slaves there': Robert Latham and William Matthews (eds), *The Diary of Samuel Pepys* (10 vols, 1970–83), II, 33–4.

48 'An account of Mr Russell's Journey from Gibraltar to Sallee [sic]', Bodleian Library, MS Eng.hist.d.153, fol. 1; Proclamation, 12 March 1692, Bristol RO, EP/A/31/4.

49 *Gleanings in Africa . . . with Observations . . . on the State of Slavery* (1806), 149; Morgan Godwyn, *The Negro's & Indian's Advocate* (1680), 28. I am grateful to Professor Dror Wahrman for the former reference.

50 Betton Charity Papers, Guildhall Library, London, MS 17034, bundle 4.

51 Ottoman historiography is in rapid and exciting flux as the archives in Istanbul become better known. Useful guides to current revisionism include Donald Quataert, *The Ottoman Empire, 1700–1922* (Cambridge, 2000); Virginia H. Aksan, 'Locating the Ottomans among early modern empires', *Journal of Early Modern History*, 3 (1999); and Halil Inalcik and Donald Quataert (eds), *An Economic and Social History of the Ottoman Empire. 1300–1914* (Cambridge, 1994).

52 In his *The Perspective of the World* (1984), 467.

53 'The Barbary states', *Quarterly Review*, XV (1816), 151.

54 [Matthew Barton], *An Authentic Narrative of the Loss of His Majesty's Ship the Litchfield* (London, n.d.), 2.

55 Andrew C. Hess, 'The Forgotten Frontier: The Ottoman North African Provinces during the Eighteenth Century', in Thomas Naff and Roger Owen (eds), *Studies in Eighteenth-Century Islamic History* (Carbondale, IL, 1977), 83.

56 Bodleian Library, Rawl. c.145, fol. 21. On Morocco's dynamic military development in the early modern era, see Weston F. Cook, *The Hundred Years War for Morocco* (Boulder, CO, 1994), and Allan Richard Meyers, 'The 'Abid al-Bukhari: Slave Soldiers and Statecraft in Morocco, 1672–1790', Cornell University PhD dissertation, 1974.

57 'Papers regarding the redemption of English captives', Corporation of London RO, Misc. MSS 156.9; Redington, *Calendar of Treasury Papers*, VII, 62.

58 *Mediterranean and the Mediterranean World, passim.*

59 See pp. 126–132.

60 The best studies in English are George Hills, *Rock of Contention: A History of Gibraltar* (1974), and Desmond Gregory, *Minorca: The Illusory Prize* (1990). Anyone interested in the diplomatic, naval and commercial history of the Mediterranean after 1700 should make a point of consulting the copious archives in the Governor's Library at Gibraltar. At present, they are virtually untouched by scholars.

61 Gregory, *Minorca*, 207–9.

62 On this, see Janet Sloss, *A Small Affair: The French Occupation of Minorca during the Seven Years War* (Tetbury, 2000).

63 Paul M. Kennedy, *The Rise and Fall of British Naval Mastery* (1976), 109.

64 J.A. Houlding, *Fit for Service: The Training of the British Army, 1715–1795* (Oxford, 1981).

65 PRO, SP 71/20 Part I, fol. 182.

3 Telling the Tale

1   See, for instance, *Francis Brooks* (1693), 7. On the English belief that Barbary corsairs could find them by magic, see Basil Lubbock (ed.), *Barlow's Journal* (2 vols, 1934), II, 55.

2   *Adam Elliot* (1731), xxiii.

3   For the activities of other denominations, see Kenneth L. Carroll, 'Quaker slaves in Algiers, 1679–1688', *Journal of the Friends Historical Society*, 54 (1982), 301–12; and B. Gwynn (ed.), 'Minutes of the Consistory of the French Church of London . . . 1679–92', *Huguenot Society Quarto Series*, 58 (1994), 271, 275, 280 and 342. I am grateful to Randolph Vigne for this latter reference. Charles Henry Hull (ed.), *The Economic Writings of Sir William Petty* (2 vols, 1964 repr.), II, 512.

4   Accounts of money collected, Corporation of London RO, GLMS/284 and 285.

5   On this device, see W.A. Bewes, *Church Briefs, or, Royal Warrants for Collections for Charitable Objects* (1896); and Mark Harris, '"Inky blots and rotten parchment bonds": London, charity briefs and the Guildhall Library', *Historical Research*, LXVI (1993), 98–110.

6   R.N. Worth, *Calendar of the Tavistock Parish Records* (Plymouth, 1887), 56–7.

7   *Ibid.*, 56–63. The prominence of women in these ransoming campaigns, both as donors in church collections, and through clauses in wills, is very marked.

8   For a classic account of the social breadth of British abolitionism after 1780, see Seymour Drescher, *Capitalism and Antislavery: British Mobilization in Comparative Perspective* (1986).

9   Guildhall Library, London, Proc. 23. 20.

10 See for instance the reports of the processions in *Daily Post*, 5 December 1721, and *Daily Journal*, 12 November 1734.

11 *The great blessings of redemption from captivity* (1722), 3 and 22.

12 *Daily Journal*, 12 November 1734; William Sherlock, *An Exhortation to those Redeemed Slaves who Came in a Solemn Procession to St. Paul's Cathedral* (1702), 16.

13 This paragraph draws on an unpublished paper by Gillian Weiss: 'From Barbary to France: processions of redemption and early modern cultural identity'.

14 Joseph Morgan, *Several Voyages to Barbary* (2nd edn, 1736), 142.

15 I have reconstructed Jukes' story from two sources: William Gouge, *A Recovery from Apostacy* (1639); and Richard Gough, *The History of Myddle*, ed. David Hey (New York, 1981), 115. I owe the latter reference to Professor David Underdown.

16 The verses quoted come from a *c.* 1790 version of 'Lord Bateman' called 'Young Baker', Bodleian Library, Harding B 6 (86). The ballad remained sufficiently popular for the young Charles Dickens and the artist George Cruickshank to combine their formidable talents in a new version: *The Loving Ballad of Lord Bateman* (1839).

17 I have found useful the approaches to narrative contained in Lewis P. Hinchman and Sandra K. Hinchman (eds), *Memory, Identity, Community: The Idea of Narrative in the Human Sciences* (Albany, NY, 1997).

18 R.L. Playfair, *The Scourge of Christendom* (1884), 135.

19 I owe this transcription of a destroyed Greenwich Hospital memorial inscription to Barbara Tomlinson of the National Maritime Museum.

20 See the account of his examination, Lancashire RO, QSP 1223/7.

21 See G.E. Hubbard, *The Old Book of Wye: being a record of a Kentish country parish* (Derby, 1951), 130–1: 'For the rest of the seventeenth century and throughout a good part of the eighteenth the Wye churchwardens' accounts are seldom quite free of entries relating to Turkish slaves'.

22 W. Petticrew to Lord Holderness, 2 October 1753, PRO SP 71/19, fols 123–6, enclosing 'A declaration made here by two Moors . . . before the Governor and Chief Justice [sic]'.

23 *Ibid.,* fols 125–6.

24 *Francis Knight* (1640), preface.

25 See *Strange and wonderfull things happened to Richard Hasleton . . . penned as he delivered it from his owne mouth* (1595).

26 Simon Schama, *Dead Certainties, (Unwarranted Speculations)* (1991).

27 *William Okeley* (1676), preface and opening verse.

28 *Thomas Troughton* (1751), 6–8.

29 For an example of an early New England captive seemingly able to take notes while in Barbary, see *Narrative of Joshua Gee of Boston, Mass.* (Hartford, CT, 1943), 26–7; *William Okeley* (1676), 26.

30 *William Okeley* (1676), preface.

31 *Ibid.,* 1764 edn, x–xi.

32 See Lennard Davis, *Factual Fictions: The Origins of the English Novel* (New York, 1983).

33 P.J. Marshall and Glyndwr Williams, *The Great Map of Mankind* (1982), 53; Percy G. Adams, *Travel Literature and the Evolution of the Novel* (Lexington, Kentucky, 1983), 97.

34 For a valuable discussion of these arguments, see the introduction to Stuart B. Schwartz, *Implicit Understandings: Observing, Reporting, and Reflecting on the Encounters between Europeans and Other Peoples in the Early Modern Era* (Cambridge, 1994), 1–23.

35 *Thomas Pellow* (1890), 186; P. Mercer, 'Political and Military Developments

within Morocco during the early Alawi Period', London University PhD dissertation, 1974, 41.

36 Magali Morsy, *La relation de Thomas Pellow: Une lecture du Maroc au 18e siècle* (Paris, 1983).

37 See Daniel Nordman, 'La mémoire d'un captif', *Annales*, xli (1986). It is suggestive that Brian Keenan's modern narrative of his four-year Beirut captivity also reveals a lack of attention to Western calendar time: see *An Evil Cradling* (1992).

38 *Thomas Pellow* (1890), 235; Morsy, *La relation*, 205n.

39 Joan Brady, *The Theory of War* (New York, 1993), 94.

40 *Thomas Pellow* (1740), 385.

4 Confronting Islam

1 On Rich, Covent Garden and *The Beggar's Opera*, see John Brewer, *The Pleasures of the Imagination: English Culture in the Eighteenth Century* (1997), 325–56, 428–44.

2 'English Slaves in Barbary', *Notes and Queries*, March 5 1921, 187. Troughton and his comrades arrived back in London on 22 March 1751.

3 *Poems on Several Occasions* (1734), 271.

4 *Thomas Phelps* (1685), preface; *John Whitehead MS*, 4 and 16.

5 Edward Said, *Orientalism: Western Conceptions of the Orient* (1995 edn), *passim*. Discussions of this rich and suggestive text are now legion. Those I have found most valuable include: Sadiq Jalal al-'Azm, 'Orientalism and Orientalism in Reverse', in Jon Rothschild (ed.), *Forbidden Agendas: Intolerance and Defiance in the Middle East* (1984), and Dennis Porter, '*Orientalism* and its Problems', in Francis Barker *et al.* (eds), *The Politics of Theory* (Colchester, 1983).

6 James Grey Jackson, *An Account of the Empire of Morocco* (3rd edn, 1814), 153. For an excellent discussion of the ubiquity of prejudice at this point, but also its limited impact on contact and collaborations in practice, see Rhoads Murray, 'Bigots or informed observers? A periodization of pre-colonial English and European writing on the Middle East', *Journal of the American Oriental Society*, 110 (1990).

7 Verses by Lord Hervey, quoted in my *Britons: Forging the Nation 1707–1837* (1992), 35.

8 For an elaboration of these points, see K.N. Chaudhuri, 'From the Barbarian and the Civilized to the Dialectics of Colour: An Archaeology of Self-Identities', in Peter Robb (ed.), *Society and Ideology: Essays in South Asian History* (Delhi, 1994).

9   See Nabil Matar, *Islam in Britain 1558–1685* (Cambridge, 1998), 74–86; and G.J. Toomer, *Eastern Wisedome and Learning: The Study of Arabic in Seventeenth-Century England* (Oxford, 1996).

10 Matar, *Islam in Britain*, 73–83.

11 *Devereux Spratt*, 25–6; Nabil Matar, *Turks, Moors & Englishmen in the Age of Discovery* (New York, 1999), x, 170.

12 *Sentences of Ali, son-in-law of Mahomet* (1717), preface. Ockley, who merits a biography, was anxious to stress the intellectual calibre of 'polite Asiaticks (amongst which the Persians do most deservedly claim the preference . . .)' even when denouncing Barbary captive-taking: see *An Account of South-West Barbary* (1713), xix.

13 Quoted in Albert Hourani, *Islam in European Thought* (Cambridge, 1991), 10.

14 *The Koran, commonly called the Alcoran of Mohammed* (1734), preface; *The Life of Mahomet, translated from the French* (1731), dedication.

15 *A Compleat History of the Piratical States of Barbary* (1750 edn), v; see, too, Morgan's *Mahometanism Fully Explained* (2 vols, 1723–5).

16 'Moors', those one-time Spanish Muslims who had settled in North Africa, were usually imagined as dark-skinned, but as Shakespeare's *Othello* suggests, in some contrast with sub-Saharan blacks, this was not necessarily seen as evidence of inferiority or lack of power. See Khalid Kekkaoui, *Signs of Spectacular Resistance: The Spanish Moor and British Orientalism* (Casablanca, 1998).

17 *John Whitehead* MS, fol. 26; *The Memoirs of Sir Hugh Cholmley* (1787), 137.

18 *Elizabeth Marsh* MS, unfoliated.

19 On British toleration of North African Jewish and Muslim traders on the Rock, see George Hills, *Bone of Contention: A History of Gibraltar* (1974).

20 Yale University's Map Library, for instance, holds a late eighteenth-century embroidered map which explicitly includes North Africa within an image of Europe. *The Adventures of Mr. T.S. an English merchant, taken prisoner by the Turks of Algiers* (1670), 157.

21 Michael Adas, *Machines as the Measure of Men: Science, Technology and Ideologies of Western Dominance* (1989).

22 BL, Add. MS 47995, fols 30 and 39.

23 *A Compleat History*, 255–6. For pre-1750 British instability, see J.H. Plumb, *The Growth of Political Stability in England, 1675–1725* (1967); and Paul Monod, *Jacobitism and the English People, 1688–1788* (Cambridge, 1989).

24 *Edward Coxere*, facing p.60.

25 *Devereux Spratt*, 11–13, 33–4.

26 'Islamic Law and Polemics over Race and Slavery in North and West Africa', in Shaun E. Marmon (ed.), *Slavery in the Islamic Middle East* (Princeton, NJ, 1999), 43.

27 *James Irving* MS, 29; *Elizabeth Marsh* (1769), I, 38–9.

28 N. J. Dawood (ed.), *The Muqaddimah: An Introduction to History* (Princeton, NJ, 1989), 59–60; *Joseph Pitts* (1704), 24.

29 See, for instance, John Braithwaite, *The History of the Revolutions in the Empire of Morocco* (1969 reprint of 1729 edn), 214–15: '[We] were sure to be affronted as we passed the streets, three or four hundred fellows setting up a great scream together, and crying Cursed are the unbelievers. Sometimes the common people would fling stones and brickbats.'

30 *William Okeley* (1684), 12–14.

31 *James Irving* (1995), 128.

32 Said, *Orientalism*, 11.

33 Michelle Burnham, *Captivity and Sentiment: Cultural Exchange in American Literature, 1682–1861* (Hanover, NH, 1997), 2.

34 *William Okeley* (1684), 41, 46–7.

35 *Joseph Pitts* (1704), 142, 156, 158–62, 171.

36 Pierre de Cenival and P. de Cossé Brissac (eds), *Les sources inédites de l'histoire du Maroc: archives et bibliothèques d'Angleterre* (3 vols, Paris, 1918–35), III, 68; *Devereux Spratt*, 26.

37 *Genesis*, 41, v. 52.

38 William Nelson, *Particulars of the hardships and sufferings of William Nelson . . . who was afterwards taken prisoner by an Algerine galley* (Grantham, 1820?). The British Library holds the only copy known to me, but has mislaid it. Not being able to consult it, I cannot say whether it is genuine.

39 See Peter Linebaugh and Marcus Rediker, *The Many-Headed Hydra: Sailors, Slaves, Commoners, and the Hidden History of the Revolutionary Atlantic* (2000); for Saphra, see Thomas Pocock, *The Relief of Captives, especially of our own countrymen* (1720), 10–12.

40 A.R. Meyers, 'The 'Abid al-Bukhari: Slave Soldiers and Statecraft in Morocco, 1672–1790', Cornell University PhD dissertation, 1974, 142–4; *James Irving* (1995), 119; *Thomas Troughton* (1751), 14–16.

41 See Ian Duffield and Paul Edwards, 'Equiano's Turks and Christians: an eighteenth-century African view of Islam', *Journal of African Studies*, 2 (1975–6). For Equiano's likely American birthplace, rather than the African setting he described in his published narrative, see the introduction to Olaudah Equiano, *The Interesting Narrative and Other Writings*, ed. Vincent Caretta (1995).

42 This point should not be over-stressed. There was a wider spectrum of opportunities open to black slaves in North Africa, but the majority seem to have been treated less well than white captives. Moreover, black Britons, like white Britons, reacted to captivity here in different ways. Thomas Saphra, for instance, reputedly a fervent Christian, chose to return to Britain.

43 PRO, SP 71/14, Part Two, fol. 221.

44 For one aspect of this, see Nicholas B.Harding, 'North African piracy, the Hanoverian carrying trade, and the British state, 1728–1828', *Historical Journal*, 43 (2000).

45 Guildhall Library, London, MS 17034, Betton Charity Papers, Bundle 3.

46 Fernand Braudel. *The Mediterranean and the Mediterranean World in the Age of Philip II* (2 vols, 1995 edn), II, 889.

47 For the Butlers, see PRO, FO 113/3, fol. 272.

48 See, for instance, BL, Egerton MS 2528, fol. 97.

49 In the 1710s and '20s, there was a considerable debate in Britain on the overlap between Unitarianism and Islam: see J.A.I. Champion, 'The Pillars of Priestcraft Shaken: The Church of England and its Enemies, 1660–1730', Cambridge University PhD dissertation, 1992.

50 *Joseph Pitts* (1704), 14, 82, 104 and 130.

51 Quoted in F.E. Peters, *The Hajj: The Muslim Pilgrimage to Mecca and the Holy Places* (Princeton, NJ, 1994), 116–17.

52 *Joseph Pitts* (1704), 68, 86, 115, 182–3.

53 See Carlo Ginzburg, *The Cheese and the Worms: The Cosmos of a Sixteenth-Century Miller* (New York, 1982), 50–1.

54 For the Hyde Parker incident, see P.G. Rogers, *A History of Anglo-Moroccan Relations to 1900* (1970), 96–9.

55 John Hughes, *The Siege of Damascus* (London, 1720), 6. For a detailed account of Marsh, see my 'The Narrative of Elizabeth Marsh: Barbary, Sex, and Power', in Felicity Nussbaum (ed.), *The Global Eighteenth Century* (forthcoming, Baltimore, MD, 2003).

56 *Elizabeth Marsh* (1769), II, 18–94.

57 I discuss this point in more detail in 'The Narrative of Elizabeth Marsh'.

58 Maija Jansson (ed.), *Proceedings in Parliament, 1614* (Philadelphia, 1988), 200; 'To the Right Honourable the Commons', Guildhall Library, London, Broadside 12.12.

59 *Francis Knight* (1640), 50; C. R. Pennell, *Piracy and Diplomacy in Seventeenth-Century North Africa* (1989), 62.

60 William Chetwood, *Voyages and Adventures of Captain Robert Boyle* (1726), 34; Paul Rycaut, *The Present State of the Ottoman Empire* (1668), 81. I am indebted for this reading of *Robinson Crusoe* to Ben Holden of Merton College, Oxford.

61 For recent discussions of this point, see Stephen O. Murray and Will Roscoe (eds), *Islamic Homosexualities: Culture, History and Literature* (New York, 1997).

62 One aspect of this was portraiture. Before 1750, high-ranking and ambitious British males, such as Lord Sandwich, sometimes chose to be

portrayed in Turkish costume. After 1760, however, it was overwhelmingly women who were represented in this mode of 'oriental' dress.

63 *Letters from Barbary 1576–1774: Arabic Documents in the Public Record Office,* trans. J.F.P. Hopkins (Oxford, 1982), 84.

64 Piers Mackesy, *British Victory in Egypt, 1801* (1995), 21; for the 1816 bombardment, see Roger Perkins and K.J. Douglas-Morris, *Gunfire in Barbary* (1982).

5 *Different Americans, Different Britons*

1 For Bird and his work, see R. Gunnis, *Dictionary of British Sculptors 1660–1851* (1968 rev. edn), 53.

2 On Britain's imperial power – and its limits – by 1713, see *OHBE*, I, 423–79.

3 For an excellent survey that attempts to get beyond this, see Colin G. Calloway, *New Worlds for All: Indians, Europeans, and the Re-making of Early America* (1997). Readers wanting to explore some of the new work on Native Americans can profitably begin with J.C.H. King, *First Peoples, First Contacts: Native Peoples of North America* (Cambridge, MA, 1999), and Carl Waldman, *Biographical Dictionary of American Indian History to 1900* (New York, 2001 rev. edn), which are both well illustrated, before moving on to periodicals such as *Native Peoples* and *Ethnohistory*. But perhaps the best introduction is through objects and images. The Chase Manhattan Gallery of North America in London's British Museum, and the National Museum of the American Indian, New York, are both excellent.

4 This literature is vast and still growing. Good introductions which reprint sections from the narratives are Alden T. Vaughan and Edward W. Clark (eds), *Puritans among the Indians: Accounts of Captivity and Redemption, 1676–1724* (Cambridge, MA, 1981), and Richard VanDerBeets, *Held Captive by Indians: Selected Narratives, 1642–1836* (Knoxville, Tennessee, 1994). An influential though now disputed attempt to offer a distinctively American interpretation is Richard Slotkin, *Regeneration through Violence: The Mythology of the American Frontier, 1600–1860* (Middletown, CT, 1973). For a recent, expert attempt to breathe new life into (for Americanists) an old source, see John Demos, *The Unredeemed Captive: A Family Story from Early America* (New York, 1994).

5 See K.O. Kupperman (ed.), *Captain John Smith: A Select Edition of his Writings* (1988). It is possible that Smith's life was never in real danger, and that he was rather exposed to a symbolic execution before being reclaimed by Pocahontas as a prelude to rebirth as an Indian.

6 See K.O. Kupperman, *Settling with the Indians: The Meeting of English and*

Indian Cultures in America, 1580–1640 (Totowa, NJ, 1980); James H. Merrell, '"The Customes of our Countrey": Indians and Colonists in Early America', in Bernard Bailyn and Philip D. Morgan (eds), *Strangers within the Realm: Cultural Margins of the First British Empire* (1991).

7 Kupperman, *Captain John Smith*, 72; Anthony McFarlane, *The British in the Americas 1480–1815* (1992), 57.

8 Quoted in the introduction to K. O. Kupperman (ed.), *America in European Consciousness, 1493–1750* (Chapel Hill, NC, 1995), 17; Alden T. Vaughan, 'From White Man to Redskin: changing Anglo-American perceptions of the American Indian', *AHR*, 87 (1982).

9 *CSPC*, V, 97.

10 For a useful survey of how Native Americans adapted to European styles of warfare, see Patrick M. Malone, *The Skulking Way of War* (1991).

11 King, *First Peoples*, 34.

12 *OHBE*, I, 195, 390, and 328–50 *passim*.

13 For a wonderful account, see Jill Lepore, *The Name of War: King Philip's War and the Origins of American Identity* (New York, 1998).

14 *CSPC*, XXXIV, 220–1; *OHBE*, II, 352.

15 On this point, see William Cronon, *Changes in the Land; Indians, Colonists, and the Ecology of New England* (New York, 1983).

16 Infants unable to walk or feed themselves might also be killed because they were too much trouble to take captive: see Demos, *Unredeemed Captive*, 7–27.

17 See Alexander Hamilton's account of how the Indians who captured him and four others at Kennebac River in 1722, on French instructions, were rewarded with food and tobacco: *CSPC*, XXXIII, 407–15.

18 Gregory H. Nobles, *American Frontiers: Cultural Encounters and Continental Conquest* (New York, 1997), 35–6, 74.

19 *Jonathan Dickenson* (1700), 12, 28, 37.

20 *Ibid.*, 40–1, 70.

21 Alden T. Vaughan and Daniel K. Richter, 'Crossing the cultural divide: Indians and New Englanders, 1605–1763', *Proceedings of the American Antiquarian Society*, 90 (1980).

22 Ian K. Steele, 'Surrendering Rites: Prisoners on Colonial North American Frontiers', in Stephen Taylor *et al., Hanoverian Britain and Empire: Essays in Memory of Philip Lawson* (Woodbridge, 1998), 141.

23 *Mary Rowlandson* (1997), 111; Vaughan and Richter, 'Crossing the Cultural Divide', 82.

24 *OHBE*, II, 291; and see Michael Zuckerman, 'Identity in British America: Unease in Eden', in Nicholas Canny and Anthony Pagden (eds), *Colonial Identity in the Atlantic World, 1500–1800* (Princeton, NJ, 1987).

25 For an excellent modern edition, see *The Sovereignty and Goodness of God by Mary Rowlandson*, ed. Neal Salisbury (Boston, MA, 1997).

26 *Ibid.*, 71, 81, 94.

27 As printed in VanDerBeets, *Held Captive by Indians*, 94, 97.

28 On this, see June Namias, *White Captives: Gender and Ethnicity on the American Frontier* (Chapel Hill, NC, 1993).

29 Lepore, *Name of War*, 5.

30 Vaughan and Clark, *Puritans among the Indians*, 153: Hannah's story is reprinted in this volume.

31 Demos, *Unredeemed Captive*, 49.

32 It should be noted however that American colonial captivity narratives were sometimes reprinted as additions to British-authored books. Thus Richard Blome, a London-based publisher with a marked interest in topography and empire, included Quentin Stockwell's narrative in his *The Present State of His Majesties Isles and Territories in America* (1687).

33 On the Deerfield attack, see Demos, *Unredeemed Captive*; L.F. Stock (ed.), *Proceedings and Debates of the British Parliaments respecting North America* (5 vols, Washington, DC, 1924–41), III, 73.

34 *CSPC*, XXV, 73–5.

35 J.H. Elliott, *The Old World and the New 1492–1650* (Cambridge, 1970). R.C. Simmons, *British Imprints Relating to North America 1621–1760* (1996) is a useful guide which demonstrates the surge in publications on this area after 1750. Books printed in Britain on France, Spain and Italy remained however far more numerous throughout.

36 Lepore, *Name of War*, 48–56.

37 See his *Pastoral Letter to the English Captives in Africa* (Boston, MA, 1698); and *The Glory of Goodness* (Boston, MA, 1703).

38 I am sure for instance that one of the reasons for the unusual success of Jonathan Dickenson's narrative, which was repeatedly reissued in Britain throughout the eighteenth century, was that the events recorded in its pages occurred in Florida rather than in New England. Dickenson's text and subtitle also made much of episodes of shipwreck and cannibalism and of one of his fellow captives, a leading English North Country Quaker.

39 Charles Fitz-Geffrey, *Compassion towards Captives, chiefly towards our brethren and country-men who are in miserable bondage in Barbarie* (Oxford, 1637), 2–3.

40 'The British Empire and the Civic Tradition, 1656–1742', Cambridge PhD dissertation, 1992, 35.

41 *Mary Rowlandson* (1997), 64; VanDerBeets, *Held Captive by Indians*, 96.

42 Stock, *Proceedings and Debates*, II, 438. Even the most forceful exponent of the view that British empire in America was military in ethos from the start, describes the regular army presence in the colonies thus: 'The

garrisons were diseased, dispersed, and undisciplined, and their numbers were small. In the seventeenth century there were seldom more than one thousand regular soldiers in the North American continent. Often there were no more than three hundred.' Stephen Saunders Webb, *The Governors-General: The English Army and the Definition of the Empire, 1589–1681* (Chapel Hill, NC, 1979), 454.

43 Stock, *Proceedings and Debates*, II, 435.

44 See Appendix B of J.A. Houlding, *Fit for Service: The Training of the British Army, 1715–1795* (Oxford, 1981), 410–13.

45 Stock, *Proceedings and Debates*, III, 359–60.

46 *Ibid.*, V, 257.

47 Vaughan and Richter, 'Crossing the Cultural Divide', 51.

48 *OHBE*, I, 215.

49 See Lepore, *Name of War*, 173–4.

50 See Eric Hinderaker, 'The "Four Indian Kings" and the imaginative construction of the First British Empire', *WMQ*, 53 (1996); and, for the Verelst and other images of the 'kings': Bruce Robertson, 'The Portraits: An Iconographical Study', in John G. Garratt, *The Four Indian Kings/Les Quatre Rois Indiens* (Ottawa, 1985), 139–49.

51 Hugh Honour, *The Golden Land: European Images of America from the Discoveries to the Present Time* (1976), 125.

52 Richard P. Bond, *Queen Anne's American Kings* (Oxford, 1952), 77; for a classic analysis of cross-cultural relations in North America stressing the 'nexus of relations and transactions' rather than conflict, see Richard White, *The Middle Ground: Indians, Empires, and Republics in the Great Lakes Region, 1650–1815* (Cambridge, 1991).

53 Quoted in P.J. Marshall and Glyndwr Williams, *The Great Map of Mankind* (1982), 195.

6. War and a New World

1 *Susanna Johnson* (1797) *passim*. I have also drawn on *A Narrative of the Captivity of Mrs Johnson* (Lowell, MA., 1834) which includes additional material.

2 *Susanna Johnson* (1797), 65–70.

3 H.V. Bowen, 'British conceptions of global empire, 1756–83', *Journal of Imperial and Commonwealth History* 26 (1998), 6. The best recent accounts of the Seven Years War as American colonists and Britons at home experienced it are Fred Anderson, *Crucible of War* (New York, 2000), and Eliga Gould, *The Persistence of Empire* (2000).

4 *An Inquiry into the Nature and Causes of the Wealth of Nations*, ed. R.H.

Campbell and A.S. Skinner (2 vols, Oxford, 1976), II, 708. For the down-turn in Western admiration for China after 1760, see Jonathan Spence, *The Chan's Great Continent* (1998).

5   R.C. Simmons and P.D.G. Thomas (eds), *Proceedings and Debates of the British Parliaments respecting North America 1759–1783* (6 vols, 1982–6), I, 71.

6   See, for instance, *Treaty and Convention for the Sick, Wounded, and Prisoners of War* (1759).

7   *Jean Lowry* (1760), 17; PRO, T1/391.

8   For pre-Revolutionary American visitors to Britain in general, see Susan Lindsey Lively, 'Going Home: Americans in Britain, 1740–1776', Harvard University PhD dissertation, 1997.

9   Richard C. Simmons, 'Americana in British Books, 1621–1760', in Karen Ordahl Kupperman (ed.), *America in European Consciousness 1493–1750* (1995).

10 John Brewer, *Party Ideology and Popular Politics at the Accession of George III* (Cambridge, 1976), 139–60.

11 See, for instance, *Elizabeth Hanson* (1760); [Arthur Young], *The Theatre of the Present War in North America* (1758), iv-v.

12 See *Mary Rowlandson* (1997), 69, 75, 76, 79, 81. For the distinctiveness of colonists' pre-1776 experience: see Jon Butler, *Becoming America* (Cambridge, MA, 2000).

13 *John Rutherfurd* (1958), 233; *Peter Williamson* (1996), 11n; *Henry Grace* (1765), 12.

14 *Thomas Morris* (1904), 315, 318. Morris's initial text was written soon after the events he described, in 1764. A version was sent to George III in 1775, but the narrative was only published in 1791. Since the original manu-script seems not to have survived, we cannot know what – if anything – he added in the interval.

15 For a balanced account of this débâcle, see Daniel J. Beattie, 'The Adaption of the British Army to Wilderness Warfare, 1755–1763', in M. Ultee (ed.), *Adapting to Conditions: War and Society in the Eighteenth Century* (Alabama, 1986); *Thomas Morris* (1904), 316.

16 Anderson, *Crucible of War*, 151–2.

17 See W.J. Eccles, 'The social, economic, and political significance of the military establishment in New France', *Canadian Historical Review*, 52 (1971).

18 See, for instance, John Shy, *Toward Lexington: The Role of the British Army in the Coming of the American Revolution* (Princeton, NJ, 1965), 1–40.

19 NLS, MS 6506, fol. 38.

20 *Gentleman's Magazine* (1758), 259–60; *John Rutherfurd* (1958), 226–7.

21 *Henry Grace* (1765), 47–8; Ian K.Steele, 'Surrendering Rites: Prisoners on Colonial North American Frontiers', in Stephen Taylor *et al.* (eds), *Hanoverian Britain and Empire: Essays in Memory of Philip Lawson* (Woodbridge, Suffolk, 1998), 141.

22 Williams' account of this episode and his own Indian captivity are in Huntington Library, Pasadena, LO 977, box 21, deposition dated 5 Feb. 1757, and LO 5344, box 115, examination dated 5 Jan. 1758.

23 Ian K. Steele, *Betrayals: Fort William Henry and the 'Massacre'* (Oxford, 1990); for an example of British desertion in the face of a possible Indian attack, see Robert R. Rea, 'Military deserters from British West Florida', *Louisiana History*, 9 (1968), 124–5.

24 On these, see Eileen Harris, *The Townshend Album* (1974).

25 Though this was by no means a unanimous view in Britain: see, for instance, [Horace Walpole], *Reflections on the different ideas of the French and English, in regard to cruelty* (1759).

26 See *Proceedings of the Committee . . . for Cloathing French Prisoners of War* (1760); Francis Abell, *Prisoners of War in Britain 1756 to 1815* (1914), 449–50.

27 *The Law of Nations* (2 vols, 1760 edn), Book III, 26, 49–56.

28 PRO, CO/5/50, fols 579 and 611.

29 Beattie, 'The Adaption of the British Army to Wilderness Warfare', 74n; W.A. Gordon, 'The siege of Louisburg', *Journal of the Royal United Service Institution*, LX (1915), 125.

30 The verdict on Amherst is in Michael J. Mullin, 'Sir William Johnson, Indian Relations, and British Policy, 1744 to 1774', University of California, Santa Barbara, 1989 PhD dissertation, 244; Anderson, *Crucible of War*, 546.

31 For Amherst and genocide, see Bernard Knollenberg, 'General Amherst and germ warfare', *Mississippi Valley Historical Review*, XLI (1965); for John Stuart, see J. Norman Heard, *Handbook of the American Frontier: The Southeastern Woodlands* (1987), 344, and James W. Covington, *The British meet the Seminoles: Negotiations between British Authorities in East Florida and the Indians, 1763–8* (Gainesville, FL, 1961).

32 For a British colonist's casual admission of how he and a companion killed and scalped a defenceless Indian woman, see *A Journal of Lieutenant Simon Stevens . . . with an account of his escape from Quebec* (Boston, MA, 1760), 12; and for an example of the ferocity of British regular army warfare in America, see P.G.M. Foster, 'Quebec 1759', *JSAHR*, 64 (1986), 221–2.

33 Quoted in Richard L. Merritt, *Symbols of American Community 1735–1775* (Westport, CT, 1966), 164.

34 *Man of the World* (2 vols, 1773), II, 169–83; Tobias Smollett, *The Expedition of Humphry Clinker* (Oxford, 1966), 192–4.

35 J. Bennett Nolan, 'Peter Williamson in America, a colonial odyssey', *Pennsylvania History*, XXX–XXXI (1963–4), 24–5. Williamson merits a proper biography as a Scottish, imperial and cultural phenomenon. The 1762 version of his narrative was reprinted with a useful introduction by Michael Fry in 1996.

36 *Peter Williamson* (1757), 10, 14, 20, 24.

37 *Peter Williamson* (1996), 14, 87, 89, 92–3, 108 *seq.*

38 *The trial of divorce at the instance of Peter Williamson* (Edinburgh, 1789), xxiii.

39 For his story, which was also made into a (sadly neglected) film with Pierce Brosnan, see Lovat Dickson, *Wilderness Man: The Amazing True Story of Grey Owl* (1999).

40 Some of Rutherfurd's family background and Detroit experiences can be reconstructed from the James Sterling letter-book at the William Clements Library, Ann Arbor.

41 *John Rutherfurd* (1958), 227, 229, 233–43.

42 *Ibid.* (1958), 220–1, 241, 247, 249.

43 Peter Way, 'The Cutting Edge of Culture: British Soldiers Encounter Native Americans in the French and Indian War', in Martin Daunton and Rick Halpern (eds), *Empire and Others: British Encounters with Indigenous Peoples 1600–1850* (1999), 142–3; S.H.A. Hervey (ed.), *Journals of the Hon. William Hervey in America and Europe* (Bury St Edmunds, 1906), 144.

44 Rea, 'Military deserters', 126; James Sullivan (ed.), *The Papers of Sir William Johnson* (14 vols, Albany, NY, 1921–65), IV, 428. For a useful survey of these kind of crossings, see Colin Calloway, 'Neither red nor white: white renegades on the American Indian frontier', *Western Historical Quarterly*, 17 (1986).

45 [William Smith], *An historical account of the expedition against the Ohio Indians* (1766), 27 and *passim.*

46 *Ibid.*, 28.

47 PRO, WO 34/27, fol. 150.

48 On this, see Philip Lawson, *The Imperial Challenge: Quebec and Britain in the Age of the American Revolution* (Montreal, 1989); and Robert L. Gold, *Borderland Empires in Transition: The Triple Nation Transfer of Florida* (Carbondale, IL, 1969).

49 Merritt, *Symbols of American Community*, 119 *seq*; see also T.H. Breen, 'Ideology and nationalism on the eve of the American Revolution: revisions once more in need of revising', *Journal of American History*, 84 (1997).

50 Based on population figures in *OHBE*, II, 100.

51 On this, see Bernard Bailyn, *Voyagers to the West: A Passage in the Peopling of America on the Eve of the Revolution* (New York, 1988), 3–66.

52 John Mitchell, *The Present State of Great Britain and North America* (1767), viii, 114; for Grenville's warning, see L.F. Stock (ed.), *Proceedings and Debates of the British Parliaments respecting North America* (Washington, DC, 5 vols, 1924–41), V, 566–7.

53 R.W. Chapman (ed.), *Boswell Life of Johnson* (Oxford, 1970), 592.

54 The best account of London's thinking on these points is still Jack M.

Sosin, *Whitehall and the Wilderness: The Middle West in British Colonial Policy 1760–1775* (Lincoln, NE, 1961).

55 See Fernand Ouellet, 'The British Army of Occupation in the St Lawrence Valley', in R.A. Prete (ed.), *Armies of Occupation* (Kingston, Ont., 1984), 38–9.

7 Revolutions

1 For André's story and cult, see Horace W. Smith, *Andreana* (Philadelphia, PA, 1865); William Abbatt, *The Crisis of the Revolution: Being the Story of Arnold and André* (New York, 1899); James Thomas Flexner, *The Traitor and the Spy* (New York, 1953).

2 Flexner, *Traitor and Spy*, 146; Abbatt, *Crisis of the Revolution*, 68.

3 Stephen Conway, *The War of American Independence 1775–1783* (1995), 48.

4 *Ibid., passim.*

5 Two valuable studies placing the Thirteen Colonies in a wider imperial context are D.W. Meinig, *The Shaping of America: A Geographical Perspective on 500 Years of History* (1986); and A. J. O'Shaughnessy, *An Empire Divided: The American Revolution and the British Caribbean* (Philadelphia, PA, 2000).

6 Conway, *War of Independence*, 157.

7 George Adams Boyd, *Elias Boudinot, Patriot and Statesman 1740–1821* (Princeton, NJ, 1952), 45. There are many studies of American Revolutionary prisoners of the British, far fewer of their opposite numbers. A rare and useful comparative essay is Betsy Knight, 'Prisoner exchange and parole in the American Revolution', *WMQ*, 48 (1991).

8 PRO, CO5/105, fol. 171.

9 Richard Sampson, *Escape in America: The British Convention Prisoners 1777–1783* (Chippenham, Picton, 1995), 193; BL, Add. MS 38875, fols 74–5.

10 James Lennox Banks, *David Sproat and Naval Prisoners in the War of the Revolution* (New York, 1909), 116.

11 For the Spanish estimate, see PRO, ADM 98/14, fol. 199; Franklin's opinion is cited in PRO, ADM 98/12, fol. 262.

12 Ray Raphael, *A People's History of the American Revolution* (New York, 2001), 114; W.V. Hensel, *Major John André as a Prisoner of War* (Lancaster, PA, 1904), 13.

13 Newberry Library, Chicago, Ayer MS 728, vault box.

14 Charles H. Metzger, *The Prisoner in the American Revolution* (Chicago, IL, 1971), 4; Memorial of John MacGuire, PRO, 30/55/82. The American Revolutionary Terror – and how it impacted on all the protagonists and ethnic groupings involved – still awaits its historian.

15 Larry G. Bowman, *Captive Americans: Prisoners during the American Revolution* (Athens, OH, 1976), 59.

16 [Allan Ramsay], *Letters on the Present Disturbances in Great Britain and her American Provinces* (1777), 20. I owe this reference to Professor Eliga Gould.

17 *William Widger* (1937), 347.

18 *Thomas Hughes* (1947), 17.

19 *Charles Herbert* (1847), 19–20; *John Blatchford* (1788), 9.

20 *Charles Herbert* (1847), 34.

21 Olive Anderson, 'The treatment of prisoners of war in Britain during the American War of Independence', *Bulletin of the Institute of Historical Research*, 28 (1955), 63; *An Authentic Narrative of Facts relating to the Exchange of Prisoners taken at the Cedars* (1777), 5.

22 Howe to Lt.-Col. Walcot, 26 January 1777, PRO, 30/55/4, fol. 388; K.G. Davies (ed.), *Documents of the American Revolution 1770–1783:Vol. XI Transcripts, 1775* (Dublin, 1976), 73.

23 For example, Washington to Howe, 10 February 1778: PRO, CO5/95, fol. 322.

24 See Raphael, *People's History, passim*.

25 Robert John Denn, 'Prison Narratives of the American Revolution', Michigan State University PhD dissertation, 1980, 61–2. For an attempt to reach beyond the propaganda to a more reliable estimate of American casualties in prison and on the battlefield, see Howard H. Peckham, *The Toll of Independence* (Chicago, IL, 1974).

26 *Substance of General Burgoyne's Speeches at a Court Martial . . . at the Trial of Colonel Henley* (Newport, MA, 1778); Boyd, *Elias Boudinot*, 45.

27 Boyd, *Elias Boudinot*, 57.

28 See the evidence assembled in PRO, CO5/105, fols 315 *seq*.

29 *Thomas Anburey* (1791), I, preface.

30 Thus a Resolution of 5 January 1781 accused the British of ignoring 'the practice of civilized nations [and] . . . treating our people prisoners to them with every species of insults', Anderson, 'Treatment of Prisoners of War', 75.

31 Washington to Cornwallis, 18 October 1781, PRO, 30/11/74, fol. 124; Lee Kennett, *The French Forces in America 1780–1783* (1977), 155.

32 Denn, 'Prison Narratives', 28–30.

33 For examples of British atrocity accusations against the Revolutionaries, see [John Lind], *An Answer to the Declaration of the American Congress* (1776), which went through five editions that year. For American propaganda networks: Philip Davidson, *Propaganda and the American Revolution, 1763–1783* (New York, 1973 edn).

34 Catherine M. Prelinger, 'Benjamin Franklin and the American prisoners

of war in England during the American Revolution', *WMQ*, 32 (1975), 264.

35   As Richard Sampson remarks, 'most British military historians appear to have been satisfied to "write off" these men' – and not just military historians: *Escape in America*, xi–xii. *Parl. Hist.*, 19 (1777–8), 1178.

36   Raphael, *People's History*, 135, 332.

37   For Allen, see Raphael, *People's History*, 18–21; Michael A. Bellesiles, *Revolutionary Outlaws: Ethan Allen and the Struggle for Independence on the Early American Frontier* (1995).

38   *Ethan Allen* (1930), 37, 40, 82, 118.

39   Howe to Washington, 1 August 1776, PRO, CO 5/93, fol. 487.

40   For McCrea, see June Namias, *White Captives: Gender and Ethnicity on the American Frontier* (Chapel Hill, NC, 1993), 117 *seq.*; *Parl. Hist.*, 19 (1777–8), 697.

41   BL, Add. MS 32413, fol. 71B.

42   Revd Wheeler Case, *Poems occasioned by . . . the present grand contest of America for liberty* (New Haven, CT, 1778), 37–9.

43   Carl Berger, *Broadsides and Bayonets: The Propaganda War of the American Revolution* (San Raphael, CA, 1976 rev. edn), 199.

44   *John Dodge* (1779), 14; *John Leeth* (1904), 29–30; Neal Salisbury (ed.), *The Sovereignty and Goodness of God by Mary Rowlandson* (1997), 51–5.

45   *Benjamin Gilbert* (1784), 12; *Ebenezer Fletcher* (1798), 6.

46   See Sidney Kaplan and Emma Nogrady Kaplan, *The Black Presence in the Era of the American Revolution* (Amherst, MA, 1989); and Raphael, *People's History*, 177–234.

47   There has been an explosion of published work on these aspects of the Revolution in recent decades. For some of the best, see Kaplan and Kaplan, *Black Presence*; Sylvia R. Frey, *Water from the Rock: Black Resistance in a Revolutionary Age* (Princeton, NJ, 1991); Gary B. Nash, *Race and Revolution* (Madison, 1990); Colin Calloway, *The American Revolution in Indian Country* (Cambridge, 1995); and see Kirk Davis Swinehart's forthcoming Yale University PhD dissertation 'Indians in the House: Empire and Aristocracy in Mohawk Country, 1738–1845'.

48   BL, Add. MS 32413, fol. 73; [Lind], *Answer to the Declaration*, 96, 108.

49   Sidney Kaplan, 'The "Domestic Insurrections" of the Declaration of Independence', *Journal of Negro History*, XLI (1976), 244–5; Benjamin Quarles, 'Lord Dunmore as Liberator', *WMQ*, XV (1958).

50   Quoted in Lester C. Olson, *Emblems of American Community in the Revolutionary Era* (Washington, DC, 1991), 80; Burke quoted in Ronald Hoffman and Peter J. Albert (eds), *Peace and the Peacemakers: the Treaty of 1783* (Charlottesville, VA, 1986), 9–10.

51 James W. St. G Walker, *The Black Loyalists* (1976), 4; Jack M. Sosin, 'The use of Indians in the War of the American Revolution: a reassessment of responsibility', *Canadian Historical Review*, 46 (1965).

52 Raphael, *People's History*, 140.

53 Robert W. Tucker and David C. Hendrickson, *Empire of Liberty: The Statecraft of Thomas Jefferson* (Oxford, 1990), 305.

54 Abbatt, *Crisis of the Revolution*, 83.

8 Another Passage to India

1   See *Sarah Shade* (1801), a 45-page pamphlet that I have drawn on throughout this chapter.

2   See Matthew Stephens, *Hannah Snell: The Secret Life of a Female Marine, 1723–1792* (1997); and Dianne Dugaw (ed.), *The Female Soldier* (Los Angeles, CA, 1989).

3   Like all people operating in a mainly verbal culture, Sarah often mis-remembers dates. Thus her own narrative has her born in 1741, whereas the Stoke Edith parish register reveals that she was baptised on 30 November 1746. But all the characters and major events in her story can be verified. For example, her first husband John Cuff is down on a Madras army muster roll as arriving in India in 1764, five years before Sarah: IOL, L/MIL/11/110. I make these points to stress how possible it is – despite assertions sometimes made to the contrary – to uncover and investigate imperial histories from below.

4   *OHBE*, II, 542.

5   C.W. Pasley, *Essay on the Military Policy and Institutions of the British Empire* (1810), 1–4.

6   IOL, L/MAR/B/272G and L/MAR/B/272S (2).

7   For two expert and colourful evocations of the East India Company's maritime evolution, see John Keay, *The Honourable Company* (1991) and Anthony Farrington, *Trading Places: The East India Company and Asia 1600–1834* (2002). Those interested should visit the National Maritime Museum at Greenwich and ask to be shown the many canvases of East Indiamen, by no means all of which are normally on display.

8   For a succinct and valuable survey, see Philip Lawson, *The East India Company: A History* (1993).

9   Brian Allen, 'The East India Company's Settlement Pictures: George Lambert and Samuel Scott', in Pauline Rohatgi and Pheroza Godrej (eds), *Under the Indian Sun* (Bombay, 1995).

10 *OHBE*, II, 487–507.

11 As the future Lord Macaulay put it: 'After the grant, the Company was not, in form and name, an independent power. It was merely a minister of the court of Delhi.' Its transformation into something very different, was 'effected by degrees, and under disguise': *Hansard*, 3rd ser., 19 (1833), 507.

12 P.J. Marshall, *East India Fortunes: The British in Bengal in the Eighteenth Century* (Oxford, 1976), 217–18.

13 P.J. Marshall (ed.) *The Writings and Speeches of Edmund Burke: Madras and Bengal, 1774–85* (Oxford, 1981), 402. For a powerful evocation of mortality rates, see Theon Wilkinson, *Two Monsoons: The Life and Death of Europeans in India* (1987 edn).

14 William Fullarton, *A View of the English Interests in India* (1788 edn), 49–50.

15 'In calculating the relative power of England over that country [India], we were too apt to commit the fallacy of estimating our own strength in one balance, and placing in the other the resources of 150,000,000 of inhabitants': *Hansard*, 3rd ser., 64 (1842), 449. It is interesting that Disraeli still felt this was a problem at a time when British hegemony in the subcontinent was virtually complete. C.A. Bayly, *Indian Society and the Making of the British Empire* (Cambridge, 1988).

16 Marshall, *East Indian Fortunes*, 43; Om Prakash (ed.), *European Commercial Enterprise in Pre-Colonial India* (Cambridge, 1998); S.Arasaratnam, *Maritime Commerce and English Power: Southeast India, 1750–1800* (Aldershot, 1996), 242.

17 C.A. Bayly (ed.), *The Raj: India and the British 1600–1947* (1991), 130. On the military labour market in India, see D.H.A. Kolff, *Naukar, Rajput and Sepoy* (Cambridge, 1990); and Seema Alavi, *The Sepoys and the Company* (Delhi, 1995).

18 NLS, MS 2958, fol. 77.

19 At least three British civilians caught up in the Patna 'massacre' of 1763 produced captivity narratives, for instance, but none of these was published until the twentieth century: W.K Firminger (ed.), *The Diaries of Three Surgeons of Patna* (Calcutta, 1909).

20 See Kate Teltscher, '"The Fearful Name of the Black Hole": Fashioning an Imperial Myth', in Bart Moore-Gilbert (ed.), *Writing India, 1757–1990* (Manchester, 1996); and S.C. Hill (ed.), *Bengal in 1756–1757* (3 vols, 1905), especially vol. III.

21 Hill, *Bengal*, III, 303 and 388.

22 *Ibid.*, III, 380; Robert Orme, *A History of the Military Transactions* (3 vols, 1803 rev. edn), II, 76.

23 G.J. Bryant, 'The East India Company and its Army 1600–1778', London University PhD dissertation (1975), 36, 247; and his 'Officers of the East India Company's army in the days of Clive and Hastings', *Journal of Imperial and Commonwealth History*, 6 (1978); *OHBE*, II, 202.

24 K. K. Datta *et al.* (eds), *Fort William–India House Correspondence . . . 1748–1800* (21 vols, Delhi, 1949–85) VIII, 287. For nervousness in London about the pace of expansion, see H.V. Bowen, *Revenue and Reform: The Indian Problem in British Politics 1757–1773* (Cambridge, 1991).

25 *British India Analysed* (3 vols, 1793), III, 839.

26 A.N. Gilbert, 'Recruitment and reform in the East India Company army, 1760–1800', *Journal of British Studies*, XV (1975).

27 *Ibid.*, 92; *British India Analysed*, III, 827. Losses at sea virtually every year can be traced in Edward Dodwell and James Miles, *Alphabetical List of the Officers of the Indian Army* (1838).

28 Gilbert, 'Recruitment and reform'.

29 IOL, MSS Eur. D 1146/6, fol. 111; James Forbes's Memoirs, Yale Center for British Art, New Haven, Rare Books and Manuscripts Department, IV, fol. 8.

30 *Proposal for Employing Mallayan or Buggess Troops* (Edinburgh, 1769), 2.

31 *Interesting Historical Events relative to the Provinces of Bengal* (1765), 181.

32 On these trends, see Stewart N. Gordon, 'The slow conquest: administrative integration of Madras into the Maratha empire, 1720–1760', *MAS*, 11 (1977); Burton Stein, 'State formation and economy reconsidered', *MAS*, 19 (1985); Pradeep Barua, 'Military developments in India, 1750–1850', *Journal of Military History*, 58 (1994).

33 BL, Add. MS 29898, fol. 41.

34 Quoted in Randolf G.S. Cooper, 'Wellington and the Marathas in 1803'. *International History Review*, II (1989), 31–2 (my italics); BL, Add. MS 38408, fols 243–4.

35 See Judy Egerton's description of one version of this work in Christie's of London's sales catalogue, *British Pictures*, 8 June 1995, 84–7.

36 For Stubbs and his contemporaries on tigers, see Christopher Lennox-Boyd, Rob Dixon and Tim Clayton, *George Stubbs: The Complete Engraved Works* (1989); Edwin Landseer, *Twenty Engravings of Lions, Tigers, Panthers and Leopards* (1823).

37 Landseer, *Twenty Engravings*, 30.

38 Egerton, sale catalogue entry, 86; Edmund Burke, *A Philosophical Enquiry into the Origin of Our Ideas of the Sublime and Beautiful*, ed. J.T. Boulton (1958), 66 (my italics).

39 Landseer, *Twenty Engravings*, 8.

40 Lennox-Boyd *et al.*, *George Stubbs*; Amal Chatterjee, *Representations of India, 1740–1840* (Basingstoke, 1998), 78.

41 Edmund Burke in 1781: *Parl. Hist.*, 22 (1781–2), 316. For Tipu and his tigers, see Chapter Nine, and Kate Brittlebank, 'Sakti and Barakat: the power of Tipu's Tiger', *MAS*, 29 (1995).

9 The Tiger and the Sword

1 For the prominent Scottish presence in this and other Mysore battles, see Anne Buddle *et al.*, *The Tiger and the Thistle* (Edinburgh, 1999). See, too, note 66 for this chapter.

2 NLS, MS 38408, fol. 31. I have benefited from discussing these murals, and many other matters Indian, with Professor Christopher Bayly and Dr Susan Bayly.

3 *Parl. Hist.*, 22 (1781–2), 114; W.S. Lewis *et al.*, *The Yale Edition of Horace Walpole's Correspondence* (48 vols, New Haven, CT, 1937–83), XXIX, 123.

4 See M.D. George, *Catalogue of Prints and Drawings in the British Museum: Political and Personal Satires* (11 vols, 1978 edn), VI, prints 7928, 7929, 7932 and 7939; P.J. Marshall, '"Cornwallis Triumphant": War in India and the British Public in the Late Eighteenth Century', in Lawrence Freedman *et al.*, *War, Strategy, and International Politics* (Oxford, 1992), 65–6.

5 *Narrative of all the Proceedings and Debates . . . on East-India Affairs* (1784), 89.

6 *Parl. Hist.*, 21 (1780–1), 1173; P.J. Marshall, *The Impeachment of Warren Hastings* (Oxford, 1965).

7 For three rather different approaches to these rulers, see Nikhiles Guha, *Pre-British State System in South India: Mysore 1761–1799* (Calcutta, 1985); Burton Stein, 'State formation and economy reconsidered', *MAS*, 19 (1985); and Kate Brittlebank, *Tipu Sultan's Search for Legitimacy* (Delhi, 1997).

8 Pradeep Barua, 'Military developments in India, 1750–1850', *Journal of Military History*, 58 (1994).

9 *Appendix to the Sixth Report from the Committee of Secrecy . . . into the Causes of the War in the Carnatic* (1782), 335, No. 11; C.C. Davies (ed.), *The Private Correspondence of Lord Macartney* (1950), 20; *Descriptive List of Secret Department Records* (8 vols, Delhi, 1960–74), III, 36.

10 Quoted in C.A. Bayly, *Indian Society and the Making of the British Empire* (Cambridge, 1988), 97.

11 For an illuminating account of Haidar by one of his Portuguese mercenaries, see BL, Add. MS 19287.

12 See *Descriptive List of Secret Department Records*, III, 80, 129, 156; K.K. Datta *et al.* (eds), *Fort William–India House Correspondence . . . 1748–1800* (21 vols, Delhi, 1949–85), XV, 541.

13 [Jonathan Scott], *An Historical and Political View of the Decan, South of the Kistnah* (1791), 15–22.

14 *Parl. Hist.*, 21 (1780–1), 1201–2; and see the reasoning of Lord Wellesley in 1799: Edward Ingram (ed.), *Two Views of British India* (Bath, 1970), 189.

15 Contemporary estimates vary. These are taken from an account by a former captive: *Innes Munro* (1789), 351; NLS, MS 13615A, fol. 32.

16 *Robert Cameron MS* (unpaginated).

17 *Innes Munro* (1789), 277.

18 IOL, H/251, fol. 699.

19 Spandrell's damning verdict on his military stepfather in Huxley's novel *Point Counterpoint*.

20 Michel Foucault, *Discipline and Punish: The Birth of the Prison* (1977), 169.

21 Robert Darnton, *The Business of Enlightenment* (1979), 292–3, 297. For army officers as cultural producers in another European power, see László Deme, 'Maria Theresa's Noble Lifeguards and the Rise of Hungarian Enlightenment and Nationalism', Béla K.Király and Walter Scott Dillard (eds), *The East Central European Officer Corps 1740–1920s* (New York, 1988).

22 Lewis Namier and John Brooke (eds), *The House of Commons 1754–1790* (3 vols, 1964), II, 142.

23 'An essay on the art of war', IOL, Orme O.V. 303, fols 109–111; IOL MSS Eur.C.348, fols 1 and 7.

24 See his *The Story of the Malakand Field Force* (1898), and *London to Ladysmith* (1900).

25 See G.V. Scammell, 'European exiles, renegades and outlaws and the maritime economy of Asia *c.* 1500–1750', *MAS*, 26 (1992).

26 Seringapatam/Srirangapatna should be visited and deserves to be a World Heritage site. For an efficient, modern guide in English, see L.N. Swamy, *History of Srirangapatna* (Delhi, 1996).

27 See *James Scurry* (1824), 48–68.

28 John Howard, *The State of the Prisons* (Abingdon, 1977 edn), iii; *Gentleman's Magazine* 54 (1784), 950. For a broader discussion of POW treatment in Europe at this time, see Michael Lewis, *Napoleon and his British Captives* (1962).

29 For the plight of the wounded, see for example BL, Add. MS 41622, fol. 52 *seq.*

30 BL, Add. MS 39857, fols 317–18.

31 *Cromwell Massey* (1912), 24.

32 [William Thomson], *Memoirs of the Late War in Asia* (2 vols, 1788), II, 45.

33 IOL, Eur. MSS E. 330. Indian intermediaries transported messages for whites during the insurrections of 1857 in an identical fashion: see Jane Robinson, *Angels of Albion: Women of the Indian Mutiny* (1996), 81.

34 This emerges in virtually all Mysore captivity narratives, see Thomson, *Memoirs* (1789 edn), I, 122, 179–80.

35 For the details of Massey's text, see Appendix.

36 See also the account of these developments in *John Lindsay* MS.

37 *Cromwell Massey* (1912), 12–30.

38 See *Robert Gordon MS*, fol. 36.

39 Abdelwahab Bouhdiba, *Sexuality in Islam* (1985), 180.

40 *Cromwell Massey* (1912), 18.
41 On Tipu's religious politics, see Brittlebank, *Tipu Sultan's Search for Legitimacy.*
42 I owe this suggestion to Nigel Chancellor of Cambridge University.
43 *Cromwell Massey* (1912), 23; Felix Bryk, *Circumcision in Man and Woman: its History, Psychology and Ethnology* (New York, 1934), 29.
44 Marshall, '"Cornwallis Triumphant"', 70–1.
45 *John Lindsay* MS (unpaginated).
46 *Ibid.*
47 Though there is evidence that he revised his original prison notebook with a view to publication, but then did not go through with it: see IOL, MSS Eur A94, fol. 149.
48 *Ibid.,* fols 41–4, 69, 84, 88, 108, 137.
49 See Kate Teltscher, *India Inscribed: European and British Writing on India 1600–1800* (Delhi, 1997), 157–91, 230–33.
50 *An authentic narrative of the treatment of the English who were taken prisoners . . . by Tippoo Saib* (1785), advertisement and 70.
51 *A Vindication of the Conduct of the English Forces Employed in the Late War* (1787), 34.
52 For a survey of this world crisis, see my 'Yale, America, and the World in 1801', in Paul Kennedy (ed.), *Yale, America, and the World* (New Haven, CT, forthcoming).
53 See Marshall, '"Cornwallis Triumphant"'.
54 For a revisionist interpretation of these French ventures, see Maya Jasanoff, 'Collecting and Empire in India and Egypt, 1760–1830', Yale University Ph.D. Dissertation, 2003.
55 For British notions that Mysore and Revolutionary France were inter-linked, see C.A. Bayly, *Imperial Meridian: the British Empire and the World 1780–1830* (1989), 113–14.
56 *Times,* 10 April 1792; *Fort William–India House Correspondence,* XVI, 422–3; and XVII, 184, 230.
57 NLS, MS 13775, fol. 274; BL, Add. MS 41622, fol. 245.
58 *Innes Munro* (1789), 51, 119; *Robert Cameron* (1931), 19.
59 Anne Buddle, *Tigers round the Throne: The Court of Tipu Sultan* (1990), 11. For a shrewd and subtle British defence of Tipu by an East India Company officer, see Edward Moor, *A Narrative of the Operations of Captain Little's Detachment* (1794), 193 *seq.*
60 NLS, MS 13790, fols 177–9, 355–6.
61 For British official acceptance that the verdict on Tipu was still mixed, see *Copies and Extracts of Advices to and from India relative to the . . . war with the late Tippoo Sultaun* (1800).

62 The British Library copy of this piece of children's drama appears to have been published *c.* 1827. C.H. Philips (ed.), *Correspondence of David Scott Director and Chairman of the East India Company* (2 vols, 1951), II, 372.

63 See the Appendix.

64 'There were two officers with us dressed in the Highland garb who appeared particularly to attract Tippoo's attention. He said he was acquainted with the good qualities of this people as soldiers, and enquired how many men we had of this description.' NLS, MS 13775, fol. 271.

65 For Thomson, see *DNB*, 56, 274–5.

66 *Memoirs* (1st edn), I, iv-v, and *passim*; (2nd edn), 8 *seq.*

67 For Richardson's novels and their impact, see Terry Eagleton, *The Rape of Clarissa: Writing, Sexuality and Class Struggle in Samuel Richardson* (Oxford, 1982).

68 For details of Bristow's narrative, see Appendix.

69 See also my *Britons: Forging the Nation 1707–1837* (1992), 177–93.

70 Mildred Archer, *Tippoo's Tiger* (1983).

71 *Narrative of all the Proceedings and Debates*, 386.

72 *Oriental Miscellanies: Comprising Anecdotes of an Indian Life* (Wigan, 1840), 177.

73 Eagleton, *Rape of Clarissa*, 14–15.

74 Theodore Hook, *The Life of General . . . Sir David Baird* (2 vols, 1832), I, 43.

75 See the article on this phenomenon in the London *Guardian* supplement of 21 August 2001.

76 See, for instance, *Harry Oakes* (1785), 28.

77 NLS, MS 13653, fol. 5; *OHBE*, II, 202–3

10 Captives in Uniform

1 William Hazlitt, *The Spirit of the Age*, ed. E.D. Mackerness (Plymouth, 1991 edn), 165.

2 *An Essay on the Principle of Population. First edition* (1996 edn), and the introduction by Samuel Hollander. For contemporary reactions, see D.V. Glass (ed.), *Introduction to Malthus* (1953).

3 For an illuminating discussion of the connections between the population debate and Britain's perceptions of its power, see J.E. Cookson, 'Political arithmetic and war in Britain, 1793–1815', *War & Society*, I (1983).

4 *Ibid.*; A.N. Gilbert, 'Recruitment and reform in the East India Company army, 1760–1800', *Journal of British Studies*, XV (1975), 99.

5 Colquhoun, *Treatise*, especially vi, 7, 16 and 196; *Memoir on the Necessity of Colonization at the Present Period* (1817), 1.

6 *PP*, 1831–32, XIII, 319.

7 On this phase of expansion, see *OHBE*, II, 184–207.

8 James D.Tracy (ed.), *The Political Economy of Merchant Empires* (Cambridge, 1991), 163.

9 M.F. Odintz, 'The British Officer Corps 1754–83', Michigan University PhD dissertation, 1988, 45–6; Peter Burroughs, 'The human cost of imperial defence in the early Victorian age', *Victorian Studies*, 24 (1980), 11.

10 See C.A. Bayly, 'Returning the British to South Asian history: the limits of colonial hegemony', *South Asia*, XVII (1994).

11 Miles Taylor, 'The 1848 revolutions and the British empire', *Past and Present*, 166 (2000), 150–1.

12 'Military forces of the civilized world', *East Indian United Service Journal*, I (1833–4), 94–5. The British also employed a growing number of police in India. But, again, these men were overwhelmingly Indian.

13 The term is Paul Kennedy's: see *The Rise and Fall of the Great Powers* (1989).

14 *PP*, 1836, XXII, 8 (my italics); *Hansard*, 2nd ser., 18 (1828), 629.

15 See C.A. Bayly, *Imperial Meridian: The British Empire and the World 1780–1830* (1989); and my *Britons: Forging the Nation 1707–1837* (1992), 147 *seq.*

16 'A grenadier's diary 1842–1856', IOL, MS Photo Eur 97, fol. 40.

17 P.J. Marshall, 'British immigration into India in the nineteenth century', *Itinerario*, 14 (1990), 182.

18 'Foreward', in Ranajit Guha and Gayatri Spivak (eds), *Selected Subaltern Studies* (Oxford, 1988), vi.

19 *PP*, 1806–7, IV, 427; for deserter details, see PRO, WO 25/2935–51.

20 H.G. Keene, *Hindustan under Free Lances, 1770–1820* (1907), xiii; cf. S. Inayat A. Zaidi, 'Structure and organization of the European mercenary armed forces in the second half of eighteenth-century India', *Islamic Culture*, 63 (1989).

21 Braudel is cited in Ellen G. Friedman, *Spanish Captives in North Africa in the Early Modern Age* (Madison, WI, 1983), 46.

22 G.V. Scammell, 'European exiles, renegades and outlaws and the maritime economy of Asia *c.* 1500–1750', *MAS*, 26 (1992).

23 C.S. Srinivasachariar (ed.), *Selections from Orme Manuscripts* (Annamalainagar, 1952), 33.

24 Coote's journal, 21 January 1760, IOL, Orme India VIII. For the miscellaneous composition of the Company's forces before the 1760s, see G.J. Bryant, 'The East India Company and its Army 1600–1778', London university PhD dissertation, 1975, 292–3.

25 K.K. Datta *et al.* (eds), *Fort William–India House Correspondence . . . 1748–1800* (21 vols, Delhi, 1949–85) XV, 507.

26 William Hough, *The Practice of Courts-Martial* (1825), 138; and his *The Practice of Courts-Martial and Other Military Courts* (1834), 74.

27 *Act for punishing mutiny and desertion* (Madras, 1850), 19–20.

28 In London, there was even profound concern about half-pay Company officers advising 'friendly' Indian states, because of the 'extension of the European system of military discipline' it would foster. IOL, L/MIL/5/380, fol. 136.

29 See, for instance, the report in N.B. Kay, *The Allies' War with Tipu Sultan 1790–1793* (Bombay, 1937), 475.

30 John Pemble, 'The Second Maratha War' in Maarten Ultee (ed.), *Adapting to Conditions: War and Society in the Eighteenth Century* (Alabama, 1986), 393.

31 *Henry Becher* (1793), 185, 188; *James Scurry* (1st edn, 1824), 60–2.

32 NLS, MS 13775, fols 193 and 368.

33 Gilbert, 'Recruitment and reform'; *James Scurry* (2nd edn, 1824).

34 This paragraph is based on Whiteway's narrative appended to *James Scurry* (2nd edn, 1824).

35 See for instance Sir Francis Burdett's speech in *Hansard*, 20 (1811), 703.

36 Irish desertion was never only or even mainly a political, anti-British act. Irish-born soldiers appear also to have deserted George Washington's Continental army in disproportionate numbers: see Charles Patrick Neimeyer, 'No Meat, No Soldier: Race, Class and Ethnicity in the Continental Army', Georgetown University PhD dissertation, 1993, 2 vols, I, 101.

37 PRO, WO 90/1: General Courts Martial abroad, entry for 21 November 1796.

38 *Memoirs of the Extraordinary Military Career of John Shipp* (3 vols, 1829), II, 78; Charles J. Napier, *Remarks on Military Law and the Punishment of Flogging* (1837), 127n.

39 For Thomas, see BL, Add. MSS 13579 and 13580; and William Francklin, *Military Memoirs of Mr George Thomas* (Calcutta, 1803).

40 See Rudyard Kipling, *The Man who would be King and Other Stories*, ed. Louis L. Cornell (Oxford, 1987).

41 I am indebted to my former Yale student Eric Weiss for information on William Francklin; BL, Add. MS 13580, fols 117, 144b.

42 *Ibid.*, fol. 145; Francklin, *Military Memoirs*, 250.

43 See, for instance, a similar romanticisation of the wayward, charismatic white leader of 'natives' in the fictional *Narrative of the Singular Activities and Captivity of Thomas Barry among the Monsippi Indians* (Manchester, 179?).

44 See, for instance, the remarkable account by a Portuguese mercenary officer serving Haidar Ali: BL, Add. MS 19287.

45 NLS, MS 8432, fols 116–17.

46 T.E. Lawrence, *Seven Pillars of Wisdom* (New York, 1991), 31–2.

47 BL, Add. MS 13579, fol. 56.

48 The following paragraphs are based on *The Trial of Lieutenant-Colonel Joseph Wall* (1802); and *Genuine and Impartial Memoirs of the life of Governor Wall* (1802).

49 Not least because British deserters were sometimes sentenced to be branded with the letter D; and the brand, like the whip, was known to be inflicted as well on slaves.

50 For Cochrane's case, see NLS, MS 8460, fols 54 and 56; Long's collections for the history of Jamaica, BL, Add. MS 18270, fol. 83.

51 Though see Scott Claver, *Under the Lash* (1954); and J.R. Dinwiddy, 'The Early Nineteenth-century Campaign against Flogging in the Army', in his *Radicalism and Reform in Britain. 1780–1850* (1992).

52 'Free Labor vs Slave Labor: The British and Caribbean Cases', in Seymour Drescher, *From Slavery to Freedom* (1999). Comparisons between black slaves and the white soldiery were made in other European imperial powers at this time: see C.R. Boxer, *The Dutch Seaborne Empire 1600–1800* (1965), 212.

53 *Hansard*, 21 (1812), 1275.

54 *Ibid.*, 1282; Napier, *Remarks on Military Law*, 191–2.

55 *Letters from England*, ed. Jack Simmons (Gloucester, 1984), 64.

56 *Statistical report on the sickness, mortality and invaliding among the troops in the West Indies* (1838), 10, 49; and *Statistical report on . . . the troops in . . . British America* (1839), 10b.

57 Peter Stanley, *White Mutiny: British Military Culture in India, 1825–1875* (1998), 69; Dinwiddy, 'Campaign against flogging', 133.

58 *Ibid.*, 137–8; James Walvin, *Questioning Slavery* (1996), 56.

59 *Hansard*, 3rd ser., 22 (1834), 239.

60 Hough, *Practice of Courts-Martial* (1825), 157–8; *East Indian United Service Journal*, 4 (1834), selections, 76–9.

61 Douglas M. Peers, 'Sepoys, soldiers and the lash: race, caste and army discipline in India, 1820–50', *Journal of Imperial and Commonwealth History*, 23 (1995), 215; for white as well as sepoy mutinies in India, see Alan J. Guy and Peter B. Boyden (eds), *Soldiers of the Raj: The Indian army 1600–1947* (1997), 100–117. It is possible that white deserters were prosecuted more aggressively than sepoys, and this is partly why more charges were brought against the former.

62 *Hansard*, 3rd ser., 11 (1832), 1229–30.

63 See their 'Height and health in the United Kingdom 1815–1860: evidence from the East India Company army', *Explorations in Economic History*, 33 (1996).

64 Hough, *Practice of Courts-Martial* (1825), 154.

65 The classic account is of course E.P. Thompson, *Making of the English Working Class* (1965).

66 *PP*, 1831–2, XIII, 158; *A Narrative of the Grievances and Illegal Treatment Suffered by the British Officers* (1810), 153.

67 C.H. Philips (ed.), *The Correspondence of Lord William Cavendish Bentinck* (2 vols, Oxford, 1977), II, 1351; for a vivid account of the life-styles of the white soldiery in India, see Stanley, *White Mutiny*.

68 Philip D. Curtin, *Death by Migration: Europe's Encounter with the Tropical World in the Nineteenth Century* (Cambridge, 1989), 8.

69 For an interesting attempt, see, Kenneth Ballhatchet, *Race, Sex and Class under the Raj* (1980); P.J. Marshall, 'The white town of Calcutta under the rule of the East India Company', *MAS*, 34 (2000).

70 IOL, L/MIL/5/390, fol. 25.

71 IOL, L/MIL/5/376, fol. 238. Harshness to soldiers' common law wives was not unique to India or necessarily racist in intent. Economy was also a factor. The troops who fought with Arthur Wellesley for years in Spain during the Napoleonic Wars were similarly forced to leave their local partners and children behind them when they left.

72 'A grenadier's diary', 132.

73 *PP*, 1831–32, XIII, 397–8.

74 Douglas M. Peers, '"The habitual nobility of being": British officers and the social construction of the Bengal army in the early nineteenth century', *MAS*, 25 (1991).

75 M. Monier-Williams, *A few remarks on the use of spiritous liquors among the European soldiers* (1823), 6; *PP*, 1831–32, XIII, 82, 172.

76 M.L. Bush (ed.), *Serfdom and Slavery: Studies in Legal Bondage* (1996), introduction, 2.

77 *A Soldier's Journal . . . to which are annexed Observations on the Present State of the Army of Great Britain* (1770), 180–1.

78 IOL, L/MIL/5/397, fols 317–18.

79 *Hansard*, 3rd ser., 32 (1836), 1043.

80 *Ibid.*, 934; *Hansard*, 3rd ser., 31 (1836), 892.

81 'A grenadier's diary', 126, 132–3.

82 *Ibid.*, 141–2.

83 See, for instance, Carolyn Steedman, *The Radical Soldier's Tale* (1988) for how a seemingly conventional and committed soldier in India gained from his experiences there both a knowledge of Indian religions and a critique of the British state.

84 See Hew Strachan, *The Reform of the British Army 1830–54* (Manchester, 1984).

85 *Statistical report on . . . British America*, 10b.

86 *Report . . . into the System of Military Punishments*, 187; IOL, L/MIL/5/384, fols 273–7.

87 *Comparative View of the Extent and Population of the Colonial Possessions of Great Britain and Other Powers* (1839): Wyld's commentary on the map.

88 See Olive Anderson, 'The growth of Christian militarism in mid-Victorian Britain', *English Historical Review*, LXXXVI (1971).

Epilogue: To Afghanistan and Beyond

1   Louis Dupree, *Afghanistan* (Oxford, 1997) is the best introduction to the history of this region in English. For the background to the 1838 invasion, see M.E. Yapp, *Strategies of British India: Britain, Iran and Afghanistan. 1798–1850* (Oxford, 1980); and J.A. Norris, *The First Afghan War, 1838–1842* (Cambridge, 1967).

2   For the British at Kabul, see Patrick Macrory, *Kabul Catastrophe: The Story of the Disastrous Retreat from Kabul* (Oxford, 1986).

3   Today the best known version of this thesis is probably George MacDonald Fraser's, *Flashman* (1969), which draws heavily on the classic Victorian indictment of the campaign by Sir John Kaye.

4   *E.A.H Webb* MS (unfoliated); James Lunt (ed.), *From Sepoy to Subedar: Being the Life and Adventures of Subedar Sita Ram* (1970), 12.

5   Lunt, *From Sepoy to Subedar*, 115 *seq*. This contains a rare example of a sepoy's captivity narrative.

6   Peter Collister, 'Hostage in Afghanistan', IOL, MSS Eur C573, fol. 127; Patrick Macrory (ed.), *Lady Sale: The First Afghan Wars* (1969), 109.

7   *Vincent Eyre* (1843), viii.

8   J.H. Stocqueler, *Memorials of Afghanistan* (Calcutta, 1843), 280.

9   See the information in a modern edition of her captivity narrative: Macrory, *Lady Sale*. Even before it was published in 1843, Lady Sale's letters from her Afghanistan prison to her husband, General Sir Robert Sale, had been passed on to the governor-general of India and sent by him back to the ministers in London. She went on to inspire several celebratory songs and poems, as well as a circus act in her honour at Astley's amphitheatre in London.

10 *William Anderson* MS (unfoliated).

11 Some of these 'lost' captivity narratives are quoted copiously in J.W. Kaye, *History of the War in Afghanistan from the Unpublished Letters and Journals of Political and Military Officers* (2 vols, 1851).

12 'The English Captives at Cabul', *Bentley's Miscellany*, XIV (1843), 9, 159.

13 Lunt, *From Sepoy to Subedar*, 86.

14 Macrory, *Kabul Catastrophe*, 141 and 173.

15 *Tait's Edinburgh Magazine*, X (1843), 458; *Blackwood's Magazine*, 51 (1842),

103, 254. On the inadequacies of men, wages, and ammunition among the British in Afghanistan, see *A Narrative of the Recent War in Afghanistan . . . By an Officer* (1842).

16 *Quarterly Review* (1846), 509.

17 Quoted in Dupree, *Afghanistan*, 391n.

18 Louis Dupree, 'The retreat of the British Army from Kabul to Jalalabad in 1842: history and folklore', *Journal of the Folklore Institute*, IV (1967).

19 'English Captives at Cabul', *Bentley's Miscellany*, XV (1844), 189.

20 Eyre published the revised drawings separately as *Prison Sketches. Comprising Portraits of the Cabul Prisoners* (1843). See, for instance, General Sir Charles James Napier's furious scribbled notes on his copy of Eyre's captivity narrative: 'God forgive me but with the exception of the women you were all a set of sons of bitches . . . I never put much faith in your half and half fellows who pretend to be *moderate* and tell "only what they saw" – if you speak truth your history is not worth a damn.' Napier was at this stage an imperial hero and warrior of a conventional stamp. IOL, MSS Eur B199, fol. 450.

21 *E.A.H. Webb* MS (unfoliated).

22 Stocqueler, *Memorials of Afghanistan*, iii-iv; *Bentley's Miscellany*, XIV (1843), 149.

23 Henry Lushington, *A Great Country's Little Wars* (1844), 9–10.

24 Yapp, *Strategies of British India*, 452 seq.; *Tait's Edinburgh Magazine*, X (1843), 370; *Illustrated London News*, II (1843), 359.

25 Warren Christopher *et al.*, *American Hostages in Iran: The Conduct of a Crisis* (New Haven, CT, 1985), 1.

26 *Report of the East India Committee of the Colonial Society on the Causes and Consequences of the Afghan War* (1842), 29.

27 W.R. Louis (ed.), *Imperialism: The Robinson and Gallagher Controversy* (New York, 1976), 6; Dr Arnold is quoted in William Hough, *A Review of the Operations of the British Force at Cabool* (Calcutta, 1849), 154.

28 'The failure of the English Guiana Ventures 1595–1667 and James I's foreign policy', *Journal of Imperial and Commonwealth History*, XXI (1993).

29 The French drove them out in 1756; while the Spanish expelled them during the American Revolutionary War.

30 Quoted in H.V. Bowen, 'British Conceptions of Global Empire, 1756–83', *Journal of Imperial and Commonwealth History*, 26 (1998), 15.

31 See, for instance, C.W. Pasley, *Essay on the Military Policy and Institutions of the British Empire* (1810).

32 Peter Yapp (ed.), *The Traveller's Dictionary of Quotation* (1983), 457.

33 Charles James Cruttwell, *Io Triumphe! A Song of Victory* (1842).

34 See, for instance, Kaye, *History of the War*, II, 489.

35 Kenneth Pomeranz, *The Great Divergence: China, Europe, and the Making of the Modern World Economy* (Princeton, NJ, 2000), 4; Paul Kennedy, *The Rise and Fall of the Great Powers* (1988), 190.

36 *Hansard*, 3rd ser., 44 (1842), 492; Michael Adas, *Machines as the Measure of Men: Science, Technology and Ideologies of Western Dominance* (1989), 136.

37 Quoted in Macrory, *Kabul Catastrophe*, 48.

38 See George Buist, *Outline of the Operations of the British Troops* (Bombay, 1843), 291.

39 Rosemary Seton, *The Indian 'Mutiny' 1857–58* (1986), xi–xii.

40 For an example of a later 19th-century working man's imperial narrative that remained in manuscript, see Carolyn Steedman, *The Radical Soldier's Tale* (1988).

41 The link between demographic take-off and industrial growth emerges strongly in E.A. Wrigley and R.S. Schofield, *The Population History of England, 1541–1871* (Cambridge, 1981).

42 Frederic Bancroft (ed.), *Speeches, Correspondence and Political Papers of Carl Schurz* (6 vols, New York, 1913), VI, 19–20 (my italics).

43 *The Howard Vincent Map of the British Empire* by G.H. Johnston (7th edn, 1902), 'Explanation'.

44 Ronald Robinson and John Gallagher with Alice Denny, *Africa and the Victorians* (2nd edn, 1981), 11–12.

45 Charles Dickens, *The Perils of Certain English Prisoners* (1890 edn.), 245, 281, 318–20. See Peter Ackroyd, *Dickens* (1990), 799–800, for the circumstances of its composition.

46 See my 'The Significance of the Frontier in British History' in W.R. Louis (ed.), *More Adventures with Britannia* (1998), 15–16.

47 Quoted in Correlli Barnett, *The Verdict of Peace* (2001), 81 (my italics); Paul Kennedy, 'Why did the British empire last so long?' in his *Strategy and Diplomacy 1870–1945* (1983).

48 These points are expanded on in Dominic Lieven, 'The Collapse of the Tsarist and Soviet Empires in Comparative Perspective', in Emil Brix, Klaus Koch and Elisabeth Vyslonzil (eds), *The Decline of Empires* (Vienna, 2001) 100; and see his *Empire* (2000), vii–86, 413–22.

49 Quoted in David Reynolds, 'American Globalism: Mass, Motion and the Multiplier Effect', in A.G. Hopkins (ed.), *Globalization in World History* (2002), 245.

INDEX

Page numbers in *italic* indicate illustrations and captions.

Abenaki Indians 151, 152–3,
   168–70, 180
Abercromby, General James 185
Adams, John 230
Adas, Michael 110
Adler, Alfred 11
Adlercron, Colonel John 279
Afghanistan, British invasion of
   17, 347–9, 354–6, 361–2, 364–5,
   366, 368
      Afghan captives 357, *358*
      British captives *348*, 349–50,
         356–7, *359*, 359–61, *360*,
         362, 363–4
      captivity narratives 350–2,
         353, 354, 361, 367, 369
Alam II, Shah 249
Alaouite dynasty 36
Algiers 33, 43, 44, *49*, 44, 66, 98,
   109, *133*
      army 68–9
      bombardment by Royal
         Navy (1816) 66, 132–3
      captives and slaves 44, 50,
         52, 56, 57–8, *58*, 64–5, 77,
         82, 84, 85, 88, 117, 118,
         121–2, 129, *133*
      corsairs 36, 44–5, 49–50,
         52, 53, 54, 60, 61, 73, 105,
         114

   plague 55
   1682 treaty with England 52,
      53, 73
Algonquin Indians 144, 177, 181,
   228
Allen, Ethan 225–6, 236, 382
Allin, Sir Thomas 61
Amelang, James 16–17
America, North:
      Anglo-French wars 152,
         158–61, 169, 170–1, 172–3,
         177–8, 208
      colonists 19, 140, 148, 150,
         154–5, 160, 161, 167,
         200–1, 207, 216
      see also American
         Revolutionary War;
         Native Americans; United
         States
American Revolutionary
   War/War of Independence
   10, 19, 203–38, 244,
   366, 368
      American prisoners 207,
         209–10, 214–15, 216–17,
         218–20, 222, 223, 224–6,
         227–8
      blacks 232–6
      British prisoners 208,
         209–13, 214, 217–18,

220–1, 222, 224, 227, 228
European immigrants 232,
236
Loyalists and Loyalist prisoners 213–14, 220, 221,
224, 225, 231–2
Native Americans 228, *229*,
230–1, 232–3, 234–5
propaganda, use of 225–8,
230, 232
Amherst, General Jeffrey 185, 186,
196, 406n
Amos, James 53
Anantpur massacre 295, 303
Anburey, Thomas 222, 382
Anderson, Captain William 352
narrative 352, *353*, 356–7,
384
André, John 203–5, *204*, *206*, 207,
233, 237–8, 241
Anne, Queen 162, 163
Annual Register 294
Archer, Mildred 303
Armatage, John 119
Armitage, David 47, 155
Armstrong, Sergeant Benjamin
329–30
Arnold, General Benedict 203,
205, 207
Arnold, Dr Thomas 365
Attakullakulla, Chief 186
Auckland, George Eden, earl of
348, 357, 366
Aylmer, Gerald 51

Baillie, Colonel William 269,
304
Baird, General Sir David 305
Baker, Thomas 129
ballads 63, 75, 82–4, 87, 119, 380
Bampfield, Joan 77

Barbary 43, 44, 71–2, 101, 109
captives 44, 45, 46, 47, 48–9,
51, 55–6, 61–2, 78–80,
114–16, 118–20, 154
corsairs 1, 44, 50–1, 54, *61*,
185, 365
galley slaves 60–1
see also Algiers; Morocco;
Tripoli; Tunisia
Barber, Mary: 'On seeing the
Captives, lately redeem'd from
Barbary' 101
Baugh, Daniel 8
Bayly, C.A. 253
Becher, Henry: narrative 277, 384
Belaney, Archie (Grey Owl) 192
Bengal 38, 130, 171, 242, 247,
248–9, 251, 256, 268, 335, 336
tigers 263–5
Bentinck, Lord William
Cavendish 341
Berrington, William 79
Bewick, Thomas 264, 265
Bird, Francis: statue of Indian
137, *138*, *139*, 139–40
Blake, Admiral Robert 67
Blatchford, John 218
Bolton, John 245
Bombay 25, 38, 247, 248, *249*, 336
Boston Gazette 223
Boudinot, Elias 209
Boulainvilliers, Henri de, Count:
Life of Mahomet 107
Bouquet, Colonel Henry 196–8,
197
Bowyer, Lt Richard Runwa 292,
293
prison notebooks 292–3, 384
Brabrook, Joan 50
Braddock, General Edward 177,
179

Brady, Joan 96
Braudel, Fernand 33–4, 35, 48,
  66, 69, 318
Brewer, John 8, 174
Bristow, James: *Narrative* . . . 302,
  384
Britain:
    army *see* British Army
    attitudes to other cultures *see*
      Muslims/Islam; Native
      Americans
    class and empire 54, 60, 78,
      85, 117, 190–1, 289–90,
      313–14, 316, 321–3, 327,
      332–45, 356
    gender and empire 59,
      126–31, 148–50, 212–13,
      241–4, 251, 269–70,
      288–9, 304–5, 337, 350,
      352, 354, 369
    industrialisation 343, 367–8,
      369–70
    navy *see* Royal Navy
    population and empire 6–8,
      141, 144, 200–1, 252, 258,
      306–10, 342, 370
    press and empire 79, 82,
      88–97, 105, 148–52,
      173–6, 224, 280, 294, 297,
      300–1, 320, 363, 368–9,
      376–7
    race 9–10, 16, 63–5, 83, 96,
      102–17, 119, 139–43,
      161–4, 180–8, 196–8, 218,
      229–36, 263–7, 293–5,
      328–33, 337–42, 357–61,
      373–4
    religion and empire 38–9,
      53–4, 75–9, 92, 121–6,
      146–7, 150–1, 199, 288–9,
      292, 373

and sea 10–11, 47, 65, 246–8
size 4–7, 133–4, 155, 232,
  370–2, 376
technology and empire 9,
  68–9, 273, 355, 367–8
trade 25, 34, 49–52, 65,
  68–71, 105–6, 110, 122,
  246–8, 261
British Army 8–9, 10, 11–12, 68,
  311–13, 322, 344–5, 346
    in Afghanistan 348–52, 354,
      355–6
    in America 158–9, 160, 161,
      171, 172, 177, 195–6,
      201–2, 208–9, 231–2
    deserters and renegades 317,
      319–20, 321, 326–7, 333–4,
      343
    flogging 314, 330, 331–3,
      341–3, 344
    in India 38, *275*, 276, 277,
      312, 314–16, 334–5, 337,
      339, 340–1
    writing skills 278–80, 284,
      316
Brooks, Francis 89, 381
Brown, Louisa *279*
Burgoyne, General John 213, 228,
  232, 278
Burke, Edmund 171, 226, 228,
  233, 251, 265, 294, 304
Bush, M.L. 340
Butland, Mary 77
Butlers, the (merchants) 121
Buxar (India), battle of (1764) 249,
  268
Byng, Admiral John 70

Calcutta, India 247, 249, 255–6,
  334
Calloway, Colin 232

Camden, battle of (1780) 207, 210
Cameron, Lt Robert 298, 384
Canada 130, 158, 167, 171, 181,
    207, 208, 209, 234
Caribbean 4–5, 18, 132, 171, 209,
    211, 310, 345
Carlisle, Fredrick Howard, earl of
    216
Carr (gun-founder) 60
Carr, William 146–7
cartography 2–7, 280, 346, 371
Case, Reverend Wheeler: *Poems* . . .
    230
Castro, Lorenzo A: *Seapiece 74*
Catherine of Braganza 24, 25, 247
Catholicism 104
        and Islam 121–3, 125
Charity Briefs 76–8
Charles I, of England 50, 113,
    122
Charles II, of England 38, 53,
    142, 318
        and Tangier 24, 25, 28, 30,
            32, 33, 40, 72
Charleston, battle of (1780) 207,
    210
Chaudhuri, K.N. 253
Cherokee Indians 164, 178, 186,
    188, 235
Chetwode, William: *The Voyages
    and Adventures of Captain Robert
    Boyle* 129
China 5, 171, 367, 371, 378
Chippewa Indians 176–7, 178, 179,
    193–5
Choctaw Indians 164, 196
Cholmley, Sir Hugh 23–4, 25, 33,
    36, 108
        constructs Tangier mole 24,
            30–2, 35
Christopher, Warren 363

Churchill, Winston 280, 376
Clark, Ensign George 320
Clinton, General Henry 203, 210,
    221
Clive, Robert, later 1st baron,
    249, 264, 315
Cochrane, Basil 331–2
Cockayne, Sir Francis 91
Colquhoun, Patrick 309, 370
Conway, Stephen 208
Cook, Captain James 9
Coote, Sir Eyre 284, 318
Cornwall 49, 85
Cornwallis, Charles, marquess
    222, 296, 303, 320, 321, 335
Coxere, Edward: narrative 89,
    113, 381
Creek Indians 164, 196, 235
Cromwell, Oliver 143
        New Model Army 26, 38
Cruttwell, Charles: 'Io Triumphe!'
    366
Cuff, Sergeant John 251, 253, 263
Cumberland, William Augustus,
    duke of 264, 279
Cunningham, Provost Marshal
    221
Curzon, George Nathaniel (1st
    marquess Curzon of
    Kedleston) 255

Darnton, Robert 278
Dartmouth, George Legge, earl of
    30, 40
Davers, Sir Robert 195
Daves, Captain 86
Davis, Lennard 92
Deerfield, Massachusetts: Indian
    attack (1704) 152–3
Defoe, Daniel 10, 14–15, 50, 164,
    387n

Robinson Crusoe 1, 14, 58, 129, 345

Tour of the Whole Island of Great Britain 93

Degrave (East Indiaman) 15

Delaware Indians 178, 188, 189, 190, *191*, 192, 193, 196–8

Dempster, Alexander 321, 323

Denmark: and Barbary corsairs 63

Devon 49, 77, 85, 217

Dickens, Charles: 'The Perils of Certain English Prisoners' 373–4; 396n

Dickenson, Jonathan: *God's Protecting Providence, Man's Surest Help and Defence* 145–7, 382, 403

Disraeli, Benjamin 252, 412, 403n

Dodge, John 230, 382

Dost Muhammad Khan 348, 357, *358*

Douglas, Mary 12

Drake, Midshipman William 297

Drayton, Michael 142

Drescher, Seymour 332

Drury, Robert: *Madagascar: or Robert Drury's Journal 14*, 14–15

Dundas, Henry, 1st viscount Melville 300

Dunmore, John Murray, earl of 233

Eagleton, Terry 304

Earle, Peter 45

East India Company 103, 242, 246, 247–8, 251–3, 308
  in Afghanistan 352, 354–5
  army 249, 251, 257–62, 273, 295, 300, 303, 312, *315*, 316, 322, 323, 334, 335–7, 341, 345; *see also* sepoys (*below*)
  army deserters and renegades 318–19, 321, 334, 335
  British attitudes to 253–6, 271, 273, 294–5, 297
  coastal bases 36, 247–8, 249
  and flogging 328–32
  sepoys 248, 260, *260*, 261, 274, 276, 285, 306–7, 312, 316, 319, 334, 337, *338*, 340, 341, 343, 344, 372
  ships 245–6, *247*, 248, 258, *259*
  see also Mysore campaigns

Eden, Emily 357, 366
  water-colour of Afghan captives 357, *358*

Egerton, Judy 266

Elizabeth I, of England 122, 155, 246

Elliot, Adam 73, 89, 381

Elliott, John H. 153

Elphinstone, General William George Keith 354

Empire, global variations of 6, 19, 35–6, 65–6, 130, 155, 160, 171, 236–7, 249, 252, 346, 378

Equiano, Olaudah 119, 399n

Exeter, Devon 76

Eyre, Lt Vincent *360*
  Prison Sketches . . . 357, *359*, 359–60, *362*, 384

Fairbourne, Sir Palmes 37

Fay, Eliza: narrative 277, 384

Fès, Morocco 62, 68

Fitz-Geffrey, Charles: *Compassion towards Captives . . .* 154–5

Fort St John 207, 209

Fort William Henry: British surrender 181

Foucault, Michel 278
Fox, Henry 159
France 6, 25, 45, 62
    Anglo-French conflict in
        America 152, 158–61,
        169, 170–1, 172–3, 177–9,
        189,
        208
    and Mediterranean 45–6,
        53, 68, 70, 80–1, 132
    and Mysore campaigns 269,
        274, 275, 276, 296–7
    Napoleonic Wars 19, 244,
        296, 309, 310, 347–8
    Revolution 296
    treatment of prisoners 173,
        182, 184–5, 283
Francklin, William: *Military
    Memoirs of Mr George Thomas*
    324–5, *325*, 326
Franklin, Benjamin 201, 210–11,
    224
Freud, Sigmund 289

Gage, General Thomas 219
Gallagher, Jack 365
Gates, General Horatio 228
Gay, John: *The Beggar's Opera* 99,
    101
George I's War (1722–4) 158
George II, of England 70, 80,
    132, 279
George II's War (1740–8) 158, 161
George III, of England 19, 202,
    205, 214, 219, 220, 227–8, 230,
    231
Gibraltar 35, 69–71, 81, 98, 103,
    109, 120, 121, 122, 126, 132, 158,
    365, 394n
    straits of 23
Gilbert, Benjamin 231, 233, 383

Gillray, James: print *223*
Glen, James 87
Goree, Africa 328–9
Gough, Richard 82
Grace, Henry: narrative 176, 180,
    383
Grenville, George 200–1
Grey Owl *see* Belaney, Archie
Gyles, John: narrative 149–50, 151,
    155, 383

Haidar Ali, ruler of Mysore 253,
    258, 269, 273–4, 276, 280,
    282, 284, 285, 287, 294, 298,
    366
Halifax, George Saville, marquess
    of 10
Halsewell (East Indiaman) 258
Hamet (Moroccan sailor) 86–7
Hamilton, Alexander 19
Hancock (vessel) 218
Hancock, John, Governor of
    Massachusetts 215
Hannibal, HMS 282
Hanson, Elizabeth: narrative 151,
    383
Hardinge, Sir Henry 334
Harris, Edward 84–5
Harris, Elizabeth 77
Harvey, Sir Daniel 104
Hastings, Warren 273, 294
Hawkins, Ellen 50
Hazlitt, William: *The Spirit of the
    Age* 308
Hebb, David 49–50
Hendrick (Iroquois) *187*
Henley, Colonel 221
Herbert, Charles: narrative 218,
    383
Hervey, John, Baron: verses 104–5
Ho Chi Minh: *Prison Diary*

(quoted) xix

Hoare, Captain Matthew 245

Hobhouse, Sir John 368

Hollar, Wenceslaus: *Tangier 24, 26–7, 26–8, 29*

Holwell, John Zephaniah: *A Genuine Narrative of the deaths . . . in the Black Hole* 255–6, 384

Hook, Theodore: *The Life of General . . . Sir David Baird* 305

Howard, John 283

Howard, Lady Mary 77

Howe, Sir William 219, 227

Huddy, Captain Joseph 221–2

Hughes, John: *Siege of Damascus* 127

Hughes, Thomas 217–18, 383

Hunwick, John 115

Huron Indians 177, 178, 195, 196

Huxley, Aldous 278

Hyder Ali *see* Haidar Ali

Ibn Khaldûn: *Muqaddimah* 115

Illustrated London News 363

Inchiquin, William O'Brien, earl of 54

India 241–2, *250*, 378
 Anglo-Indians 337, 339
 British imperialism in 241–344 *passim*, 366, 368–9, 372
 'Mutiny' (1857–9) 369, 372, 373–4
 tigers 244, 263–5, *264, 266*, 267–8
 see British Army; East India Company; Maratha Confederacy; Mughal empire; Mysore campaigns

Inspector (privateering ship) 62, 119

Ireland 5, 7, 65, 112, 120, 310, 370, 419n
 Barbary captives 50, 59
 soldiers and mercenaries 39, 121–2, 310, 323–4, 342, 345, 377

Ironmongers' Company of London 120

Iroquois Indians *187*
 'kings" visit to court of Queen Anne 162–4, *165, 166*

Irving, James: narrative 89, 115, 116, 119, 382

Islam *see* Muslims/Islam

Jacobite Rebellion (1715), 112, 159; (1745–6) 112, 125–6

Jamaica 332

James I, of England (VI of Scotland) 49

James II, of England 120, 158, 318

Jefferson, Thomas 232, 233, 236

John of London (vessel) 73

Johnson, James 168–9

Johnson, Dr Samuel 106, 179, 182, 201

Johnson, Susanna: *The Captive American* 168–70, 173, 383

Johnston, G.H. 371

Jones, David 228

Jones, Philip 223

Jones, Thomas 119

Joyce, James (quoted) 1

Jukes, Vincent 82–3, 84, 382

Kabul, Afghanistan 347, 349, 350, 351–2, 354, 355, 356

Kay, John 85

Kearnan, Corporal 335

Keene, H.G.: *Hindustan under Free*

Lances, 1770–1820 317

Kennedy, Paul 376

King Philip's War (1675–6) 144, 148, 153, 160, 161–2

Kipling, Rudyard: *The Man who would be King* 324–5

Knight, Francis 60, 88, 89, 129, 382

Lambert, George, and Scott, Samuel: East India Company paintings 248, *249*

Landseer, Edwin 264
  Engravings of Lions, Tigers, Panthers and Leopards 266

Laroui, Abdallah 46

Lawrence, T.E.: *The Seven Pillars of Wisdom* 325–7

Lepore, Jill 150

Lindsay, Lt John: prison diary 291, 304, 384

Linebaugh, Peter *see* Rediker, Marcus

Litchfield, HMS 67–8

Littlehales, Colonel John 180

Liverpool: first newspaper 174, 190

London 11, 63, 76
  Covent Garden Theatre 99, 101, 102–3
  Hampton Court 110
  National Army Museum 317
  Newgate prison 40
  redemption processions 79, 80
  St Paul's Cathedral 79, 137, *138*

London Chronicle 224

London Gazette 153, 297, 320, 321

Long, Edward: *History of Jamaica* 330–1

Lorimer, Joyce 365

Louis XIV, of France 36, 62, 110

Lowry, Jean: narrative 173, 383

Lurting, Thomas 89, 382

Lushington, Henry: *A Great Country's Little Wars* 362

Macaulay, Thomas Babington, Baron 255, 367–8, 412n

McCrea, Jane 228, *229*, 230, 232

Mackenzie, Henry: *Man of the World* 188

Madagascar 15

Madras (Chennai), India 247, 253, 262, 274, 283, 336
  St Mary's church 252

Maguire, John 213

Malcolm, General Sir John 341

Malta 35, 45, 310

Malthus, Thomas: *Essay on the Principle of Population* 308, 309, 310, 370

Maratha Confederacy 262, 299, 320, 324

Marlborough, Charles Churchill, duke of 264

Marsh, Elizabeth: *The Female Captive* 89, 90, 109, 115, 126–8, 130–1, 382

Massey, Cromwell 285, 291–2
  prison journal 285–7, *286*, 289, 384

Matar, Nabil 106

Mather, Cotton 147, 148, 154, 161
  Good Fetched out of Evil . . . 151
  Magnalia Christi Americana 152

Mediterranean, 8, 17–18, 23, 25, 33–6, 41, 47–8, 70, 121, 125, 126, 144, 360

Meknès, Morocco 55, 60, 61, 110,
    111
Menocchio (Italian miller) 124
Mercedarians 53–4, 80
Metacom's war (1675–6) *see* King
    Philip's War
Miami Indians 177, 193
Minorca 35, 69–70, 81, 98, 103,
    120, 122, 132, 158, 272, 365,
    423n
Mokyr, Joel 334
Monamy, Paul: *East Indiaman 247*
Monmouth's rebellion (1685) 143
Monongahela, battle of (1755)
    177–8, 179
Montcalm, Louis Joseph, marquis
    de 185
Montgomery, General Archibald
    178
Morgan, Joseph 107
    A Compleat History 107, 108,
        112–13
Moriscos 44, 45, 107
Morocco 43, 51, 104
    army 64, 68–9, 95, 119
    British captives 55, 69, 71,
        76, 90, *90*, 91, 93, 95–7,
        109, 120, 126–8, 131
    corsairs 44, 45, 46, 52, 53,
        58, 59, 73, 127
    naval bombardment 67–8
    treaties with Britain 87, 126
    see also Fès; Meknès; Moulay
        Ismaïl; Rabat; Tangier
Morris, Thomas 177, 201, 405n
Morsy, Magali: *La relation de
    Thomas Pellow* 95
Moulay Ismaïl, Sultan of
    Morocco 36, 52, 60, 61, 68, 93,
    96, 120
    city-palace complex 110, *111*

Mozart, W.A.: *The Abduction from
    the Seraglio* 131
Mughal empire 18, 36, 47, 103,
    130, 171, 248, 249, 252, 253,
    256, 262, 265, 318
Muhammad, Prophet 107, 122,
    126
Munro, Innes 298, 384
Muslims/Islam 28, 36, 43
    British attitudes to 41, 43,
        45–6, 47–8, 79–80, 98,
        101–3, 104, 105–10,
        112–13, 114, 122–5, 126,
        131–3, 361
    Catholic attitudes to 121,
        122, 125
    and Catholic redemptionist
        orders 53–4
    as slaves 38–9, 45–6
    treatment of captives and
        slaves 58–60, 62, 82,
        83–4, 113–19, 126–30,
        393n
    see also Algiers; Barbary;
        Morocco; Mughal
        empire; Ottoman empire
Mysore campaigns 261, 262, 263,
    269–75, 296–7, 299–300, 303,
    305, 306–7, 366
    British captives/captivity
        narratives 275–8, 280,
        282–92, 295, 296, 300–2,
        304–5, 320, 321–3, 327

Nairne, Thomas 145
Napier, General Sir Charles 324,
    332, 423n
Napoleon Bonaparte 19, 244, 296,
    297, 309
Nash and Parker (merchants) 59
Native Americans 106, 114, 140,

401n
American colonists' attitudes
to 140, 141–3, 161–2, 164,
167, 172, 202, 236–7
in American Revolutionary
War 228, *229*, 230–1,
232–3, 234–5
Bird's statue 137, *138*, *139*,
139–40
British attitudes to 139–40,
161–4, *175*, 176–7, 178–9,
185, 186, *187*, 188, 190,
192, 193, 196–9, 202
conflict and war 144–5,
152–3, 158–9, 160, 168–9,
177–8, 181, 201
deaths from disease 143
treatment of captives 114,
140–1, 145–55, 160,
169–70, 173, 179–80, 189,
196–8
New Devonshire (East Indiaman)
245–6
New York Gazette 223
Niebuhr, Reinhold 378
North, Frederick, Lord (2nd earl
of Guildford) 215, 271
Northcote, James 264

Oakes, Harry: *A Vindication of the
Conduct of the English Forces
Employed in the Late War* 295,
384
Ockley, Simon 106
O'Connell, Daniel 342
Ogilby, John: *Africa* *42*, 43
ó Gráda, Cormac 334
Okeley, William 89
Eben-ezer . . . (narrative) 90,
91–2, *100*, 116, 117–18,
382

Oran, Algeria 121
Orme, Robert 280
Osterly (East Indiaman) 258
Oswego, battle of (1756) 178, 189
Otis, James 234
Ottawa Indians 177, 178, 181, 182,
183, 193
Ottoman empire 35–6, 43, 48,
65–6, 81, 98, 103–4, 112, 125,
171
see Barbary; Muslims/Islam

Paget, General Sir Edward 340
Palmerston, Henry Temple,
viscount 313, 332
Parker, Captain Hyde 126, 127,
130, 131, 132
Patterson, Orlando 63
Pauli, Ensign 195
Pearson, Mike Parker 15
Peers, Douglas 339–40
Peewash (Chippewa) 193–4, 195
Pellow, Thomas 89
The History of the Long Captivity
93, *94*, 95–6, 97, 382
Pennant, Thomas: *History of
Quadrupeds* 267
Pepys, Samuel 25, 393n
Pequot massacre 143
Petticrew, William 87
Petty, Sir William 47, 75
Phelps, Thomas 89
A True Account 102, 382
Philadelphia (ship) 119
Phoenix (brig) 216–17
Pilsberry, Joshua 213, 225
Pindar, Sir Paul 88
Pitt, William, the Elder (earl of
Chatham) 131, 132
Pitt, William, the Younger 244,
335

Pitts, Joseph 89, 118
    *A True and Faithful Account of
    the Religion and Manners
    of the Mohammetans* 107,
    108, 115, 118, 122–5, *124*,
    382
Plassey, battle of (1757) 249, 259,
    276
Plymouth, Devon 49, 217
Pocahontas 83, 141
Pollilur, battle of (1780) 269, *270*,
    271, 273, *275*, 275–6, 291, 300,
    301
    mural 269–70, *272*, 276–7,
    304
Pondicherry (East Indiaman) 258
Pondicherry, siege of (1748) 242,
    257
Pontiac's War (1763) 178, 193, 195,
    201
Powhatan 141
Prakash, Om 253
Pratt, Mary Louise 13
Price, Richard 309
Purchas, Samuel 44

Quebec Act (1774) 234
Queen Anne's War *see* War of
    Spanish Succession
Qur'an translations 105, 107

Rabat, Morocco: Souk el Ghezel
    57
Ram, Sita 354–5
Ramsay, Allan 214
Rediker, Marcus, and Linebaugh,
    Peter: *The Many-Headed Hydra*
    119
Rich, John 99, 101, 102–3
Richardson, Samuel 301, 304
    Clarissa 301, 302

Rivington, James 223
Robertson, Captain Charles 193
Robinson, Ronald 365
Robson, John 84
Roettiers, John: silver medal 38
Romer, Colonel William 155
Ross, Alexander: translation of
    Qur'an 105
Routh, E.M.G.: *Tangier: England's
    Lost Atlantic Outpost* 33
Rowlandson, Joseph 148
Rowlandson, Mary 148, 154
    *A True History . . . / The
    Sovereignty and Goodness of
    God* 148–9, 150, 151, 155,
    162, *163*, 176, 231, 383
Rowlandson, Thomas: *The Death
    of Tippoo or Besieging a Haram!!!*
    294, 295
Royal Navy 8, 9, 11, 51, 118, 158,
    208, 312–13, 322
    and American Revolutionary
        War 210–11, 214, 216–17
    and Barbary powers 46, 47,
        50, 51, *61*, 67–8, 71, *74*,
        132–3
    base at Tangier 24, 34–5, 36
    blacks 119
    captives in India 276, 278,
        284, 293, 297, 321
    deserters 324–6
    flogging 332, 342, 344
    Muslim slaves 45, 46
Rushdie, Salman 375
Russia 5, 66, 130, 208, 236, 296,
    311, 348, 371
Rutherfurd, John 193, 201
    narrative 176–7, 179, 192–5,
        383
Rycaut, Paul: *Present State of the
    Ottoman Empire* 129

Said, Edward 132, 316
    Orientalism 102, 397n
St Asaph, Wales 76
Sale, Florentia, Lady *351*
    A Journal of the Disasters in
        Afghanistan 351–2, 369,
        384, 422n
Sale, George: translation of *Qur'an*
    105, 107
Sale, General Sir Robert 351
Saphra, Thomas 119, 399n
Saratoga, battle of (1777) 207,
    210, 212, 213, 222, *223*, 224,
    225, 278
Scammell, G.V. 318
Schama, Simon 89–90
Schurz, Carl 370
Scotland 7, 50, 53, 85, 269, 300,
    417n
Scott, Samuel, *see* Lambert,
    George
Scurry, James 282, 321, 384
Seeley, Sir John 375
Seneca Indians 178, 193, 196–8
Seringapatam, India 282, 298,
    299, *299*, 327
        Darya Daulat Palace and
            mural of Pollilur 269,
            272, 276–7, 304
        prison *281*, 282, 283–4,
            285–7, 291–2
Seven Years War (1756–63) 130,
    132, 161, 170–3, 174, 176,
    178–81, 185, 186, *187*, 188, 189,
    192, 195–6, 200, 202, 214, 283,
    328–9
Shade, Sarah: *Narrative* . . . 241–2,
    244, 245, 248, 251, 253–4, 256,
    257, 263, 267, 384, 411n
Shawnee Indians 177, 178
Sheeres, Henry 32

Shelburne, William Petty, earl of
    366
Sherlock, William 54, 79
Shuja ul-Mulkh, Shah 348–9, 355,
    363
Sidi Muhammad, Sultan of
    Morocco 69, 126, 127–8, 131–2
Siraj-ud-Daulah, Nawab of
    Bengal 248–9, 253, 255, 256
slave trade, transatlantic 48, 55–6,
    62, 63–4, 78, 86–7, 231–36,
    367, 377
Smith, Adam: *Wealth of Nations* 10,
    70, 171
Smith, Captain John: *The General*
    Historie of Virginia 140–1, 383
Smith, William: *An historical account*
    of the expedition against the Ohio
    Indians 197–8
Smollett, Tobias: *Expedition of*
    Humphry Clinker 188
Snell, Hannah: *The Female Soldier*
    242, *243*
Snelling, Sergeant James 320
Southey, Robert 332
Spain 6, 23, 25, 34, 36, 44–5, 46–7,
    49, 53, 56, 66, 68, 69, 80, 105,
    107, 122, 145–6, 171, 209
    see War of Spanish
        Succession
Spectator 368
Spratt, Reverend Devereux 89,
    114, 117
    Autobiography . . . 106, 114,
        118, 382
Sproat, David 210
Stoop, Dirck: *Demolishing Tangier's*
    mole 39
Stormont, David Murray,
    Viscount 224
Stuart, John 186

Stubbs, George:
  Lion and Dead Tiger 266
  Portrait of the Royal Tiger 264,
    264
Suffren de Saint Tropez, Admiral
  Pierre de 274, 283
Summerton, Margaret 38
Sutherland, Lt James 89, 382
Swarton, Hannah: narrative
    150–1, 383
Swift, Jonathan: *Gulliver's Travels*
    1–3, 92–3

Tangier 23, *24*, 24–5, 28, *29*, 30,
    33, 34–5, 43, 69, 72, 109, 365
  fortifications *26–7*, 26–8, 32
  mole 24, *30–1*, 30–2, 35, *39*
  Muslim slaves 38–9, 46
  siege and evacuation 32,
    36–41, 130
Tavistock, Devon 77
Tellicherry, India 248
Temple, Sir Richard 317
Teviot, Andrew Rutherford, earl
  of 36–7
Thirty Years War (1618–1648) 143
Thomas, George 323, 324–8, *325*
Thompson (renegade) 321
Thompson, E.P. 335
Thomson, James: 'Rule Britannia'
  47
Thomson, William: *Memoirs of the
  Late War in Asia* 300–2
Times, The 297, 368
Tipu Sultan Fath Ali Khan 267,
  269, 273, 274, 280, 282, 285,
  287, 288–9, 295, 296–300, 302,
  303, 305, 308, 320, 327, 366
  palace 269, *272*, 276–7, 304
Tomocomo 141
Townshend, General (later

marquis) George: paintings of
  Native Americans 181–2, *183*
Trinitarians 53–4, 80, 81
Tripoli 35, 43, 44, 55, 66, *67*, 98,
  129
Troughton, Thomas 89, *90*, 91,
  99, 101
  Barbarian Cruelty 91, 382
Tunis/Tunisia 35, 43, 44, 66, 67,
  98, 109
Turner, J.M.W.: *The Loss of an
  East Indiaman 259*

Underhill, Captain John 143
United States 5, 296, 306, 311,
  312, 363, 371, 378
  see also America, North;
    American Revolutionary
    War; Vietnam War
Utrecht, Treaty of (1713) 69, 137,
  152, 159

Vanderlyn, John: *The Murder of
  Jane McCrea* 228, *229*
Vattel, Emeric de: *The Law of
  Nations* 184–5
Verelst, John: portraits of Iroquois
  'kings' 163–4, *165*, *166*, 181
Victoria, Queen 312, 346, 348,
  351, 369, 370
Vietnam War 66–7, 276, 294, 305,
  306

Walker, James: *The Black Loyalists*
  235
Wall, Joseph 328–30, *329*, *331*, 332
Walpole, Horace 270–1
Walvin, James 333
Wampanoag Indians 148, 161
War of Austrian Succession (King
  George II's War) 158, 161

War of Spanish Succession (Queen Anne's War) 69, 76, 107, 137, 158, 159, 160, 161

Ward, James 264
    Fight between a Lion and a Tiger 266, *265*

Washington, George 205, 209, 219, 221, 222, 227

Waterloo, battle of (1815) 104, 310

Way, Peter 195

Wellesley, Richard Colley

Wellesley, marquess 307, 325, 326

Wellington, Arthur Wellesley, duke of 10, 320, 333, 421n

West, Benjamin:
    General Johnson saving a wounded French officer from . . . a North American Indian 184
    The Indians delivering up the English captives to Colonel Bouquet 197

Whitehead, John 55, 89, 108–9, 382

Whiteway, William 321–2
    narrative 322–3, 385

Widger, William 216–17, 383

Wilkes, John 224

William III, of England 110, 120, 158

William's War (Nine Years War) (1689–97) 76, 158, 159, 160

Williams, Reverend John: *The Redeemed Captive Returning to Zion* 153, 383

Williams, Richard 180

Williamson, Peter 188–9, *191*, 192
    French and Indian Cruelty . . . 176, 188, 189–90, *191*, 192, 198, 202, 383, 406n

Wyld, James: map of British Empire 346

Yamasee War (1715) 144, 145, 158–9

Yapp, M.E. 363

Yorktown, battle of (1781) 70, 210, 222, 270

Young, Arthur: *The Theatre of the Present War in North America* 174